# THE COMMUNIST PARTIES OF
# SCANDINAVIA AND FINLAND

The History of Communism
Edited by F. W. Deakin and H. T. Willetts

# The Communist Parties of Scandinavia and Finland

A. F. Upton

With contributions by Peter P. Rohde and
Å. Sparring

Weidenfeld and Nicolson    London

Copyright © 1973 A. F. Upton

First published by Weidenfeld and Nicolson
11 St. John's Hill London SW11

ISBN 0 297 99542 1


Printed in Great Britain By
Redwood Press Limited
Trowbridge, Wiltshire

CONTENTS

# ABBREVIATIONS

ASS:     Akateeminen sosialistinen seura, Academic Socialist Society

GATT:    General Agreement on Trade and Tariffs

ILO:     International Labour Organisation

IKL:     Isänmaallinen kansanliike, Patriotic People's Movement

ISH:     International Seamen's Organisation

MRA:    Moral Rearmament Movement

NATO:   North Atlantic Treaty Organisation

NEP:    Novaya Ekonomicheskaya Politika, New Economic Policy

NKP:    Norges kommunistiske parti, Norwegian Communist Party

SAJ:     Suomen ammattijärjestö, Finnish TUC

SAK:    Suomen ammattiyhdistysten keskusliitto, Central Organisation of Finnish Trade Unions

SAP:    Sveriges socialdemokratiska arbetarparti, Swedish Social Democratic Workers' Party

SD:     Social Democrat

SDP:    Suomen sosiaalidemokraattinen puolue, Finnish Social Democratic Party

SF:     Socialistisk Folkeparti, Socialist People's Party

SHAEF:  Supreme Headquarters Allied Expeditionary Force

SKDL: Suomen kansan demokraattinen liitto, Finnish People's Democratic League

SKP: 1) Sveriges kommunistiska parti, Swedish Communist Party
2) Suomen Kommunistinen puolue, Finnish Communist Party

SNS: Suomen-Neuvostoliiton rauhan ja ystävyyden seura, Finnish-Soviet Peace and Friendship Society

STP: 1) Suomen sosialistinen työväen puolue, Finnish Socialist Workers' Party
2) After May 1923, Suomen työväen puolue, Finnish Workers' Party

SSV: Sveriges socialdemokratiska vänsterparti, Swedish Left-social Democratic Party

VPK: Vänsterpartiet Komunisterna, The Left Party, the Communists

VS: Venstresocialisterna, Left Socialists

WFTU: World Federation of Trade Unions

When this volume was planned it was agreed that the major part of it should be devoted to a fairly full history of the Communist Party of Finland, and that the parties of Denmark, Norway and Sweden should be dealt with in extended essays. The reasoning behind this decision is illuminated by Dr Sparring's remarks on the Swedish party, when he says that it 'has never belonged with the major parties of the international communist community' and that its 'national role has been marginal'. The same is true of the parties of Denmark and Norway, with some reservations over their activity in their respective wartime resistance movements. The histories of these parties have, of course, many features of undeniable interest, as the distinguished contributions to this volume clearly demonstrate, but taking the very broadest view one may suggest that even if they had never existed, it cannot be imagined that the history of their own countries or of the communist movement as a whole would have been much different.

On the other hand, the historical significance of the Communist Party of Finland would seem to be much greater. The history of independent Finland since 1918 cannot be understood without taking into account the major role of the Finnish communist movement—whether actively or passively, its existence has always been a factor of the first importance. This is partly because the party belongs to that select group of western parties which have always had a genuine mass following among its own working class, and in their trade unions, and on the basis of this popular following has participated in coalition governments under a bourgeois parliamentary system. On the international stage, the Finnish party is a unique specimen of a communist party, operating in a European country bordering on the Soviet Union, which has preserved substantial political independence and a capitalist economic system. This has conferred on the party its peculiar and ambiguous role in the relations of Russia and Finland. On grounds such as these it seemed that the Finnish party merited special attention.

I should like to record here my gratitude to the two Scandinavian contributors to this volume; it would have been difficult indeed to find more helpful or obliging collaborators. Peter P. Rohde, who wrote the essays on Denmark and Norway, is now a freelance writer and historian. He joined the communist movement in Denmark during the Munich crisis, and became a prominent publicist for the party. He has a distinguished record of activity in the Danish resistance to the German occupation, and was for a time a prisoner of the Gestapo because of this. Mr Rohde was expelled from the party in 1953 for protesting against its condonation of the Doctors' Plot and the Slansky affair. Dr Åke Sparring is a Swedish academic with an international reputation, who is currently director of the Swedish Institute of International Affairs, and is the acknowledged authority on the subject of Swedish communism, and also well known for his work on European communism generally. Dr Sparring's essay has been translated from the original Swedish by my wife, and this is just one of her many contributions to this volume.

ANTHONY F. UPTON
*St Salvator's College*
*St Andrews*

# PART ONE:
# THE COMMUNIST PARTIES
# OF SCANDINAVIA

# 1. THE COMMUNIST PARTY OF DENMARK

PETER P. ROHDE

Industrialism on a large scale began in Denmark as late as the 1870s, impeded as it had been by legislation which favoured the craft guilds and derived from medieval times. But in 1859 a new, progressive trade act was introduced which granted full freedom of trade and free competition. From that time, after a short pause for breath, industrialism broke through with great speed and transformed economic life, creating modern capitalism, with its accompanying social structure, producing a proletariat and a class of property owners, and a modern political structure with, for the first time, genuine political parties—a conservative party, a liberal party, and a socialist party. A former lieutenant in the Danish army, Ludvig Pio, who had volunteered for the French army during the war with Germany in 1870, and on whom the Paris commune in 1871 had made an enormous impression, formed in the same year in Denmark a branch of the International and started a paper, *The Socialist*, in which he exposed capitalism and called upon the masses to fight it. The movement spread rapidly in the capital, but two years later a clash between a demonstration and mounted soldiers—remembered as the 'Battle on the Common'—provided a suitable pretext for the government to charge the leaders with sedition and have them imprisoned, while the International was declared illegal and dissolved.

For some years this damped the revolutionary fervour, but in the 1880s the labour movement gathered momentum again. In 1884 the first two labour members of Parliament were elected, and the party supported the Farmers' Party in its fight for parliamentary government and for the reintroduction of the progressive constitution of 1849, which had been largely nullified through conservative amendments. The party programme, adopted about this time, indicates the passing from a somewhat utopian scheme of starting labourers' 'Unions of Production', which would run parallel with and independent of capitalist undertakings, to a demand for the taking over of the means of production by expropriation. In the same way it claimed that all entailed estates should be parcelled out in smallholdings and credit institutions established which would make it possible for people to acquire them without cash payment. Uncultivated areas were to be confiscated and granted to agricultural labourers, who should be given financial help to acquire the working equipment. This agricultural programme of the Social Democratic Party is interesting—it actually foreshadowed the agricultural policy of the next fifty years and placed the socialists in the vanguard of the rural proletariat as well as of the urban.

These demands made the farmers of the liberal Farmers' Party consider matters thoroughly. Until that time, they had been the spearhead of political progress and carried on a stubborn fight against the conservatives. As a matter of fact, the party had appropriated the name of 'the Left'—*Venstre*—and was indeed a left party. But the socialist agricultural programme was not what they had been looking for, and although the two parties had been cooperating to bring the conservatives down, many of the farmers began to wonder whether, in the end, they had not more in common with the conservatives than with these socialist rioters, who turned the heads of the agricultural workers. Thus in 1901, when the liberal Farmers' Party succeeded the conservatives, and for the first time formed a government, they began to take up a definitely hostile attitude to the socialists, and their democratic zeal was badly diluted. In fact, from that time on, 'the Left' became more and more a party of the right, and although even to this day it officially calls itself 'the

Left', it is and has remained a solidly conservative party, heavily backed by vested interests.

But for those in the party who still nourished democratic ideals, this was too much to swallow. Some members broke away and formed a new party, 'the radical Left' which, though it never became a very large group, has had an important part in political development by helping the socialists to power during a long alliance which in fact did not break up until 1967. Its following was a rather odd, though attractive mixture of smallholders, the liberal town population, and the intelligentsia. It stood for democracy, free trade, social reform and pacifism. It was formed in 1905 and represented a liberalism much like that which, a few years later, Lloyd George introduced in England with his finance bill of 1909. The general election in 1913 gave the democratic parties a majority, and a radical government was formed with socialist support. It was this government which had to cope with the problems created by the first world war, and it did so with success, in so far as it did manage to keep the country out of the war. But the war also promoted the extremist tendencies within the working-class movement.

Already in 1913, the Social Democratic Party had changed its programme: it had always been in contact with the German sister party, and had gone through the same stages of development. It had originally formulated its own principles according to the Gotha programme: now in 1913 it drafted its new programme after the model of the Erfurth programme, and took the road of revisionism, as outlined by Edouard Bernstein in his famous book after 1899. This was an inevitable development, as everything seemed to indicate that the ideas of orthodox Marxism had grown out of date, and that revolution had been supplanted by the struggles in Parliament and the trade unions, while the international brotherhood of the workers would make war impossible for all future time. But the year after the radical government had been formed with socialist support, one of these illusions was thoroughly exploded: when the war broke out, the belief in workers' international solidarity collapsed, and even if this did not affect the government directly, it stimulated whatever there had been of opposition to the line of compromise, which the Social Democratic Party had taken under the leadership of Thorvald Stauning, who was for thirty years to be the dominant figure in the Danish, and partly in the Scandinavian workers' movement.

Some opposition there had been already before the war began. In 1910 there had been established a group of dissidents, calling itself 'the Trade Union Opposition League', which was clearly inspired by syndicalist ideas. It is implicit in the nature of syndicalism that it should carry on with the struggle in the trade unions and not bother about the debates in Parliament, which it considers as mere gossip and waste of time. There was however one political personality who also moved leftwards in these years and at last broke with the party. His name was Gerson Trier, an intellectual who had been a friend of Friedrich Engels and had for years carried on a correspondence with him. In 1916 he resigned from the party and wrote an open letter to Stauning, in which we find the following explanation:

> My resignation is not the outcome of a sudden impulse. From the moment when the Social Democratic Party broke the party programme by agreeing to the military appropriations, and from the moment when the party adopted a conciliatory attitude to the monarchy, and from the moment it gave up the class struggle for a bourgeois compromise policy— I have had the feeling that we moved along a path which, in spite of the socialist phrases which are still high-sounding on solemn occasions, will turn out to be fatal for the future of the Social Democratic Party as a socialist workers' party.

The Russian revolution, in November 1917, had its immediate repercussions. Two new parties arose in the wake of the great event: 'the Independent Social Democratic Party', and 'the Socialist Labour Party'. Both of them contested the general election in 1918, but received an infinitesimal number of votes. The Comintern tried to reconcile them and amalgamate them, but failed. Soon a third party was added to them. It was the 'Social Democratic Youth', which had been started in 1906, but opposed the revisionist line of the party it was linked to, joined the Zimmerwald movement and at last, in 1919, inaugurated the 'Left Socialist Party of Denmark', which half a year later absorbed the Socialist Labour Party, joined the Comintern, and finally adopted the name 'the Communist Party of Denmark'—*Danmarks kommunistiske Parti*—a name it has preserved to this day.

It had only got as far as that because the Comintern insisted upon the unification of the existing groups, and those which did not obey soon withered away. But even then it was not a very impressive party, and the revolutionary leaders in the Comintern and in the bolshevik government realised it. Lenin never thought much of it. He had had some experience of political conditions in Denmark for in 1910 he had participated in a social democratic congress in Copenhagen. On photographs from that event he is seen trudging along behind the imposing figures of Stauning and his colleagues, corpulent and long-bearded, self-confident and domineering as they were. The party newspaper had mentioned his name but seemed unable to spell it correctly. The affairs of the Danish party were too small for him to waste time on, so he left that to comrade O. W. Kuusinen, who, at the fourth world congress of the Comintern, said:

> The tasks of the Danish party are very great and the party itself very small. It is not yet a mass party, and it may take a long time until it can become the spokesman for the broad masses. We must not forget that Denmark has a very strongly organised Social Democratic Party, perhaps better organised than in any other country in the world, and it also dominates

the trade unions. Of course there are oppositional currents, but our comrades there have not so far managed to exploit the situation and have so far not been able to contact the oppositional elements.

That was a very sober analysis: if all the later reports from the Comintern had been equally sober the communist movement in Denmark might have been in a more favourable situation than it actually is. Kuusinen's words can be read as an analysis of Danish communism today, when, after a considerable boom, it has sunk down to the level it had reached in 1922. But Kuusinen's sobriety was not typical of Comintern ideas generally. Zinoviev, its leader, had missed his chance when there really existed the possibility for a European revolution in the years immediately after the war. Now, after 1924, when the situation was stabilising, he only gave the impression of a little man devoid of ingenuity and understanding, only able to demand renewed offensive and initiative. Stalin, indeed, was quite conscious of that, and fully occupied in rendering him harmless. So, gradually, Manuilsky was drawn in to replace him.

The Comintern was in fact a web of intrigue and factional struggles, and this was bound to be felt everywhere. In Denmark the unity of the party had been a formal fact from 1923, but only on the surface. Behind the facade there were just the same intrigues and internal struggles as in the Comintern—with the result that membership figures fell to about seven hundred. At the election in 1926 the party obtained six thousand votes, or 0.4 per cent of the total figure. The contest for the leadership in the party was particularly harmful: the principal antagonists were on one side Thøger Thøgersen, a rhetorical genius, even if rather histrionic, but ignorant of ideological questions and impossible as an organiser, and Richard Jensen, leader of the stokers' union, a simpleminded, straightforward personality of unquestionably proletarian origin, who as a prominent member of the leadership of ISH, the International Seamen's Organisation, had

several secret and illegal jobs to see to. And on the other
side was, first of all, Axel Larsen, a former railway worker.

First, Thøgersen and Jensen succeeded in bringing the
original batch of party leaders to downfall. They were
three, who soon turned back to the Social Democratic
Party from which they had come, and where they were
all well received and all got good jobs, one of them,
Ernst Christiansen, becoming deputy foreign minister
after the second world war. That was in 1927, and now
the two new leaders were able to have Axel Larsen
expatriated to the Soviet Union to acquire a better
understanding of what communism is. He attended the
Lenin school in Leningrad for four years, together with
Martin Nielsen, an unskilled worker, who like Larsen was
to play an important role in later years. While these two
men were on the school bench in the Soviet Union, things
went from bad to worse for the party at home. While
the election in 1926 had been miserable, the results of
the election in 1929 were even worse, with only 3,700
votes, or 0.2 per cent. This caused the Comintern to
interfere once more: at the end of the year it sent a long
letter urging the party to fight the social democrats, or,
to use the expression of those years, social fascists. The
new slogans should be seen in connection with a new
trend in the policy of the Comintern. Stalin, who had by
the removal of Zinoviev, and in Germany of Ruth Fischer,
settled accounts with the left-wing deviationists, now
tried to paralyse the right-wing deviationists—Bucharin
fell and pulled several communists in other countries
with him, such as Kilbom in Sweden and Brandler in
Germany. And as two small items in the big game, Larsen and Nielsen were sent back to Denmark, presumably
to replace Thøgersen and Jensen, and reorganise the
party. This was successfully carried through.

It was a most opportune moment for the new men.
The international economic depression, with its consequent unemployment, provided a most fertile field of
work, and they knew how to exploit the situation. The
previous leaders had been agitators and nothing else: they

had been thundering against the Church, social legislation, and the monarchy. Instead of that, the two new
men tried to get away from broad generalisations to the
concrete situation, took advantage of the behaviour of the
public assistance officials, and organised unemployment
demonstrations. Larsen, who was—and still is—a man of
great gifts, an acute intellect, a keen debater, a sly
tactician, and often considered the finest parliamentarian
in the Danish Folketing—House of Commons—now the
sole chamber of Parliament, realised that the uncompromising line of fighting the democratic parties would not
do. His greatest difficulty was that the Social Democratic
Party, which had for the first time formed a government
in 1924, did so again, following the timetable of the
British Labour Party, in 1929, with the solid support of
the vast majority of the labouring masses.

It was a most critical time, as the great economic crisis
swept the country only a few months after the formation of the new government under Stauning. But it
tackled the problems, and succeeded in introducing comprehensive social legislation, which contributed to miti-
gate the hardships of the depression. Stauning had started
his career as a cigar-maker and a trade unionist: he had
become a member of Parliament in 1906, and leader of
the party in 1916. His greatest assets were tactical agility
combined with violent ruthlessness, and a fine instinct
for being agile and ruthless at the proper times. While
he proved able to preserve complete unity in his party
(with agility), he fought all kinds of extremist tendencies,
and particularly the communists (with ruthlessness). Thus
it was a formidable opponent Larsen was confronted
with, but he soon proved that he was in possession of
exactly the same qualities which made Stauning such an
outstanding leader: the difference being that while Stauning had taken over a big and well-organised party, Larsen
found himself at the head of a party that hardly existed,
and, in so far as it did exist, was utterly disorganised,
with everybody fighting everybody. Thus the fact that
at the general election of November 1932, the commu-

nists could poll seventeen thousand votes and obtain two seats in the Folketing—almost fifty years after the social democrats had won their first two seats (1884)—proved that the party had now recovered from its children's diseases and got on to the adolescent stage. It pursued the line of advance at the following elections: 1935, 27,135 votes (1.6 per cent) and 1939 (the last election before the German occupation), 40,893 votes (2.4 per cent). This last election also secured the party a third seat.

The two first communists to be elected were Larsen and Arne Munch-Petersen, an intellectual and son of a professor of law. He was, however, too much of a theoretician and did not fit in with the more pragmatic line that Larsen had sponsored. He had to resign his seat, and in 1937 he went to the Soviet Union, never to come back. What actually happened is not known, he disappeared altogether and is assumed to have been a victim of the Stalinist purges. Thøgersen was more fortunate: he was completely outmanoeuvred by Larsen and exiled to the Soviet Union, where he stayed for the next five years. After coming back he never regained his position or got any influence. He was an anarchist more than a communist; his lyrical temper soared high in the first years after the Russian revolution, but when the catchwords were organisation, order, discipline, he could not cope with his younger competitors. It was more difficult for Larsen to get rid of Richard Jensen, who was one of the instruments of the Comintern, and directly responsible to that formidable monster, so Larsen could not just put him aside, as was the case with Thøgersen. He tried to several times, but Jensen always popped up again with his diabolical grin. At last, however, Larsen got his chance. In 1938, some ships which belonged to the Spanish government, but which Franco claimed and which might be handed to him, were sabotaged by a group of Danish communists, who were afterwards identified, arrested and sentenced to many years imprisonment. Somehow Jensen's name was connected with the group, and in the end he was sentenced to sixteen years' imprisonment.

That was in 1941, but in 1944 he succeeded, together with some others, in escaping, helped by a communist resistance group, and got off to Sweden. For a few years Larsen had got rid of his most dangerous competitor and enemy.

No doubt it was a benefit to the party that Larsen had become its leader. He had however, his limitations. They came out most clearly in his attitude to the question of national defence, particularly after the nazis had taken over in Germany. A look at the map will convince anybody that the little outgrowth of the north German lowlands, which is called Denmark, was in a hopeless situation. But Larsen did not see it like this. First he turned furiously against the Social Democratic Party, which had begun a cautious re-orientation regarding the defence question. For half a century it had been taken for granted that Denmark could not possibly defend itself against its southern neighbour, and as Germany was the only possible enemy, the outcome of this line of thought was that neutrality was the only conceivable principle to be followed in Danish foreign policy. The Social Democratic Party, when forming a government for the first time in 1924, accordingly introduced a bill advocating disarmament, and although this was not adopted in full, the military apparatus was gradually reduced to something like a frontier police or gendarmery. After Hitler's coming into power, the party began to re-think its position. On 13 October 1933 Larsen could still see no reason for changing his attitude, and declared in the Folketing:

> Denmark, like all 'fatherlands', is a capitalist country, ruled by an upper class, while the workers have to carry all the burdens and deliver the cannon fodder when the 'fatherland' calls for defence. The workers have never had any advantage in defending their country.

But then, four years later, Larsen had changed his attitude in this matter and advised a strong defence against the danger from the south. He had not, however, arrived at this conclusion thanks to his own deliberations. In the meantime the popular front tactics had been introduced. Starting in France, it was taken up by the Soviet government, which realised it was the best possible means of defence, and an instrument for meeting the war danger and for avoiding an isolated confrontation with Germany. But Larsen did not see this for himself: he had to be called to Moscow and told that they were interested in dragging Denmark into the network of powers which wanted to contain Hitler's aggressions. Thus, from one day to another, the Danish Communist Party changed its defence policy. It was rather late to join up, and accordingly it must have had a particularly shocking effect when, on 23 August 1939, Stalin concluded his non-aggression pact with Hitler, which put an end to all popular front tactics. The next couple of months were marked by confusion, and the very existence of the party was endangered when, at the end of the year, the Soviet Union attacked Finland. The party seemed to have spoiled any sympathy it might have nourished in wider circles, and a good many people, especially among the intellectuals, returned their membership cards.


The German occupation of Denmark and Norway on 9 April 1940 brought the crisis in the party to bursting point. It confronted the party with the question whether it should immediately go underground, and do whatever it could to take up the fight against the occupation forces, as members of all other political parties did, or whether it should exploit all the possibilities which its position as a legal party offered, particularly in fighting the 'collaborators', which meant carrying on the attacks on the Social Democratic Party under different conditions. This involved a line of strict neutrality towards the German occupation forces, and after some consideration the party leaders sponsored the latter alternative and accepted the full consequences of their choice: a couple of days after the occupation, the daily paper of the party—*Arbejder-bladet*—had a leading article which laid the full responsibility for the occupation on the shoulders of Winston Churchill and his Danish followers, the Social Democratic Party. The attitude of the party towards Finland was equally provocative in the eyes of the population, and the progress of the party since the 1930s stopped altogether. No doubt the party would have disappeared completely if the international situation had not changed altogether with the German invasion of the Soviet Union on 22 June 1941.

The first consequence of the new phase, as far as Denmark and its Communist Party was concerned, manifested itself at the very same hour as the Germans crossed the Russian border: three hundred leading communists were arrested by the Danish police, but at German request, and the party was declared illegal. A so-called 'Communist Act' was hurried through Parliament, and after the release of almost two-thirds of those arrested, the remainder were detained in an internment camp in a forest not very far from the town of Elsinore. But some of the most important people avoided arrest, among them Axel Larsen, and thus it was possible immediately to constitute a new leadership and agree on the new party line. In contrast with the case in Norway, the leaders soon saw that the illegal struggle they had been forced into overnight could not be carried on within a narrow party framework, but would have to take on a national character and be fought in cooperation with the widest possible circles.

Thus, while the first home-made bombs were tried out and began exploding in workshops and factories working for the Germans, and while the first illegal papers were circulated, the various resistance groups, which had come into existence sporadically and independently of each other, established a certain measure of cooperation. The chief organisers of this were Axel Larsen and a professor of neurology and member of the party, Mogens Fog. Their first achievement was to come to an agreement with the leader of the Conservative Party, Christmas Møller, about launching an illegal paper, *Frit Danmark*, which was to serve the common aims of all resistance people and contribute to create a united front against the Germans, as well as to indoctrinate the population against nazi ideology, and also try to formulate the ideas on which the country was to be developed when once the war had come to an end. Soon afterwards, however, Møller was urged to come to England; he left illegally for Sweden in a fishing boat and was brought from there by plane to Great Britain. That meant that communist control of *Frit Danmark* became even closer, but it was carried on in a most intelligent way so that it did become the means of communication for the nation which it was intended to be. Besides this paper, the communists ran their own illegal paper called *Land og Folk*—Country and People.

In the meantime, the arrested communists in the internment camp fought another struggle. Among those arrested in the first place was Martin Nielsen, who had been editor of *Arbejderbladet*, and also Thøger Thøgersen. But even in the camp the fractional struggle went on. Thøgersen became isolated from the main body, together with a group which had joined him: most remarkable among them was Kaj Moltke, an aristocrat by birth, belonging to the famous family which had for centuries contributed generals and statesmen to the country. Kaj Moltke, a man of high intelligence, had spent years in Moscow together with Thøgersen, but now they were pushed into outer darkness—for heresy there was no forgiveness, not even in a concentration camp and not even at a time when the lamb and the lion could graze together outside.

At the end of 1942 the illegal struggle took on sharper forms, the Gestapo became more alert, and among those who fell into their hands was Axel Larsen. During the first half of 1943 the resistance took such dimensions and penetrated the population to such a degree that a crisis was inevitable. After a series of incidents the government declared officially that it did not have the confidence of the people any more and resigned, no other government being formed to take its place. This happened on 28 August 1943, and on the following night the Germans took over everywhere. They also took over the control of the communist internment camp, which up to that time had been guarded by Danish police under German supervision. Out of the two hundred and fifty still interned, less than a hundred succeeded in escaping; the others, less successful, were sent to the German concentration camp at Stutthof, among them Nielsen, Thøgersen and Moltke. On the home front the crisis and the German takeover necessitated and made possible a further step towards a complete fusion of the various fighting forces in the underground struggle. In September, a common coordinating council was established, called the Freedom Council, and here again the agile personality of Mogens Fog was a driving force. Each group had a representative, but as Fog pretended to be outside the party the communists in fact were well dug in and could, thanks to their experience in illegal work, be the dominant force behind the scenes.

This became of importance when the end of the war was approaching, when the imminent prospects for the final culmination, including the allied invasion in western Europe, and the Russian armies which were approaching at still greater speed, brought about a crisis inside the Freedom Council and the underground forces. One wing of the illegal army had hesitated to submit itself to the Freedom Council. It was the military groups, which had been formed to carry out a number of special operations in case of a British invasion. These groups comprised a large number of officers from the army and navy, for the country had surrendered so suddenly that these had never been set in action, and a great many officers felt that the only way in which they could justify their right to existence was by joining the illegal army and fighting when they were called. But they never were called upon—except for building up the underground intelligence service in Denmark (and Sweden) which functioned so well that, according to General Montgomery, it proved to be second to none. The invasion was expected to start by the beginning of 1944—in March—on the western coast of Jutland. This expectation made it a natural thing that the military groups should be subordinated to the British command. But the Freedom Council did not endorse this idea and it was only when the British seemed to lose patience that the council hesitatingly gave in and accepted that a Danish general should be appointed head of the military groups and that they should be subordinated to SHAEF. The invasion did not come in March, and when it did come it was not on the west coast of Jutland. Denmark was somehow pushed out of the picture, at any rate as seen from the west.

But in the east the Russians had a keen eye turned on the Baltic, and accordingly on the Scandinavian countries in general, but on Denmark in particular as the guardian of the entrance to the Baltic. The Danish communists realised this very well: at no time during the occupation had they lost contact with the Soviet government. Their radio communications functioned all through the war, their link with Moscow being most often Stockholm, where the Russian embassy was entrusted to Madame Kollontai. So the Freedom Council, with its communist dominance, accepted a suggestion that Denmark should have a diplomatic representative in Moscow, as she had in London and Washington, where the Danish ambassadors had opted for the allied cause when their country had been occupied. This had not happened in the Soviet Union, and it was an open question whether the Soviet Union would be willing to receive an ambassador from Denmark, which had succumbed to German pressures, and until August 1943 had carried on a subtle kind of collaboration with the Germans. It was soon made clear that the Russians would on no condition receive a man who represented what was in those days termed 'the old statesmen', that is, those who were responsible for the political line followed until August 1943. Some suggestions were made, and dropped, but in the end all the parties agreed to send Mr Døssing, a man who had never engaged himself in actual politics but who belonged to the extreme Left. This was well known to the communist members of the Freedom Council, who had proposed him, but probably not to the others. When in Moscow, Døssing had conversations with the deputy foreign minister and chief of the Scandinavian department in the foreign office, Dekanozov, who expressed astonishment to hear that some Danish statesmen 'consider Denmark a British sphere of influence and an Anglo-American field of military operations. The latter is by no means certain, and the former we do not understand at all'.

This was said at a time when the Russian armies were approaching at a rapid rate along the coasts of the Baltic, while the western forces had been halted temporarily on the other bank of the Rhine. The possibility of being liberated by the Russians was therefore a thing to be considered. It was also pointed out to Danish negotiators, among them Christmas Møller, that at the Yalta Conference no agreement about Denmark and its liberation had been reached. Obviously this was a matter that had been left open in order not to create further trouble, and in actual fact this indicated that the partner who first arrived on the spot would have to be accepted as the liberator, whatever the consequences. This caused the former prime minister, Mr Buhl, to try to persuade the Swedish authorities to promise military occupation of Denmark, in order to avoid a Russian liberation and in order to avoid the capital becoming 'another Warsaw'.

At the same time representatives of the Freedom Council were negotiating—also in Stockholm—about what shape the future Danish government should have, and after prolonged talks it was agreed that it should consist half of old-line statesmen and half of members nominated by the Freedom Council out of its own ranks. But the communist members at any rate had by that time fully realised that in case of a Russian liberation such a government would never be formed, and by the middle of April 1945 everything seemed to indicate that the Russian army would be the first-comer; its northern flank was aiming directly at Lübeck, which lies at the entrance to the peninsula of Jutland. On 17 April the Freedom Council met and had a discussion about the future, and the communists laid before the rest a plan for the future of Denmark which could be said to anticipate a coming Russian liberation. The plan was violently opposed by Frode Jacobsen, a social democrat, and actually the first man in Denmark to have begun the organised resistance. Now he stood up and declared that this plan for Denmark's future was a betrayal of the principles they had all agreed on from the beginning, and which had a democratic development as its foundation stone. Frode Jacobsen won the day: what would have happened to him if the Russians had arrived first is anybody's guess. But they did not. Only two days later, Churchill wrote to Eden: 'There is no reason why the Russians should occupy Denmark, a country which should be liberated and regain its independence. . . .' At the same time Eisenhower sent an American force northwards to support Montgomery, whose troops entered Lübeck six hours before the Russians arrived, so they had to keep out of the town.

Thus some communist expectations were not fulfilled, but even then they had a tremendous time. The fifty-fifty government was formed according to plan, including three communists, among them Fog and Larsen, recently returned from Sachsenhausen. Fog, however, still officially stood outside the party, only supporting it, whatever that meant. Nobody could doubt that the party had done excellent work during the occupation, and as the people were completely ignorant of the fact that its members in the Freedom Council had been eager to transform Denmark into a People's Democracy the party had gained an enormous reputation. This was seen at the first general election in October 1945 when, with a party membership of merely five thousand, it polled 255,000 votes, or 12.4 per cent of the total. This meant that it won eighteen seats in the Folketing. This was the heyday of the party, and the conferences in Yalta and Potsdam had given room for some expectations of a more harmonious relation between east and west, while the fact that the Comintern had been dissolved in 1943 suggested that the various communist parties all over the world would no longer just consider themselves tools of Soviet interests but might develop into national parties, which could appear in the role of His Majesty's loyal opposition.

Something like this may have loomed in the mind of Axel Larsen, who was not insensitive to his unaccustomed position as the hero of the whole people. In spite of having spent three years in a German concentration camp he immediately took over the leadership of the party and indicated the outlines of the party for the future. He was wise enough to see that the republicanism, which he had so loudly propagated during the 1930s, would not do at a time when the royal house had gained immensely in prestige, thanks to the brave attitude of the king and his German-born queen. So Larsen decided that the republic was not on the agenda. As far as the Social Democratic Party was concerned it would seem a natural thing to continue the line of collaboration which the Freedom Council had succeeded in establishing. But here again it turned out that Larsen was not the creative personality and born leader but the agile disciple who understood how to follow an order, for the idea of collaboration, and indeed amalgamation of the workers' parties, was not an idea born in his own mind; it derived from Moscow and was followed everywhere in Europe: the thought behind it being that the whole working-class movement should be conquered from within by the communists. But once more the lack of genuine knowledge about the conditions in the rest of the world prevailing in Moscow was only too obvious, and the fact that the parties in the various countries pursued this hopeless endeavour revealed the emptiness of their claims to be truly national parties. The old foxes in the Social Democratic Party in Denmark saw right through the beautiful slogans and refused to commit themselves.

That was the first defeat of the communists after the war. The old divisions began to come through once more, and at the same time the international horizon began to look rather gloomy: it was obvious that the eastern countries which had been invaded by Russian troops at the end of the war had been not so much liberated as occupied once more: the civil war in Greece indicated Soviet and Yugoslav interference, and Churchill's Fulton speech and the Truman doctrine inaugurated a less peaceful era. All this was reflected in the election to the Folketing in 1947, which was a setback for the communists. Their share of the vote dropped to about half of what it had been two years before, their seats in the Folketing being exactly halved to nine. But worse was to come. Under the inspiration of Zhdanov, the Soviet government entered a new phase of aggressive expansionist policy, which culminated in the coup in Prague, the blockade of Berlin, the expulsion of Yugoslavia from the eastern community, and the resurrection of the Comintern under the name of Cominform. The western answer was the establishment of NATO, the cold war and the clash in Korea.

Under the impression of these events, the elections in the spring of 1950 saw the communist vote very nearly halved again, falling to ninety-four thousand. The high spirits of the time immediately after the war had gone, and some differences of opinion began to arise, even though for quite a long time they were well concealed from the masses. Larsen, whose strength was his capability as a parliamentarian, saw with apprehension the number of voters decrease at every election, and wanted, in order not to frighten the voters further, to carry on a cautious policy. But he had a group against him, partly of a younger generation, with Ib Nørlund as their spokesman. Nørlund had started his career as a scientist, a student of atomic physics, which he had studied in Niel Bohr's institute of theoretical physics; indeed Bohr happened to be his uncle.

But already before the war young Nørlund seemed more inclined towards politics and soon became the leader of the communist youth organisation. During the war he was active in the underground, and now, as there was small hope of ever entering the Folketing, he and some others decided that it was not in the Folketing at all but among the labouring masses that the struggle was to be fought. They discovered that Parliament was a bourgeois institution which it was not worth wasting time on. They wanted to return to various forms of spontaneous action which had been used with success in the 1930s. This implied that the party was to be a small elite, which could, in the decisive hour, become the spearhead of the masses and thus carry through a revolution—such as Lenin had done in 1917. They considered themselves as the disciples of the great revolutionaries of those days. Ib Nørlund has cultivated his connections with Moscow and must be considered, indeed wants to be considered, the grey eminence who does not stand forth in the limelight but gathers all the threads in his hand and all the power. This is the man as he is today but in 1950 he still did not count for very much, apart from the fact that he was one of the group which turned critically against Larsen and his policy of caution. Perhaps it should be mentioned that Richard Jensen was still there, and that after his return from Sweden he turned very critically and openly against Larsen, whom he accused of being responsible for his own imprisonment. Also Thøgersen and Moltke had come back alive from Stutthof, Thøgersen only to die, while Moltke entered political life again but with mental reservations against Larsen, who thus found himself surrounded by a growing circle of critics and enemies.

But even then, Larsen won the first round. Frightened by the resolute American intervention in Korea the Soviet government wanted to strike a more conciliatory line, in order not to run any risk. So they caused the Stockholm appeal to be drawn up, with its slogans of peaceful coexistence and mobilisation of peace partisans, who tried, with very primitive but also very militant methods, to knock into the heads of people that it was peace and nothing but peace which the tycoons in Moscow were fighting for. The new line strengthened Larsen against his critics in the party, and it started assiduously manipulating such organisations as 'Les partisans de la paix', the Danish branch of which was led by Mogens Fog, and the 'Democratic World Federation of Women', which succeeded in acquiring a number of non-party sympathisers, so that in the election of 1953 the party raised its share of the vote from 4.6 per cent to 4.8 per cent, a short-lived increase, as in a second election the same year the percentage came down to 4.3 per cent.

It was as if rock-bottom had been reached, where a handful of diehards were willing to uphold the party, no matter what happened. They also seemed to be very little concerned about such events as the Slansky trial in Prague and the Doctors' Plot in Moscow. The daily paper, which had by now adopted the name of the illegal *Land og Folk*, proved quite willing to print all the trash which had been published in the Russian papers, including the anti-Semitic accusations and attacks on Zionism and on the recently established state of Israel. A few persons who could not swallow this criminal nonsense, and protested, were expelled from the party, but the vast majority of members found it acceptable. At Stalin's death Martin Nielsen wrote an obituary which gave the reader the impression that the author had been struck by such a degree of despair at the news of the death that he could not possibly survive for another hour.

It was, of course, an unpleasant discovery, revealed by Khruschev a few months later, that the whole story about the Doctors' Plot was made up from beginning to end and that not one of the fifteen accused doctors could be held responsible for a single crime and had to be released—apart from the two or three who had obviously been tortured to death in prison. A few months later the June revolt in Berlin made a bad impression but could be explained as the work of American agents. All such irregularities, however, were as nothing in comparison with the chain of reactions which followed in the wake of

Khruschev's secret speech at the twentieth party congress in January 1956. Everything which the party had tried to defend and justify was here ridiculed, scorned and condemned. The events in Hungary at the end of the year made things still worse, and in 1957, when an election was held once more, it turned out that the hard rock-bottom had still not been reached, as the communist voters decreased to seventy-two thousand, or 3.1 per cent, which meant the loss of two seats.

Was there any hard rock-bottom at all? It did not make it any easier for the party that the split inside the leadership now came up to the surface and could no longer be hidden from the public. Immediately after the secret speech one would get the impression that the thaw, which had already been proclaimed previously, would continue with increased acceleration, and all the western parties followed up more or less willingly, but when the crisis over Hungary once more led to a sharpening of the hard line it was a manoeuvre which proved too much even for an experienced tactician. Larsen was among those who had adapted themselves to the liberal course of the thaw, and he had come forward with declarations about his having been fooled by Stalinism. His tactical sense told him that it would mean self-destruction to re-call what he had re-called and thus make himself the laughing-stock of everybody with his common sense left intact. He had to stick to his word if he were not to lose all his authority. On the other hand, his opponents pressed in the opposite direction, fully realising that now they had trapped him. They branded him as a revisionist, a dirty word which has a long story, as old as the communist movement itself, and has now been taken into use again by the Chinese, who started using it about Tito though in reality they were referring to Khruschev. And it is true enough that Larsen had wanted to revise party tactics, which had only led from one defeat to another. But on that point his comrades would not give in. The central problem was the relationship with the

Soviet Union, that is, whether the party should try to carry through a somewhat independent line so that it could be accepted as a genuine Danish party, or whether it should be satisfied to be considered merely as an off-spring of the Russian party.

By this time, Larsen had to defend himself on many sides. In the Folketing he was held responsible for the Russian intervention in Hungary; he answered that 'Hungary has been thrown into a situation which can only be characterised as civil war, where the fate of the country is at stake, events which can release a European war, and which in the end has necessitated that Soviet troops intervene so that peace and order could be maintained'. In contrast with the complicated situation in Hungary, Larsen found the events in the middle east, which took place at the same time, extremely simple, and he liked to draw them into the discussion as an effective demonstration. He said in a speech on 11 November:

> The war in Egypt started as a brutal imperialistic attack on one of those countries which were formerly colonies, and still have not obtained their full national and economic independence. No excusing lies can conceal that Britain and France, with Israel as their helper, have, following a carefully worked out timetable and plan, begun the most flagrant war of aggression with a purely predatory aim.

Larsen, in this example of historical interpretation, seems to follow the official Soviet view, and he does not care to distinguish between the aims of Britain and France, and those of Israel; neither does he care to mention the share of responsibility the Soviet Union has in the affair in giving such huge quantities of arms to a country which made no secret of its intention to use those weapons against another country. Larsen continues:

> This war of aggression has now been brought to an end. World opinion, the resolutions in the General

Assembly of the United Nations, the violent opposition to the war in the British and the French
peoples, and the ultimative warnings of the Soviet
Union to the aggressors have worked this out.

This is history written from a very personal point of
view: the attitude of the United States, which was the
really decisive fact in bringing to an end the Anglo-
French undertaking, is not even hinted at—that would
have been to play the game of the imperialist enemy. In
the same way it was a little inopportune to touch on the
violent opposition of the British Labour Party to the
affair, while a vague reference to the indignation and
will to peace of the people would always be acceptable
as an interpretation of historical events. As will be seen,
Larsen did not move far away from the orthodox line;
others went further. Some left the party altogether and
Mogens Fog, who had always been a close friend of and
adviser to Larsen, wrote at this time an article in which
he called for a revisionist attitude to Marxist and Leninist writings. This was hot stuff, and even though Larsen
probably in his heart agreed with Fog he remonstrated
against the word revision and explained that what was
needed was not a revision but an interpretation of these
writings in the light of recent experiences; thus the task
was to bring the Marxist-Leninist system up to date.

In April 1958 the Communist Federation of Yugoslavia
held a congress in connection with the adoption of a new
constitution for the country, and the Danish party, like
most other parties, received an invitation to send a delegation. Axel Larsen was appointed to go, together with
Knud Jespersen, one of the younger members, whose attitude was at that time not quite clear but which did
not agree with Larsen's. The invitations were, however,
not accepted by all who had received them; first the
Soviet Union refused to send a delegation, because of
the new constitution which had been drafted and which
was not considered to be a genuinely socialist document;

after the Soviet refusal many other parties retired. The Danish party did not refuse to attend, but it changed its delegation by substituting another man for Larsen, who was considered too unreliable to expose to the Yugoslav poison. After it had returned, the delegation reported to the central committee and afterwards Larsen gave his opinion, in which he criticised several points in the draft of the Yugoslav constitution but on the whole expressed himself in such a way that one can see how the lesser spirits in the party could be persuaded that Larsen had become a Titoist; and one need not doubt that the die-hards did whatever they could in order to confirm this impression.

Larsen used the opportunity to explain his own position, and it is particularly interesting to see how, trying to make his points of view clear, he found it convenient to base himself on what Mikoyan had said to the twentieth party congress in 1956, which Larsen had attended. Indeed, Mikoyan's contribution was highly interesting, and in a way much more sensational than Khruschev's secret speech, as it dealt with much more fundamental problems than the cult of personality and such stuff. His was really a discussion of Marxist principles, and it is worth noticing how Larsen was attracted by this piece of deep-searching analysis, which, if put forward by some minor figure, would have been branded as sheer heresy. But it is also worth noticing that Larsen, however attracted he might be, avoided mention of the most dangerous of the heresies, such as Mikoyan's new doctrine about the possibility of a peaceful transition from capitalism to socialism. In fact the doctrine, which had also found its way into the Yugoslav draft, was refuted by Larsen and characterised as a 'social democratic theory'. In other words, one gets the impression that Larsen was wavering between what he would have liked to say and what he dared say or considered opportune to say at a moment when his leadership was in the balance.

Even then, his speech caused a mighty stir, and it

forced him to try to explain his points of view even more explicitly. So he sat down and conceived a memorandum which can be said to be his declaration of faith. His principal claim was that the Danish party should emancipate itself from dependence on Moscow and become a genuinely Danish party. He writes:

> We know that the most important propagandist weapon against us is the slogan that we are not a Danish, not an independent party, but that the Danish communists receive their orders from Moscow. It is no use our insisting in the most vehement way that we are a Danish and an independent party. Even the most correct political line on our part does not guarantee that we will earn the confidence of the Danish people, as long as most of them think and say: yes, but even then—we cannot trust the communists, for they fetch all their thoughts, ideas and politics from Moscow. But we are responsible for that ourselves. Our own behaviour makes it easier for our opponents to make us suspect.

The memorandum was published in *Land og Folk* on 28 August 1958. At first the editor had refused to publish it, but he had to do it after Larsen had appealed to the executive of the party. However, the executive agreed only after having—the day before—printed a declaration which had been adopted by the central committee, by twenty-seven votes against seven, with one abstention. In the declaration the executive says:

> We are against all trends which will make it possible to undermine and weaken the unity of the world communist movement, and in this connection we condemn the Yugoslav draft for a constitution, whose most important points of view are wrong and can only harm the international movement

through its confusion and lack of clarity. These revisionist points of view have also been heard in our
own discussions. . . .

In this way the antagonistic attitudes were underlined,
so that everybody felt a reconciliation to be impossible
and that Larsen's days as general secretary of the party
were coming to an end. In the last days of October the
party held a congress. Piotr Pospelov, a secretary to the
Soviet central committee and an expert on revisionism and
how to deal with it, was invited, and Larsen was officially
deposed, Knud Jespersen being made his successor.

But this was not the end of Larsen, rather of the
Danish Communist Party. He did not leave the party
as a lonely man, for he was followed by a considerable
retinue of trade union people and intellectuals, as well
as by so many of the rank and file that there seemed to
be good prospects for forming a new party, a socialist
party on a national basis, as suggested by Mogens Fog.
How good the prospects were was seen at the election
in 1960, when the new party got 150,000 votes, or 6.1
per cent, while the communists dropped from seventy-two
thousand votes in 1957 to twenty-seven thousand, or 1.1
per cent, which meant that they would not get any
representation in the Folketing, while Larsen won no less
than eleven seats. The official name of the new party is
'Socialistisk Folkeparti'—Socialist People's Party—usually
called merely SF. It is an anti-capitalist party, but grants
that the general development has not in all respects
followed the prognoses of Karl Marx. On the other hand
it criticises the Social Democratic Party for having stopped
being a socialist party and for having become too dependent on the trade union movement. It still hopes to
get in touch with the progressive wing of the party in
the Soviet Union, and thus to promote a continuing
dialogue within the socialist world.

SF has a rather mixed composition—on the one hand there are many intellectuals: among those who helped Larsen to establish the party was his old friend Mogens Fog, who is still a valued adviser but has refused to take part in actual politics in public. He had continued his scientific career and became in 1967 the rector of Copenhagen University. Kaj Moltke also joined SF, in spite of his many conflicts with Larsen, and became a member of the Folketing. The deputy chairman of the party is a professor of zoology, Morten Lange. The other part of the membership are youngsters, hippies and flower children, who have been keen partakers in all kinds of demonstrations, CND marches, Vietnam protests and so on; this rather unruly crowd, which may have joined the party on false premisses, could not in the long run support parliamentary procedures, which SF relies on. So there was a break, and at the following election they launched a party of their own, called 'Venstresocialisterne'—the Left Socialists. VS, as it is called, managed to get four seats, one of them going to Kaj Moltke, but this party soon split in two and the general impression is that VS will go down at the next election while SF has come to stay.

As already mentioned, the Communist Party only obtained 1.1 per cent of the votes at the election of 1960; this was exactly the same figure as in 1932 when the party started its career under Larsen, and it has not been able since then to get enough votes to be represented again in the Folketing. The new leader, Knud Jespersen, has proved quite capable, but behind him stands the grey eminence, Ib Nørlund, and it is his hand which is discernible behind the proclamations, resolutions and speeches which have poured out plentifully with all their empty verbiage. Much of what Nørlund has said and written through the last ten years is directed against SF; quite naturally, as SF has nearly killed the Communist Party and deprived it of its natural right of existence, has—to use Marxist terminology—deprived it of its objective conditions. Even when addressing an international audience Nørlund still directly or indirectly hints at sf and Larsen. Thus in 1960, at a communist conference in Moscow, Nørlund said:

> For our party it has been evident that revisionism has been the chief danger. In order to win in the struggle against revisionism, it has been necessary for our party to liberate itself from sectarian impediments. The revisionistic groupings have, in our country, developed more and more into unprincipled opportunism, which in the interests of the bourgeoisie is to bear witness against the communists and the socialist world. In their endeavours to create confusion, they often borrow the theories which have been first formulated by the Yugoslav revisionists.

But the very same accusation—the accusation of being the instrument of the revisionist devil—has also been directed against the Communist Party itself:

> Exactly in this situation, when the creation of the socialist camp, the growing unity of the peoples against imperialism and reaction, the great victories of the liberation movements of the colonial peoples have created the best possible conditions for new, great victories in the struggle of the working class and the labouring masses against oppression and war, for peace and socialism—exactly in this situation modern revisionism has been resurrected, and has grown strong within the communist movement in a number of countries, among these also in the Communist Party of the Soviet Union.

These lines have been taken from a pamphlet called 'To All Communists in Demark', and it comes from a group of supporters of the Chinese outlook, who had established a small circle of people which in 1964 constituted itself as a party called the 'Communist Working Group'. Its two leaders, Gotfred Appel and Benito

Scocozza, are both intellectuals, and the new party has so far had no appeal to the working class. But it should not be forgotten that inside the Danish Communist Party there are a certain number of young people who are in doubt about the line which the party is following, and who have some sympathy with the Chinese point of view. Whether they will ever speak up, or whether they will stick to the official line, or one day leave the party, all depends on what kind of policy the leaders pursue, and this again is dependent on the international scene and what troubles the Russian party leaders go on creating. In that respect they have so far been quite insensitive to the problems of the western parties. Thus the fall of Khruschev and the way it was done caused much criticism, and Knud Jespersen had to go to Moscow and ask for an explanation. He came back and told his audiences that they could go home and sleep quietly, that the new leaders had done what they had done because of Khruschev's mistakes, an explanation which did not by any means satisfy everybody. While the peculiar debate with China was going on the whole time, so that most communists got accustomed to it, considering it as one of the curses sent by heaven, the invasion of Czechoslovakia came as a shock and once more created much misgiving and anxiety. This necessitated another of Jespersen's and Nørlund's trips to Moscow, followed by explanations meant to calm shattered nerves.

In May 1969 Jespersen was once more in Moscow as a delegate to the international communist congress. He also contributed to the stream of oratory, but in contrast with his Norwegian and Swedish comrades, who expressed themselves in very critical terms, he had not one word to say about the Soviet occupation of a socialist country and spent most of his time in prophesying the collapse of the capitalist world. The leaders of the Danish Communist Party do not neglect any chance of announcing that they are a purely Danish party, taking no orders from other countries, and will not, as Ib Nørlund expressed it, 'allow themselves to be conducted by Moscow's baton', but the louder these announcements, the more they have clung to the orders issued from the Kremlin. This is also the experience which the great majority of the former members of the party seem to have had—they have drawn their conclusions from them and left the party. It is a very small and insignificant group which has remained. The theoretical experts such as Ib Nørlund like to talk a lot about the old idea of the withering away of the state: so far it is only the withering away of the party which has taken visible shape before our eyes.

## 2. THE COMMUNIST PARTY OF NORWAY

PETER P. ROHDE

In 1848, in Norway, Henrik Ibsen, a young student of pharmacy and still completely unknown, wrote his first drama, *Catalina*, inspired by the February revolution in France. The poet Bjørnstjerne Bjørnson was full of enthusiasm for the revolution, and a young student of literature and music, Marcus Thrane, a utopian socialist much influenced by Saint-Simon, felt himself compelled to do something for the oppressed classes. 'Socialism', he wrote, 'will bring the downfall of the old rule that one should have the wages, the other the work, and instead introduce the rule that everybody should receive according to his work. For only a society which is based on such a rule is based on justice and truth. Only in such a society will there be true freedom, equality and Christian fraternity among men'. The great thing about Thrane was that he saw this problem as a political problem, which could only be solved through the class struggle. His historical significance is that for the first time he stirred the lower classes in Norway to class-consciousness and political struggle. He started the first labour unions, and the movement ran like wildfire all through the country until the bureaucratic forces, frightened by the socialist threats, had Thrane and his intimate collaborators arrested and sentenced to four years' imprisonment. And when at last Thrane was released the whole movement had collapsed and there was no chance of restoring it to life again. But even so, this opening chapter in the history of the Norwegian labour movement has had its effect and been an inspiring force. It has had no parallel in the other Scandinavian countries. In Denmark there was a kind of revolution in 1848, which forced the king to

relinquish his absolute powers and allow a free constitution, but it all happened in a day, and it was a national
and bourgeois revolution, with no apparent involvement
of the working classes. In Sweden there was nothing of
this kind.


The next decades witnessed the breakthrough of industrialism in Norway, involving a much heavier exploitation
of the working classes. The Liberal Party, called Venstre—
the Left—as in Denmark tried to adopt the cause of the
labourers in much the same way as the British liberals did
under Lloyd George before the first world war; they were
also quite successful for a long time, and this will account
for the fact that a socialist party was not established
until 1887. In that year, Det Norske Arbeiderparti—the
Norwegian Workers' Party—was launched by amalga-
mating a number of small political groups and some
equally small trade unions. They were still in many ways
dependent on the Venstre, and it remained one of their
problems for the future how to emancipate themselves
from the political and ideological leadership of that party.
The leader of the Venstre, Sverdrup, had got his first
great inspiration from Marcus Thrane and thus was about
as much of a socialist as most of the members of the new
Arbeiderparti. This was one reason why the new party
had a slow and difficult start; another reason was that the
political energies of all the parties in these years was
absorbed by one great national problem, the relation of
the country to Sweden. Norway had been linked to
Sweden through a personal union since 1814, but the
Norwegians felt they were discriminated against; they
much regretted the Swedish supremacy and at last declared unilaterally that the union had been dissolved. It
nearly developed into a war but Sweden refrained, being
urged by the great powers to find a peaceful solution.
Norway, however, received the support of the great powers
after having declared that she would remain a kingdom,

and thus the Arbeiderparti was outmanoeuvred and had to see its hopes of a republic disappear.

This was in 1905, but 1905 was also the year of the first Russian revolution, which made its reverberations felt everywhere; in Norway in particular it caused a radicalisation of the youth movement of the Arbeiderparti, which in turn had an effect on the party itself. From 1906 there was a strong left wing inside the party, whose most talked-about man and strongest personality was the leader, Martin Tranmael, then twenty-seven years of age, a young craftsman of unusual rhetorical gifts, with a vision of the future and a humanitarian outlook. He had his stronghold in the trade unions and he was a resolute protagonist of violent methods if these were required. He was much influenced by syndicalist ideas and aimed at a social revolution. He found in the wages struggle the most convenient instrument for promoting the revolutionary spirit and saw in the general strike the effective means to bring about the social revolution.

But the party itself was, for a long time to come, still a relatively insignificant factor in political life. In 1903 it had won its first four seats in the Storting, out of 117, a number which the following elections increased to ten, eleven and twenty-three in 1912, but which then sank slightly in the next two elections. It was the war, and particularly its aftermath, which transformed the Arbeiderparti into an important political force, and that did not happen immediately. The defeat of the socialist attempt to declare war upon war by a universal strike in the name of international brotherhood at first had a rather paralysing effect on the socialist movement; the Second International seemed to be completely dead. Late in 1915, however, an international conference was called together in Zimmerwald, in Switzerland, by the 'Italo-Swiss Committee', which set up a permanent secretariat and issued a manifesto against the war. The Arbeiderparti was invited to attend, but refused; then the youth movement was invited, who accepted. From that moment the two wings within the party had their own foreign contacts; the left-wingers nourished relations with the Russian refugees in Norway, such as Bucharin, who wrote several articles for their paper under the pseudonym Nota Bene.

The Russian revolution created a dangerous situation in Norway. The food situation was serious, and prepared the ground for disturbances, and in a good many industries workers' councils sprang up spontaneously. They did not in fact achieve much, but were symptomatic of the atmosphere, and of a new and more aggressive mood. This was demonstrated at the congress of the Arbeiderparti at Easter 1918, when the former minority, under the guidance of Tranmael, succeeded in capturing the party leadership, and introduced a more revolutionary ideology. The debate turned mostly around the use of the general strike; the former leaders had maintained as their point of view that a social democracy could never use violent methods, or accept dictatorship whether of the upper class or from the lower class. Tranmael retorted that the workers could not renounce their right to proclaim a general strike as a means of preventing oppression on the part of the minority. He explained that as a revolutionary party, a socialist party could not endorse the right of the propertied classes to exploit and oppress the working classes, even if the former were supported by a majority in Parliament. Accordingly the party would have to prepare itself for revolutionary mass action in the struggle for the economic emancipation of the working class, though as a party the social democrats would try to gain political power by way of elections.

The question of the dictatorship of the proletariat had never been discussed previously in the Arbeiderparti, but came on the agenda as a result of the bolshevik revolution. Tranmael declared that dictatorship by a minority was out of the question, but still he left open the possibility of some form of workers' dictatorship. Nobody insisted on formulating a clear conception of what the idea implied. The same thing happened with the notion of revolutionary mass action. Some people interpreted it as meaning a rising with armed force, but for most of Tranmael's followers this was unthinkable. Most people in Norway were strongly anti-militarist, but from a pacifist point of view, which was irreconcilable with an armed rising. Still, Tranmael carried the day at the congress, and the basic principles he had suggested were adopted by 159 votes against 126. Thus the Arbeiderparti had, at least in principle, become a revolutionary party.

The principles which had been discussed so ardently at the 1918 congress, but not sufficiently clarified, were soon seen in practice in their naked reality elsewhere, particularly in Hungary, where a general strike prepared the way for a dictatorship by a minority. And out of the convulsions of the terrible events of 1919 was born the Communist International. Creating an International had been a difficult job, particularly because the German communist group, the Spartakusbund, had been violently against it. This group was quite small, but influential because of the outstanding personalities of its leaders, above all Karl Liebknecht and Rosa Luxemburg. Rosa Luxemburg was the most consistent adversary of Lenin's plan for a Communist International, because she feared the bolshevik dictatorship and its consequences if applied to western communism. It was not the idea of a Communist International which she opposed, but she wanted it to be established only when some strong, revolutionary mass parties existed in the west to counterbalance the bolshevik pressure. So when the constituent meeting was called to Moscow she persuaded her group to send two delegates with a mandate to oppose the formation of the International, and to refuse to join it if it should, nevertheless, be founded. This act of defiance of the bolsheviks was about the last thing she managed to achieve —three days later she was killed.

In the event, the Communist International was founded, with Zinoviev, a brilliant speaker and a master of double-dealing and intrigue, as its president, and with Bucharin and Radek as his deputies. Bucharin, who had an intimate personal knowledge of Scandinavian, and especially of the Norwegian workers' movements, was the great theoretician of the Bolshevik Party, but lacked real political understanding; Radek, who had an acute grasp of political matters, and many brilliant qualities, lacked that deep-rooted moral balance which knows how to distinguish between right and wrong, that is, he lacked moral character. It was significant and fatal that the leadership of the Comintern was thus entirely in the hands of the Russians, which meant that the so-called International was used by Moscow as an instrument in the hands of, and a support for, Russian bolshevism.

However, expectations were high in the beginning. In the first number of the Comintern newspaper, Zinoviev prophesied that within a year not only would all Europe be a Soviet republic but it would already be forgetting that there had ever been a fight over it. The first outside party to adhere to the new organisation in 1919 was the Bulgarian Communist Party, and the second was the Norwegian Arbeiderparti. This seems rather odd, and indeed it is, for there is a blatant contrast between the Bulgarian and Norwegian parties: the former had evolved under the constant influence of the Russian brother party, while the latter was not even properly Marxist—it was a curious blend of reformism and anarcho-syndicalism with a dash of Marxist doctrine. In many ways the Norwegian party was the antithesis of bolshevism, being against civil war and for pacifism, against ideological unity and for a certain amount of individualism, and against the subordination of the trade unions to the political movement. Yet, curious as it may seem, the same phenomenon is seen in other countries as well: in Italy, Holland and France it was the syndicalist groups which in the beginning felt themselves attracted and joined the Comintern. This meant that Lenin had been successful in the tactics expressed in *The State and Revolution*, where he says that on the international battlefield, bolshevism would have to seek the support of the anarchists against the social democratic 'traitors'.

But this tactic could not be pursued successfully for long. It was true that when the second congress of the Comintern met in Moscow in July 1920 it was quite an impressive crowd which gathered round Lenin's platform. There were, apart from Italy, Bulgaria and Norway, delegations from all the Balkan countries, from the French socialists, the German independent socialists, the socialist Left in Czechoslovakia, from several Asian countries, and from small communist parties in Germany, Austria, Hungary and Poland. It was a very heterogeneous crowd, counting a good many syndicalists and pacifists, and it was not easy to see how such a rabble could be made to stick together and follow one authority. This had been painfully realised in the executive committee of the Comintern, particularly because Lenin had just started his campaign against the ultra-Left by publishing *Left-wing Communism, an infantile disease*. The moment was thought ripe for action, and it was a critical moment, not only for Russia, but for Europe, as the red army was rapidly advancing on Warsaw, the collapse of Poland was considered imminent, and the German communists were preparing to launch the revolution as soon as the red cavalry was in sight.

At this critical point the Comintern leaders had made up their minds to challenge the workers of the world to break up their traditional organisations. They were convinced that most European social democratic leaders were incompetent traitors, who ought not to be admitted to the Comintern, so they sought to make the conditions of admission as acceptable to the masses as possible while making them unacceptable to the leaders. The outcome of this tactic was the Twenty-one Theses, which were to be accepted or rejected by all aspirants to membership of the Comintern. They insisted on the most absolute obedience to orders from the Comintern, underlined the duty of all member parties to support the Soviet Union, insisted that every party which joined the

Comintern must call itself a communist party, and must break with all social democratic organisations, including the trade unions, and that they must be prepared to carry out purges from time to time even if this meant repeated splits every few years.

These theses caused great consternation in most western countries. When the leaders of the Norwegian party learned about them, they were shocked, the one most shaken being Tranmael, who saw the foundation of everything he had fought for being shattered. He had wanted a democratic federalism and a revolutionary humanism, while the Russians wanted a robot-like discipline and obedience, not only to the leadership of the Comintern but to the Russian party first of all. His immediate reaction, therefore, was to turn the theses down. But the majority of the party leadership felt that it would be suicidal to break with the Russians at this moment. They had themselves contributed towards creating goodwill and a feeling of solidarity with the Russians; there was still a civil war going on and a break with the Comintern would, in the eyes of most party members, look like a betrayal of a people that was fighting with its back against the wall. A split in the Arbeiderparti seemed unavoidable, but it would be smallest if membership of the Comintern was continued and some modifying conditions procured to preserve cooperation with the trade union movement. Such conditions were in fact granted by the Comintern, and Tranmael agreed, even if reluctantly, to accept the theses. They were then endorsed by the party congress by 281 votes against 20, but such a majority was only possible because the right wing of the party had already seceded.

After a conference, which they had summoned as soon as it became clear that the majority was willing to swallow the theses, the right-wing resolved by 136 votes to 18 to establish a party of its own; they called it Norges socialdemokratiske parti, a name which indicated that they meant to create a party on the lines of the Swedish and Danish social democratic parties, and in collaboration with them. At the next elections in 1921 the new party obtained eighty-three thousand votes and six seats in the Storting, while the vote of the Arbeiderparti was reduced from 217,000 to 192,000, which gave them twenty-nine seats. Together the two labour parties secured 30 per cent of the votes, slightly less than at the previous election. The attitude of the Arbeiderparti to the Twenty-one Theses had still another effect, as Tranmael refused to continue as secretary of the party and expressed the wish to go back to journalism, where he had started. Officially he based his decision on the fact that the party had refused to follow his line but the real reason was presumably that he anticipated all the trouble that would follow in the wake of the continued discussions about the theses and preferred to meet this from a more favourable strategic position. So he was made editor of the party newspaper, *Arbeiderbladet*, while his former postion was shared among four people, of whom Trygve Lie, later secretary general of the United Nations, was made leader of the party bureau.

The fourth congress of the Comintern in 1922 had put the Norwegian case on its agenda as a special problem; it was discussed in a committee headed by Bucharin and with Trotsky among its members. The committee did not pay any attention to the opinions of the Norwegian delegation and put strong pressure to bear on it to accept the resolutions which the Comintern had prepared. Among the new aspects of these resolutions there was one point in particular which seemed to be quite unacceptable to the Norwegians: that the trade unions should be subordinated to the communist parties. This was a demand which had its roots in the strategy of the second Comintern congress of 1920, when the tactic of splitting all the workers' organisations was launched. The Comintern leadership seemed to make a special point of splitting the trade unions; in the end this endeavour destroyed the chances of the Comintern but it is fairly easy to see what caused the leaders to make the attempt.

For at about the same time there were endeavours to

reorganise the Trade Union International, and they proved successful; the reconstructed organisation was born in Amsterdam and was usually referred to as the Amsterdam International. The Russians quite rightly saw that this would become one of the strongholds of the non-communist workers' movement and accordingly they set their minds on destroying it from the very beginning. That was why the Communist Trade Union International, or Profintern, as it was called, was established; its purpose was underlined in the tenth of the Twenty-one Theses, according to which all communists must 'emphatically urge the break with the yellow Amsterdam International' and advocate support of the red Trade Union International. It is characteristic of the confusion within the Comintern leadership that the directive contained in Thesis 10 was in strict contradiction to the rules which Lenin himself had laid down, that all workers should remain within the existing unions. The Comintern had its explanation ready when met with this argument: they claimed there was no real contradiction, as it was quite possible to combine unity at the national level with an international split. However, this piece of Marxist dialectics proved too much for simpler minds and the international split was followed by national splits in several countries; of all the undivided trade union movements only the Bulgarians definitely affiliated to the Profintern.

When confronted with the new and more acrimonious demands, the leaders of the Arbeiderparti, who had had no end of trouble up to then from the Comintern, and uninterrupted interventions from its executive committee in internal Norwegian affairs, took it for granted that the party could no longer remain within the Comintern. But they were too far ahead of their followers; even at this point the majority of the members felt themselves in duty bound towards the bolshevik revolution and could not conceive of a break, so that it was postponed once more. The Russians, feeling that something was going wrong in Norway, sent Karl Radek to Oslo in the hope that he might avert a break, and he succeeded. Radek brought about a compromise; Tranmael, who had been the principal spokesman for a break, acknowledged that the proposal had been premature, it was withdrawn and formal unity re-established. But every such compromise is likely to be unworkable. In order to create a clear line, Tranmael and his sympathisers worked out a programme which was meant to be an interpretation of the compromise but which in effect implied a dissociation from the Twenty-one Theses, and this programme became the main issue at a national party congress in February 1923.

The Comintern found it advisable to be represented at a high level at this meeting, and sent Bucharin, because he was well known and liked in Oslo. At the congress, Tranmael, as the representative of the majority, though rather an uncertain one, gave an account of his new programme, while the viewpoints of the minority were expounded by a young and comparatively unknown person, a joiner who had come fresh from the youth organisation, Peder Furubotn. He had been entirely won over by the ideas behind the Twenty-one Theses, and he propounded his views with immense oratorical skill and assurance, even though he sometimes gave his listeners the impression that he was not always fully the master of his subject. There is no doubt that he made an impression on his audience, but the majority did not give in to his rhetoric, nor did they submit to Bucharin's, and when it came to a vote, the programme which Tranmael had submitted to the congress was passed by 94 votes to 92.

On a strict interpretation of the Comintern theses, which involved the excommunication of all dissenters, this should have been the end, but it was not. The Comintern had already lost so many adherents on account of the unhappy theses that the leaders, in striking contrast with what the theses proclaimed, were willing to go a long way to keep the flock inside the pen and accepted the Tranmael programme. In spite of this acceptance, the Comintern could not refrain from interfering in the internal affairs of the Norwegian party, sometimes condemning unacceptable persons, sometimes demanding changes in the organisational or editorial arrangements. Thus the executive of the Comintern asserted that the party should start an anti-religious campaign by declaring atheism to be part of Marxism. The Arbeiderparti leadership could not swallow all this and called an extraordinary congress to be held towards the end of 1923.

By this time there were many, both of the former majority and of the minority of the previous congress, who realised that a break was inevitable, and indeed not only inevitable but desirable. Those who were still ardent adherents of the Comintern had sent a man to Moscow just before the congress was due, to urge the executive to do something to have Tranmael and his followers deposed or silenced. His name was Arvid G. Hansen. The Comintern did what it could, and nominated the famous French communist Marcel Cachin to go to Norway as its representative. But Cachin did not turn up and the executive then sent a German communist and former clergyman, by the name of Edward Hoernel; Hoernel started by distributing a letter from the Comintern which declared the congress to be incompetent to adopt any proposal which was contrary to the theses of the Comintern. These theses were to be accepted and consented to formally, and if they were turned down the majority would automatically cease to be affiliated to the Comintern which would from then on consider the minority group to be its branch in Norway.

This was an ultimatum, and Tranmael branded it as an immoral act, which must be withdrawn, so that the members of the congress could make their decision 'as free persons on their own responsibility'. He then moved a motion rejecting the ultimatum and this motion was passed by 169 votes to 110. The defeated minority left the congress hall, singing the 'Internationale'. The very next day, Sunday, 4 November 1923, the minority held a closed meeting which, while unholding its right to consider itself the real Arbeiderparti, because it was acting in accordance with the party statutes, and the majority were heretics, finally resolved to change its name to Norges kommunistiske parti—NKP.

NKP was quite a strong party in the beginning. Of the twenty-eight members of the Storting who had represented the Arbeiderparti, thirteen decided to join the new party, and already on the day following its establishment the party was able to launch a new paper, called *Norges Kommunistblad*. Sverre Støstad, one of the younger people who had made their entry into political life at the election of 1921, was elected chairman of the party. But it was not he who left his mark on NKP, but Furubotn, who became party secretary, and Arvid Hansen, both of them intransigent communists. There was great uncertainty about the relative strengths of the three workers' parties which now existed, and also about the ideological attitudes of the Arbeiderparti and NKP, both of them claiming to be communist parties, and both revolutionary parties which subscribed to the theory of the dictatorship of the proletariat. They could not disagree about Marxist ideology, their dispute concerned only the obligation to obey the Comintern and their right to decide their own internal affairs. Thus when the youth organisation of the Arbeiderparti, which had lost more than half its members to NKP, was reconstructed, it took the name of Venstrekommunistisk Ungdomsfylking—Left Communist Youth League—in order to demonstrate that they were even more communist than the communists. So the whole controversy boiled down to this: was the revolutionary class struggle to be directed by the Arbeiderparti or by Moscow?

There was great excitement about the next general election, which would reveal the true strength of the three parties. It was held in 1924 and was a great triumph for the Arbeiderparti: although there was a small decrease in its vote, from 21 to 18 per cent, considering that about half its members in the Storting had joined NKP one might have expected the vote to drop by half, so this was a satisfactory result. It proved that the vast majority of the working population accepted the policy laid down by Tranmael and his followers. The Social Democratic Party got 8 per cent as against 9 per cent in 1921, and NKP got 6 per cent. The three parties got twenty-four, eight and six seats in the Storting respectively. Three years later there was another election and the popular vote for NKP fell to 4 per cent. In 1930 it fell to 1.4 per cent, which did not give it any representation in the Storting at all, and it remained unrepresented until after the war. At its lowest point, in 1936, the NKP vote fell to 0.3 per cent—4,376 votes. At the same time the Arbeider-parti had increased its poll from 18 per cent in 1923 to 43 per cent in 1936, with seventy seats. This very con-siderable progress was partly due to the fact that the social democrats, who had seceded from the Arbeider-parti because of its acceptance of the Twenty-one Theses, now found no reason why they should still continue as an independent party and in 1927 they joined their old party again.

This inspired some of the people who had been active in forming NKP to re-join the Arbeiderparti, because they wanted to contribute to the re-union of the working-class movement. Among those who left NKP in 1927 was Sverre Støstad, the chairman, together with a great num-ber of intellectuals. And more followed in 1928, when for the first time the Arbeiderparti was called on by the king to form a government, which it did—the most short-lived of all Norwegian governments. It lasted only eight-een days, being forced out by a flight of capital ar-ranged by the great financiers and owners of capital, who were frightened to death at the thought that a semi-com-munist government might let the revolution loose. NKP had done everything it could to prevent the amalgamation of the two workers' parties, and their tactic had been to urge the establishment of what they called a coalition party. This was natural for them in the 1920s, as it was the time of the Comintern endeavours to establish a united front everywhere in Europe, but in Norway it was a complete failure.

In 1928 the Comintern changed its policies. The united front tactic had failed not only in Norway but all over, so the social democrats were now to be exposed to the workers as 'class-enemies'. This was a prelude to the great purges in the Soviet Union, and the leaders of the Arbeiderparti were exposed to vile smear campaigns and branded as the most effective and willing instruments of the capitalists. But in 1935, when Hitler had taken over in Germany and threatened Europe, events led to the next stage in the tactical meanderings of the Comintern, which now promoted the popular front of all democratic parties to fight the fascist danger. NKP faithfully followed the new line; it took up negotiations with the Arbeiderparti and even declared itself willing to join the Second International if necessary for unity. In fact the only thing which NKP could not possibly accept was any mention of Trotsky; this was a point of some importance at that time because Trotsky had been given a residence permit in Norway after being expelled from the Soviet Union, and one of his enthusiastic admirers, the author Helge Krog, had even started a Norwegian branch of the Fourth International.

The political situation in Norway had been transformed in 1935 when a second labour government had been installed, to remain firmly in office for many years. It is easy to understand that the NKP could not achieve much against such massive strength on the part of the Arbeiderparti, and that it was reduced to commenting on events and trying to put its spoke in the wheel of its more successful rival for the allegiance of the working masses. In fact with its infinitesimal number of members and of voters NKP only just existed in the 1930s.

During the years when the Arbeiderparti formed the government, a change took place in it: responsibility always has a sobering effect and the party gradually adopted the same shape as the Swedish and Danish Social Democratic parties, even if its ideology was still nearer to

the communist model. The fundamental difference between it and NKP, however, was not of an ideological nature, for NKP had gone so far as agreeing to join the Second International to bring about a popular front; basically
their differences were still over their respective attitudes
to the Soviet Union. The Arbeiderparti insisted on remaining absolutely independent, a party which took no
orders from abroad, while the NKP, as was obvious from
its manoeuvring, did nothing else. That came out more
clearly than ever when the Molotov-Ribbentrop pact was
signed on 23 August 1939. This sudden somersault caught
NKP napping; the leaders were at first at their wits' ends
but they soon accepted the new situation and thus served
to isolate NKP even more. There were, of course, valid
arguments in favour of the Russian decision to keep out
of the approaching clash, since the endeavours of the
Soviet Union to bring about a military agreement with the
western powers had been cold-shouldered and ignored,
so that the Russians could form the impression that the
western powers meant to let the .nazis loose upon them
and allow the Germans a free hand in the east. But even
then, the agreement served to isolate the communists,
and in Norway this was even more the case when, at the
end of the year, the Russians attacked Finland, which, in
spite of the people speaking a language that is absolutely incomprehensible to the Swedes, Norwegians, Ice-
landers and Danes, is considered a part of the Scandinavian quintet. The Arbeiderparti identified itself
completely with the Finnish cause, as did all the other
political parties except NKP, which equally ardently advocated the Russian viewpoint.

The nadir of the political line of NKP was reached when
the Germans occupied Denmark and Norway. The official
viewpoint of the party was that the war between Germany
and the western powers was an imperialistic war, and
when the Norwegian government showed more friendly
feelings towards Britain than towards Germany it meant
that it was putting itself at the disposal of British imperialism. Consequently it was in the interests of the

Norwegian people to avoid all resistance to the occupation forces, even passive resistance. This attitude was possibly taken in the hope of avoiding repressive action on the part of the Germans, but it was labelled treachery by the rest of the population and anyhow it did not save the communists. While in Denmark the Communist Party was left in peace until the war against the Soviet Union was launched, in Norway the Germans struck down the communists in August 1940. One would think that this was enough to arouse the party from its torpor, but it was not. There was still a non-aggression pact between the Soviet Union and Germany, and the party obviously felt itself bound to respect that. But from June 1941 that agreement did not exist any more.

It was not immediately evident what line of policy the party wanted to adopt. Furubotn, who had spent some years in the Soviet Union, had come back in time to take over the leadership of the party during the war. He was appointed chairman of the party at a secret session of the Central Committee in December 1941. His aim had been, from the autumn of 1940, to form militant groups to fight the Germans and to establish large-scale sabotage. He realised that such a policy would mean great hardship for the civil population and all kinds of reprisals; that it would aggravate the general situation and might lead to civil war, such as was the case in Yugoslavia at about the same time. And that was exactly what he wanted to happen. Accordingly Furubotn fulminated against the bourgeois 'home front', which tried to build up a united front against the occupation forces and their Norwegian followers, the Quislings. But the passivity for which Furubotn was blaming them, backed up by the so-called 'freedom transmitter' which broadcast from Russian territory, was in fact directed from London. After three weeks of heroic but hopeless fighting in 1940, the Norwegian troops with their king and the whole government had retired northwards and had at last been transferred to Britain, where they continued their resistance. Thus the Norwegian people had a king and government in active struggle against the Germans. That was why the Norwegians never had a comprehensive freedom council like in Denmark, where the king and the government were put out of action when they became the prisoners of the nazis. For the whole of the war the Norwegians received their orders, what to do and what not to do, from Britain.

In 1943 Furubotn wanted to see a freedom council formed, comprising groups from the extreme right to the communists, and his proposals were put before the London government, but his suggestions were cold-shouldered and ignored. It was too easy to see that Furubotn was fishing in troubled waters and aiming at goals that were not in accordance with the national needs of the Norwegian people as a whole. But Furubotn was not in agreement with the whole of his own party either. A group opposed the extremists, though it is rather difficult to tell what they actually wanted to substitute for their policy. But when Furubotn finished one of his rhetorical appeals with the slogan 'down with the imperialist war', it was not easy to make out which of the warring parties he was talking about and consequently exactly what kind of struggle he wanted. It is very difficult to give everyone his due in this controversy, but not so very important either, since it was not so much ideological differences as personal animosities that lay behind the discord. But it was a disagreement which cast a long shadow, continuing even after the war and reaching its climax as late as 1949.

There can be no doubt about Furubotn's personal courage. He was the only underground leader who operated all through the war under his own name, and it was to a great extent due to his activities that the communists were quite popular for a limited period after the war, even if their share in the actual fight had been rather dubious. No doubt their prestige was also to a great extent due to the Russians, who had helped to liberate Norway by

chasing the Germans out of the northern parts in the
Finnmark—and had then withdrawn. The coalition government which was formed immediately after the end of
the war under the leadership of Einar Gerhardsen, who
for the next two decades was to be the central personality
in the Arbeiderparti, included two communists, Strand
Johansen and Kirsten Hansteen, whose husband had been
executed by the Germans. Gerhardsen had been in a
concentration camp during the greater part of the war,
together with some of the leading communists, and they
had discussed the possibilities of a merger of the two
parties after the war. Now the discussions were taken up
again. But nothing came out of them; this was entirely
due to Furubotn's negative attitude, as he feared, and
with good reason, that NKP would not be able to maintain
its identity and policy when confronted with the experienced leaders of the Arbeiderparti.

At the first postwar election in 1945 the communists
polled 177,000 votes, or nearly 12 per cent, which gave
the party eleven seats in the Storting, an enormous jump
from the miserable position held before the war. But it
did not last: at the next election in 1949 the number of
votes had already dropped to 103,000, or 6 per cent and
the election in 1953 showed a further drop to ninety
thousand, or 5 per cent. This decline in popular support
precipitated the showdown which would have taken place
in any case at some point. In 1946 Furubotn had been
elected general secretary of the party, and his wartime
policy was highly praised, particularly by the member of
the Storting Emil Løvlien, who on that occasion made
some highly critical remarks about the general line of the
party at the beginning of the war, implying that the faults
and weaknesses which the party had committed during
the first phase of the occupation had been corrected by
the policy which Furubotn had introduced.

But Furubotn's triumph did not last for long. Even in
1946 some of his closest collaborators were expelled from
the party, but the strife did not come out into the open
until October 1949, after the first electoral defeat had

given the opposition a favourable background for launching an attack on Furubotn. On 24 October, Strand Johansen a communist member of the first postwar government gave a speech to one of the leading trade unions, which was followed by a resolution against the 'second centre' inside NKP, meaning the Furubotn group. The next day this group, which was actually a majority, offered their resignations, and on 26 October there followed the formal expulsion of Furubotn and his adherents. These unexpected and sudden events, which must have taken the great mass of the members of the party by surprise, were explained on 27 October in an article in the party newspaper, *Friheten*, in which the expelled leaders were accused of having constituted an opposition inside the party which had been 'unmasked and denounced ten months ago' but had continued its activities. It was said to have aimed at forcing on a 'policy which eliminates the class struggle and replaces it by bourgeois nationalism' and of having been in reality 'a Trotskyist, bourgeois-nationalistic, Titoist centre', which had paralysed the party central committee by endless and futile discussions.

These accusations were followed by the disclosure of other crimes, such as having formed secret military forces during the occupation, which of course was quite true; but Strand Johansen came out with these revelations because now, in 1949, four years after the war, he could reveal something more, namely that Furubotn had aimed at overthrowing the established order as soon as the Germans had been driven out—which was probably also quite true. In other words, what at that time had won immense prestige for Furubotn could be used four years later as a criminal charge against him. Johansen even added: 'When we take over in Norway these people will be held responsible and sentenced to hanging'. After this effort Johansen was taken to hospital; he had been seen at a window of his home calling for help against attackers, though the police, when they entered the house, found no trace of the persons alleged to be concerned. A statement issued by Emil Løvlien on 30 October said that

Strand Johansen was merely overworked after the election campaign and the purge of the Titoists, but the fact is that in spite of having won the day inside NKP, Johansen never returned to political life, and Løvlien, having thus in a most unexpected way got rid of both his competitors, was elected general secretary of the party. Under Løvlien's leadership an extensive purge was carried out of Furubotn supporters. This was paradoxical because Løvlien, in 1946, when Furubotn was elected secretary, had praised the new leader and his policies at the expense of the Strand Johansen group. But now, with the latter in an asylum and the former still free and resentful, Furubotn became the primary enemy. So Løvlien dissociated himself from his previous statements and now claimed that the party had been following the correct line before Furubotn had returned during the occupation: 'We had extended and strengthened the fighting instrument against fascism' from the very beginning of the occupation.

The Norwegian purge must be seen in connection with the purges which took place about the same time in all the eastern European countries at the instigation of Stalin and Beria. The connection is clearly brought out in an article entitled 'What the process against Rajk can tell us' in the party newspaper *Friheten*, written by the chairman of the Oslo branch of the party, Knut Willoch. He writes:

> It is obvious that inside our party also there must exist nationalistic, petty bourgeois, Trotskyite and Titoist elements, enemies of the Soviet Union and of socialism, who can form the starting point for recruiting agents of the counter-revolution, and for the secret services of the bourgeois states—for instance, the Yugoslav embassy, which has managed to get hold of a survey of our party organisation.

It is a well-established fact that when somebody in the Soviet Union has become suspect and is brought into court there is no end to what he can be accused of. The same happened in the case of Furubotn. The 'second centre' was charged with attempted murders and criminal plans, and the homes of suspects were searched at night by armed men. Furubotn personally was said to have been an agent for the Gestapo. In his own camp it was not much better; they claimed that leading party people had planned to kill Furubotn and that his opponents were a network of spies working for the British Secret Service. The campaign against him had its effect: it broke Furubotn, who took to drinking. For a long time he hoped that the Soviet government and the Cominform would come to his assistance, but this only proved that he did not know the rules of the game completely, for even though he continued praising Stalin—'Never in its history has the Norwegian people had such faithful friends as the Soviet Union, the Bolshevik Party and Stalin, the man'—and condemning Tito, the very fact that he had lost control of the party apparatus was enough for the realists in the Soviet government to drop him. The purge of his followers went on into 1950, and many of Furubotn's admirers left him, some in order to stay in the party, others to leave the communist movement altogether; a few, perhaps about a hundred, remained faithful to their leader. Thus there was still a Furubotn group, and time and again it gave vigorous demonstrations of its survival, though the real significance of the group was that it embodied the guilty conscience of the NKP.

Thus, after Khruschev's secret speech at the twentieth congress of the Soviet Communist Party, and particularly after the Russian intervention in Hungary, it dawned on many party members that there might also be something wrong in Norway, and in the Norwegian Communist Party. But the continued existence of Furubotn and his group partly accounts for the fact that de-Stalinisation of the Communist Party could not make any real progress in Norway. Some people would draw a parallel between the defamation and disgraceful treatment of Imry Nagy

and that of Furubotn. Whatever the substance, the forms
in which the action against Furubotn had taken place
were equally disgusting, and it was generally understood
that if the communists had held power in Norway,
Furubotn would, as Strand Johansen had predicted, have
shared the fate of the Hungarian statesman and of
Trotsky. And just as the great Russian hero of the period
of the revolution was blotted out from official history
writing, so also was his Norwegian fellow sufferer: when
in 1963 the party celebrated its fortieth anniversary, the
name of Furubotn was not mentioned once, nor was the
purge of 1949–50.

All this put a heavy strain on the party and its leaders,
and it will in part explain the new decline in electoral
support at the election of 1961. From the ninety thousand votes of 1953, the party had sunk to sixty thousand in
1957 and now in 1961 to fifty-four thousand; its support
had declined from the peak of 12 per cent in 1945 to
3 per cent in the space of fifteen years. The election of
1961 was remarkable on account of the appearance of a
new party, the Socialistisk Folkeparti—Socialist People's
Party—which is identical in name with the Danish party
which Axel Larsen had launched with such success after
his expulsion from the Danish Communist Party in 1958.
The new Norwegian party was in fact inspired by its
Danish prototype, but there was a difference. The Danish
SF was basically a group of communists who had broken
away from the body of the party, while the Norwegian
SF had come from the Arbeiderparti. Nor was it such a
sudden phenomenon as it might at first appear. The
movement behind it had started some seven or eight
years earlier around a periodical called Orientering—
Guidance—which could be compared with the British
Left Book Club, having the same left-wing trend and
working through similar means. The editor, and the
man who became the founder of SF, Finn Gustavsen, said
that the party could have been founded already in 1949,
the year when Norway was 'fooled into NATO'. SF carries
on the old traditional pacifism of the Arbeiderparti at a

time when the latter had changed its policy in that direction and joined with the bourgeois parties in supporting armaments and the North Atlantic Treaty Organisation. Accordingly SF could call upon the support of the old pacifists who remained faithful to the original programme. But after the 1949 purge in NKP, Gustavsen's movement could equally well be attractive to those communists who were dismayed by the Stalinists inside the Communist Party. At the election of 1961 the SF scored a major success, even though it only obtained two seats in the Storting, for the Arbeiderparti had won seventy-four seats and the bourgeois parties held seventy-four seats, so that the two SF members held the political balance. But at the next election in 1965 the growing support for SF so split the labour vote as to give the bourgeois parties together a majority over the Arbeiderparti and the SF together, so that the labour government had to resign after thirty years in office and let the bourgeois parties form a coalition government. But the SF had equally damaged the NKP in this election, in which it suffered a catastrophic defeat. Its vote fell to twenty thousand, or 1.4 per cent; and it lost all representation in the Storting.

At this point NKP changed its leader. Løvlien had not proved a success and he gradually left the stage to be supplanted by the nondescript figure of Reidar Larsen, who was known to make a good impression when performing on radio or television. But apart from that he had little to his credit, and he was just as tainted with a Stalinist past as his predecessor had been. It is therefore no surprise that so far no significant change can be observed in the party. Reidar Larsen seems to know no way of avoiding the apparent destiny of NKP, which is gradually withering away. It may be some relief to him that SF suffered a split in February 1969, when at the party congress a minority of 67 out of 198 delegates walked out singing the 'Internationale'. Most of them were young people, but perhaps the few older ones among them would have some vague memories of the Sunday, 4 November 1923, when a splinter group of the Arbeiderparti in exactly the same way left the congress singing the 'Internationale', and constituting itself as an independent party adopted the name of Norges kommunistiske parti.

The consequence of this split was seen at the election held 8 September 1969, when SF lost nearly half of its vote and forfeited its two seats in the Storting. It is extremely probable that the SF has now lost whatever influence it may have had and that it will never revive. The voters who left SF have gone over to the Arbeiderparti, which increased its share of the vote from 43 to 47 per cent; they certainly did not transfer to the NKP, whose share in the vote sank from 1.4 to 1 per cent, a most remarkable development when one considers that in 1923, at the foundation of the new party, it persuaded nearly half the members of the congress of the Arbeiderparti to follow its call to form a new party. The result of this election is that Norway is the first Scandinavian country in which both the Communist Party and the SF have been defeated to such an extent that they have lost the whole of their representation in the national Parliament.

# 3. THE COMMUNIST PARTY OF SWEDEN[1]

## Å. SPARRING

The Swedish Communist Party—Sveriges kommunistiska parti (SKP)—has never belonged with the major parties of the international communist community. Great commitments are lacking in its history. Party members have no heroic time to look back on in wonder and pride. Their banners have never flown on any barricade. No period of illegality has brought out their courage and their cunning. They have never made any contributions of their own to the shaping of the history of Marxism or produced a leader in whose deeds and thoughts new generations could be trained.

SKP's national role has also been marginal. Nor have external circumstances favoured the party. During its full fifty years of existence two world wars have shaken European society while Sweden has enjoyed unbroken peace. Favourable external and internal circumstances have contributed to a rapid and stable economic development. During the greater part of the party's history, down to the present day, Sweden has been led by a social-democratic regime which has known how to combine moderation and reform in such a way that the welfare state has come about without any major birth pangs—and without the party's left-wing being tempted to jump off. Whereas the Swedish Social Democratic Workers' Party—Sveriges socialdemokratiska arbetarparti (SAP)—has until now stood close to the trade union movement, SKP has been branded by the overwhelming majority of the workers as splitters, a fact which has not been without importance in elections when the social democratic majority has been threatened by the bourgeois opposition.

In these circumstances there has been meagre nourish-
ment for revolutionary feelings. One would underrate the
sense of reality of the communist leaders if one did not
believe that they have had a clear idea of the situation.
There has always been a wide gap between SKP's revolutionary rhetoric and its daily work in Parliament and the
trade unions. With a certain degree of justice one can
view the party's whole history as an unbroken fight between 'reformers' and 'dogmatists'. During the 1920s the
struggle led to three party ruptures. In the 1940s the
party leadership, by using the 'peaceful road' as its platform, was well on its way to transforming the SKP into
a parliamentary party. After pressures from the Cominform the party unwillingly sounded a retreat. The 1950s
was the decade of impossible compromises. In the 1960s
SKP accepted a new programme and new rules, in which
the party presented itself as a parliamentary party, un-
fettered by international loyalties, and with real internal
democracy. But now, as earlier, the 'dogmatists' rallied to
the fight, and in the last party congress the clear line was
blotted out. To a great extent this picture resembles the
development of other communist parties in the indus-
trialised world. In certain respects the common problems
stand out especially clearly in SKP. This study can therefore be read as an illustration of what has also happened
in parties whose historic importance is incomparably
greater than SKP's.

### i. From opposition to subordination

The Swedish Social Democratic Workers' Party began as
a revolutionary party, though the inaugural congress of
1889 did not exclude the possibility of a peaceful transformation to socialism in Sweden. But reformism got an
early footing in the party and it did not take long before
the party was united on a practical reform policy. But the
unity was not complete. While the majority of the party
during the years before the first world war moved towards
the Right, the Social Democratic Youth League went very

firmly to the Left, and its paper *Stormklockan*—The Assault Bell—became the foremost organ of the social democratic Left. In 1912 a fraction sprang up in the party, the Alliance of the Social Democratic Left, and among its more outstanding members there were the later leaders of the Swedish Left Social Democratic Party, Zeth Höglund, Carl Lindhagen, Fredrick Ström and Ivar Vennerström. Without being revolutionary this phalanx was more impatient and less convinced of the benefits of parliamentarism than the majority in the party leadership. Above all, the party leaders were considered much too willing to compromise on the current question of defence.

In the youth league anti-militarism had strong roots. In Sweden, as elsewhere, the collapse of the International on the outbreak of war in 1914 came as a shock to the young socialists. When the defence bill was debated in 1915, and the Diet and SAP accepted re-armament in practice, the gulf between the young socialists and the party majority was much too wide to be bridged over. The Social Democratic Youth League began to carry out its own policy. In September 1915, the league was represented at the Zimmerwald Conference, where both its delegates, Zeth Höglund and Ture Nerman, adhered to the Left which was directed by Lenin. As a curiosity it may be mentioned that the first contribution—two hundred Swedish crowns—to Lenin's fraction in the Zimmerwald International was made by the Swedish youth league. For the social-democratic opposition in Sweden, however, which was to a large extent pacifist, the radicalism of the Zimmerwald Left would have been much too strong a brew, which may well be the explanation why Höglund and Nerman kept quiet about their connection with Lenin after coming home. Nor did the peace conference which the youth league convoked against the wishes of the party in spring of 1916, call for a revolutionary war. Its slogan was 'peace at any price'. They would wage the fight against the 'war activists' with extra-parliamentary mass actions.

The peace conference brought about the final break-up

within the party. Those social democrats who sympathised with the youth league left their places both on the editorial staff of *Socialdemokraten* and in the leadership of the party. The SAP congress in February 1917 could only confirm the break-up by expelling the Left opposition. Practically the whole youth league went with it. It was a very heterogeneous collection of politicians who, in May of the same year, formed the Sveriges socialdemokratiska vänsterparti—Swedish Left-Social Democratic Party (ssv). Vennerström was a pacifist, Carl Lindhagen a humanist, Fabian Mansson was deeply rooted in the old Swedish peasant democracy, nor was Zeth Höglund, the central figure in the new party, a dogmatic revolutionary. What they had in common was their opposition to the leadership of SAP. Fifteen members of Parliament came over, and over five hundred local party organisations, with a membership of about twenty thousand, joined ssv, which was not a bad start.

Although the left-wing party was born in a moment when distress and inflation were creating unrest in the ranks of the Swedish workers, its first programme can hardly be called revolutionary, and its constitution was anything but Leninist. Lindhagen, who played a predominant part in the programme committee, wished the rules and programme to be 'without rigorism'. What worried him most was the 'philosophy of power' which had taken possession of the 'democratic movements'. The new party should therefore avoid anything that had a flavour of authoritarianism and oppression by a majority. Only after the party had created a complete democracy in its own ranks could it lay a claim to show the way to others:[2]

> Not the power of the leaders, which degenerates into authoritarianism and suppression of the minority, killing the movement's vital nerve, spiritual freedom, or stiffens into sterile bureaucracy, but only the working masses' own growing insight, strength, and ability to take its fate into its own hands is the way

to the objective. Extra-parliamentary mass action is a necessary complement, in the present-day class struggle, to parliamentary activity, which is not sufficient by itself to lead the working class to victory. Mass action, which is dependent on the growing extent and intensity of the class struggle, is likely to develop the individual's sense of responsibility and feeling of solidarity and by doing so brings about the addition of moral strength of the greatest importance for the socialist movement, which for its future must build on a morally and spiritually strong working class.

Although the party's leading men received with sympathy the message of the October revolution and even defended the dissolution of the Russian Constituent Assembly, they had at this time little in common with Lenin's bolsheviks. But within the Left-Socialist Youth League were forces that wished for a more purposeful revolutionary policy, and already at the second party congress in July 1918, conflict came into the light of day. Höglund's attempt to define the party as both revolutionary and parliamentary was a compromise which, faced with the ultimatum of the Twenty-one Theses, was doomed to fail.

ssv's third congress in June 1919 had decided to affiliate the party to the Comintern. This had not gone entirely smoothly. The decisive trial of strength between the party's two wings was, however, first occasioned by the publication of the Twenty-one Theses, with their strong demand for discipline in the ranks. This was not what Lindhagen had dreamed of. Before the congress of May 1921, which was to take a decision about the theses, a vote was held within the party; 4,318 members voted for acceptance while 2,041 voted against. Considering the importance of the question, participation in the election was not overwhelmingly large, since at this time the party declared its membership to be twenty thousand. But the congress confirmed the result: by 173 votes to 34 it decided to accept the theses. With this the minority was considered expelled, and after a half-hearted attempt to operate an independent left-wing socialist party they rejoined SAP in 1923.

As we know, the Twenty-one Theses *inter alia* provided that those parties which joined should give up their previous names and call themselves the communist sections of the Comintern. Their programme and rules should harmonise with the International's. In the new programme which the congress now approved, they regarded 'the working masses' extra-parliamentary direct action as the way to the overthrow of class society and the accomplishment of socialism'. They warned against 'bourgeois-democratic and reformist illusions', because bourgeois democracy was only class tyranny in a veiled form, and as such useless when it was a question of the final showdown with the capitalist system. To the extent that the party took part in parliamentary sessions it did so only in order to guard the interests of the working classes and to make use of the possibilities for revolutionary propaganda which this platform offered.

Whether it would be necessary to resort to force or not depended entirely on the opposition, and since experience showed that the bourgeois class defended its privileges with all available means, the party considered that the accomplishment of the revolution with the 'smallest possible sacrifice' demanded the arming of the working class. For the same reason the party should, with all its might, support the building up of military resources. Dictatorship of the proletariat was 'a necessary passageway' to socialism. Naturally, the organisation rested on democratic centralism.[3]

Therefore SKP was—on paper—'a revolutionary party both in means and aims'. In reality no attempt was made at all to exploit the revolutionary tidal wave which, according to the programme, was immediately approaching. Nor does the congress seem to have been particularly well acquainted with what Lenin regarded as democratic centralism and discipline generally. The party constitution warned explicitly that centralism could easily lead to dictatorial authoritarianism if proper vigilance was not observed—a reminder of the first party programme. A couple of years later it became clear even to the most optimistic revolutionary that the hopes that had been entertained at the end of the war about the immediately approaching world revolution had been an illusion. In the Soviet Union war communism was liquidated and the 'new economic policy' followed, with concessions to kulaks and foreign capitalists. Stalin launched the theory of 'socialism in one country' and Trotsky was manoeuvred out. The Comintern adopted a 'rightist course'; it was now a question of working for the long term, of seeking co-operation with social democrats for so-called common demands, and generally building up and strengthening the organisation. Sections should be 'bolshevised' and the Comintern's central organ be given power to act. Debate was reined-in and ideology dogmatised.

The dogmatising of ideology and the directions issued by delegates of the Comintern became more than the independently minded Höglund could stand. Within the leadership of SKP irritation at the behaviour of the Finnish and German delegates from the Comintern was general.[4] Already in 1923 an open conflict broke out about the party's relations with the Comintern, which ended with Höglund's downfall and expulsion at the congress of 1924. With that almost all of the leading men of 1917 had left the party. Like the expelled minority of 1921, Höglund and his followers also tried to keep going as an independent left socialist party before they gave up and secured re-admission to SAP.

SKP's official histories consider the schism of 1924 as a significant event in the development of SKP towards a party 'of a new type'. This assessment is no doubt correct, but the final bolshevising was to be completed only after 1929. The men who took over the leadership after Höglund—Karl Kilbom, Oskar Samuelsson, and Nils Flyg —were more 'faithful to Moscow' than Höglund and the group around him, but they were no weak-minded copycats. Thus the party chairman, Kilbom himself, was often critical about Russian policies, but then he also regarded the Soviet Union as 'the foremost bastion of the international working class' and was determined to defend the Soviet Union. Kilbom says in his memoirs that there were many who in 1924 would have liked to follow Höglund. Why they did not was partly due to the fact that they did not believe that there was a place for a party between the communists and the social democrats, and partly because they did not want to leave the road open for the servile follower of the Comintern, Hugo Sillén.[5]

The current rightist course in the Comintern's policy made it possible for Kilbom to work together with the Comintern without friction for some years; he himself was in general a diligent and popular delegate to the Comintern, and was close to Bucharin. An administratively gifted man, he used most of his energy for building up the party organisation—which, however, never had a secret section—and the press. When necessary, he did not hesitate to borrow money from the capitalist banks and—as an act of gratitude—give them some help in their trade with the Soviet Union. He had noteworthy successes. When communism in Europe in general was in retreat, in Sweden it could mark up some handsome achievements. In the elections for the Second Chamber in 1928, SKP doubled its votes, and the party organ *Folkets Dagblad*—People's Daily—was able steadily to increase its circulation. On the other hand, Kilbom failed completely in his attempts—in full accordance with the Comintern's directives—to infiltrate and break up the Swedish trade union movement.[6]

The 'leftist course' which was inaugurated by the sixth congress of the Comintern became the beginning of the end for the Kilbom epoch in SKP. According to the new line the capitalist world faced an immediate economic crisis—which it did—with growing antagonism of the capitalist states against one another, and between the capitalist states and the Soviet Union. Kilbom, Flyg and Samuelsson believed neither in the economic crisis nor in the accusation that Sweden was an imperialist country which was taking part in a conspiracy against the Soviet Union, and they said so. This was more than the Comintern's executive committee could stand. On 9 October 1929 a Comintern executive delegation announced in Stockholm that Kilbom and his nearest hangers-on had been 'suspended' and with that the third split in the party was a fact. In both the previous party splits the majority had gone along with the Comintern. This time it went against, and in spite of the vehement protests of the Comintern, supported by the Sillén phalanx, the majority refused to give up the party name.[7] Up to 1934 therefore, Sweden had two communist parties, which both claimed to be sections of the Comintern. Finally Kilbom resigned and the party was named Socialist Party. This broke up in 1937 and was then led by Nils Flyg in a nazi direction, while Kilbom and his followers, like their predecessors, joined the SAP.

The 'Sillén communists' called their people to a party congress at the turn of the month November–December 1929, which now proceeded under 'the signs of complete unity'. On the reasons for the schism in the party the congress declared that:[8]

> ... instead of promoting the bolshevising of the party, the Kilbom-Samuelsson-Flyg leadership has continued the old left-socialist traditions in many fields. ... Their activity was *limited mainly to* the numerical strengthening of the party, likewise to raising the party's share of the vote at elections, and increasing subscriptions to the party press. To bring up the party in a spirit which would raise its fighting fitness and revolutionary determination, and create a clear bolshevik line was considered by this party leadership a secondary task. ...

Briefly, the old party leadership had neglected to change SKP into a party of 'the new type'. With Kilbom, the social democratic tradition disappeared in SKP and a new era began.[9]

In Italian party slang this period goes under the name of the 'long night', in other words, the period of Comintern domination as distinguished from the 'short night' or period of Cominform domination. In all its actions and dealings, SKP became humbly submissive to the Kremlin and the Comintern. Social democrats became 'social fascists', and 'Swedish imperialism' was taking an active part in the war preparations against the Soviet Union. The ninth congress raised cheers for 'Soviet Sweden' and had comrades Stalin and Thälmann on its honorary presidium. No protests were heard when the seventh and last congress of the Comintern, in 1935, made a political about-turn and recommended the popular front policy. And naturally SKP defended the bloody purges in the Soviet Union in the 1930s. The final test came with the Ribbentrop Pact. Obviously the pact put SKP and its leadership in a difficult situation, but however much some might have doubted its justification this was not expressed openly. For many years SKP had fought tirelessly against nazism and fascism. The Swedish volunteers to Spain, who overwhelmingly consisted of party members, had extorted an unwilling admiration even from the party's opponents. The government had been attacked with biting arguments for its passive neutrality in the expected showdown between fascism and democracy.

SKP was manifestly in no way prepared for what was to come. Only a few days before the signing of the pact it was stated in *Ny Dag*, the party's main organ since 1929:

> In the present situation our country's independence is threatened. The threat comes from nazi Germany, whose boundless desire for expansion is also directed to the north. We communists have stood in the front rank when it came to encouraging the struggle for defence of our frontiers from the fascist danger. . . .

It would be naive to believe that the nazi threat is remote. The thunderclouds of war are accumulating. Lightning can strike down on the Swedish people sooner than we suspect. In such a situation it will be resolved who is anti-fascist and who is an idle talker and a verbal-radical.

But, seemingly without difficulties, the party leadership found themselves in the right in this new situation as well, and soon repeated the Comintern declarations. Where the popular front had said that it was willing to defend bourgeois democracy against the fascist assault, according to the new style Germany's war with the western powers was an 'imperialist war' without any justification. 'The talk about an Anglo-French war for democracy and against fascism and for the freedom of nations is nothing else but deceit against the people', the central committee declared in November 1940.[10] For Sweden's part it was appropriate to act realistically, maintained Sillén's successor to the post of party leader, Sven Linderot:[11]

> . . . Sweden's foreign policy must follow the advice that Molotov once gave, namely that it pays in foreign policy to gather as many friends as possible. Because whatever kind of a regime has power in Germany, Sweden must, even from the viewpoint of the revolutionary working class, follow a foreign policy which aims at friendly relationships with Germany, diplomatically correct relations, not 'friendship' with nazi ideology and methods of oppression, but governmental and diplomatic friendship, which offers mutual advantages. . . .

SKP could live up to these fine distinctions to such an extent that polemics against the Swedish nazis continued as though no Ribbentrop Pact had been made, which of course was in line with the Comintern directives. But they also had to take a stand on concrete actions on the part of the German regime, and in this the party in its statements went farther than was necessary. For *Ny Dag* it was not only impossible to condemn the German attack on Denmark and Norway on 9 April 1940: the paper could among other things report from Oslo on 24 April 1940 that the Norwegian workers and German soldiers were discussing the situation that had arisen in a fully comradely way in the beerhouses and on street corners.

To defend the Russian conquest in Poland, Finland and the Baltic states was obviously much easier. In Poland the red army was met by red banners and the Internationale, in Finland hundreds of thousands of workers and peasants waited impatiently for its arrival, and in the Baltic states the people were deeply grateful for being freed finally from the oppression of the imperialist powers. The intensive feelings of Nordic solidarity which in these years dominated the Swedish public left Linderot cold: for him they were mere emptiness and generally speaking no 'Nordic idea' existed.[12]

It was hardly surprising that in these circumstances doubt should be thrown upon SKP's loyalty to Sweden. After Finland had been defeated in the winter war and Norway and Denmark occupied by the Wehrmacht, the country was surrounded and it was impossible to know what fate the Ribbentrop Pact had prepared for Sweden.[13] Although the communists in the Diet and elsewhere expressed their solidarity with Sweden, their utterances were now and then ambivalent. In the speech quoted above, Linderot had presumably meant that communists could fight for national independence even if Sweden was a bourgeois country, but independence must not be considered as a dogma, but as something subjected to the laws of development. In the same way that tribes merged into nation states, so must national states merge into larger entities. Independence could only be defended so long as it was necessary and progressive.[14]

Linderot did not trouble himself to specify by what criteria one should judge the degree of necessity and progressiveness of a national state. Remembering the communists' behaviour in the then occupied countries, and what had actually happened in Poland and the Baltic states, it was hardly preposterous if people outside the party interpreted Linderot's statements as clearly disloyal. Nor did reaction fail to appear. SKP escaped being declared criminal by a narrow margin. In the Diet the threat of dissolution hung over the party. In the central trade union organisation the possibility of expelling the communists from the trade unions was discussed; they contented themselves with recommending unions to exclude communists from top positions. Public places were closed to party meetings and a transport ban was put on the party newspapers. Police carried out checks on the party offices and individual communist's homes. Considerable numbers of communists in the northern frontier area were put in internment camps. In addition there was all the persecution—particularly during the winter war—to which individual communists were exposed in their places of work. Fortunately the arson which was committed against the newspaper *Norrskensflamman* in the winter of 1940, in which five people were burned to death, was unique.

The lot of the individual communists was anything but enviable during this period. What it involved in broader terms is difficult to say. It can only be established here that during the days of the German-Soviet Pact the rising trend that the party had shown in the 1930s was broken. It is true that in the elections for the Second Chamber in 1940 SKP did collect a few more votes than in 1936—101,424 against 96,519—but here one has to note that the Socialist Party, which in 1936 had collected 127,832 votes, had in the meantime been reduced to an unimportant nazi sect, and that SAP in the 1940 elections had got more than 1.5 million votes. SKP's membership figures may have been halved.

## ii. The peaceful road

The German attack on the Soviet Union in June 1941 not only changed Sweden's subsequent strategic position, but also the public's attitude to the Soviet Union and the SKP. After some time the transport ban on the party newspapers was lifted, the public places were open again for their meetings, the dissolution threat disappeared, and the central trade union organisation recalled its discriminatory circular. Not without satisfaction could Sven Linderot point out that in the so-called informational session of the Diet in the autumn of 1942, they no longer discussed 'the communist danger' but the 'danger of inflation'.[15] In the local elections before that SKP had nearly doubled its admittedly feeble vote of 1940, something which is probably explained by widespread dissatisfaction with the government's prices and incomes policy. But the election also showed the SKP had started to regain a position as a legal opposition party, although it could not yet pick up all the votes that had gone to parties to the left of SAP in the 1930s. To this it must be added that SKP, after the sudden end of the Ribbentrop Pact, began to emerge as a partially new party. This became obvious most of all in the final stage of the war.

After the dissolution of the Comintern in May 1943, SKP was faced with the task of formulating a new party programme—the old Comintern programme was just no longer acceptable. In the prevailing 'national front' atmosphere it was to be expected that SKP, in its new programme, would appear more national and less revolutionary than before. Even so, the new party policy was introduced cautiously at the party conference in June 1943. Here a programme commission was set up in which the later party leaders, Hilding Hagberg and C. H. Hermansson, acted as chairman and secretary respectively, and which, before the twelfth party congress of May 1944, could present new principles for the party. The programme, which is not a party programme in the usual sense but rather a statement of principles, was exceptionally short. It states that SKP is based on a Marxist outlook, that the party's aim is a classless society, that Sweden has already reached the stage of state monopoly, and that the material requirements for a socialist 'transformation' of society are thus present. The capitalist state is described as an organ for the preservation of the 'economic and political domination of the bourgeois class' which the working class is to replace by its own 'democratic state'. Inside the bourgeois state the workers have succeeded in conquering important bourgeois-democratic freedoms and rights, which they defend against the forces of reaction. They also defend the national right of self-determination.

The text contains no positive statement of a 'revisionist' character, if one does not count the appreciative words about bourgeois freedoms and rights, but the programme is strikingly vague on certain points. The term 'dictatorship of the proletariat' had been dropped, it says nothing about the arming of the working class, the word 'revolution' does not occur, and the programme does not contain a single reference to the Soviet Union. The positive 'revisionist' innovations were confined to the commentaries on the principles that Hilding Hagberg gave to the congress,[16] and the resolutions which were framed there.

The congress met in the shadow of revolutionary events which were impending in Europe. It was only a question of months before Germany would surrender, the red army was advancing, old states were falling apart, the resistance movement in the occupied countries began to reveal its postwar policies, and social democracy on the continent became more radical. With this wind blowing in the world, it was believed among SKP's leaders that Swedish social democracy too would be pushed to the Left. Therefore cooperation should be offered to SAP, 'unity from above'—but at the same time pressure should be created from below. To show that the party meant business, the congress took the surprising step of accepting the social democrats' postwar programme, which had just been published, as a foundation for a united front.

The new policy did not rouse undivided enthusiasm within the party. Many communists remembered with bitterness the treatment they had been subjected to during the war and wished for a systematic purge of the responsible politicians; their bitterness was particularly directed against Gustav Möller, one of the social democrats' strongest men, who during the war had occupied the post of minister of the interior and thereby been responsible for the work of the police. These demands for revenge were not easily quieted. 'One of the factors fatal for cooperation with social democracy is that social democrats in general, at least the leading social democrats, are enemies of the cause of the working class, or in any case potential enemies of socialism', Sven Linderot warned as late as two years afterwards.[17] It was well understood among the leadership of SKP that real cooperation with social democracy demanded far-reaching concessions on the communist side. The offerings that were made were certainly not small; they can be found, to a significant extent, in Hagberg's commentaries on the principles.

Besides the mutual animosity founded on many years of conflict, SKP's revolutionary ideology and its ties to Moscow stood in the way of the desired cooperation with the SAP. The Comintern had not minced words when in 1928 it described the socialist revolution:[18]

> The proletariat's seizure of power is no peaceful 'seizure' of the existing bourgeois state machine through a parliamentary majority. The bourgeoisie will use all the means of violence and terror to secure and consolidate the property it has stolen and its political power. The bourgeoisie is unable, any more than the feudal nobility, to surrender its place in history to the new class without the most desperate, embittered struggle. Therefore the violence of the bourgeoisie can be broken only through the determined use of the violence of the proletariat. The seizure of power is the violent destruction of bourgeois power, the breaking up of the capitalist state machine (the bourgeois army, police, bureaucracy, legal system, Parliament, etc.) and their replacement by the new organs of the power of the proletariat,

which above all are the instruments for keeping down the exploiters.

In the SKP programme of 1921 the formulation was as follows:[19]

> Whether the change from capitalism to socialism in our country can take place without using force depends entirely on our opponents. Force and terror are characteristic of bourgeois society, which rests entirely on capitalist exploitation, militarism, on the organised violence and terrorism of the police force and the prison system. And experience shows that the bourgeois class defends with extreme measures —by blood-baths of the workers and the atrocious murder of their leaders—its privileges and its class power. Therefore the working class must, with the experience it has already gained from various quarters, be prepared to meet force with force in such a situation. The accomplishment of the revolution and socialism with the least possible number of victims will, according to our understanding, demand the arming of the working class. At the same time, the party rejects all unplanned violence, all attempted *coups*, and individual acts of terrorism, declaring that its aim is not destruction of persons, not revenge against individuals, but the abolition of the capitalist system and its ramshackle institutions.

The corresponding paragraph in the principles of 1944 reads quite briefly:

> The capitalist state is an organ for the preservation of the economic and political domination of the bourgeois class. It is the historical task of the working class, together with other exploited and plundered classes, to capture political power and create its own state for achieving a socialist order of society.

So the 1944 formulation gives no intimation whatever how SKP imagined that the 'working class' would capture political power. This is reserved for the commentaries. Like the writer of the 1921 programme, Hagberg repudiated 'desperate *coups* on the part of a minority group' and stressed that the achievement of socialism could take place only on the basis of the conscious will and action of the great mass of the working class and its natural allies. In this there was nothing especially new. What was new was that Hagberg announced as a belief of the party that in the situation that would arise as a consequence of the collapse of nazism, the peaceful transformation of Swedish society would become possible, or according to Frithiof Lager's more cautious phrasing, was 'not excluded'.[20] The party could therefore pledge itself without reservation to make use of the 'so-called democratic methods', if it would help, and redeem the enterprise from the capitalists. Whether it would be necessary to resort to the use of force depended on the strength and resistance of the capitalists against the legal power. But, as Lager pointed out hopefully in the above mentioned article, the Swedish capitalist class would now, for the foreseeable future, be characterised by a 'general reduction in power', for which reason the risk of a counter-revolution was not terribly great. The force in question was therefore the force a legally elected government could if necessary use against a rebellious capitalist class.

None of the statements from the twelfth party congress can be interpreted as meaning that the party abstained from violence on principle. They implied only that it was believed that under existing circumstances socialism could be achieved in a peaceful and—although the word was not used—a parliamentary way. But even this belief contained risks of 'right-opportunism'. Therefore it was only as it should be that Sven Linderot, in the first number of the party's ideological periodical *Vår Tid*—Our Times—which appeared in January 1945, pointed out that the periodical was founded in order to fight such 'right deviations' as 'trade unionism' and 'parliamentary cretinism'; and the party secretary, Gunnar Öhman, underlined in the following issue of the periodical: 'We are, and we remain, a Marxist party, and nothing has changed in our principal conception'. The party had only applied 'flexible tactics'.[21] Hagberg himself assured the congress that in every particular situation there were concrete circumstances which would determine the party's tactics, and Linderot warned explicitly about the changes the immediate future could bring in its lap, with the consequent need for quick changes on the party's side.[22] It is therefore not significant that the 'peaceful road' is not mentioned among the basic principles. Such discretion could be regarded as natural for other reasons. Too pronounced an emphasis on the 'peaceful road' would unmistakably contain a 'revisionist' or—in the language of the day—'right opportunist' deviation, and could thereby, as later developments showed, jeopardise the unity of the party and its international relations.

However it is probable that SKP's leaders—and certainly not only the leaders—during the period 1944–8, believed that the postwar era would bring about in Sweden a bloodless transformation to socialism. This is admitted rather bluntly and with appreciable bitterness in the foreword to the 1953 programme, 'Sveriges väg till socialismen'—Sweden's Road to Socialism:

> When the second world war was over, the Swedish people hoped that a new society would be built up with work, security, and rising living standards for all. The people would become masters in their own house and the well-being of the people would come before that of big business.
> Already during the war years, the two workers' parties had got a majority in both chambers of the Diet. To this majority were pinned the hopes of socialist transformation of society.
> The people's hopes, however, were not fulfilled. The

social democratic government . . . has followed policies which on decisive questions are in contradiction
with the real interests of the people. . . .

In September 1944 the Swedish people had a parliamentary election and SKP brought home its greatest victory
of all times: 318,000 votes, or 10.5 per cent of the
electorate, a threefold increase since the previous election. New members poured in. In 1940 the membership
might not have been above ten thousand; by the time of
the 1946 congress the number had got up to forty-four
thousand. Belief in the peaceful road strengthened in
step with external successes. This was revealed by the
later very dogmatic Set Persson in a speech of 24 March
1945:[23]

> I will therefore stress: we give our support to the
> efforts to go forward by the peaceful road, that is by
> the usual democratic means, through trade unions,
> contractual agreements, legislation, parliamentary res-
> olutions, government orders, and so on, and we
> acknowledge that this road can be successful. But
> this does not imply, naturally, that the Swedish Com-
> munist Party is not a revolutionary party. We have
> certainly, in the manner I have pointed out, accepted
> a peaceful development. In addition we have also,
> for our part, declared openly that we do not wish
> anything else than to be able to compete with other
> parties for the people's support for our policies, and
> have therefore never contemplated the use of other
> instruments of power. Only those who represent a
> policy directed against the interests of the majority
> of the people can find it necessary to gain the
> acceptance of the people with the help of force and
> coercive measures.

Later, when Set Persson was forced to leave the party,
after a hard struggle, he described the moods during the
period after the end of the war thus:[24]

When the red army and the people of the Soviet Union, after unheard-of sacrifices, had crushed the fascist war machine, a pleasant idyll began to unfold in Sweden. Communists were given places on official committees, even on the defence committee, they could occupy the post of *borgarråd* in the capital, etc. New members poured into the party, and the number of seats increased in the elections. At that time however, intoxicated by the victories of the Soviet soldiers, the party leaders formulated the slogan of 'the peaceful road to socialism' for Sweden.

The 'intoxication' reached its peak at the thirteenth congress in 1946, when Sven Linderot affirmed that SKP did not envisage any socialist transformation of society to which less than a majority of the people had consented.[25] In this he was very close to repudiation in principle of other ways to socialism than the parliamentary. Development had been swift. Only three years earlier Linderot had maintained, quite orthodoxly, that parliamentary sessions should be considered in the first place as appropriate platforms for agitation.[26] As the belief in the peaceful road grew stronger, so also a gradualist outlook developed in the party and this gradualism staggered close to the despised theory of the 'peaceful growth of socialism'.

The social democratic postwar programme, which the 1944 congress had accepted as its own action programme had, according to the non-communist way of speaking, many socialist features. For Linderot, speaking in 1944, the programme contained no forward steps on the road to socialism,[27] and also Hagberg had supposed at that time that the accomplishment of socialism would be a revolutionary process, since 'between the present economic order and that of socialism there is no intermediary stage'.[28] For him, the nationalisation of private enterprise in a bourgeois society was only an expression of the needs of the capitalists. The decisive question was which class had power in society. Political power was by no means won because the working class had an elected majority in the Diet and set up a government on this basis. Only when the working class came to occupy all the decision-making organs of society had it secured power. This need not necessarily imply that—as had happened in the Soviet Union—the capitalists should be deprived of their civil rights. But it meant that the new socialist legislation would not permit activity which aimed at disturbing the new economic and social order, which might fairly reasonably be interpreted that bourgeois parties would exist only to the extent that they ceased to be bourgeois.

These views were consistent with the acceptance of the SAP postwar programme only so long as this programme was understood as reform activity within the framework of a bourgeois society. But in the long run it would prove impossible to preserve the distinction between the positive reforms for the working class and purely socialist measures. The Swedes also learned, from the respected leader of the Danish Communist Party, Axel Larsen, that they were rather sectarian.[29] Already, in the above quoted statement by Set Persson, the slide is obvious; when the speaker referred there to contractual agreements, government orders, parliamentary resolutions, etc., he was obviously thinking of activities within the framework of existing society. And if the bourgeois state machine could be used for socialist reforms, was it bourgeois in the ordinary sense? In the general 'intoxication' the demand for the crushing of the state machine disappears, and all that is left is the demand for certain 'dismissals' and 'transfers' in the administration.

Linderot appeared full of assurance when at the thirteenth congress he declared his belief in what the Italian communists called 'structural reform':[30]

> Full employment, economic efficiency, democracy, a higher living standard, state planning and direction of production and consumption when necessary from the viewpoint of the public good, in order to bring

about the desired results—these guidelines open the road for a peaceful transition to socialism.

Linderot stressed also that this was the Swedish way:

> But we shape our party's policy out of the historic and social conditions that prevail in Sweden, which in many cases are very different from those which apply for example to America or the Soviet Union. It is therefore absurd that our Swedish policy should be decided in either Washington or Moscow.

Undeniably, in this way SKP had gone far to meet social democracy. But SAP was cool. They declined cooperation in elections, they declined cooperation in government, and there was no question of an amalgamation of the parties. At the party congress in 1946 Linderot went further than ever when he declared that SKP, a party responsible for carrying through the postwar programme, could not be considered as an opposition party. But in 1946 favourable circumstances had in fact already passed and even this hint was left unanswered. There were many reasons for the negative attitude of the social democrats. The wish for trustful cooperation often expressed by the communists contrasted sharply on occasion with the fight they carried on in the trade unions against social democratic delegates. Their attitude to Swedish democracy was still ambivalent. And in spite of the dissolution of the Comintern, the leaders of the SAP were far from convinced that SKP was a purely Swedish party. Out in the places of work suspicion was less, and doubtless there was, especially in 1945, a certain desire for closer cooperation between the parties. The communists' chances to become a powerful factor in Swedish politics depended entirely on the relations they were able to build up with the social democrats. When the social democrats said 'No', and moreover started to campaign actively against them, it gradually became clear that the 1944 policy had been a mistake.

The party's election successes immediately before and

after the end of the war probably depended to a large extent on the prestige of the Soviet Union, gained by defeating Hitler's Germany. As the cold war hardened, and the reports of the terror behind the 'iron curtain' became prevalent in the Swedish press, the prestige of the Soviet Union began to sink, and the communists' voting figures to decline in step with it. The election to the Second Chamber in 1948 reduced SKP to what it had been before the war, a sect out in the cold on the fringes of Swedish political life.

The dilemma of the communists became all the more obvious: if the party wished to keep in touch with the Swedish public it had to prove its independence, in effect to show that it had the courage also to criticise the actions of the Soviet Union. But by doing this the party would place itself outside the international communist community. If the communists wanted to work together with the social democrats, this must be cooperation on terms set by the social democrats, and then one could legitimately ask why should the communists preserve their own party? There was no obvious solution to this dilemma. After the active years around the end of the war the party began to go into hibernation; it did not wake into life until the early years of the 1960s. But then the circumstances had changed.

### iii. The impossible compromise

In 1947 the first signs were noticeable that Linderot had begun to doubt the workers' front. The 1948 congress proceeded under the signs of pessimism, and a cautious ideological retreat had its beginning. It is true that the congress considered that there was still a peaceful road to socialism, but it was a mistake, which 'certain party comrades' had been guilty of, to confuse the 'peaceful road' with the reformists' 'peaceful growth' towards a socialist society.[31] That 'certain party comrades' were, in this case, identical with the party leaders could hardly have escaped even the most dim-sighted congress delegates. There was a last faint hope just before the 1948 election. But the election was a catastrophe, and with that the party adapted its external propaganda to the directives put out by the Cominform. This happened, however, only after direct pressures. In a conference of the Nordic communist parties in February 1948, the leader of the Finnish delegation, Hertta Kuusinen, had delivered a bitter attack on the Swedish communists. It was no secret that Kuusinen was close to the Kremlin. Now that the period of cooperation had come to an end it was the duty of the parties, without any opportunism, to join the fight that the Cominform had indicated. The Swedish delegates asked for a period of grace until the coming election. After that the time for waiting was over.

The last years of the 1940s were the time of great showdowns in the communist parties both in eastern and western Europe. SKP was no exception though the forms were milder. It was said in the executive's analysis of the election defeat of 1948 that the party had not drawn the political consequences of the sharpening of class conflicts in the postwar years in time. 'The growth of fascism' which the bourgeois class had undergone had been underrated, and also the role that 'right-social democracy' played in the 'reactionary offensive'. Nor had they directed sufficient attention to the decisive significance of the Soviet Union for peace and the socialist struggle for freedom.[32] Both ideologically and organisationally the party was in need of a shake-up. This was a document entirely in the spirit of the Cominform.

The task the party now set itself was not to seek a place in the government through cooperation with this or that element; the objective now was to fight the growing American influence in Europe. In the slogans this became a fight for freedom and national independence against the United States and its social democratic 'lackeys', together with the glorification of life on the other side of the iron curtain. A propaganda which was based on panegyrics on the socialist countries and maledictions —it is difficult to find a more adequate expression—on the

social democrats, was doomed to fail in its task. In the
1948 election SKP had got 6.3 per cent of the votes, in the
local elections of 1950 the figure was 4.9 per cent and in
1952 only 4.3 per cent. With that, all the gains made during the 1940s were rubbed out.

SKP played out its role as a conformist communist party
quite splendidly in front of the general public. Even so
sober a judge as Leif Kihlberg, the political editor of *Dagens Nyheter*—the leading Swedish daily—regarded the
party as one big Soviet espionage organisation.[33] This
impression was strengthened by a couple of espionage
cases at the beginning of the 1950s, in which communist
party members played an active role. The violent language
in the communist press concealed, however, an increasing
passivity. 'When the cold war began, many members went
underground and sank into a coma, and many have not
awakened yet', a party veteran wrote in the 1963 'congress
debate'.[34] The 'mass battle' against 'right socialists' and
'American imperialism', which should have been organised
'from below' did not take place at all. At their employments communists were exposed to constant provocations,
got at loggerheads with others, and became even more
isolated. The workers' communes were in danger of turning into 'discussion groups' for the dedicated.[35] In spite
of continual exhortations in the party press, no improvement came about.

That was not all though. The painful defeat of 1948
and the disobedience to the Cominform demanded its
scapegoats. In many parties, among others the Norwegian
one, widespread purges had already taken place. Something
similar seemed to be approaching in SKP. One of the
party's most dangerous and implacable critics was Set
Persson, who according to his own statement had opposed
the party line which was introduced in 1943–4 all the
time.[36] Set Persson had belonged to the party leadership
ever since the beginning of the 1930s and during his political career had won respect even outside the party. As a
*borgarråd* in Stockholm in the period 1946–50 he had
given proof of a creditable administrative ability. At the

same time he had never belonged to the inner circle of the party leadership or to the groups of people who had shaped the 1944 policy. Because of this he was somewhat more dangerous as an opponent.

In October 1949 Persson succeeded in extorting a decision in the central committee to set up an inquiry to evaluate the policy which had been decided upon in the congresses of 1944 and 1946. The commission, which was composed of people the majority of whom were favourable to the party leadership, worked for a year without being able to agree on a common conclusion. The majority used this dissension as a pretext for deciding not to submit the report to the central committee. The committee was, however, presumably in order to avoid an open breach in the party, induced to put out a declaration according to which the conditions for a peaceful road to socialism in Sweden had never existed. A number of party comrades had made mistaken statements, without being corrected in time.[37] This was regrettable but now the mistakes had been put right.

But with this the struggle was not over. For the inner circle it was important to get rid of Set Persson, and in the autumn of 1952 he began to be subjected to veiled attacks in the party press. Already before this a somewhat softer policy towards the social democrats had been introduced: in the unions the communists could vote for a good social democrat; also communists could join the social democratic May Day processions, even when the banners attacked the communists, etc.[38] Set Persson fought against these tactics, first in the central committee and then in the sixteenth congress of April 1953. Another question over which Persson and the majority of the central committee stood opposed to one another concerned the agitation on behalf of the Soviet Union. While Persson maintained that agitation for the Soviet Union must be put first, because a friendly attitude to the Soviet Union led to a friendly attitude towards communists, the majority in the party leadership thought that the Soviet Union could well defend itself. 'Our opponents will represent us as a Russian party. We must show that we are a Swedish party by putting the question of the interests of the Swedish workers first on the order paper'.[39] It is probable that the majority of the party leadership was supported by the majority of the party members, but Set Persson was not quite alone. Thanks to a skilful if not especially comradely trick at the congress, it was possible to isolate Persson, and he was forced to ask for his own release from the party. The slander campaign which was directed at him after this, and the drastic measures which were taken against his followers, bear witness that the party leadership did not want any discussion on the matter.

The party now began cautiously to grope its way back to the 1944 policy. In the autumn of 1953 Hagberg, who had now succeeded Linderot in the post of party leader, characterised their relations with SAP as 'cooperation without agreement'—a new variant on the theme of a non-opposition party—and two years later he let it be understood that the communists certainly regarded SAP as a party of the workers, and therefore it was not in the interests of SKP that the party should be destroyed.[40] In the party congress of the same year people again began to talk cautiously about the peaceful road to socialism.[41]

So came the fatal year 1956, with the twentieth congress of the Soviet Communist Party, peaceful coexistence, the parliamentary road, the disclosures on Stalin, and—in the autumn—the upheavals in eastern Europe. These events activated practically all SKP's problems: its relation to democracy, its relation to the Soviet Union, its ideological foundations, and—in the last analysis—the party's existence.

The legitimation of the 'parliamentary road' belonged to the welcome contributions from the twentieth congress. When SKP, in the 1940s, had discussed the peaceful road to socialism, the use of the word parliamentary had been avoided, even though it had been understood that it was the Diet that hopes were pinned on. In the 1953 programme, which is modelled upon the British, the importance of the Diet had been toned down and the 'people's democracies' were now presented as the model. After Stalin's death talk about the Diet began again. It was therefore hardly surprising that *Ny Dag*, shortly after publishing Khruschev's report at the twentieth congress, let it be understood that Sweden's road to socialism 'can in all probability be parliamentary—not soviet'.[42] Hagberg was very inclined to tone down the commotion about parliamentarism. The role of force, parliamentarism, the peaceful transformation, etc. had already some time back ceased to be 'a problem in the old sense' for SKP.[43] C. H. Hermansson gave assurance that SKP—parliamentarism notwithstanding—was still a revolutionary party, because every changeover from capitalism to socialism involves revolution.[44] In May the central committee was ready with an authoritative statement:[45]

> The central committee welcomes and agrees with the analysis by the twentieth congress of the possibilities which have arisen through historical development of following other roads to socialism than that followed by the Soviet Union and the peoples' democracies.

The 'scientific analysis' which was demanded inside SKP, and which would definitely affirm that Sweden belonged to the countries which had the prerequisites for achieving socialism by the parliamentary road, was circulated in a publication entitled *Nutid-Framtid*, which was published at the end of 1957. The book had come into being on the initiative of the central committee, to work out 'certain questions on the programme', an indirect acknowledgement that the 1953 programme was out of date. Under the heading 'The Diet and popular power', a central committee member, P. O. Zennström, declared that 'SKP had as its objective a peaceful parliamentary transformation to socialism arising fom Sweden's own conditions'. Force could only come into question if the 'capitalist minority' rose against the will of the people expressed by the democratic Diet, and 'democratic Diet' meant a Diet which had been chosen at a general election. This implied that

Sweden neither could nor would follow the example of the Soviet Union and the people's democracies, from whose mistakes, however, one could learn a great deal. Not even the openly reactionary parties should be repressed but they should be defeated in an open struggle.[46]

Zennström's thoughts reappeared in a more ambiguous form in the 1961 'Programförklaring'[47]—explanation of the programme—accepted by the nineteenth party congress. The ambiguity can probably be clarified by the 'Declaration' of the eighty-one parties, which was issued in Moscow shortly before the congress, with its hostile attitude towards 'revisionism'. The 'Programförklaring' avoids using the word 'parliamentary' and replaces it with 'peaceful, democratic'. The significance of the Diet is reduced to its being only one instrument among others for breaking down the position of monopoly capital. While the Moscow statement strongly emphasises the necessity of the dictatorship of the proletariat, the 'Programförklaring' says that the achievement of socialism does not prevent the independent existence of several parties. Now, the peoples' democracies are counted among the states with a multi-party system, though Zennström had rejected them as suitable models for Sweden. The future of parliamentarism in a socialist Sweden was thus anything but guaranteed; and with this a source of conflict remained inside the party.

If the Swedish communists in 1956 accepted with pleasure the parliamentary road, and in large measure seized upon Khruschev's exhortation to enter into cooperation with social democrats, they were no less grateful for the doctrine of peaceful coexistence and for the appreciative words which the Russian party boss had uttered about the neutral states. That these are now recognised as welcome partners in the struggle for peace made it possible for SKP to present itself as a defender of Swedish neutrality against the plots which, according to SKP, the bourgeois parties had been guilty of.[48] In principle SKP could place itself on the same platform on foreign affairs as SAP. But on concrete questions the communists came to occupy the same isolated position as before.

Khruschev's disclosures on Stalin were, on the contrary, all the more disagreeable a surprise. In the case of Stalin the party leadership had no alibi and it was therefore scarcely to be expected that the central committee should take the initiative for a more deep-going self-criticism. Harald Rubinstein, about whom more later, described in the great showdown of 1963 the actions of the party leadership in the following way:[49]

> After the 'revelations on Stalin' (the writer apologises for the unpardonably simplified expression) the walls of faith crumbled and the cornerstones were considerably disturbed from their former positions. But the communist party did not seize the opportunity to endeavour to analyse the changes. Neither did any soul-searching, constructive self-criticism occur. Would it not have been justified to examine fairly thoroughly the question of the degree to which we must learn anew? Were our critical senses not dulled, our scientific approach inadequate, our demands upon ourselves small—I repeat that this argument is mainly in respect of the postwar period—since we did not suspect that something was gravely wrong in the socialist countries? All of which I say without overlooking in any way the impressive progress made in many sectors within these countries.
>
> When at last the party was helped toward the truth, virtually the only things spoken of were those deemed to be unavoidable. The entire question, in all its breadth, was rapidly swept under the mat, miscellaneous skeletons were locked in cupboards, and the personality cult was duly condemned. Now everything would certainly right itself again.

The central committee's statement on the Stalin question was, as Rubinstein said, extremely feeble.[50] Obviously the party leadership did what it considered to be the

only thing possible in the circumstances. Partly they tried
to put the criticism of Stalin in as mild a form as
possible, partly they tried to cut short, as bourgeois
propaganda, self-evident questions about the Soviet system
itself. But this official attitude did not correspond with
what was stirring inside the party. Discussions only increased in intensity.

Ferment in Poland, but most of all the revolt in Hungary, caused even the party leadership to waver, though
only for a moment. The violent storm of opinions which
blew up against SKP in connection with the Hungarian
tragedy no doubt put a great strain on the internal
solidarity of the party. But though many turned deserters
and others became passive the party leadership succeeded
in keeping its grip on the organisation. What it could
not prevent—to quote Rubinstein once more—was the
crumbling to pieces of 'the walls of faith'. The open
discussion on Stalinism, and SKP's relations with the socialist countries, which should have taken place in 1956,
first happened at the beginning of the 1960s, when the
communist world movement was shaken by new antago-
nisms and SKP was, by mortal judgement, on its way out of
history.

### iv. The great showdown

The opposition's chance came in the autumn of 1962
when SKP again did badly at the elections: the party's
share of the electorate now fell to 3.8 per cent, which was
the lowest figure the party had ever scored in a regular
election. This was another consequence of the twentieth
congress. Khruschev's exhortation to the communist parties to cooperate with the social democrats had led, on
SKP's part, to their whole agitation being directed against
'big business' and its 'tools' the bourgeois parties. In the
Diet SAP was supported come rain or shine. When at the
end of the 1950s the social democrats found themselves
in a minority in the Second Chamber, help was not un-
welcome, but this policy forced the communists to sup-

port less welcome measures, like the defence agreement of 1958 and the introduction of purchase tax in 1960. SKP reduced itself to a small, absurd auxiliary party, and its services earned small thanks in return. SKP's faltering attitude to democracy and the nation meant that the party was continuously kept outside the community of the 'four democratic parties' and the gains were made by SAP.

After the 1962 election defeat the party leadership tried to cheer up the faithful by saying that the most important objective had been achieved, namely that the right wing had been beaten back and the 'workers' parties' had gone ahead. Bo Gustafsson, an economist and one of the party's younger forces, concluded very rightly that 'one more left-wing victory and we are lost'.[51] But where were the causes of defeat to be found? Gustafsson meant that the party had lost its socialist image by putting forward only its immediate demands. What was required was a really socialist perspective. But after these introductory phrases other correspondents took up the really burning question, namely the party's relationship with the socialist states in general and the Soviet Union in particular. Many party members, wrote one of the contributors to the cultural pages of Ny Dag, Sam Johansson, considered that SKP, in its attitude to foreign policy, should assume a more 'neutral' position.[52] And the paper's correspondent in Peking, Sture Källberg, warned explicitly against neglecting their own country. In countries where the socialist revolution had triumphed through their own resources, the parties had stood on a markedly nationalist basis and these countries had therefore avoided the problems that had arisen in the places where the socialist order had been brought in with the help of the red army.[53]

Such language could not have been read before in Ny Dag, and that these articles were printed could be taken as the result of the fact that the opposition had now grown so strong that the party leadership no longer dared to stand against it. At the end of 1962, or the beginning of 1963, the central committee received a letter, signed by Sven Landin and Yngve Johansson, with a summary of what could be called the demands of the left-socialist opposition. It is stated in it, briefly and bluntly, that the party isolated itself from the Swedish workers and Swedish democracy by defending everything that happened in the socialist countries. The central committee ought to reconsider its international relations, and above all, wind up the secret diplomatic ties with the sister parties in the east. The letter ended with a demand for 'renewal and rejuvenation' at the top of the party, in the course of which the chairmanship should also be brought up for discussion.[54]

The letter was first published much later but it is obvious that quite a few party members soon knew about its contents. And because the struggle between the majority of the central committee and the opposition now came to concentrate on the question of SKP's relations with the Soviet Union, the question of the Swedish attitude to the current Russo-Chinese conflict became at the same time a struggle between dependence and independence, between the party leadership and the opposition. The struggle was not about any ideological question, because on the whole the opposition had little sympathy with the Chinese attitude. It was the party's independence that was being protected by refusing to take a stand in the conflict.

The mediatory position which the central committee tried to hold between Peking and Moscow at the beginning became more difficult to hold when the Soviet Union, after the Cuba conflict in the autumn of 1962, increased its pressure on the other communist parties. An unqualified line-up on the Soviet side, however, demanded a great deal of preparation. In the autumn of 1962 some of the 'dogmatists' were purged, among them Knut Senander, who was later to propagate openly his pro-Chinese views. In the spring the central committee made a statement in which it defended Yugoslavia against the Chinese attacks—and at the same time took the opportunity to regret that SKP had, a long time before, 'made an unjust and damaging statement on Yugoslavia and its leading party'.[55]

The abusive public debate which Russia and China started in the summer of 1963 made the earlier restraint of *Ny Dag* impossible, as far as information about the conflict was concerned. An effort was made to educate their own party members by a series of articles, and 'neutralist' tendencies expressed by the opposition were energetically condemned. Hagberg made repeated trips to Moscow. The campaign reached a peak in a declaration from the Nordic parties, in which the leadership of the Chinese Communist Party was condemned unanimously. This took place only a couple of months before SKP was to hold its twentieth congress.

But there was deep antagonism among the party leaders. While the campaign against the 'neutralists' was at its height, C. H. Hermansson wrote a leader in *Ny Dag* which was quickly to make him the opposition's rallying point. The leader carried a headline: 'About the deeply tragic and the deeply necessary':[56]

First they [the communists] had to learn that the nationalisation of the means of production and the foundation of socialist conditions of production were not sufficient to guarantee a developed socialist democracy in a socialist country, and that the leader of a communist party could develop into a tyrant who brutally liquidated party comrades, and under cover of his position of power shook the cause of socialism over many years.

Now they had learned another bitter lesson. The establishment of workers' power and socialism does not automatically guarantee that the relations between states become harmonious and characterised by trustful cooperation. . . .

Tension and antagonism between the Soviet Union and the Chinese People's Republic continue to develop ever more strongly. It is not just a question of an interlude which resembles the village brawls of former days, or the disorders of conscripts going on leave. Far worse are the accusations which are levelled by both sides of treason to the cause of socialism, and the nationalist tendencies which stand out more and more. . . .

What is deeply necessary is that this regrettable development must not paralyse the communist party's contributions to the important problems which now face the Swedish working class and the Swedish people. . . .

When, four days later, in a notice in *Ny Dag*, the central committee invited the members to a discussion about 'Congress '64', the storm broke out in earnest.[57] The previously quoted article by Rubinstein indicated the tone and content. The questions central for the party were now taken up in open debate: its attitude to democracy, the inner life of the party, its relations to the other parties and above all to the Soviet Union, its policy in relation to the social democrats, and the need for a socialist action programme.

The debate was dominated by what we shall here call the left-socialist opposition, and plain language was spoken. There must be an end to the ambivalent attitude towards democracy, both inside the party and in the party's relations with the country; there must be an end to the humiliating dependence on Moscow; an end to organised fraction activity in the trade unions; and an end to the whitewashing of the socialist states and the blackguarding of Sweden. The implications of the 'national road to socialism' must be finally accepted and the members themselves be allowed to control the party—and not to let it be controlled by the paid officials. The existing party leadership was worn out, it was not only that its speech was 'difficult to understand to the point of incomprehensibility', worse than that was that it wavered noticeably when journalists came with so-called delicate questions. Briefly, what the opposition demanded was a thorough settlement with the past and a new set of leaders.

After this violent outburst, the congress itself became something of an anti-climax, and its statements on the central questions wavered. The men of the old guard still dominated the party apparatus and its important executive committee. But Hagberg was forced to resign when he came up for re-election and C. H. Hermansson came into his place. And the renewals which were to take place in the party after the congress bore Hermansson's stamp to a very high degree. During his first months as leader Hermansson worked hard to give the party a new image, and in his many statements for radio, press and other channels put himself a long way from the 'Programförklaring' of 1961. The attitude of the general public changed from suspicious hostility to benevolent interest, and without doubt Hermansson became a popular politician on the TV screen. Surely this fact should have made the orthodox majority in the apparatus passive. The first reward came at the elections for the Second Chamber in 1964, when the party polled 5.2 per cent of the electorate—which was not a remarkable success in numbers of votes (at the 1960 elections for the Second Chamber the party had had 4.5 per cent of the vote) but it was significant because the declining trend had been broken and the victory was counted a personal success for Hermansson.

Three elements could soon be distinguished in the Hermansson line. He lost no opportunity to demonstrate the party's independence and took the liberty on many occasions of criticising the Soviet Union's actions in foreign policy and even the internal political conditions in the socialist states. He made an open acknowledgment of Swedish democracy, and inside the party he encouraged a freedom of debate unheard of until then: both the 'dogmatists' and convinced 'revisionists' were allowed a hearing in the columns of Ny Dag. By allowing prominent party members to work in the 'Socialist League', an association in the first place of socialist intellectuals, many of whom belonged to the social democrats, he sought an opening to the Right. This became very much easier as a group of younger Swedish intellectuals, influenced by the Vietnam war and the increasing social disturbances in the United States, began at this time to shift their position to the left. The results were soon there to be seen. In the 1966 local elections the communists could gather 6.4 per cent of the vote, which, compared with the 1962 election, meant near enough a doubling.

The new policy—if not indeed the new party—was endorsed at the 1967 congress, which like the 1964 congress was held with open doors. Here a new programme and new rules were approved. The rules, which were probably unique for a communist party, carefully stressed the individual members' freedom and rights. Naturally the members are obliged to conform with the programme, but not as before to the tactical line which the party leadership has laid down. It is possible to appeal to the congress against every expulsion of a member. The cells which had formerly been the party's basic organisations may continue if the members so wish. All elections of delegates take place by secret ballot. At the party congresses members of the apparatus have the right to speak but cannot take part in the voting. The party cannot order its representatives in the trade unions and the Diet to vote in a prescribed way. All party congresses are public, along with the proceedings and the records. Obviously there is no talk of 'democratic centralism'.

There is nothing in these rules that is contrary to the accepted practices of Swedish associations. Therefore it is no surprise that the programme binds the party to liberal freedoms and rights and to the Swedish type of parliamentary government. That the party's ideological foundation is Marxism-Leninism is not mentioned on the whole. Its international solidarity embraces all 'social and national liberation movements' which, however, are not defined more closely. It is perhaps not to be wondered at that 'American imperialism' still remains the foremost threat to the peace and freedom of the peoples, but it is

significant that the socialist countries too are criticised
in the programme. Among their negative features are
'indefensible differences' in incomes and social standing,
bureaucratic encroachments on justice, and limited freedom of press and speech. As to socialism in Sweden, the
party supposes that this will be accomplished through
'structural reforms'—a conception taken over from the
Italian party, whose influence on SKP during the 1960s
has, generally speaking, been significant.

The 1967 congress thus meant a radical break from the
'new type of party' that the Comintern had set up as a
model in the 1920s. Therefore there is no need for wonder that a great number of members wanted to change
the party's name, a symbolic settling of accounts with the
past. But the proposal was met with strong opposition
and the result was a compromise: from 1967 onwards
the party's official name has been 'Vänsterpartiet Kommunisterna'[58]—the Left Party, the Communists—or VPK.

### v. The pendulum swings back

To all outward appearances, with the congress of 1967
the party had finally found a solution to all the problems
it had had to struggle with since the dissolution of the
Comintern during the second world war. Its attitude to
democracy and to the Soviet Union had been defined, its
isolation broken down, and the party's new slogan of
'socialist renewal' had gained a certain response. The
communist visage had been replaced by a left-socialist
one, resembling what had been done earlier in Denmark
and Norway, and behind it had collected together most of
the opposition to the left of social democracy.

But the party's new image was only a part of the
truth. It was obviously difficult to create trust and cooperation between the old party members and the new
forces that Hermansson had gathered round himself. And
the core of the party was still formed of old 'traditionalists', for whom it was very difficult to get their
bearings in this new world. The 'dogmatists' or 'Marxist-

Leninists' had on previous occasions raised objections and formed their own associations, which were partly composed of old party members like Nils Holmberg and Knut Senander, partly of young intellectuals like the above mentioned Bo Gustafsson. Their numbers and influence are, however, scarcely in proportion to the attention they aroused, even if the Marxist-Leninists were partly born of the revolutionary wave which the Vietnam movement brought after itself. More serious for Hermansson was the opposition which later developed with the old party leader Hilding Hagberg as its standard-bearer, and which was constituted above all from what, in place of something better we may call the traditionalists. The strength of the traditionalists is to be found most of all among the old guard and among the membership in Norrbotten, by tradition the reddest district in Sweden, whose newspaper *Norrskensflamman* had earlier aired its dissatisfaction with Hermansson and the new policy.

It was easy for the traditionalists to point out a series of organisational mistakes which Hermansson had been guilty of, but this criticism would presumably have been less dangerous in the autumn of 1968 if the party had not met with a painful electoral defeat. The causes of the defeat are certainly numerous. The bourgeois parties cherished good hopes of being able to put the social democrats in a minority, which made it easy for SAP in its propaganda to present the election as a choice between 'workers' rule' and 'bourgeois rule', a vote for the communists was a vote for the bourgeoisie. A few weeks before the election came the invasion of Czechoslovakia: despite the fact that Hermansson dissociated himself violently from the invasion, and recommended the 'freezing' of diplomatic relations with the Soviet Union, it is quite probable that to a certain extent the invasion influenced the electors. But still more important, presumably, was the fact that the inner struggle in the party created uncertainty about the party's aims. When the votes were counted, it turned out that VPK's share of the electorate had been halved, and it finished up with only 3 per cent, the lowest figure in the party's history. This was very much more serious because the electoral law which comes into force in 1970 excludes from the Diet those parties which collect less than 4 per cent of the electorate.

Clearly it took some time before the seriousness of the situation dawned on the party leadership.[59] Then Hermansson began to seek a middle way, in the hope of being able to strike a compromise with the traditionalists. But in doing this the line of 1967 has been compromised, and the attitude to democracy and the Soviet Union is not as self-evident as before. This in turn has led to many of the men who outwardly have symbolised the new line either leaving the party or falling back into passivity. And the old image has emerged anew. The party's trade union policy points to a return to the classical fraction activity, almost an act of desperation in the present-day situation.

At the moment of writing it is impossible to say whether the developments after 1967 should be regarded as the travail of a new party or the beginning of a return to old positions. In view of the similarities which exist between the circumstances of the Scandinavian countries it would be reasonable to forecast a 'Norwegian' or 'Danish' solution. This would mean a reasonably strong 'Left Party' with 5 to 6 per cent of the electorate and a 'Marxist-Leninist' organisation of some type with a few hundred members and ten to twenty thousand voters.

# PART TWO:
# THE COMMUNIST PARTY
# OF FINLAND

A. F. UPTON

For more than a century prior to 1917 Finland had been an autonomous grand duchy, whose ruler was the tsar of Russia. For most of this period the relationship had been remarkably free from strain and tension, but after 1897 the Russian government had initiated a campaign of russification in Finland aimed at undermining Finland's constitutional rights, and this in turn generated in the Finns a movement of national resistance. Parallel with this development was the rise of an independent workers' movement, which formed a political party in 1899, and in 1903 adopted the name Finnish Social Democratic Party (SDP), with a revolutionary, Marxist programme:[1] this committed the party to an unrelenting pursuit of the class war in every department of its activity. Unlike other social democratic parties of that era, with which in any case its contacts were not very close, the Finnish party resisted the revisionism of the Bernstein school and sternly rejected ministerial socialism; such weak tendencies to revisionism as existed within the Finnish party were unable to shake the monolithic orthodoxy of its doctrine— on the contrary, circumstances tended to harden the militant posture of the party.

During the great revolutionary crisis which shook the Russian empire in 1905–6 Finland extorted from the weakened tsarist government the abandonment of its russification policies and a new democratic constitution for Finland, the central feature of which was a unicameral legislature, based on universal suffrage and proportional representation. The Finnish workers were proudly conscious that these concessions had been won by their efforts in the main, and especially by the general strike

which they had launched in 1905, which had forced their
own bourgeoisie into joining the workers in demands for
radical reform. The workers had felt their power and
entered the elections for the new Parliament confident
that, as the largest political party, they would dominate
their divided bourgeois opponents. So it proved, but as
soon as the Russian government had recovered its grip the
success began to prove illusory. In a series of Parliaments
between 1907 and 1914, major reform legislation was
carried, only to be vetoed by the Russian-dominated
executives. Before long a new russification campaign began and the whole achievement of 1905–6 seemed to be
in danger; and when Russian military government was
imposed, on the outbreak of war in 1914, the situation
had become desperate.

The political experiences of this period left the workers'
movement in Finland important legacies; these arose from
the way in which, after 1906, the Russian government
became the obvious major obstacle to the realisation of
the aims of SDP. This led straight to the idea that only
Finnish independence could create conditions in which
the programme of the party could be realised, and independence from Russia became a fundamental aim of
the workers' movement, as it did of most patriotic Finns.
Finnish national feeling came to be defined and expressed in terms of a rejection of Russia, an enduring
characteristic which has been the worst handicap under
which the subsequent Finnish communist movement has
laboured. Yet, by an irony of history, a second legacy
of the situation was one of collaboration between SDP
and those forces in Russia opposed to the tsarist regime.
SDP had contacts with the Russian socialists from an
early stage of its history, the best known example of
which is the meeting of bolsheviks at Tampere in 1905,
under the protection of the Finnish workers' movement—
the occasion when Lenin and Stalin first met. After 1907
the number of such contacts fell off sharply, the controversies of bolsheviks and mensheviks passed the Finns
by, and, most important for the future, Lenin's writings

remained virtually unknown in Finland before 1918; but the idea that Finnish and Russian socialists could work together against their common enemy remained alive. A third legacy was that in the eyes of the workers the Finnish bourgeoisie, with honourable exceptions, had shown a disposition to collaborate with the tsarist regime in order to frustrate the advance of socialism in Finland; this added a new dimension of bitterness to the concept of class war and kept it burning bright in its pristine, Marxist purity. Finally, the years of frustrated parliamentary activity from 1907 to 1912, compared with the glorious revolutionary successes of 1905–6, kept the revolutionary aspects of Marxist socialism very much alive in the Finnish workers' movement. It seemed too obvious that the unnatural and treacherous alliance of domestic reaction with the foreign oppressor could only be defeated by force.

One more special factor brought the Finnish workers' movement to 1917 with its faith in undiluted Marxist socialism unshaken, for it had been exempted from the general socialist cataclysm of 1914. Finland, though technically at war as part of the Russian empire, was in fact in an almost unique position as a special kind of non-belligerent. There was no military service, so the Finns did not have to fight for either side and their socialists could preserve their internationalism intact. They adhered to the anti-war Zimmerwald international when it developed, and denounced without any embarrassment the imperialist war and the traitors among the socialist parties of the belligerents who had supported it. Thus in some ways the SDP was in an almost uniquely favourable position in the year 1917; it had survived all the troubles of its early years with its organisation and doctrine monolithically intact. Further, in the wartime election of 1916, it had crowned its achievement by winning an absolute majority of seats in Parliament, 103 out of 200. It is true that this caused little immediate excitement, because nobody expected that the tsarist regime would permit Parliament to meet, or if it did that anything substantial could be achieved. But it was a sign pointing the way forward: history was on the march and in the end it would carry socialism in Finland to its final triumph. Yet the leadership of the SDP was quite unprepared for the sudden shift of fortune that now overtook it.

The Russian February revolution had two main effects on Finland: at the governmental level, the provisional government promised the full restoration of Finland's autonomy and could be expected in the long run to extend that autonomy by constitutional reforms; as an immediate measure, the Parliament of 1916 with its socialist majority was convened. At the popular level, Russian revolutionary enthusiasm swept the Finnish workers. Partly it was an infection spread through Russian troops and workers in the military establishments, but perhaps above all through the radical sailors of the Russian squadrons stationed in Helsinki; partly it was carried by Finnish migrant labourers who had been on war work in Russia, or employed on the extensive fortification projects in Finland itself. Fraternisation developed fast, while the wave of enthusiasm and the collapse of governmental restraints brought workers flooding in to the SDP and the trade unions; these found themselves swamped by the influx of enthusiastic, impatient, revolution-minded recruits.

The leadership of the party was overwhelmed from both sides at once. Power was dumped into their laps from above, when in consequence of their parliamentary majority but against all their revolutionary and class-war traditions they were forced into a coalition government with the bourgeois parties, while at the same time their members from below were urging them to take power and institute a socialist revolution. Innocent of Leninist teachings, they naively clung to the view that Finland had still to pass through the phase of bourgeois capitalism, that she was not ripe for socialism, that the proletariat, in an overwhelmingly agrarian society, was insufficiently developed. So, in spite of the radical voices from below the leaders of SDP hesitated and fumbled: in the so-

called *valtalaki*, the centre of their parliamentary programme for 1917, they proposed to be content with internal self-government for what would still be a bourgeois
Finland, together with such interim reforms as democratic local government, prohibition and an eight-hour
law. To do the leadership justice, they were acutely conscious that the eventual outcome of the Russian revolution was uncertain and that Finland's eventual fate was
bound up with it. Even so, their reforms were too radical
for the Russian provisional government, urged on by some
elements of the Finnish bourgeoisie. At the end of July
Kerensky dissolved the Finnish Parliament and ordered
new elections. SDP had to decide whether to submit or
venture on revolutionary resistance; they hesitated, fumbled, and gave in. At a general election in October 1917
the united front of a thoroughly frightened bourgeoisie,
aided by revulsion in the socialist ranks against the apparent futility of parliamentary politics, produced a bourgeois majority in the new Parliament.

At this critical point came the October revolution in
Petrograd which transformed the situation. The bolshevik
regime at once urged the Finnish socialists to follow
its example: now that the Finnish bourgeoisie had lost
their Russian protectors, the way to a seizure of power
was wide open. Driven from below, the SDP presented
a series of radical demands to the new Parliament
and proceeded to enforce them with a revolutionary general strike. It was entirely successful and the Finnish
workers, encouraged and armed by the Russian soldiers,
took over control of the country. Once more the leaders
of SDP found power thrust upon them, and once more
they fumbled. All the old doubts persisted, and perhaps
more important the bolshevik regime in Petrograd might
collapse and leave them out on a limb; so when the
bourgeois parties conceded the immediate reform demands,
the general strike was called off and a bourgeois government was installed.

SDP paid a bitter price for this lack of revolutionary
confidence. Their own radicals, encouraged from Petro-

grad, continued to press for a seizure of power and en-trenched themselves in the red guard organisation, which rapidly built up into a semi-independent political force. On the other side, the bourgeois government was pre-paring to meet force with force, secretly developing its own militia organisation and negotiating in Sweden and Germany for foreign assistance against the socialist dan-ger. Something like an arms race developed between red and white, armed clashes occurred, and on 26 January 1918 both sides, independently, decided to strike. The SDP leadership declared the bourgeois government de-posed and set up a provisional workers' government.[2] Full-scale civil war developed, with the bolsheviks supply-ing arms and instructors to the reds, the Germans giving outright military assistance to the whites. When the treaty of Brest-Litovsk compelled the bolsheviks to stop all in-tervention in Finland, and a German expeditionary force had landed in the rear of the red front, the defeat of the reds was speedy and total. The red government moved to Russia in face of the white advances, and on 26 April 1918 it held its final session in Petrograd. It decided to disband the government and set up temporary committees for the care and resettlement of the thousands of refugees who had followed it over the Russian frontier.[3] When the immediate task of caring for the refugees was got under control, a body entitled the Central Committee of the Foreign Organisation of Finnish Social Democrats, or Finnish Workers' Executive Committee, was established in Moscow, though various other committees of exiles also functioned in Petrograd.[4] These bodies now began to consider the reasons for the appalling catastrophe they had brought down on the Finnish workers' move-ment and the means by which its recovery could best be promoted.

Most of the leaders of the Finnish workers were in Russia
in 1918, apart from the handful of revisionists who had
dissociated themselves from the revolution. There were a
few who had fallen into the hands of the whites, and
those who were not killed, like Y. Mäkelin, faced years in
prison. A few managed to live underground in Finland,
like K. Wiik, and surfaced when the worst of the reprisals
were over, or, like E. Gylling, the only member of the
red government who deliberately stayed behind to share
the fate of its followers, managed to get out to Sweden
and eventually joined the others in Russia. Of these, the
most important for the future was O. W. Kuusinen. Although he had only been deputy for education in the red
government several observers rate him as one of its ablest
members and its main driving force. He had made a
reputation as a theoretician, and was to become an acknowledged expert on dialectical materialism and a politician with an astonishing flair for backing the winning
line. This kept him alive right through the Stalin era and
beyond, one of the tiny minority of old-guard communists
who survived. In 1918 Kuusinen's abilities made the exiles
look to him above all for guidance in finding a new
policy to replace the one which had ended so badly.

The nominal leader was K. Manner, who had been
speaker of the 1916 Parliament, chairman of the red
government and, in its last days, dictator. Manner had
charm and presence but his impressive facade covered a
weak and irresolute man, who was repeatedly thrust into
prominence by events, when without exception he proved
unequal to the challenge. Though fated to become the

figurehead for those who opposed or resented the pre-eminence of Kuusinen, Manner was never more than a tool manipulated by stronger personalities. Much nearer in abilities to Kuusinen was Y. Sirola, the deputy for foreign affairs in the red government. He was a rather academic politician, of whom nearly everyone speaks with affection and who had been visibly distressed by the violence and cruelties of civil war. Sirola lacked the lust for power necessary for political success. It was fitting that he was to become an educator, directing the training of party cadres until his death in 1936 on the eve of the purges. He was generally content to follow and support Kuusinen and never presented any challenge to the latter's political dominance.

Two eminent figures were quickly lost to the new movement: one was another bourgeois intellectual, E. Valpas-Hänninen, who had built up a great reputation since 1906 as a stern class warrior and leader of the hard-line radicals in the SDP. But when it came to action this fire-breathing demagogue repeatedly discovered that the correct historical moment had not yet come. Typically, when the revolution broke out Valpas was lurking on the fringe of events, successfully avoiding any active role in the revolutionary regime, to such an extent that he believed that it was safe for him to return to Finland when developments among the exiles displeased him; he was mistaken, and he received a heavy prison sentence. A more proletarian figure was O. Tokoi, who had come to prominence as a trade union leader and had presided over the coalition government of 1917. Tokoi figures in Finnish communist demonology as the first major defector, for almost at once he was sent on a mission to Murmansk and got involved in the affairs of the Murmansk legion, a force of red guard refugees, organised and armed by the British forces in north Russia. Instead of carrying out his mission to direct this force in the interests of the revolution, Tokoi entered into contact with the Finnish government with a view to arranging an amnesty for the legion, while at the same time negotiating with the

British for its possible use against the bolsheviks. Tokoi was therefore regarded as having gone over to the enemy and was formally declared a traitor by the newly formed Communist Party on 24 September 1918.[1] Thus a potential leader of considerable stature was lost to the movement.

The violent red guard wing of the revolution also lost a major figure in A. Taimi, who had been a deputy for military affairs in the red government. Taimi had begun his political career with the Russian bolsheviks, and he was now taken away again to serve in the Russian civil war, as were many other red guards among the exiles. Among those who remained were the Rahja brothers, Eino and Jukka, whose persistent preference for violence and direct action, and dubious personal lives, ensured them a stormy career in the subsequent history of the movement.

As the exiles debated what had gone wrong, some understandably felt that they had been betrayed by the bolsheviks at Brest-Litovsk, or even that the red government itself had sold out to Imperial Germany:[2] others, led by Valpas, took the pre-Leninist line that the revolution had been premature, because capitalism in Finland had not been ripe for overthrow, so that the task before the movement was to rebuild on reformist lines and prepare the proletariat for action in the future when the circumstances were right. Valpas was propagating this view in his newspaper *Vapaus*, circulating in the Petrograd area in June and July of 1918, in opposition to the opinion being formed by the majority group among the exiles.[3]

This group had discovered the answer to its problems in the writings of Lenin, which most of them were reading for the first time, discovering there both the explanation of their failure and the recipe for future success: they must purge themselves of the old social-democratic illusions and reconstruct the movement on correct bolshevik principles. Kuusinen wrote the classic exposition of this view in his 'Self-criticism', in which he analyses the ideological immaturity of the old workers' movement, which had amounted to a Kautskyite deviation, so that in 1917, in spite of its honourable traditions, SDP had departed from its class-war principles:[4] 'In reality, our social democrats descended to whoring with both the Finnish bourgeoisie and, initially, with the Russian bourgeoisie . . . the Finnish coalition government served as the bed for this immoral coupling'.

Under Kuusinen's dominant influence, Manner, Sirola and the bulk of the exiles had adopted this opinion by the time when, on 25 August, in a former seminary near Moscow, there was held an advisory conference of Finnish socialists. This seems to have had more than a hundred participants to begin with, but when the crucial vote was taken on 29 August the number recorded as present is ninety-four, though some of the minority may already have left once they saw how things were going.[5] The conference had before it two drafts for a programme of future action, one drawn up in Moscow and the other in Petrograd. Both envisaged that revolution should be the central aim of the movement but the Petrograd draft had a section, inserted at the instance of the trade union wing, which set out a programme of immediate reforms to be secured within the capitalist system, since they envisaged an immediate revival of a legal trade union movement in Finland.[6]

Kuusinen opened the debate with a scornful denunciation of the muddled, Kautskyite-centrist thought embodied in the Petrograd document. It would lead the movement straight back to the ideological contradictions that had just brought it to disaster:[7]

> In the class struggle, the battle for total power has come to the front. Now force must be opposed to force. Nothing rallies the masses like this type of revolutionary class war, which involves the suppression of the whole capitalist structure, the total destruction of the power of the bourgeoisie, the taking of all power into the hands of the workers, and the creation of a socialist order.

Of course, a revolution had to be carefully prepared and launched at the right historical moment, but to include the reformist proposals of the Pertrograd draft would only lead to confusion and weakness—'a communist programme cannot be anything other than revolutionary. A programme of democratic and social reforms set up alongside it would be like a demand by slaves who need to be liberated for an alleviation of their slavery'. Kuusinen assumed that the revolution was now at hand all over Europe, so they could tell the oppressed workers in Finland, 'Help is coming. A new revolution can be launched. It can bring salvation'.[8] But it took five days of debate before the meeting was ready, on 29 August, to vote on the five theses of the Moscow draft. A motion by the trade union opposition to send them to committee, to be amended on the lines of the Petrograd draft, was defeated by seventy-four votes to sixteen, with four abstentions. The majority then resolved to convert the meeting into the founding congress of the Finnish Communist Party and ruled that only those who unreservedly accepted the five theses would be allowed to participate. In this way the Finnish Communist Party came into existence, on 29 August 1918.[9] The text of the five theses runs as follows:[10]

1. The workers are to prepare energetically for an armed revolution and in no way to fall back into the old parliamentary, trade union, and cooperative struggle which was the basis of the Finnish workers' movement before the revolution.

2. Only that kind of workers' movement and activity which is guaranteed to promote the spread of communism and the achievement of the victory of the workers' socialist revolution can be approved and must be energetically promoted—activity among the workers on any other basis must be severely condemned, exposed, and resisted.

3. Through the revolution, all power must be gathered into the hands of the working class and the iron dictatorship of the workers must be established—the

aim must be the destruction of the bourgeois state, and not the establishment of democracy either before or through the revolution.

4. Through the dictatorship of the workers, a communist society is to be erected by the immediate confiscation of all land and capitalist property, and all production and distribution is to be run through the activity of the organised workers.

5. The initiation and victory of the workers' international revolution is to be promoted with the utmost energy, and also the socialist, soviet state of the Russian proletariat is to be supported by every means.

It can be seen that this was a very uncompromising document and gave ample grounds for the Finnish courts to rule, as they did, that the Finnish communist movement was from its inception illegal and that membership of it automatically constituted the crime of sedition at least.[11] The Marxist observer will also perceive that this document is riddled with what Lenin later defined as 'left-infantilism'. The party now agrees that it was a mistake to have condemned democracy in those terms and to have rejected all forms of non-revolutionary activity; it accounts for the error as an overreaction to the experience of defeat and the still very imperfect understanding by the members of bolshevik ideology.[12] They should have made proper provision for the public activity of the movement in the pre-revolutionary period.[13]

The first congress of SKP consisted of the seventy-one who had voted for the five theses plus thirteen others who declared their acceptance of them.[14] It is claimed, with considerable justification, that it represented the great majority of the elected leadership of the old workers' movement, especially as some of the important absentees, like Gylling, or the trade union leader Lumivuokko, gave their adherence later. Consequently, although it had admittedly no direct contact with the workers in Finland, the congress had a good right to speak in their name even though, as subsequently emerged, it had badly misinterpreted their current mood. One cannot seriously contest the claim of SKP to be a legitimate heir of the old Finnish workers' movement.

The congress then got down to business, electing Manner and Sirola as joint chairmen,[15] after which J. Rahja opened proceedings by regretting the necessity of breaking with some old comrades of the minority, but claiming that it was a price which had to be paid for the ideological unity which was the only basis for effective action.[16] They then began to discuss the forms of this action, and Kuusinen elaborated its ideological basis, stressing that revolution required careful and responsible preparation and that this would of necessity largely take the form of underground activity. It followed that 'everyone who concedes the necessity for secret activity must also accept the total concentration of power in the party leadership'.[17] This extreme form of democratic centralism was thus inserted into the party's traditions at its very inception. Kuusinen also pointed out that recruitment would have to be very selective, although they must never lose sight of the eventual aim of creating a mass party. A committee of three, Kuusinen, Rahja and L. Letonmäki, was entrusted with the drafting of the action programme. The draft defined the party as the party of the proletariat, concerned only with organising the proletariat for armed insurrection and the establishment of a proletarian dictatorship.[18] The means must be first of all a massive spread of propaganda among the masses, the widest possible military training of the workers, and the recruitment of sympathetic workers into the party.[19] Then when the revolution did come, there would be no compromises but the socialist order would be ruthlessly enforced by the workers' dictatorship. This programme was adopted unanimously and they elected a central committee consisting of Kuusinen, Sirola, J. Rahja, L. Letonmäki and K. M. Evä.[20]

This congress also held an interesting discussion of the question of Finnish independence. J. Rahja condemned the old concept of independence as outdated by the rise of imperialism. Manner held that since the idea of independence had shown itself to be very attractive to the Finnish workers, the party must take account of this. He thought that even between socialist states it would not be possible to abolish national frontiers at once, though there should be the closest collaboration. But of course in the end frontiers would disappear, and as communists they knew that there could be no real independence for small countries like Finland.[21] No resolutions were passed on this crucial topic but a modern communist would see in the discussion further evidence of the ideological immaturity of the participants, who showed a failure to grasp the teachings of Lenin and Stalin on the nationality question. Their gropings also illustrate a dilemma that has hung, albatross-like, round the neck of SKP since its inception—namely how to reconcile loyalty to world communism and its original fatherland, Soviet Russia, with the sometimes contradictory demands of Finnish national feeling. In Marxist theory there is no real problem but in hard political fact there is a contradiction which cannot be talked away and has done the communist cause in Finland incalculable damage over the years.

On 3 September the congress which had been promised a visit from Lenin, heard that he had been shot. Kuusinen then drafted on their behalf an open letter to Lenin, summarising their past errors and telling him all that they owed to his teachings:[22]

> For us former Finnish social democrats, acquaintance with communist doctrine has meant at one blow the opening up of a new perspective on the world. It has made a socialist revolution in us as well. Only now that we are awake do we see the full light of socialism, which at most we had only dreamed of before.

Nobody could mistake the mood of Pauline conversion, or the high faith and idealism in which SKP set out on its long mission. In closing the congress Manner said: 'The decisions made in this meeting make it the most important gathering of the Finnish workers' movement. We have left

one phase of its development behind us, and begun another'. If the first assertion is open to discussion, the second can scarcely be challenged.

At first SKP had important work to do in Russia itself,
among the refugees; teams of agitators were sent round to
introduce the new party to them. At the same time SKP
sought to fulfil its mission to give military training to
able-bodied workers, and to enlist them for service in the
immediate defence of the Russian revolution. SKP established a 'military section' of the central committee, and
apart from encouraging individuals to enlist in the red
army direct, they raised two full regiments of Finns,
which served in Karelia and on other fronts. More than
six thousand men were recruited for these and other units
down to 1921, when most of them were demobilised. SKP
was politically responsible for them and looked on them as
cadres for its own revolutionary struggle.[23] But these activities were increasingly seen as an unfortunate diversion
of energy from Finland itself, which the party held was
'the only field of activity of this party'.[24] The second
congress of SKP in 1919 decided to wind up its work among
the refugees and transfer it to special organs to be super-
vised by the Russian Communist Party.

The fundamental task of SKP was to establish itself as
the leader of the workers inside Finland. There, the vic-
torious whites had unleashed a massive repression against
their defeated enemies. Exact figures cannot now be recovered but it is beyond dispute that between seventeen
and twenty thousand reds were murdered, judicially executed, or allowed to die of hunger and the disease of mal-
nutrition in prison camps during the course of 1918. Some
eighty thousand experienced the miseries of the hastily
improvised camps and thousands of these eventually suffered terms of imprisonment. In addition SDP, the trade
unions, the socialist newspapers and the youth movement
were suppressed and their assets confiscated. How much the
eventual success of SKP owes to the bitterness engendered
by the treatment of the defeated reds is one of those
questions which defies quantification; but there is no

doubt that significant sections of the Finnish working class came to see, in support of SKP, their only effective means of expressing the resentment and hatred which they so justifiably directed against the bourgeois regime.

The more optimistic among the victors imagined that socialism had been crushed in Finland for decades to come, but they were mistaken. There was a small group of social democrats who had always dissociated themselves from the revolution of 1918, and took no part in it. This group, led by V. Tanner, had already tried, in April 1918, to restart a workers' movement, publishing a manifesto which described the revolution as a criminal mistake and calling on the workers to commit themselves to peaceful reform. In November 1918 the Helsinki Workers' Council was revived,[25] and at the end of December a provisional congress of a revived SDP was held.[26] The communists and many other socialists outside their ranks could never forgive Tanner and his colleagues for repudiating the revolution and spitting on its memory in the moment of defeat. A deep and vicious feud was born between the two legatees of the old workers' movement. The December congress of SDP specifically denounced the exiles and the SKP; T. Tainio, in a typical speech, said that 'the communists are the most dangerous enemies of the Finnish workers and the Finnish social democratic movement, at this time more dangerous than the bourgeois'.[27] Earlier, in June 1918, the Finnish trade union movement had been revived under the chairmanship of another socialist who had stood aside from the revolution, M. Paasivuori, while the youth movement began to revive in Helsinki during the autumn, and, significantly, although still without contact with SKP showed signs of dissatisfaction with Tanner's revisionism.[28] This was the background to the launching of SKP in Finland itself.

One essential step towards realising the programme adopted was to publish suitable literature. SKP already had a periodical, Kumous,[29] but in addition they set to work translating the Marxist classics, especially the works of Lenin, and put out a series of explanatory pamphlets on

the new theory and practice of communism, the programme of the Bolshevik Party, and the aims of the SKP.[30]
But before the fruits of this crash programme of transla-
tions and commentaries could be distributed, SKP needed
an organisation inside Finland. The first moves antedate
the foundation of SKP, for links were established between
the group of exiles in Stockholm and supporters in Finland in June and July, mainly concerned with organising
relief for the red prisoners and helping them to escape.[31]
The Stockholm group came to be recognised as the 'Stockholm bureau' of SKP, which was from then on a main link
between the central committee and Finland. In November
the first regular SKP organisers were sent in from Stockholm, under orders to build up a network of underground
cells on a troika system; in this system each party member
recruited two others, and in theory nobody would be acquainted with more than five other members, yet there
would be a pervasive network of cells. The system promised tight security, but it had its drawbacks; as one participant put it: 'It was so secret that even the workers did
not know about it'.[32] In truth, the members of SKP were
complete novices at underground work,[33] and as commonly
happens with novices tended to overdo the conspiratorial
techniques.

A second line of communication was directly over the
frontier from Russia. This was dangerous, for the frontier
areas were under martial law until 1920, and the local
authorities had few scruples in dealing with SKP emissaries
who fell into their hands, several of whom were 'shot
while trying to escape'.[34] But there was a group of skilled
smugglers in the frontier regions, then unemployed and
willing to sell their services to SKP.[35] With their aid, supplemented by direct corruption of the frontier authorities,
the evidence is that it was possible for SKP at all times to
pass men, literature and even arms across the frontier,
though the degree of risk involved varied according to the
political situation. It was also possible to ferry men and
materials in and out by motorboat, since the thousands of

islands of the archipelago which covers the Finnish coast-
line make interception extremely difficult.

It is obviously impossible to assess objectively the results of this early activity of SKP. The party readily concedes that it was very haphazard, depending as it did on
the work of scattered individuals who had very little inter-
communication; it was an affair of devoted and hunted
men moving around the country and starting little groups
of enthusiasts. There is evidence that on the one hand the
stern exhortation to prepare for the next round in the
revolution came as an inspiration to many who had been
shattered by their defeat, though they tended to assume
that it meant the imminent return of the red guard with
all the armed strength of Russia behind it. On the other
hand, some felt that to talk of a new revolution after such
a bloodletting was unrealistic, and found the dogmatic insistence of the SKP emissaries that this was the only correct
line of action unacceptable.[36] The party now recognises
that it was badly infected with ultra-Leftism, and that this
did damage its work and prevented it getting through to
the masses. Indeed SKP must have felt this quite early, for
in December and January instructions were transmitted
to widen the scope of party activity by participation in
trade union activities and public meetings, in addition to
building up underground cells, but the call was not much
heeded.[37]

However, even at this early stage the biggest obstacle to
effective work inside Finland was the effectiveness of the
government's security police. Individual party agents were
being arrested from the time they first appeared in Finland, but the 'domestic centre', painfully formed in Helsinki by March 1919 as the coordinating body for all
SKP activity, and which was the forerunner of the 'Finnish
bureau' of the party set up in 1921, survived a bare two
months before the security police arrested its members in
May. This led to the first formal trials of SKP members by
the Finnish courts, which ruled that SKP was a criminal
conspiracy and membership of it a criminal act.[38] Finland is a poor theatre for underground conspiracy, for al-

though in a geographical sense there is plenty of room to hide in, in a social sense it is a very tight-knit community where strangers are quickly noticed. There is not enough privacy or anonymity in Finnish life to provide the necessary cover for the conspirator, while an agent who sought refuge in the backwoods simply put himself out of action. Although SKP came to develop a high level of skill in dodging and deceiving the authorities, the battle between SKP and the security police proved an uneven one, with the police well on top until its conclusion in 1944.

In February 1919 SKP held a party conference, made up exclusively of emigrants, and considered its attitude to the parliamentary elections to be held in Finland in March. They approved a manifesto published under the title of 'The Red Voting Ticket',[39] which elaborated the five theses into a detailed programme for an immediate armed revolution and the establishment of a socialist society. The party now regards this manifesto as one more example of the prevailing ultra-Leftism, but at least it formulated the concept of proletarian dictatorship in a more correct, Leninist manner, describing it as 'proletarian democracy, organised and free'.[40] It would mean government by soviets elected by the workers, with a right of recall, and only the bourgeoisie would be denied political rights.[41] Its basic error was the call to the workers to boycott the election, not because communists boycott bourgeois elections on principle but because on this occasion, 'history has prepared the possibility of removing the whole bourgeois state and changing it into a workers' state . . . it follows from this that no lesser objective can come into question in the struggle of the proletariat'.[42]

It is doubtful how widely this call was circulated, but it evoked a response from the left of the SDP, whose spokesman, I. Lassy, agreed that the overthrow of the bourgeois state was the only real objective but saw tactical advantages in the workers taking part in the election; a boycott by an inadequately organised left would have no effect.[43] The workers did in fact ignore SKP's call and voted heavily for SDP, returning eighty members to the two hundred member Parliament, of whom two were in fact communists.[44] The party had, as it now admits, misinterpreted the mood of the workers and it persisted in this error for some months more, partly because of its dogmatic ultra-Leftism, partly through lack of direct contacts with Finland.

In March 1919 SKP was prominently represented at the founding congress of the Comintern.[45] The Rahja brothers opened the debate on proletarian dictatorship, which ended with the decision that bourgeois democracy was now a reactionary force and that the dictatorship of the proletariat was the only valid objective of communist policy. Sirola led the debate on the white terror. Yet despite this brave start SKP never played a very prominent part in the affairs of the Comintern, the members of its rather large delegations at Comintern congresses rarely speaking in the debate, while the Comintern itself did not waste much time or effort on Finnish affairs, except when forced to do so by internal crises in SKP. Kuusinen alone, of the various Finns who served on the Comintern executive or secretariat, played an important role in its affairs.

This first Comintern congress generally endorsed the strong revolutionary line which SKP had evolved, and during 1919 the party pressed ahead with various schemes for armed insurrection in Finland. These were stimulated by the counter-threat of intervention by Finland in the Russian civil war; in April 1919 the authorities connived at an abortive armed incursion by white militants into Russian Karelia, and there was a very real threat in the summer and autumn that Finland would join in General Judenitch's attack on Petrograd. SKP ran the political side of an officer-training school for Finns, which turned out some three hundred graduates a year while the civil war lasted in Russia. The men served in the red army, or in later years in the frontier guard and in the autonomous army established in Russian Karelia.[46] There was a persistent effort to revive the red guard in Finland itself, and in some places units did begin drilling and loads of small arms were smuggled in and concealed. It may not have amounted to much but it evoked alarmist articles in the bourgeois press in June and July.[47] At the same time the military section of SKP tried to organise subversion among the Finnish conscripts.[48] A more ambitious plan centered on the Finnish refugees in Sweden: by April 1919 a staff for a battalion of red guards was working in Sweden and men were being trained in the remote northern areas. The first idea was to invade northern Finland as a signal to start the revolution, but this was changed in September into a plan to march across Finland into Russia. Then this too was dropped and in 1920 the battalion was disbanded and those who wished were helped to migrate to Russia.[49]

Despite these activities, all the evidence suggests that in the early summer of 1919 SKP was in danger of sinking into complete futility. It was not succeeding in making a fruitful contact with the mass of the workers in Finland, partly because of organisational difficulties, partly because the rigid revolutionary line did not correspond with the mood of the workers. This became so apparent that the central committee sent Kuusinen and J. Lehtosaari on a mission into Finland to find out what was wrong. This Kuusinen mission, which managed to evade the security police for over a year, changed the history of SKP. As Kuusinen became acquainted with the realities of the situation he became convinced that a major change of tactics was needed. The party must drop its conspiratorial approach and reach the workers through active participation in public organisations and through a public press. Only in this way could SKP get its message over to the masses —'Kuusinen and his staff perceived that they had become isolated from their army'.[60] The conversion was gradual, for Kuusinen had come with the intention of enforcing the party line, and as late as October 1919 he was still defending the electoral boycott policy as correct;[51] but in the end, on his own responsibility he decided to change the line.[52] The party acknowledges now that 'SKP's representatives in Finland had no instructions from the party leadership for this, and they began to act independently.[63]

The first major success for the new line was the capture
of the Social Democratic Youth League at its conference
of 15–20 September.[54] This organisation had about 250
branches and some fifteen thousand members, and was
already highly dissatisfied with the revisionist line of SDP.
It was not difficult to get its congress to vote that 'class
conciliation between the bourgeoisie and the proletariat
must not happen. It is an economic and historical impos-
sibility', and that the league policy must be 'unwaveringly
to wage relentless class war to the end, in order to overthrow the rule of the bourgeoisie'.[55] On the question of
its relationship to SDP, the league declared its independence; its members would no longer be obliged to join SDP
on reaching the appropriate age and it would support SDP
only in so far as its policies adhered to a class-war line.[56]
The league was from this point on under firm communist
control, becoming the first big public organisation which
acted as a power base and recruiting ground for the party.
The most valuable immediate benefit was that the league
commissioned I. Lassy to run a periodical for it, the
*Socialist Journal*,[57] and left him free to put its columns
at the disposal of Kuusinen. In this way Kuusinen was
able to publish basic communist material in a legal paper
with a circulation of six thousand; for instance, on 1 October the programme of the Comintern was printed in full,[58]
and in a series of articles by Kuusinen the differences between communism and social democracy were fully elaborated. This propaganda drive was soon extended as the
communists and their allies captured such provincial SDP
papers as the Kuopio *Savon Kansa*.[59] There was then both
a daily and a periodical press putting over a strict class war
line and attacking the SDP acceptance of bourgeois society
and its institutions.

Further successes followed. In September the leftists
captured the Helsinki SDP machine, and they were gain-
ing ground fast in the Social Democratic Women's
League, the Temperance League, and the Workers' Sports
League.[60] They were also making significant headway
in the trade union movement, where in November Kuusi-

nen organised a radical takeover of the Woodworkers' Union, the fourth largest in the country.[61] But the keenest struggle was for the biggest prize of all, the control of SDP itself, through the party congress set for December 1919. For this Kuusinen was recommending a different line from that laid down for other workers' organisations. With them he had urged the radicals to capture them if they could but above all to maintain them intact. But in the case of SDP it seems clear that Kuusinen doubted whether it could be captured and that he was determined from the first, if he failed, to launch a separate radical socialist party. To charges that this involved the crime of splitting the working-class movement, Kuusinen's modern defenders can reply that he knew that if the radicals did win control at the December congress, the beaten revisionists would secede, so that a split was anyway inevitable.[62]

The fight for SDP raged all autumn. Kuusinen and colleagues were in close contact with dissatisfied social democrats like S. Wuolijoki and E. Pekkala, and a vigorous press debate was kept up. The revisionist leadership warned the party of 'bolshevik agents abundantly supplied with Russian rubles who are active among the working class' and who were concealing their communism behind a mask of radical social democracy.[63] The opposition claimed that all they were demanding was that SDP should adhere to the honoured principles it had stood for down to 1917.[64] The communists alleged that in their desperation the revisionists rigged the elections to the December congress by creating unrepresentative rural branches to pack the congress with tame voting fodder, while in Uusimaa province, when the opposition won most of the fifteen delegates, the party committee enlarged the delegation to twenty-six and itself nominated the additional eleven delegates, including Tanner himself.[65] Any student of Finnish political parties will recognise that there is nothing inherently improbable in these charges, whatever the truth may be.

The congress was held from 8 to 16 December 1919,

and Tanner won all the decisive votes. Some delegates elected as radicals defected to the establishment, leaving the opposition with about one-third of the participants.[66] The opposition also made tactical mistakes, as when they ran K. Luoto for chairman and he turned out to have a vulnerable past record which was used to get him expelled from the party in mid-congress,[67] while I. Lassy was shown to have used dubious means in getting hold of confidential party documents. But the great debate was over fundamentals, and here E. Pekkala spoke strongly for the communist concept that the working class would have to take all power into its own hands before a real democracy could be created; the job of the SDP should be to prepare the workers for this. The bourgeois constitution was a fraud, concealing the dictatorship of the bourgeoisie.[68] The revisionists, however, proved the stronger; their line was confirmed in the crucial vote by 98 to 54 and the congress closed with Tanner and his colleagues firmly in control of SDP.[69] The defeated minority had to consider what they should do.

This was a question that came up when SKP held its second congress in Russia in September 1919. Only émigrés attended, and the central committee expressed their alarm at Kuusinen's new line. They insisted that all true socialists must come out of SDP and set up a new public party, but also stressed that such a party would need a high standard of ideological maturity—in other words would need to be controlled by SKP. Thus the congress was approaching the problem of how any public political movement in Finland could be effectively controlled by SKP acting from outside.[70] The congress formally ratified SKP's membership of the Comintern and rebuffed Kuusinen by insisting that revolution was imminent and that to prepare for it should be the main preoccupation of the Finnish workers. Consequently the congress insisted that underground work must enjoy at least equal priority with developing a public political movement, and implied that Kuusinen was neglecting this. It is indeed alleged that even at this stage the split between Kuusinen and the Manner-Rahja group in control of the central committee had gone so far that SKP was cutting off funds to Kuusinen and sending in agents of its own to counter his influence and insist on a strict obedience to the party line.[71] What is certain is that by the end of 1919 there was an open threat of a split between the *émigré* leadership and the movement inside Finland.

On 16 December 1919 the leaders of the defeated SDP opposition held a meeting to consider their position, and concluding that the congress had in effect renounced the workers' cause they issued a manifesto beginning 'Comrades! There is no longer a socialist workers' party in Finland', and calling for the formation of a new political party. Eventually they succeeded in organising a congress for such a party, which assembled in Helsinki on 13 May 1920.[72] The seventy-eight delegates who attended may have represented as many as fifty thousand members of SDP organisations which had seceded since the December congress, and one may assume that most of the anti-revisionist membership of SDP took part. Communist commentators are entitled to claim, as they do, that this was a meeting of social democrats. It was decided to establish a new party, the Finnish Socialist Workers' Party, and to adopt a programme that had substantially been written by Kuusinen himself, although SKP complained later that it had got 'watered-down' in its final drafting.[73] This programme is generally reckoned one of Kuusinen's masterpieces. It is defiantly Marxist: the new party 'is the class-war party of the proletariat, whose programme is the abolition of capitalism and the building of a socialist society'.[74] It was a revolutionary party in the sense that it sought the overthrow of the existing social order, but it did not advocate violence as a means: on this point there was a masterly explanation which affirmed:[75]

> The party does not encourage the workers to anarchistic violence, disorders, riots or insurrections. On the contrary, the party seeks by educational and or-

ganisational activity to influence affairs so that the victory of the working class and socialism shall be achieved in as orderly a fashion, as peacefully and soberly, as painlessly and speedily as possible. But no party resolutions can decide beforehand the ways in which a revolutionary process embracing the whole world will develop. . . . More important to the political forms of this process will be the weapons used by the workers' enemies.

This programme, which goes on to outline the measures that will be needed after the revolution to establish a Finnish Soviet republic, is an early example of Kuusinen's inventiveness as a Marxist theoretician. It contains two concepts that were later to be of the greatest importance: the possibility of a peaceful transition to socialism, and the possibility of different roads to socialism in different countries.[76] It was therefore at that time in conflict with the current line of the Comintern and of SKP. On the other hand, the difference is one of tactics not final aims. Kuusinen had brilliantly anticipated the change of line which the Comintern itself was shortly to make, when it recognised, as he did, that the revolution might be some distance in the future and that it was legitimate for communists to participate positively in parliamentary, trade union and local government activity under a bourgeois regime in the interim—though only for the purpose of preparing the working class for its revolutionary destiny.

Up to this point in the proceedings the police, who had been present throughout on rather dubious legal grounds,[77] had not interfered. They were probably too politically illiterate to appreciate the significance of the programme.[78] But when the congress began to debate international relations, it had before it Kuusinen's proposal that it should affiliate to the Comintern, but 'on its own programme'. This has two interesting implications: first, that Kuusinen publicly revealed his disagreement with some points in the current Comintern theses;

second, that since Finland could only be represented by one party in the Comintern, he was proposing that SKP be wound up and STP taken into its place as the sole recognised party of the Finnish workers. SKP histories are reluctant to face this manifest truth, although it is the answer to charges that STP was just a cover for SKP. It was not, it was intended to replace it, and what role if any would have been left for the *émigrés*, of whom Kuusinen himself would inevitably have been one, is not clear. What is clear is that Kuusinen had now repudiated the central committee and its policies; this is merely obscured by the fact that his proposal could not be executed, for as soon as the motion to affiliate to the Comintern was carried, the police closed the meeting and arrested eleven of the organisers, who were subsequently charged with sedition and convicted.[79]

The setback was only temporary and partial, for on 19 June 1920 the Helsinki City Socialist Organisation took the name STP and adopted the programme, except for affiliation to the Comintern.[80] There is some evidence that the authorities had tacitly agreed to permit the new party on this condition.[81] J. Kivi became chairman, and A. Tuominen secretary, and a national organisation was rapidly built up, so that on 27–8 December 1920 it was possible to assemble a party council representing twelve of the sixteen electoral districts into which Finland is divided.[82] The programme was confirmed and the tactics of the party laid down: starting from the assumption that the warring classes were irreconcilable, there was no point in seeking to ameliorate the capitalist system. Therefore the purpose of STP in taking part in Parliament and local government was to educate the working class by exposing the class dictatorship concealed behind the democratic facade. The trade unions should wage relentless war on the system and reject all policies of conciliation or industrial harmony, while SDP was to be exposed continually as the betrayer of the workers' cause. The STP quickly achieved a membership of about twenty-five thousand and captured 341 seats in local elections in December 1920, against 1,032 for the SDP. It was already established as a major force in Finnish politics.

STP is one enduring monument to Kuusinen's long underground mission in Finland. The other is the capture by the radical Left of the Finnish Trade Union Congress— SAJ. In this the lead was taken by Kuusinen's colleague, Lumivuokko, who in turn found able collaborators in Tuominen and E. Louhikko. When the SAJ congress was held on 25–9 May 1920 it was a triumph for the radicals. There were seventy-five delegates, of whom SDP and Lumivuokko each controlled twenty-five, but in the struggle for the remaining twenty-five delegates Lumivuokko and Louhikko were easy victors. They picked their own chairman, M. Väisänen, and put Tuominen in as vice-chairman and Louhikko as secretary. The executive committee and the large committee were given a radical majority, and SAJ finally broke its connection with SDP, leaving the individual unions free to contribute to political parties if they wished, while the general programme was firmly based on the concepts of class war.[83] This was a major victory for Kuusinen; workers' militancy increased and strike activity in 1920 was three times the 1919 level,[84] SAJ was firmly under the control of friendly forces and was committed to a class-war doctrine; the social democrat minority was harassed and impotent. The position was consolidated in 1921 when the radicals went forward to capture control of almost all the remaining trade unions, giving the communists a grip on the trade union movement which they held unbroken until 1930.[85]

By the spring of 1920 Kuusinen had been evading the police successfully for more than a year. He had transformed the communist movement in Finland from a desperate and ineffective conspiracy into a rising mass movement, and incidentally conducted a major love affair which had produced some three hundred sheets of letters and poems.[86] He could no longer remain in Finland and left the centre of Helsinki in a small boat, and after some adventurous voyaging in the archipelago was ferried safely to Stockholm. There he established his base and continued to direct the movement he had created and had to face up to the problem of the relations of his movement to SKP and the central committee in Russia, whose emissary he had originally been.

For the *émigré* SKP in Russia, 1920 was a terrible year filled with disappointment and disaster. In contrast with the upsurge of STP in Finland, SKP seemed to be tearing itself apart. The most spectacular occurrence, though probably the least significant, was the emergence of an anti-party group in the Petrograd area. In the official view of SKP this group was petty-bourgeois/anarchist in character, and had been infiltrated by Finnish secret service agents who exploited the purely selfish and personal grievances of its members against the leadership of SKP.[87] The reality seems to be that many Finnish refugees in the Petrograd area were leading a very bleak existence in 1920, and that some of the more articulate and ambitious among them found it easy to persuade others that the local SKP leadership, above all the Rahja brothers, were living in luxury on the proceeds of loot they had brought out with them in 1918. There certainly was a group of discontented party members, several of whom had been serving in the red army, who planned to overthrow the central committee and take the leadership themselves; and they were anarchist in the sense that they had no programme beyond this. Their leader was V. Eloranta, who had been a prominent figure before 1918; in June 1920 the central committee expelled him and six of his companions from the party for organised opposition to the party line.[88] They then decided, in desperation, to kill their enemies, above all the Rahjas, and on 31 August 1920 a group of them broke into a party meeting in Petrograd, where Jukka Rahja was giving a lecture, and opened fire, killing eight people, of whom J. Rahja was the most important, and wounding nine others. The culprits were arrested and tried by the Russian authorities. Eloranta was executed and others served terms of imprisonment.[89] The enemies of SKP have often used this spectacular incident to imply either that SKP were simply a lot of political gangsters who naturally settled their accounts in this way, or that the leaders were so remote from their deluded followers, and so alienated from them, that the latter were driven to violent protest. But it is more reasonable to see this bizarre and uncharacteristic episode as an expression of the tensions, frustrations and demoralisation of two years of aimless refugee existence under wretched material conditions. The local leadership of SKP, dominated by the Rahja brothers, had been far from tactful in dealing with grievances and had become the only available target against which to discharge these accumulated passions. The long-term repercussions of the episode on the history of the party were negligible.

What really presented a mortal threat to SKP was the growing power of the Kuusinen anti-party group. By the summer of 1920 there had gathered in Stockholm a substantial minority of the party leadership, including Sirola, Lumivuokko and Letonmäki, and this group had formally defied the call of the central committee to come to Russia for a congress of SKP. On 15 July they addressed a letter to the central committee announcing that they would not recognise the proposed congress because it was STP that represented the real communist movement. They suggested instead that a new congress be assembled in Stockholm, representative of both factions of SKP and including other non-party representatives from Finland. This congress should proceed to found a new workers' party to replace SKP, modelled on the programme and organisation of STP, with control centered in Finland.[90] SKP central committee refused, and went ahead with its own, third, congress in August. Only Letonmäki agreed to come, and attempts to enlist delegates direct from Finland had little success, only a handful of quite insignificant people responding.[91]

The third congress of SKP therefore found the party in schism, as its historians now openly acknowledge.[92] The central committee report, while conceding that its lines of communication with Finland had broken down, condemned the comrades there for their 'disobedience and arbitrary behaviour'.[93] To remedy the situation the congress adopted two policy documents, one defining its policy on public, legal activity, the other laying down the ground-rules for its underground work. The first, after contemptuously dismissing any socialists who stayed with SDP as lackeys of the bourgeoisie, recognised that STP was 'really working on the lines of the revolutionary class struggle'.[94] But by its nature STP was exposed to the dangers of opportunism, especially the temptation to buy tolerance from the authorities by making compromises. SKP in fact claimed the credit for starting STP, and instructed all its members to join the party—indeed this was essential so that they could guide its activities and make of it 'the kind of public, proletarian party which can prepare recruits for the ranks of SKP and prepare the masses for the achievement of the dictatorship of the proletariat'.[95] Modern communist commentators agree that this qualified and patronising attitude was incorrect and showed that SKP was still infected with left-deviation; it was 'extreme and one-sided' in its evaluation of STP.[96]

The same faults are held to be apparent in the second document on 'the organisational structure of the party'.[97] This defines SKP as acting as 'a secret party', whose activities must at all times be strictly controlled by the central committee, subject to the overriding authority of the Comintern. The central committee must endorse all delegates to party congresses, and congress resolutions, once accepted, were binding on all members without right of dissent. In Finland the party was to be organised in small cells, based on places of work or military units, each cell linked by a single contact man to the others. Party members must be strictly disciplined, display 'moderation and decency' in their private lives, confess nothing to the authorities if arrested, but once convicted must proclaim their communist faith in open court.[98] The third congress had met the Kuusinen challenge head-on by asserting the unquestionable authority of the central committee in exile over the movement in Finland, and by emphasising the importance and priority of underground activity.

Kuusinen replied by assembling what amounted to an anti-party congress in Stockholm in September.[99] Nominally it was a party school, where Kuusinen, Sirola and Lumivuokko gave crash courses in Leninism to the leadership of STP, carefully analysing the errors of the old social democrat movement. But in the last three days the delegates held general discussions on the future course of the workers' movement in Finland. There are two interpretations of what was decided at these meetings. The official SKP version is that it was envisaged that SKP and STP would continue a joint existence, that they only affirmed that underground activity by itself was not enough and that 'alongside SKP, the STP is a necessary and correct organisation'.[100] The other interpretation is that Kuusinen conceded that SKP had followed an incorrect line from its inception and should be replaced by STP, that all the delegates from Finland endorsed this view, and that only Sirola expressed reservations about a total repudiation of the leadership in Russia. Since this is clearly what Kuusinen had intended in first founding STP, and since even the SKP historians concede that the conclusions reached at Stockholm could be interpreted in the second sense—though mistakenly as they maintain —it does seem probable that the Stockholm meeting intended that the *émigré* party should be wound up. The central committee seems to have understood this at the time, for they replied by proposing to expel Kuusinen from the party, but the Comintern declined to endorse their proposal which would have acknowledged before the world that the Finnish communist movement had split in two.

STP certainly forged ahead; in particular it built up a formidable press and distributed large numbers of basic Marxist texts.[101] In the autumn it began to publish a national daily paper in Helsinki, *Suomen Työmies*, and captured a number of provincial papers from SDP control.

In November Tanner in person beat off a determined communist attempt, at a shareholders meeting, to take over the SDP presses in Helsinki.[102] The continual harassment by the police, to which all the STP papers were subjected for alleged breaches of the press laws, and the steady stream of prosecutions of party activists for sedition—there were nearly three hundred convictions for sedition or treason in 1920[103]—could not stop the movement growing. It might have been expected that the conclusion of a peace treaty between Finland and Russia in October 1920, and the opening of diplomatic and trade relations between the two countries, would have relieved the internal political pressures, but it made no difference. On the one side, Russia was always very careful not to involve the affairs of the Finnish communists in official relations between the two states, so they made no protest at the treatment given to the communist movement. On the other hand, the Finnish authorities declined to accept at face value this official detachment, but regarded the Finnish communists as agents in a Russian design to subvert and destroy Finnish independence, and treated them accordingly. In December 1920 *Suomen Työmies* wrote:[104]

> White Finland has made peace with red Russia. Officially . . . but still the war goes on. Because the war against Soviet Russia is carried on in Finland. War against the workers' state. War against the workers' ideals. . . . Open war with the working class of Finland continues.

The initiative in healing the breach in the Finnish communist movement seems to have been taken by Lenin himself in February 1921, when he asked Kuusinen to come to Moscow to help in drafting a new programme for the Comintern, thus recognising the value of Kuusinen's theoretical work in the founding of STP. The leaders of STP agreed to his going with reluctance; their fear that they would now lose their leader was justified, for from that point on Kuusinen became increasingly tied up with Comintern work and remote from the regular direction of Finnish affairs.[105] Kuusinen did, in fact, draft the theses for the third Comintern congress of 1921, but at the same time he acceded to the demands of the Comintern that the scandalous schism in the Finnish movement must be ended. The Comintern appointed two mediators, Radek and Bela Kun, to supervise a reconciliation on the basis of the new Comintern theses, and for this purpose a congress of SKP was opened near Petrograd on 25 July 1921.[106]

The novel feature of this fourth congress of SKP was that of the eighty-seven delegates, fifty-five had been brought from Finland, and the voting rights were so defined that the delegates from Finland should have a substantial majority over the émigrés. All the fifty-five had to leave Finland illegally, which required a high degree of organisation, though fortunately a corrupt frontier guard commander was prepared to facilitate border crossings for a fixed tariff, so that many delegates could simply walk into Russia in broad daylight.[107] Both the factions in SKP naturally did their best to secure a majority of delegates favourable to themselves, but the result was a virtual dead-heat.

The Russians did not neglect the opportunities offered for impressing the visitors. A large group attended the Comintern congress to witness the acceptance of the new theses and Kuusinen's election to the secretariat. Tuominen and Sirola were given an interview with Lenin, who praised the STP as a model organisation of a public workers' party and said that it did not matter whether it affiliated to the Comintern, for, Lenin said, it was a better revolutionary party than some which were affiliated.[108] The quarrels within the Finnish movement he dismissed as superficial. Some of the Finns also took part in the founding meeting of the new communist trade union international, Profintern.[109]

The SKP congress went on for over two weeks, which, since Manner is said to have made a speech lasting fifteen hours, is perhaps understandable. The atmosphere was strained, though one hesitates to accept at face value stories that the Rahjas had tried to murder Kuusinen before he left Stockholm, or planned to kill Tuominen on the way back to Finland, or put it about that Kuusinen's mistress, newly arrived from Finland, was a police spy. Eino Rahja in particular was a violent and loud-mouthed man, but there was probably more idle talk than hard fact behind these stories. There was without question a lot of bitterness to be lived down, but with the Comintern mediators present to remind everyone of their communist duty, a reconciliation was achieved. It was done in the best dialectical manner, each side engaged in self-criticism and criticism of the others, and then the synthesis emerged.

Manner, speaking on behalf of the old central committee, confessed to ultra-Leftism, which he explained as an exaggerated reaction against the Kautskyite errors of the old workers' movement, though he did not forget to stress that Kuusinen himself had fully shared in this before he left for Finland. On the other hand, when Kuusinen proposed to transfer the leadership of the movement to Finland he had, 'under the influence of democratic illusions, bowed to petty-bourgeois primitiveness'. It was best that SKP should be directed from Russia, 'near the roots of bolshevism and the centre of the Comintern'.[110] The quarrel was now ended. 'We Rahja men have been liberated from the ultra-communism that was disturbing us in 1920–1, and since the Kuusinen men admit their mistakes, nothing else is outstanding. . . . Kuusinen has shown he possesses a sound bolshevik ability to draw back, for which he should be given thanks and respect'.[111]

Kuusinen explained how experience in Finland had cured him of his ultra-Leftism, but had then carried him too far in the other direction. 'In this Kuusinen group there have been some bad mistakes. There were traces of the old democratic poison in us. We confess these mistakes openly'.[112] The proposal to hold a congress in

Stockholm had been one of the worst mistakes, for far from promoting unity it would have split the movement irremediably. Now, however, there was no further ground for factions, the recent Comintern theses had shown the way forward. Sirola declared that 'unpleasant and painful as this split has been, I think it has been useful in forcing us all on to a more realistic footing. It is good to feel now that this is a real party congress'.[113]

The congress then proceeded to adopt a programme of action based on the Comintern theses. In accepting the report of the central committee, congress recognised that both factions had acted in good faith and their quarrels had largely arisen from bad communications; in fact they had both been moving in the direction now confirmed by the Comintern.[114] But the document emphasised that Kuusinen had been guilty of leading an anti-party group, and that he should have obeyed the call to attend the third congress even though he had appealed to the Comintern against it. This sort of thing must not happen again; the congress 'emphasises to every party member without distinction the necessity for the internal solidarity and unity of the party, which demands submission to communist discipline and support of the authority of the party leadership by the carrying out of assignments exactly and obeying orders received'.[115]

The congress carried a long and detailed programme covering all aspects of its work. Its aim was defined once more as 'to raise the Finnish proletariat into battle against the butcher-bourgeois dictatorship, in which battle the forces of the bourgeois state will be smashed and the dictatorship of the proletariat established, in the form of the soviet power of the working people'.[116] In directing this struggle SKP would follow faithfully the guidance of the Comintern in the common struggle against imperialism everywhere. They would seek to organise the unemployed and to urge the workers to prepare to take over their factories; they would be sympathetic towards appropriate sections of the petty-bourgeoisie so as to persuade them to be neutral in the class war, while the farmers and rural labourers must be brought to see that they too are exploited and that their real interests are in line with those of the proletariat; even small farmers who occasionally employ hired labour may be approached with a view to securing their cooperation.[117] In the trade unions, communists must assume the lead everywhere, and even the most trifling grievances of the workers should be taken up; but at the same time the communists must plan all their actions thoroughly, they must never expose themselves to the charge that they are reckless troublemakers.[118] STP must be guided from within by the party and used as a recruiting ground. Parliament is to be used as a platform for 'exposing boldly the rottenness of the butcher society', and parliamentary elections must be contested as keenly as possible as a means of educating and arousing the enthusiasm of the masses.[119] The same intense activity is called for in local government, but the communists must never fall into the error of making promises that cannot be performed. In the army, the conscripts must be shown how they are the tools of imperialism, but it is the duty of the workers to do their military service and 'accept all the instruction in the use of arms which can be obtained from it'.[120] Finally, it is stressed that the revolution, though not now imminent, cannot be long delayed, and SKP must at all times be ready for it.[121]

The congress ruled that SKP is essentially 'a strong underground organisation which uses energetically and skilfully both legal and illegal forms of action'; it follows that the strictest discipline must be observed and that recruits must be subjected to careful initiation and probation. The basic party unit must remain the secret party cell, which should be established inside every place of work and every public institution. Finally, the congress elected a new central committee, in which the old factions were carefully balanced; Kuusinen and Sirola were set off against E. Rahja and Manner. At the same time it was decided to establish in Helsinki a Finnish bureau of the party, to coordinate the work of the cells and act as the local executive arm of the central committee, to which it was to be strictly subordinate.[122] A strong Kuusinen man, Tuominen, was to take charge of this body.

This fourth congress can be regarded as marking the consolidation of the Finnish communist movement into its mature form. There were plenty of clashes of personality still to come, but it was never again threatened with internal disruption until the most recent times. The party's working structure had attained the form it was to keep until the party became legal in 1944, and the basic policy lines laid down—active preparation for armed revolution and no compromise in the class war—held good until the popular-front line of the 1930s. The party now faced two problems: how could it build up its underground network and keep it effective in face of intense police activity, and how could the party achieve effective control of the various public organisations within which it operated, particularly with the central committee in Moscow and the lines of communication with Finland slow and uncertain. The years between 1921 and 1944 show an uneven pattern of successes and failures in both these tasks. One important factor which the fourth congress could not take account of was that the central purpose of the party, the preparation of the revolution of the proletariat, in 1921 so confidently expected in the reasonably near future, was to become increasingly unrealistic as the prospect of revolution receded further and further from view, until eventually it was lost sight of altogether. SKP was to suffer all the bitterness and frustration of any organisation that is highly organised to meet a situation that never in fact materialises, and in part because of this fails to cope adequately with situations which do occur.

In 1921 the Finnish communist movement was still wrestling with the problems of coordination and discipline. For instance, while many of the leaders were absent in Russia in the summer of 1921, a party emissary in Finland, Hanna Malm, a close friend and later the wife of Manner, and described as a 'fiery-souled revolutionary', persuaded the radical trade union leader N. Wälläri to join her in a press campaign to shame the trade unions into radical action. In June and July fierce articles appered in *Suomen Työmies* pouring scorn on their passivity. On 22 July Wälläri wrote that the workers should take over the factories at once and that this could lead straight to revolution.[1] It was pure anarcho-syndicalist heresy, and when the leaders got back from Russia in the autumn they had to reassert their authority, closing the columns of their papers to extremist views and sending Malm back to Russia.[2]

These were not the only extremist elements still at work; there were those in the movement who were working for an immediate armed uprising. During 1921 the virtually autonomous military section of SKP was trying to revive the red guard in northern Finland, more arms were brought over the frontier and hidden away near centres like Oulu and Rovaniemi, ex-members of the Murmansk legion were enrolled to provide trained cadres, and some drilling was done.[3] This effort faded out in September, and was quickly overshadowed by the crisis that developed in Karelia.[4] This region, along the eastern borders of Finland, was still mainly inhabited by rather underdeveloped forest communities, speaking a language

closely related to Finnish. The Finnish nationalist movement had always regarded the Karelians as an integral
part of the Finnish nation. The peace treaty of 1920 had
recognised the special position of Karelia, by providing that
it was to enjoy local autonomy within Russia, which it
already did, for in June 1920, a Karelian Workers'
Commune had been established as an autonomous region
within the Soviet Union. The task of organising it had
been given by Lenin to the Finnish communist leader
E. Gylling, and under him Karelia became in effect a colonial area administered through the Finnish communist
movement.[5]

Before he went to Karelia, Gylling had worked on a
plan for a Scandinavian Soviet republic, to be based on
Karelia but to extend over the far north of Finland,
Sweden and Norway, where communism had won a lot
of support among the small farmers and forest workers.
It is an open question whether, in 1921–2, it was seriously intended to put this plan into effect. The Russian
government was not involved, for they were desperately
trying to normalise relations with the border states and
SKP officially supported their policy; but there were still
militants sufficiently undisciplined to be prepared to try
out an adventure of this kind.[6] However, if they had a
plan, it was forestalled, for the Finnish nationalists struck
first, in November 1921, when with the connivance of
the Finnish authorities they launched an armed incursion
into Russian Karelia. The local forces, many of them
recruited from or led by Finnish refugees, contained the
invaders and the enterprise quickly collapsed because the
expected uprising of the local population in favour of
the invaders did not happen. By early 1922 the surviving
raiders were back in Finland, while the Finns in Karelia
were naturally jubilant at thus humiliating their old
enemies.

In their exuberance some of them launched a counter-
attack which turned out to be pure farce. A small group
of former red guards, led by J. Moilanen, crossed the
Finnish frontier and arrived at a lumber camp at Värjö

in the remote north of Finland. They arrested the camp administration, took the contents of the safe and told the astonished workers that the communists were taking over, offering to pay all who would enlist in the new red guard. Nearly three hundred men did enlist, and a proclamation was issued declaring that this was the workers' answer to the incursions into Karelia and claiming to act in the name of SKP; there was no suggestion that the movement had Russian support. The red guards then moved on and induced the local Finnish frontier guards to surrender, but on 7 February they crossed back into Russia with their booty.[7] The Finnish and Russian governments declined to take the incident seriously; Chicherin indeed seems to have been furious at the whole affair, while although SKP officially claimed credit for it, it had more likely been a pure gamble by their activists, led by E. Rahja, who wanted to demonstrate their potential. Certainly it was the last military action led by SKP until the second world war.

In August 1923, while SKP was holding a party conference, they became excited, as did the Comintern, by what they took to be an imminent revolution in Germany, and SKP issued an instruction to its members that 'in Finland, vigorous communist activity to launch the preparations for revolution must begin at once'. New plans were made for arms deliveries and some military experts sent in to Finland, but the response was minimal.[8] The party now concedes that its efforts failed because 'belief that bourgeois democracy would survive was widespread among the masses. The error was also present within the ranks of SKP'.[9] A call by the Finnish bureau for mass street demonstrations in October 1923 produced no response,[10] and by the end of 1923 the last serious attempt by SKP to promote revolution in Finland had come to nothing. From that time forward, in the official doctrine of Finnish communists, the revolution was to remain an event in the indefinite future.

Part of the weakness which SKP showed in the autumn of 1923 was due to the misfortunes which had overtaken its activities in Finland since the fourth congress. Things had started well enough when the leaders of STP held a conference from 26–9 September 1921 and agreed that the party and its representatives in the trade unions would in future accept the Comintern line, even though they were not formally affiliated to it.[11] The Karelian crisis then presented to STP its first real test, and the party turned to SDP and proposed joint action to stop the incursions and avert the danger of war with Russia. The social democrats, who opposed the Karelian adventure, replied that as a condition of joint action STP must acknowledge that Russia too was to blame for the situation that had developed in Karelia.[12] The communists were neither surprised nor disappointed by this, for in their view SDP had been 'exposed', and the way was open to appeal to the workers over the heads of the SDP leaders, building a united front from below, as the process was called. From 6 to 8 January 1922 STP held a party council; this ratified the decision to accept Comintern leadership and authorised the party to appeal to all the workers to join in a campaign against the dangers of war.[13] The committee then drafted a manifesto, known as the 'Peace Manifesto', which they published on 17 January.[14] They called for a broad alliance of workers, farmers, and petty bourgeoisie to oppose the war danger, but did not disguise their revolutionary intent, since 'the whole class struggle of the proletariat towards the realisation of socialism will advance through this cooperation and struggle'. But what really alarmed the authorities were phrases like 'into battle for the defence of Soviet Russia', and calls for 'a common fighting front of all working people in defence of Soviet Russia'.[15] The counterstroke was swift, for on 26 January almost the entire committee of STP and its leading newspaper editors were arrested and subsequently charged with treason.[16] A few days later, right-wing extremists murdered the minister of the interior, who had ordered the arrests, with the clear intention of pinning the deed on the communists,[17] but the assassin bungled the aftermath and the truth came out. Eventually the arrested communists came to trial, on very shaky legal grounds, since the essence of treason is aiding an enemy and Finland was officially at peace with Russia ˙in 1922. The trials, in April 1922, were turned into a grand propaganda demonstration by the accused, contrasting the aggressive, imperialist dreams of the Finnish nationalists with the high-principled nationality policies of Lenin's Russia.[18] But the defendants got up to four years hard labour, which was confirmed on appeal, so that at one blow the communist movement in Finland had been decapitated.

The resulting weakness and confusion was revealed in a scandal that rocked the movement and threatened to reopen the issues settled at the fourth congress. The Helsinki branch of STP took the initiative in replacing the lost leadership by appointing a provisional committee, with N. Wälläri as chairman and K. Kulo as secretary.[19] Then, at the end of January 1922, one of the greatest of the surviving leaders of the old workers' movement, Y. Mäkelin, was released from prison. He announced his adherence to STP and was at once put in charge of one of its principal newspapers, *Pohjan Kansa*, resuming his old predominance over the working-class movement of Oulu and Pohjanmaa.[20] SKP in Russia took fright at this, for Mäkelin had never undergone any systematic conversion to bolshevism—the central committee recorded its 'alarm' at hearing of his resurrection[21]—and in June they were discussing the possibility of calling Mäkelin to Russia to be re-educated. But Mäkelin, though unswervingly loyal to the movement, went his own way and the party now admits that its attitude of suspicion was unworthy and mistaken.[22]

The scandal arose from a circular sent out by the central committee to all SKP cells on 3 February 1922. In general, it was intended to remind the underground movement of the need to step up its effectiveness, since STP was in clear danger of being suppressed by the authorities; but in a passage dealing with the raising of famine relief for Russia, it suggested that workers might steal materials and tools from their employers to make relief supplies, saying that this would have the advantage of making the capitalists pay for them.[23] A copy of this document fell into the hands of SDP, which published it on 4 March with suitable comments on the depravity of the communists who were encouraging the workers to become thieves, a line taken up with relish in the bourgeois press. STP was shaken, and their paper *Suomen Työmies* hastily repudiated the compromising passage by suggesting that SDP had forged it and that this was a typical example of its role as a lackey of the bourgeoisie.[24] Mäkelin, who was convinced that the circular was genuine, wrote an article, 'Is there something rotten in the working-class movement?',[25] which STP refused to publish.[26] But *Pohjan Kansa* openly attacked the passage on stealing for Russia as 'completely reckless and childish', and on 14 March, while insisting that the whole thing must be seen in proportion, poured scorn on SKP's agent, H. Malm, who had been peddling the circular and reproaching Mäkelin for making a fuss over it. The situation became more embarrassing when SDP was able to prove that the whole circular had been written in the offices of STP; the party hastily found a faithful woman member, E. Korhonen, to confess that she had drafted the passage without authority. SKP now agrees that this was a deliberate lie and that Manner and Malm had in fact drafted and issued the circular on the orders of the central committee.[27]

The open controversy between Mäkelin, speaking for a large section of STP opinion, and *Suomen Työmies*, led to a scandalised debate when a council of STP met on 31 March 1922. One delegate, A. Kaarne, said that the whole underground activity was useless and positively harmful: 'Coming as it does from abroad, it could at this moment be the destruction of our legal party'.[28] Wälläri, as chairman, ruled that there could be no discussion of underground activity, because STP as a party did not have any. The council went on to discuss the dispute between *Pohjan Kansa* and *Suomen Työmies* and Mäkelin vigorously defended his critical stand. Finally, a series of resolutions was carried deploring any public airing of internal controversies as damaging to the movement, and insisting that such arguments must be settled internally so that the party press would present a common front at all times.[29] It is apparent how Kaarne's initiative threatened to reopen the whole issue of the relations between STP and SKP, and to resurrect the demand for a movement free of *émigré* influences.

The central committee of SKP certainly felt this, for in an enlarged meeting held soon after they insisted that SKP, through its Finnish bureau, must strengthen its grip on STP and the trade union movement. To effect this, every party member must obey orders regardless of his personal opinions, no outside discussion of internal party affairs was permitted, and even when the party made mistakes the members must be their 'most enthusiastic defender, and with all energy and enthusiasm defend the party from the attacks of the enemy . . . any conduct other than defence of the party is regarded as the action of an enemy of the party'.[30] Communist morality was sternly insisted upon and Mäkelin, and those who shared his tendency to think for themselves, were sharply called to order.

During 1922–3 STP became a major parliamentary party, following the election of July 1922. The reconstructed leadership of STP had decided that since further repression was to be expected, which might impede electoral activity, they would set up a separate electoral organisation consisting of a nationwide network of local electoral committees with their own records and funds; then, if the authorities took legal action to suppress the STP, the electoral machinery would remain legally immune. As they said: 'The intention of the bourgeoisie to prevent our electoral activity, by suppressing the operations of the party, must be frustrated'.[31] The new organisation was duly established, but since the same personnel tended to run both the election committee and

the local STP branches the former could still be substantially damaged by proceedings against STP.

The next step was to offer an electoral alliance to SDP
for a joint defence of working-class interests. The offer
stressed that 'it does not mean that either party gives
up or compromises its independence or its principles', but
the offer was rejected; the social democrats would not
recognise the validity of any independent workers' movement.[32] So the election had to be fought by STP in isolation and under constant police harassment; for instance,
Uusimaa province went through six provincial secretaries
in little over a year, the police picking them off one
after the other, while Häme province used up five and
Satakunta three. The STP election manifesto was published on 24 May; it began with an acknowledgement of
the biggest dangers which faced a revolutionary party
when it engaged in parliamentary activity, right opportunism and reformist heresy. So they made it clear that
'the fight for a majority of parliamentary seats will not
resolve the class struggle or place political power in the
hands of the working class'.[33] But the struggle was
justified in order to relieve, however superficially, the suf-
ferings of the workers and to defend their meagre existing rights. A programme of tax reliefs and social services
was outlined but this was only 'a means by which the
struggle can be deepened and the working masses awakened and drawn along the road of uncompromising class
war'.[34]

The election results were remarkably good. STP won
over 128,000 votes, almost 15 per cent of the total cast,
and twenty-seven seats in Parliament.[35] These had all
been won from SDP, which was cut from eighty to fifty-
three seats. STP got a majority of the working-class vote
in those areas where the old SDP organisation had come
over to STP, as in Helsinki and the far north of the
country. The parliamentary group which resulted was a
constant source of anxiety to SKP, for the number of actual party members among it may have been as low as
five[36] and only a handful of them had any previous

parliamentary experience. But they proved docile enough; on 7 September the STP parliamentary group met and adopted a document entitled 'Guiding Principles for the Parliamentary Work of the Workers' Party', which followed pretty closely a draft sent out from the central committee in Moscow and was fully in line with Comintern policy.[37] The parliamentary group was 'a weapon to be used by the proletariat in carrying out the destruction of the system of capitalist exploitation'; they were not legislators in the bourgeois sense of the word, their actions were designed 'to call to account the exploiters and oppressors of the people' so as to stimulate the people to take action. In order to educate the masses, the group would work in close contact with them, stressing the repressive nature of the bourgeois state, and by proposing reforms within the bourgeois structure would prove how the bourgeoisie will never consent to them. Where the bourgeoisie makes superficial gestures designed to divert the masses from their revolutionary purposes, these will be exposed. The group was entitled to use any tactics that served their ends, and in respect to the social democrats they would seek to stiffen their purpose when they were on the right lines and expose them as allies of the bourgeoisie when they were not.

It is clear that SKP had successfully put over its line to STP and that there was little danger of any serious deviation by the group. Their chairman, Långström, in the first speech of the session, announced that the group would not accompany the speaker when he presented the formal greetings of Parliament to the president, for the speaker 'had been elected to watch over the interests of the exploiting class' and could never speak for the real needs of the people.[38] Yet even this aggressive attitude, worked out with Mäkelin, worried the central committee of SKP, for at a meeting on 28 September they discussed how Mäkelin had made small verbal alterations to the draft of the 'Guiding principles . . .' as sent from Moscow. Taimi complained that the alterations obscured the revolutionary purpose of parliamentary work—though it is difficult to see how it could have been made more explicit—and was nervous about Mäkelin's influence.[39] One sees here the neurotic fear of the émigrés that the Finnish end of the movement might get out of control.

In the outcome they had nothing to complain of. During a year of parliamentary activity the group kept up a ceaseless propaganda attack, moved twenty-eight motions for a general amnesty, urged social reforms, demanded abolition of the bourgeois militia organisation, and in one superb gesture of defiance moved to abrogate the constitution and establish a soviet republic.[40] Their tactics were utterly opportunist; on the law providing for the establishment of smallholdings to relieve rural poverty the group first opposed it, on the grounds that only nationalisation and massive redistribution of land could provide a solution, then supported it, on the grounds that the landless labourers imagined that it would bring them relief, and when they discovered that it did not their disillusion would assist 'the victory of the proletarian revolution'.[41] Långström himself, looking back after many years, concedes that the group may have overdone it. 'Perhaps we were too extreme then, indulged in the use of unnecessarily violent language'.[42] They were to pay a heavy price for their faithful fulfilment of the instructions they had received.

The authorities naturally found the endless public defiance and agitation intolerable; the supposedly illegal SKP was making fools of them before the eyes of everyone. Already in September 1922 they were contemplating the suppression of the Social Democratic Youth League, which SKP had controlled since 1919,[43] and in April 1923 the courts did suppress it for promoting illegal activities. What seems to have frightened them more was that on 19 January 1923 the committees of STP and SDP agreed to hold a week of joint demonstrations for the release of political prisoners and the reduction of tariffs on imported necessities.[44] The conservative *Uusi Suomi* wrote: 'This has got to stop. Treason must be condemned with the utmost severity and the Communist Party rendered incapable of action'.[45] The backlash had begun and on 30 January, under the joint patronage of the two white chieftains of 1918, Mannerheim and Svinhufvud, the 'Suomen Suojelusliitto'[46] was formed to coordinate all anti-communist forces. It declared that 'the communist movement is at present the greatest of our internal dangers', and this because 'our eastern neighbour incites and supports it'.[47] The league would unite all the forces of white Finland to resist the danger, and it symbolised the determination of bourgeois Finland to suppress communism, an aim which was at last realised in the 1930s. This was the response which STP had brought on itself by its very successes. The SDP was the first to run for cover; it never again responded to appeals for joint action from the communists until the very changed circumstances of 1945.

But STP too tried to erect deferences against the growing danger. It was still not legally registered with the authorities as a political party, so on 15 May 1923 a congress was assembled, attended by some eighty delegates.[48] Its main purpose was to establish and register the party legally under the name of the Workers' Party of Finland,[49] significantly dropping 'Socialist' from the title. They also re-defined their objectives and moderated the language of the programme of 1920; the purpose of the party was now 'in cooperation with other workers' parties in the country to change the capitalist system to a socialist one'. This was to be done by organising and educating the workers 'so that the workers would be able to safeguard their interests'. There was a keen debate on cooperating with other workers' groups, and a resolution to pursue this on every occasion; in order to further this the party press was directed to avoid inflammatory polemics with the social democrats, although of course the tactics of their leaders must still be analysed and exposed.[50] The party, under its new name and with the revolutionary elements of its programme toned down, was formally accepted by the authorities and officially registered.[51]

But it did not save them from the impending blow. In July the chief of the security police told the government that he could prove that STP was directed from Moscow in the interests of Russia, provided he was allowed to arrest the leaders and seize the archives. The government had doubts, but the minister of the interior agreed and on 3 August the whole parliamentary group, the party committee, the main party officials, and the editors of its papers were all arrested, and the assets and printing presses sequestered.[52] Although the government declared that it had ample proof that STP was manipulated from outside and engaged in seditious activities, they could not in fact produce any direct evidence or obtain any significant confessions. The result was that nearly ten months had to pass before the trials could be put on, when 189 accused were convicted and got prison sentences of up to three and a half years.[53] STP was ruled to have been a criminal organisation and its assets were confiscated, but the printing presses had to be released and resumed activity.

Naturally the trials were a splendid theatre for communist propaganda. Since the prosecution could not prove seditious activity it had to argue from intent, as expressed in the 1920 programme and subsequent speeches and writings, and from circumstantial evidence, that STP had in fact followed Comintern directions. The defendants lied solidly and shamelessly whenever it suited them and the case against them looked thin and unconvincing to progressive opinion abroad.[54] Yet although one admires the courage and devotion of the defendants, and their splendid defiance of the class enemy, their position looks ethically dubious. They claimed credit for being the leaders of the proletariat in its mission to destroy bourgeois society but were in effect complaining because that society chose to treat them as hostile. Nobody would wish to condone the conduct of the Finnish security police, though this was fairly restrained by comparison with the habits of many of its contemporaries, not least in Soviet Russia, but the accused had undoubtedly provoked the retribution that fell on them. The communist movement was in a self-proclaimed state of war with bourgeois Finland and intended its destruction; it could hardly complain if the intended victim fought for its life.

STP had been an impressive structure, for in its brief career it had built up over five hundred party branches with over twenty-three thousand paid-up members. Its destruction was a shattering blow to SKP, since the supposed independent network of underground cells did not really exist; the party had organised itself inside the structure of STP and was destroyed with it.[55] Fortunately, the trade unions were still intact, leaving SKP with a mutilated rump of cells from which fresh activity could be developed;[56] clearly, if new leadership could be provided the mass support which STP had shown to exist could be mobilised once more.

This seems to be the point to consider the relationship of SKP to STP and the mass movement in Finland. From the SKP point of view there is no problem; STP and the trade union movement represented the politically conscious sector of the working class, and it was the role of SKP to be their vanguard and to guide the proletariat towards its historically determined, revolutionary goal. Circumstances forced SKP to do this in a conspiratorial way and to place its headquarters outside Finland; equally, the need to act as the directing brain of the proletariat forced the party to preserve its separate identity and cohesion within the mass movement. Lenin himself had said that the relation of SKP to STP was a model of how things should be arranged in circumstances where a legal communist party was impossible.[57] The role of SKP clearly demanded eternal vigilance to prevent the untutored masses straying off along opportunist paths, and this was reflected in the anxieties of SKP over the behaviour of someone like Mäkelin.

Their enemies, on the other hand, see STP as composed of honest Finnish workers duped and manipulated by a power-hungry and unscrupulous gang of exile politicians who staked everything on their hope of subjecting Finland to the power of Russia, and returning in triumph backed by Russian bayonets. This view is a manifest caricature; SKP had indeed given its allegiance to the Comintern, as the guiding authority of the world proletarian movement, and faithfully followed its line. An outside observer is likely to conclude that the Comintern, whatever its original intentions, eventually became the tool of the narrow national interest of Russia. But one must accept that, especially in this pre-Stalin era, the leaders of SKP would not see it in this light and accepted its leadership in good faith as serving the best long-term interests of the Finnish proletariat.

If SKP had been simply a tool of Russian imperialism it would have lacked the means to manipulate a movement like STP. For the communist party image of itself as a distinct organisation within the mass body is an idealisation, an aspiration that could not be realised. For SKP in Finland was a very disorganised entity, its very membership indefinable. They could not keep registers, issue membership cards or collect dues in any systematic way. The members of the party in Finland consisted of all those who reckoned themselves such, and could secure recognition from the others. The party now admits that within the STP 'the Communist Party acting within its ranks was then relatively weak'.[58] SKP had only one effective instrument of control, and that was money. The movement needed the funds which the Comintern was prepared to feed into it as long as it held to the Comintern line and these funds were channelled through SKP. But it would be absurd to exaggerate even this factor, especially when its true extent cannot be determined.

The truth about communist achievement, then and later, is that it derives from the existence within the Finnish working class of a strong minority which refused to accept the verdict of 1918; stimulated and hardened by the white terror, these people were resolute not to accept defeat but to fight on for a reversal of that verdict. To such men and women, the revisionist SDP seemed to have betrayed the cause and they needed an ideological and organisational structure round which they could form. SKP offered them this, through Kuusinen's concept of STP and the programme of the fourth congress. These people did not have to be duped or manipulated; they shared the same heritage as the SKP leaders and followed SKP willingly because it alone expressed their determination to continue the class war against bourgeois Finland. This hard core of the Finnish workers has been in permanent, voluntary schism from bourgeois-nationalist Finland since before 1918; they have never accepted it or its values and as long as SKP has symbolised their dissent, by refusing to compromise with the established order, it has enjoyed their loyal support. None of the indignities and absurdities which SKP has been involved in through its adhesion to a party line laid down in Moscow has had any significant effect on the level of its mass support in Finland. This is no doubt partly because these people have never understood or cared about the precise doctrines to which SKP stands committed—and in this sense these people are not communists—for them it is enough that SKP stands with them and against the establishment. One can therefore assume that STP had represented the real face of Finnish communism, and that even if SKP had been legal, and its leaders operating in Finland, the situation would have been little altered. Without the persecution of the authorities, the movement would have been somewhat bigger, and a leadership based in Finland would have been a little less responsive to some aspects of Comintern direction, but the basic situation and the responses to it would have been the same. The pattern which emerged after 1944 is not so very different from that which was destroyed by the great purge of 1923.

The immediate reaction of SKP to the disaster was sluggish, for its mind was on other things in the summer of 1923. It had just worked out a new policy on the farmers. One of the hard facts of 1918 had been that the victory of the whites had rested on the support they had got from the small farmers, who were still the backbone of Finnish society. There was a natural tendency on the part of the workers' movement to write these people off as natural allies of the bourgeoisie. In 1919 the SKP election manifesto had called for an end to private ownership of land and assumed that progressive elements among the farmers would willingly go into collectives.[59] But the NEP in Russia, and the obvious tactical need to win a foothold for SKP in the countryside, pointed to a change of attitude, and in the summer of 1923 a new policy was formally adopted by SKP at a party conference.

The small independent farmer was now re-defined as the potential ally of the proletariat, because like the proletariat he too was exploited by the forces of capital through interest rates, high prices for manufactured goods and low prices for farm produce. SKP therefore recommended that existing small farmers should be guaranteed permanent possession of their holdings and that all rural labourers who wished to set up as independent farmers should be given the land to do so. The socialist state, after the revolution, would give all material assistance to help keep such small family farms economically viable.[60] On this programme SKP must encourage the rural population to organise itself, and through its own organisations to ally with the proletariat in the overthrow of their common capitalist enemy; the revolution would then set up a workers' and farmers' state.

This programme, confirmed at the fifth congress of SKP in 1925, has been the consistent basis of SKP agrarian policy ever since, and it is clear that if it ever succeeded in rallying significant sections of rural society to support SKP, that would be a major breakthrough for the party. Even so, there was resistance to the new policy inside the party. An opposition circular of the time declared: 'It is wrong to speak of the farmers in this country as the comrades-in-arms of the workers. Is it not these same farmers who, together with the real bourgeoisie, fought against the workers and the rural poor?'[61] Since one finds, even in the 1950s, SKP warnings to the workers not to speak contemptuously of their rural comrades as bumpkins, or petty-bourgeois at heart, it can be assumed that suspicion against the small farmer among the industrial workers is not easily eradicated. Perhaps that is one reason why the policy has failed over the years. The grip of the Agrarian Party on the Finnish farmers has never been shaken, and only among the semi-proletarian farmers of the far north, who are also seasonal forest workers, has SKP gathered up significant rural support.

The party conference of 1923, meeting just after the arrests, was keyed up by this major policy shift, and by the heady expectations of a new wave of revolution spreading from Germany.[62] The Comintern issued a statement that the arrests in Finland showed the nervousness of the bourgeoisie in face of the revolutionary tide, and accepted the destruction of STP without much regret. All activity in Finland would now be conducted through the underground SKP, whose central committee should be reinforced by representatives of the suppressed public movement.[63] 'Finland's embattled workers must gather under the sole flag of the revolutionary Communist Party'.[64] In fact, the movement in Finland began to revive spontaneously; on 5 September already a 'Helsinki workers' local organisation' was founded,[65] with the intention of reviving an electoral machine, and other localities followed this lead. Shortly after, V. Vuorio launched a newspaper, *Työväen Tiedonantaja*, which claimed to be neutral: 'It does not represent any particular party tendency within the working-class movement'.[66] Initially SKP did lack the machinery to assert control over the new workers' movement; its attempts to raise mass demonstrations in favour of the arrested men were a total failure,[67] and the *Tiedonantaja* was no adequate substitute for the lost newspapers,[68] particularly since its early line was often incorrect. As the party puts it: 'It was some time before the paper's tone was improved',[69] and temporarily the mass movement in Finland remained headless.

The basis of the future action of SKP was to consist of a re-built underground network, the construction of which began in 1923. It was of the essence of this that the basic underground system should no longer be tied in with the various public institutions; the party would form separate fractions inside these, which were to be subordinate to the underground cells.[70] The basic cell was to be of five or six members and they were grouped in areas and districts. The central committee sent in a number of trained organisers to get the new system started, particularly in 1924, and the party declared in 1925 that good headway had been made.[71] The cells were supposed to be based on the factory or workshop in the towns and on the village in the countryside. What inevitably happened was that the scheme was turned upside down. Instead of the underground cells controlling the fractions in the public bodies, the real work was done in the fractions and the life of the cells remained largely notional. So too did the membership of the party, which was often nominal and unamenable to discipline. In the nature of things it is difficult to quantify the resulting structure, but a variety of sources, some from SKP and some from police records, suggest that a system of some five hundred cells, coordinated by two hundred local committees, was functioning in the period 1925–8,[72] but that most of these cells were really identical with the fractions inside the public organisations and not true work-place or village cells as planned.

On May Day 1925 the central committee issued a remarkably frank statement on its underground work. It assured the workers that SKP 'is already in such condition that you need not bother about any other political party', and described how the party members were to form work-groups, whose public activities would be legal but which would be based on a revolutionary line taken direct from SKP and the Comintern, through the party cells. These latter 'invisibly steer the work of the groups', and their members must learn 'skilfully to combine legal and illegal activity'.[73] The trade union side of the movement was appalled by this public boast that they were being controlled from beneath in this conspiratorial fashion and branded the statement as 'dreadfully irresponsible' because it confirmed everything that the bourgeois enemy was alleging against them.[74]

Development of a public organisation was forced ahead when the president, because of the arrest of the STP members of Parliament, dissolved it and called an election for April 1924. SKP found that many of its old supporters were sunk in apathy: 'In many places the left-wing workers were doubtful about elections, and of the opinion that in the prevailing conditions of terror it was not worth taking part in elections'.[75] But the Helsinki local organisation issued a call, on 25 January 1924, to form local election committees and offered to act as the coordinating centre.[76] On this improvised basis the election was fought, with only the *Tiedonantaja* as newspaper, and a very creditable ninety-two thousand votes was collected; this was 10.4 per cent of the votes cast and gave them eighteen seats in Parliament. For the future it was decided that a network of 'socialist workers and small farmers' associations' would provide the permanent local electoral machinery. When necessary, they would send delegates to a central electoral council, which in turn would elect a permanent executive committee, the 'Helsinki Workers' Electoral Committee'. The members of Parliament constituted themselves as the 'Socialist Workers' and Small Farmers Parliamentary Group', and it was agreed that this parliamentary group, in consultation with the electoral council and the editors of the communist newspapers, would constitute the policy-making directory of the public political movement. It was left open, at this stage, whether they would eventually try to form a new political party.[77]

The new parliamentary group always had a majority of SKP members in it; it was led by M. Rosenberg[78] and it followed the same parliamentary tactics as its predecessor, except that in accordance with the worker-farmer alliance policy more stress was put an agrarian questions.[79] This electoral machinery worked well enough; they raised 110,000 votes and twenty seats in the 1927 elections, and 128,000 votes and twenty-three seats in 1929. They also contested local government elections, and won nine hundred seats in 1925 and 1,035 in 1928.[80] Over the country as a whole the communist vote wavered around 10 per cent of the votes cast, though this was not evenly distributed. In the far north their vote was in the range 27 to 32 per cent, in the rural east only 5 to 10 per cent, and in the more developed south and west, 11 to 15 per cent. Thus they enjoyed a substantial popular support but not on a scale that made them a real threat to the political stability of the country.

Throughout its life this rather amorphous political structure raised serious problems of control for SKP. There was always a latent tendency to resent *émigré* interference; this first flared up over the presidential election, held at the beginning of 1925. An electoral council held on 19 December rejected the orders of SKP to run Kuusinen as the worker-farmer candidate, and voted 125 to 45 to choose M. Väisänen, then a political prisoner, as their candidate, though they did accept the SKP platform calling for a worker-farmer government.[81] The election was supposed to show the power of the new worker-farmer alliance, but was very disappointing, as the communists got only forty-one thousand votes. SKP refused to be discouraged; in a statement after the election they claimed that their line had been correct, but had not been put over with sufficient vigour, because too many party members still did not understand the importance of the countryside.[82]

More alarming for SKP was the emergence of an opposition group, led at first from the Tammisaari forced labour camp by N. Wälläri.[83] Subsequently, Wällari was characterised as an 'adventurer and Trotskyite, an anti-party intriguer', and the whole group, which included Väisänen, as petty-bourgeois.[84] In April 1925 the opposition published a manifesto entitled 'Away From the *Emigrés*', which demanded a moderation of SKP policies in order to win over the left-wing social democrats as the basis for a new political movement; the *émigrés* 'should not be allowed any decisive influence in these matters'.[85]

This was the beginning of a persistent argument inside the movement. Walläri went on to criticise the whole worker-farmer alliance policy, and said that there was no point in pursuing the class war for its own sake when there was no realistic prospect of victory. SKP accused the group of concealing behind their tactical demands a fundamental tendency to 'adapt to being inside a capitalist system', and called the demand to break free from *émigré* control a concealed wish to give up the revolution as an aim. To go over exclusively to action within a legally established party was to accept to fight on the terms dictated by the bourgeoisie and to betray the workers' cause.[86] But SKP did not feel strong enough to break with Walläri at this point; on his release from Tammisaari he was even made editor of *Tiedonantaja*, and he continued his revisionist agitation.[87]

But in these circumstances it is no surprise that SKP did come out strongly against re-starting a public political party, which might well have got out of control. In March 1925 Kuusinen himself intervened to kill the idea; his central argument was that it played into the hands of the enemy by facilitating the work of repression. Kuusinen rejected the supposed dichotomy of public and underground work[88]:

> Activity must be both open and secret. . . . A revolutionary workers' movement cannot have two parts, one purely public and one purely secret. If it is split into two camps, then the public movement would no longer be revolutionary, but the secret movement would no longer be a workers' mass movement. The roots of our secret party must be deep in the public workers' movement—wherever the working masses are present. And a class-conscious public workers' movement must always be anchored in the secret communist party. Therefore fuse the public and the secret activities so tightly together that they cannot be divided.

However, Kuusinen did stress that communists were in no sense exploiting the public movement for ends of their own; within the public organisations they would serve faithfully, but 'in the right communist spirit'.[89] The youth movement presented similar problems: the Social Democratic Youth League, dissolved in April 1923, had been replaced successfully by the 'Socialist Youth League' in December, which was a legal organisation of communists and social democrats.[90] In accordance with the new line, SKP also founded an underground youth movement, the 'Finnish Communist Youth League', and its members were supposed to direct the public body. At once the basic problems emerged: either the members took the public movement seriously and neglected the underground one, or they indulged in left-opportunism and went in exclusively for conspiratorial activity, ignoring the public movement.[91]

The party congress of 1925 was very stern in its criticism of the Communist Youth League, which had scarcely begun to establish a proper cell system. Then, in November 1925, the authorities struck down the Socialist Youth League, which was condemned as an illegal organisation, and its leaders given up to three years in prison. This at least simplified the situation by proving that only underground work was possible, and in the years after 1926 quite a successful 'study-group' movement was launched for young people. These study groups were informally linked but together they made quite a considerable movement. Figures are hard to come by, but estimates of the numbers involved in study group activities range from ten to twenty thousand members, while the Communist Youth League itself claimed about two thousand members and some 110 cells. Thus the youth movement probably functioned at about the same level of activity as the party itself and was a major source of manpower for the various SKP activities.[92]

The fifth congress of SKP was held in Russia in 1925, and in contrast with its predecessors demonstrated by its near unanimity that SKP had grown to maturity as a communist party. The voting delegates consisted of some thirty brought in from Finland, plus the central committee.[93] Part of its success was due to careful advance preparation, which ran into trouble at one point only, on the failure to eliminate an opposition clique centered on Eino Rahja. He had quarrelled with his colleagues on the central committee in 1924, and the official party version is that Rahja had fallen into a right-opportunist heresy and advocated compromising with SDP.[94] But one factor was certainly Rahja's personal activities. In 1923 SKP had been involved in a plan, later abandoned, to circulate forged Finnish currency. Rahja had managed to pass off some of the forgeries to the Russian State Bank, and in addition carried on printing them on his own account, in defiance of party policy. The central committee had wanted to expel Rahja but powerful friends in the Comintern, notably Zinoviev, had intervened to save him—indeed in 1925 they insisted on his re-election to the central committee.[95] It was not until 1928 that Rahja's enemies finally brought him down for his misconduct, and secured his expulsion.[96] In 1925 their failure to do so meant Rahja and two other delegates formed an opposition fraction, but 'their fraction attacks were repelled as unfounded and unjustified'.[97]

The main policy line for the congress was worked out at an enlarged central committee meeting in June 1925, which finally rejected the Wälläri campaign and confirmed the development of the underground network.[98] The congress itself then met in September, and its theoretical starting point was the Comintern thesis that a temporary phase of stabilisation had set in in the capitalist world, the so-called 'second-phase' of capitalism. SKP recognised this as applying to Finland, but asserted that the stability of Finnish capitalism was linked with the efforts of British and American imperialism, which were supporting it because they wanted to use Finland in their plans against the Soviet Union.[99] Because of this, the revolution in Finland had been set back and this in turn faced the communist movement with the twin dangers of hope-

166    THE COMMUNIST PARTY OF FINLAND

less passivity in some workers and right opportunism in others.

The congress confirmed three main lines of policy, of which the first was the endorsement of the new agrarian policy of 1923.[100] The promotion of an independent small-farmer movement in alliance with the proletariat was the basis on which the revolution in Finland was to be achieved. An important aspect of this was that SKP must have a proper attitude to Finnish nationalism, since this was very important for the attitudes of the farmers. SKP must establish beyond question that the party and the Soviet Union stood unequivocally for Finnish independence, and that when Finland had achieved a worker-farmer government Russia would consider linking Karelia with an independent Finland.[101] The second policy line was that in politics, while SKP must never lose sight of its revolutionary aims, it was legitimate to cooperate with honest social democrats among the workers, to seek to win their confidence but at the same time to expose without mercy their leaders, with whom no collaboration was possible.[102] Thirdly, great emphasis was placed on work in the trade union movement, where absolute priority must be given to the struggle against SDP efforts to split the movement. This could only by done through the activities of the SKP fractions, by fostering trade union militancy, by backing all the workers' demands, and by keeping the trade unions on a class-war basis. The party must persuade SAJ to boycott bodies like the ILO but to seek to establish links with Profintern and the Russian workers.

On tactics, the congress stressed how the double network of party cells and party fractions in public organisations must be developed, and said that this work was only just beginning.[103] There had already been some deficiencies in the work of the fractions, notably in the parliamentary group, and they were reminded that at all times the fractions were to be subordinate to the party cells and that unconditional obedience and conspiratorial discipline were essential. Party members must remember 'that the alpha and omega of bolshevism is the Comintern and the Communist Party'.[104] There was to be no new public political party but there would be a network of 'comrades associations', which should include workers of all shades of opinion and would have no overt party affiliation; the SKP members would avoid taking the lead in these though they would actually control them through fraction activity. But there was no form of public activity which was to be immune from the workings of the party fractions; the cooperatives, women's movements, the temperance movement, the athletics movement, all offered scope for turning the workers towards revolutionary, class-war attitudes of mind. The future of SKP was clearly mapped out; a solid web of underground cells would control the work of innumerable fractions in every kind of public organisation, and all would be working towards the common objective: to prepare the workers and farmers for the revolutionary role they would have to play once the current phase of stability had ended, and to frustrate the efforts of the bourgeoisie and its social democrat henchmen to divert the masses from their destiny.

Circumstances dictated that in the 1920s the crucial field for communist activity would be the trade unions. For one thing, after the destruction of STP, the trade union movement offered the most important field within which SKP could operate on a national scale; to some extent, the control of the trade union congress, SAJ, compensated for the lack of a national political party. For another, there was intense pressure on SKP from the Russian government, because SAJ offered the nearly unique phenomenon of an undivided trade union movement embracing both communists and social democrats, and able to act as a bridge-builder, or Trojan horse according to taste, between the communists and the non-communist trade union world, which Russia aspired to influence. Hence in this brief period the Finnish trade union movement became a significant factor in international trade union politics.

The Finnish authorities naturally regarded the continued existence of this free field for legal communist activity with the utmost disfavour, and would have wished to deal with it as they had dealt with STP. In 1924 they thought they had succeeded, for in connection with a legal case arising out of a strike in 1921, the supreme court ruled that SAJ had been involved in criminal activity. Circulars were sent from the Ministry of the Interior to the prefects suggesting the local suppression of communist-controlled trade union branches, but in August SAJ alerted the ILO, and since Finland had signed the ILO agreement permitting free trade union activity the government's legal advisers ruled that suppression of trade unions would infringe this.[105] From that point on it became the hope of the authorities that the social democrats would secede and set up their own trade union movement, after which it would be possible to strike down SAJ legally.

There could be no doubt that SKP did indeed control SAJ from 1920 onwards. A typical instance of this was the capture of the transport workers in 1921, who at first were formed into one massive union representing nearly one-third of the total membership of SAJ.[106] At the inaugural congress of the new union its purposes was defined as 'to shake the whole capitalist system', and to pursue simultaneously 'both trifling wage demands and the socialist revolution'.[107] Yet this theoretical control was not absolute; attempts during 1921 by SKP to turn industrial action into political action, as the Comintern required, or to launch purely political protest strikes, had all failed.[108] This had been the background to the attacks by Wälläri and Malm on the leaders of SAJ for their apolitical attitude.[109] On the other hand, the communists in SAJ had successfully got its committee to decline to affiliate to the Amsterdam international, and early in 1922 held a successful ballot in SAJ which favoured affiliation to Profintern, where SAJ was informally represented through SKP.[110] The communist leaders of SAJ dared not implement the decision for fear of driving the social democrats into secession, thus revealing a dilemma which they never solved: the price of maintaining an undivided trade union movement was to give the social democrat minority a virtual veto power inside SAJ, since the threat of secession would bring the communists to heel. However, SDP could not use the threat recklessly, since they did not want to incur the odium of appearing as the 'splitters' in the eyes of the workers. So a long game of bluff and counter-bluff began over the secession threat.

The situation was revealed at the SAJ congress in 1923, where the communists and their sympathisers probably controlled sixty-five of the seventy-six delegates.[111] SKP could not use this strength effectively, for on 29 March SDP had stated its minimum price for staying in SAJ— full political neutrality of the movement and an equal division of places on the executive bodies.[112] The outcome was a series of compromises, although SKP won one clear victory when SAJ committed itself unequivocally to class-war policies. The relevant resolution declared:[113]

> The trade union movement's struggle must be directed against all the class forces of the bourgeoisie. . . . The final objective is to change the system of production based on private ownership into a system where production is undertaken only for the good of society. . . . The trade union movement is committed to a class-war position and so its own struggle and that of the workers who are organised politically on a class-war basis are the same.

But of the other issues, affiliation to Profintern was shelved, member unions which affiliated to a political party had to allow contracting out for their members, and after the suppression of STP this was changed to a rule prohibiting member unions from affiliating to political parties. The policy of concession to the social democrats paid off, for in December 1923 SDP formally decided that its members could stay in SAJ. They had not achieved parity of representation on the executive but there were signs in 1924 that SKP did not have control either. The

SAJ committee, against the explicit policy of the Profintern, agreed to work with ILO,[114] the communists were defeated on the drafting of the SAJ manifesto for the general election of 1924, and over the question of whether to receive a fraternal delegate from the Amsterdam international, which was anathema to SKP, the committee wavered, first voting 11 to 10 against, then 11 to 9 in favour, so that the delegate from Amsterdam was received. The party blamed this defeat on the waverings of the fellow-travellers.[115] They also conceded that in spite of their efforts SAJ refused to back militant strike action so that industrial unrest fell off in 1923–5.[116] The root of the trouble was in E. Huttunen, who had been elected chairman of SAJ with communist support in 1923, and who then steadily moved back to a social democrat position until in 1925 he broke publicly with the communists.[117] In these circumstances SKP made a bid to regain control in 1925 by proposing an extraordinary congress of SAJ, but the committee refused this, as they also refused Huttunen's proffered resignation as chairman.[118] For this reason one can see why the fifth congress of SKP was so insistent that the party, through its fractions, must prepare for the regular congress of SAJ in 1926 with the utmost care.[119] SDP was already preparing for battle, and held a preliminary conference of its own trade unionists on 30 December 1925 to prepare to fight the delegate elections. They also drew up revised terms for staying in SAJ: affiliation to the Amsterdam international, cooperation with ILO, political neutrality of the movement, and equality of places on the executive.[120]

SKP was equally active. Early in 1926 A. Tuominen was released from prison and SKP—though now they deny this—gave him the task of coordinating the party campaign for the congress which began on 3 May. In April, Manner went to Stockholm with SKP's instructions; in addition, Kuusinen sent written orders directly to Tuominen; and finally, at the congress itself, Melnitshanski attended as fraternal delegate from Russia and was in fact the official spokesman for Profintern. The line was a

clear one; SAJ must be preserved intact, and whatever
concessions were needed to keep the social democrats
from seceding would have to be made, although in the
public proceedings a hard line was to be maintained, exposing the social democrats as traitors and splitters.[121] It
is fortunately not necessary to decide how far Tuominen's account of the subsequent intrigues is literally
true, and how far SKP is justified in dismissing it as a
highly coloured fantasy, for the main facts are clear
enough. SKP failed to keep control of proceedings, partly
because its requirements were unrealistic, partly perhaps,
as Tuominen says, because communications with Moscow
were too slow and events outpaced SKP's capacity to direct
them.[122] SKP wanted a tame social democrat for chairman, and E. K. Louhikko, a tough communist, as secretary. The compromise that had to be made, without
benefit of endorsement from Moscow, was that a formidable social democrat, M. Paasivuori, became chairman,
with Tuominen as secretary. Melnitshanski had little
choice but to endorse this, as otherwise the congress
would have split. Apart from this it proved fairly easy to
compromise the other issues. The social democrats
dropped the demand for parity on the executives and
accepted one-third representation, so that they got ten
places out of thirty on the main committee and three out
of ten on the executive. On the other points SKP made
the concessions; strikes were not to be made political,
the movement would not support any political party, and
it would not affiliate to any international but would continue to work with ILO. It is known that SKP felt that these
concessions went too far, because they said so at a party
conference in 1926, condemning the Finnish bureau for
having disobeyed party orders.[123] Further, at the end of
the SAJ congress, the communists circulated a paper saying that the concessions were purely tactical to appease
the social democrat splitters and that they implied no retreat from a revolutionary class-war policy.[124] The regrets
which SKP expressed over these compromises merely demonstrate how theoretical preoccupations blinded them to

political realities, for the record shows that the compromise worked very well. While it lasted, SAJ membership rose by over 70 per cent to ninety thousand, all talk of secession by the social democrats ceased, some successful strikes were carried through, and SKP got the opening it wanted for bridge-building moves in the non-communist trade union world. But all this depended on the spirit of the compromise being maintained and this was too much to ask of the doctrinaire émigrés in Moscow.

The same lack of touch with reality shows up in the other major preoccupation of SKP in 1926, their agrarian policy. They proclaimed that the disillusion of the small farmers with the bourgeois regime was such that an independent farmer opposition movement was springing up in the countryside. The task of SKP was to assist this movement and to steer it into alliance with the proletariat; but the party must not get tied up in the actual running of it, for this must be a genuine autonomous farmer movement.[125] The Finnish bureau of the party had orders for the vigorous exploitation of this supposed opportunity and chose as its main weapon the establishment of a newspaper, the *Farmers' News*,[126] which was published weekly from late 1926, with some five to ten thousand copies, until late 1927, when SKP at last perceived that there never had been any genuine move among the farmers to break away from Agrarian Party leadership. Perhaps the most significant result of this exercise in theoretical politics was that it recruited into the movement Y. Leino, the agronomist who wrote much of the *Farmers' News* and was to play a fatal role in the history of SKP after 1944.[127]

When SKP held a party conference in late 1926 the tone was one of considerable satisfaction. While they deplored the excessive concessions over SAJ, they looked forward to exploiting the situation by raising the level of industrial militancy, for while it was not SKP policy to provoke irresponsible strikes, even an unsuccessful strike is educational for those who participate, and raises their class-consciousness.[128] The principal weaknesses noted were slack cell discipline, irregular payment of party dues, poor success in penetrating the cooperative movement, and above all failure to spread the work among the women.[129] As with the farmers, the party aspired to raise an autonomous women's movement, the 'Women Workers' Delegate Movement', which would be guided by SKP fractions but run by non-party people.[130] One senses again, in the shot-gun effect that SKP was calling for, a lack of touch with reality. They were asking far more of their members in Finland than they could possibly deliver. The resultant dissipation of members' energies and enthusiasm into so many different fields of activity could only result in poorly based and superficial organisations without real staying power in a crisis, as events were to demonstrate. The reader of the policy documents of SKP for these years must always doubt how much substance lay beneath the paper patterns of cell and fraction, and the multiple legal organisations in which they were supposed to function. The actual reminiscences of the people on the spot, forced to work in tiny conspiratorial cliques, rightly fearful of police spies, faithfully accepting party orders which they had no capacity to execute, gives a very different picture of the realities of communist activity in these years and the extraordinary faith and courage of the ordinary party member, than either the ritualistic prose of party documents or the lurid images of the bolshevik menace conjured up by their enemies.

During 1927 a fresh dimension of delusion was added from the ruling circles in Russia itself, for they became persuaded that the imperialist camp, led by Britain, was planning an attack on the Soviet Union, probably in 1929, and that Finland was involved in their plans. The Russian Communist Party central committee discussed this threat in March 1927 and debated whether they should not plan a pre-emptive strike against Finland. It seems that certain precautions were taken, some military preparations made, the SKP regime in Karelia increased its military establishment, and SKP was directed to focus its

activities on frustrating as far as possible Finland's participation in the imperialist plot.[131] The SKP party conference in 1927 explicitly endorses the thesis of imperialist
war preparations in Finland and its own duty to combat
them.[132] A speech in Parliament by the communist
member Kulmala was quite explicit, when he threatened
'unrelenting class struggle against capitalism and its mili-
tarism in every Marxist revolutionary form, before a war
and during it. In wartime there would be no reconciliation
of classes, no industrial peace, no wartime truce . . . the
coming war, if it is a war against the Soviet Union, will
be an international class war'.[133]

The new tension found expression in the work of
SKP in the Finnish army, which was the special responsibility of the military section of the central committee.
Down to 1925 little had been done except to distribute
subversive literature among the conscripts; then, in accordance with fifth congress policy, an effort was made to
establish SKP cells inside army units. In 1927, however,
there were only seventeen such cells, with 121 members,
and a mimeographed news-sheet, *The Red Soldier*, which
had a circulation of two to three hundred copies monthly.
It can be seen that SKP subversion of the Finnish army
was utterly insignificant and ineffective. This did not stop
their enemies claiming that it was a menace to national
security, and accusing SKP of constant espionage for Russia. To combat this charge, SKP published an explanation
of its military policy in 1927.[134] They denied categori-
cally that SKP ever organised espionage, not because they
had moral scruples but because 'SKP is the political revolutionary party of the workers of Finland, and espionage is
not part of its task'. When the party wanted to help the
Soviet Union it would do so by calling on the workers to
stop any imperialist war. SKP's role in the armed forces
was educational; its aim was to prevent war but if war
should come then its aim was 'to convert it into armed
revolt within each capitalist belligerent against its own
bourgeoisie.' There is no good reason to doubt the essential truth of these statements; SKP was indeed dedicated to

subverting the Finnish army if it could, but was not concerned with espionage, though of course individual Finnish communists were enlisted by Russian intelligence
and were caught and convicted from time to time. Such
slight subversive capacity as SKP did possess in the army
was smashed in October 1927 when the organisers of its
military section were arrested in Finland and tried and
convicted early in 1928.[135]

The only way in which SKP could aspire to help the
Soviet Union was to exploit its industrial power to sabotage the supposed plans of the imperialists. This task was
given an unusual twist in 1927, because for almost the
whole year Finland had a purely social democrat government. From a tactical point of view it might have been
expected that SKP would seek to keep this government in
office. Tuominen and others, working in the field in Finland, argued for this for the very good reason that this
government held the security police in check, and enormously eased the party's work.[136] The figures speak for
themselves. In 1926 there were one hundred and twelve
convictions of communists for sedition or treason and in
1928 ninety-four, but in 1927 there were only twenty.
The central committee in Moscow saw things differently,
and from a strategic point of view realistically, for if the
SDP government was a success and could ameliorate conditions in Finland, it would wholly discredit the SKP case
that the workers must seek their salvation through revolution. SKP was bound to promote the failure of the Tanner
government and to harass it in every possible way. In
their view it was 'the servant of big capital' and 'swiftly
moving towards social-fascism', and was also an active
participant in the war plans of the imperialists.[137] SKP
had good grounds for knowing that this was not the case,
since the minister of agriculture, Mauno Pekkala, was
the brother of the leading communist member of Parliament, Eino Pekkala, and through this connection all the
proceedings of the government were leaked.[138] The parliamentary group obviously had a special responsibility in
harrying the government, and inevitably they fell short of

what the party demanded,[139] but action in the industrial field offered the best openings. SKP had a programme for 1927 involving extensive strike action; the Finnish bureau sent out a circular in May emphasising that the party must keep control of all strikes.[140] That month a very promising strike in the paper industry was settled by government mediation in spite of all SKP efforts to keep it going,[141] and a similarly promising one in the nationalised railway workshops, directly involving the government, was also cleared up by a government-inspired compromise.[142]

The great success of 1927 was the metal workers lockout which began in May. This was especially suitable because it began with a dispute in the Crichton-Vulcan shipyard in Turku, which had just received an order for building submarines. SKP stressed that this was a blatant example of how the Tanner government was involved in the aggressive plans of the imperialist warmongers,[143] and thus it became from the start a semi-political strike against armaments. SKP put all its strength into this dispute, Russian money was procured to support it, and it lasted until December. Then the government mediator produced reasonably favourable terms for a settlement, and SAJ endorsed them, ending the strike; the communists in SAJ had done this without waiting for clearance from SKP in Moscow, and the following day came instructions that the strike must be kept going. Despite the uproar this caused among the members of the Finnish bureau and the SAJ fraction there was nothing to be done about it. The difficulty of directing affairs in Finland by remote control from Moscow was proved once more.[144]

The other major use of SKP's trade union influence was to exploit SAJ's contacts with non-communist trade unions. Early in 1927, when Tuominen was in Moscow, the importance of developing such links was pressed on him.[145] It seems odd that when in the spring of 1927 SAJ was invited to send an observer to the congress of the Amsterdam international in Paris, the communist fraction, having waited in vain for instructions from Moscow, decided to decline the invitation and carried this decision in the SAJ committee.[146] It is suggested that the Finns disliked having to attend such gatherings and to put over the Profintern line to hostile audiences; it is even alleged that on occasion a Profintern-provided interpreter actually substituted propaganda for what the unfortunate and incomprehensible Finnish delegate had actually said.[147] It makes a good story, even if it is not literally true, since it describes figuratively what was actually happening—SAJ was being exploited for ends alien to the interests of its members, and the local communists in control, who had the reactions of their constituents to consider, could not afford to be exposed as puppets of external forces. So in this case when Moscow ordered them to reverse their decision and go to Paris, the communist fraction, after agonised debate, decided to disobey the party line and adhere to their refusal.[148]

But some progress was made along this line; the Norwegian trade unions were persuaded to enter into co-operation with SAJ and the Russian trade unions with a view to promoting a new, comprehensive trade union international, while some individual unions, like the forest workers, agreed to enter joint committees for collaboration between Russian and Scandinavian trade unions.[149] The biggest formal success was achieved in February 1928, when a conference was held in Copenhagen between delegates of SAJ and the Norwegian and Russian trade unions, which drafted a document known as the Copenhagen Agreement. This had two parts; in the first the parties agreed to sponsor a conference designed to set up a new trade union international, based on class-war policies. In the second part the three parties entered into a mutual assistance pact among themselves and agreed to wage a common struggle against capitalism and the danger of imperialist war.[150] But even this success proved an empty one: the conference for a new international was called but the response was so poor that it was abandoned. More important, when SAJ came to consider ratifying the mutual assistance clauses it became clear that to do so would drive the social democrats into secession, in addition to which the Swedish trade unions threatened to break off relations with SAJ in case of ratification. The communist fraction in SAJ decided, in face of this situation, to postpone a decision, to circulate the Copenhagen Agreement among the individual unions, and to leave the question of ratification to the next SAJ congress in 1929.[151]

A conference of SKP held late in 1927 had still shown a considerable degree of self-satisfaction. Their analysis of the situation put the danger of imperialist war in the fore-front: 'The danger of war is a real one, even if the actual outbreak may be postponed for some time'.[152] They recognised that the fascist danger in Finland was loom-ing larger but assured themselves that SKP too was grow-ing stronger, along the lines laid down in 1925. They found time to denounce the Trotsky-Zinoviev opposition to Stalin as objectively menshevik, anarchist, and syndi-calist.[153] There was, as always in these reviews of the sit-uation, a routine list of shortcomings in party work in al-most every field, but the general impression conveyed by the document summarising the decisions of the con-ference was that things were going well for SKP; in fact it was just on the brink of destruction through the malice of its enemies and its own dogmatic blindness to reality. It was typical of this latter phenomenon that when Tuo-minen was called to Moscow, in March 1928, he was severely called to account for not getting the Copen-hagen Agreement ratified immediately, and for failing to launch a dock strike which SKP had wanted to start in the summer of 1927 but which the SAJ committee had refused to endorse, on the reasonable grounds that all ef-forts should be concentrated on the metal workers dis-pute.[154] These were both cases in which the party work-ers in Finland had backed their own assessment of the situation against unrealistic instructions from Moscow which disregarded local conditions and which were based solely on the broad policy requirements of the Russian government and the Comintern.

The blow which struck SKP at this point arose out of

the arrest of the leaders of the military section in Finland who came to trial in February 1928. The investigations into their case had opened up leads on to the underground activity of SKP, of which the party in any case openly boasted. A communist member of Parliament stated on 28 February that 'we do not hold it a crime that the workers' revolutionary activity is underground, when it cannot take place openly because of bourgeois persecution'. The party was proud of the work of its military section, and while it was not trying to raise an immediate revolution hoped that this work would 'play a very important part when the armed class struggle comes on the agenda'.[155] Unfortunately, one of the accused, J. Rasi, had turned police informer, and on 18 April 1928 the security police made nearly sixty arrests, which took in the whole underground leadership, including the trade union fractions, sparing only the members of the parliamentary group, of whom just two were arrested.[156] The party now admits that it had badly underestimated the police on this occasion, though it is claimed that the central committee had some advance warning, and had sent orders to the leadership in Finland to disperse, which were disregarded.[157] What is indisputable is that SKP in Finland had suffered a staggering blow, from which it had not recovered when worse trials beset it in 1929.

# 4. THE DESTRUCTION OF COMMUNISM IN FINLAND

The April arrests virtually put SKP out of action in Finland until late in the year 1928, by which time the training of new organisers was completed, and a new Finnish bureau and area committee network had been set up, although inevitably the quality of the new cadres was weaker than that of the old.[1] During the summer of 1928 the great dock strike had been launched, but SKP could not do much to extend it, as they wished, because their surviving fraction members in SAJ had been shocked into opportunist vacillations, which they also demonstrated, from the party's point of view, by their failure to press the ratification of the Copenhagen Agreement.[2] It was during this unhappy juncture that the Comintern proclaimed that the 'third phase' of the development of postwar capitalism had begun,[3] and said that it would be characterised by a rapid intensification of the class war and a growing danger of imperialist war. In these conditions the greatest danger for communist parties would be right-opportunism, since the social democrats, faced by growing tensions, would be pushed into social fascism and would be the most insidious enemies of the workers. It followed that to destroy the social democrats must be a first priority for all communists.

This new hard line was unflinchingly adopted by SKP, with dismal consequences. The sort of thing that happened can be shown by an analysis which the party published of its performance in the Finnish local elections of 1928. On the face of things the workers' and small farmers' candidates had done well; their vote had increased and they had secured a net gain of three hundred

seats.[4] But this in no way satisfied SKP; some of this success had been due to entirely improper electoral pacts
with SDP, when in accordance with 'third-phase' policy
they should have been emphasising the depravity of
SDP. Indeed the whole campaign had shown a tendency
to fight on local issues instead of using the opportunity to
present a fundamental exposition of the current situation
in proper Marxist-Leninist terms, thus plainly betraying
the deadly sin of right-opportunism.[5] The campaign had
shown that the workers' and small farmers' alliance 'was
not consistent and could not, as a whole, keep unwaveringly to the correct line'. The conclusion was clear: 'The
main danger is now the danger from the Right, the
danger of social democrat influence'. Thus just when
SKP in Finland was particularly weak, when the fascists
and reactionaries were gathering their strength to wipe it
out, the party leaders in Moscow, faithful to their dogma,
could only rant on about an entirely imaginary danger
from the social democrats. To do the party justice, it now
concedes that its attitude was mistaken, that instead a
popular front policy would have been correct; as it was
they were refusing cooperation even with left-social democrats and fell into policies that were 'to some extent
sectarian'.[6] But even now, they cannot leave it at this,
they argue unconvincingly that the party line was 'in its
main points correct, and to abandon it would have meant
surrender', since no amount of compromise could have
averted the fascist onslaught. On the other hand, the
uncommitted observer is left wondering how any policy
at all could have led to a worse result than that actually
produced—the reduction of the communist movement in
Finland to total impotence.

The year 1929 opened gloomily with a report by the
Finnish bureau of the party on the state of the underground network; everywhere it was crippled after the
arrests and the number of functioning cells had fallen
from around five hundred to some 380.[7] In April the
situation was reviewed at an enlarged meeting of the central committee, which formally analysed the situation in

the light of the 'third phase'. In Finland the growing economic crisis was held to prove the intensifying contradictions of capitalism, which were driving the bourgeoisie towards war with Russia at the behest of British imperialism. Rather perversely, the Finnish government had just signed the Kellogg Peace Pact; but this was a cunning trick inspired by American imperialism in its competition with British imperialism. However, it was not even as simple as that, since the signing had also been done with the active encouragement of the British, because 'Finland's joining served equally the purposes of British imperialism, which wished to conceal its own war preparations against the Soviet Union, and those other preparations which it was directing'.[8] When drivel of this kind passes for serious analysis of a situation, the subsequent policy failures need cause no surprise. They went on to assert that the growing tension was bringing more and more workers to support the revolutionary line of SKP, because the role of the social democrats as tools of the capitalists was becoming ever more apparent.[9] It followed that the left-social democrats, who still talked as if they opposed capitalism, were the worst of all: 'It is becoming clear that the left-SD leaders are the most dangerous of all the promoters of bourgeois policies to the working class'.[10] Indeed, SDP was simply building bridges for fascism: 'The prospect exists that the social democrat leaders, who are now social fascists, will move over completely to fascism'. SKP was admittedly weakened by the arrests of 1928, and this had led to an outbreak of right-opportunism in its work in all fields.[11] But the Comintern had shown what must be done; there must be unceasing struggle against the SDP, particularly its leftists, so that the revolutionary alliance of the workers and small farmers could be built up by a popular front from below; while to ensure success in this, SKP might have to be purged of some opportunist elements.[12]

The real situation, against which these fantasies must be set, was that Finland in 1928 had already begun her phase of the great depression, triggered off by the collapse of the export markets for her forest products. The economic distress—unemployment for the workers, bankruptcy for many small family farms, falling profits for industry, and insecurity for the small businessman— had produced not the imagined revolutionary upsurge on the Left but a growing mood of right-wing nationalist reaction. In this the great dock strike of 1928-9 had played a major role. The Finnish Right claimed that it had been deliberately timed to stop Finland's timber exports so that the Soviet Union could take over her markets. This is unproven surmise; SKP had wanted this strike since 1927 and had given it organisational and monetary support; but they did this to any industrial dispute, on the Leninist principle that any properly organised strike raises the class consciousness of the workers. Whatever the truth, the strike gave a new credibility to the allegation that SKP was a treasonable conspiracy and a tool of Soviet policy. Further, to combat the strike Finnish employers had organised large-scale strike-breaking. The forces which financed the strike-breaking organisation, Vientirauha,[13] went on in 1929 to finance an emergent, semi-fascist political front, which finally achieved the destruction of domestic communism. Their manager, V. Kosola, was to become the figurehead of Finnish fascism. Thus in 1929, out of economic distress, a clearly discernible fascist danger was emerging. In face of this, the obvious policy for SKP would have been a popular front of all progressive and democratic forces to resist it, but adherence to Comintern dogma forbade this. SKP now agrees that 'the theories which appeared in many party documents about a general intensification of left feeling among the workers, and an increase of revolutionary tendencies,' did not fit Finland in those years.[14] SKP, by ignoring reality, simultaneously provoked the reactionaries to new extremes and split the potential anti-fascist front.

The new policy line of SKP produced three main results, all equally disastrous. First, it shattered the Finnish trade union movement at the congress of SAJ, held on 10 May 1929. SKP instructions for this were clear;

the Copenhagen Agreement, which they valued for its affirmation of class-war policies and its call to frustrate imperialist war on the Soviet Union, must be ratified.[15] This line had been confirmed at the Profintern congress in January 1929, which insisted that there must be no concessions to reformist trade unions in the revolutionary 'third phase'.[16] But the Finnish bureau of SKP and the SAJ fraction could not bring themselves to obey these manifestly suicidal orders, and for this they were to be bitterly reproached by SKP for opportunism.[17] At a pre-congress conference, in March, the communist fraction had agreed that in the interests of trade union unity they would postpone the question of ratification, and this was the policy adopted when the congress met.[18] The communists had a clear majority of the delegates but they did not dare to steamroller a ratification decision; instead they passed a resolution confirming their support for the Copenhagen Agreement but deferring ratification until the Norwegian movement had made a decision.[19] But they made their concession in such a way that nothing was gained. The party later tried to claim credit for this compromise,[20] but in fact it was forced on SKP because their fellow-traveller allies in SAJ would not obey the party line.[21] Another recent SKP account of the episode concedes that the party line may have been a mistake, and 'perhaps our party criticised this decision too vehemently'.[22] But the party fraction, possibly to compensate and prove that their revolutionary zeal was unabated, went on to provoke the social democrats by votes condemning the Amsterdam International, by voting to cut the salary of the social democrat SAJ organiser, by expressing solidarity with the imprisoned communists—in short by showing in every possible way that SKP was determined to use its power in SAJ for party ends.[23] As a result the social democrats seceded, though they did this in stages; initially Paasivuori refused to continue as chairman of SAJ and all the social democrats refused to hold any office in it.[24]

The second consequence of adopting 'third-phase' policies was to split the communist movement in Finland itself. SKP had never eliminated the opportunist opposition trend led by Wälläri since 1926, which favoured an independent workers' movement based on Finland.[25] For this SKP reproached itself very bitterly in the 1930s, accusing itself of having been soft on this manifestation of right-opportunism.[26] The same tensions had caused a rift in the parliamentary group between the strict party liners, led by Rosenberg, and the opportunists led by E. Pekkala.[27] At times the opportunists won, as in early 1929, when the group voted in favour of a health insurance bill, superficially the obvious thing for a workers' group to do. Then SKP pointed out that objectively the law was reactionary and persuaded the group to reverse its attitude.[28] By the summer of 1929 this situation had become too much for the Wälläri group, which perceived—correctly—that SKP policy was playing right into the hands of the reactionaries and would end in disaster for the workers. So Wälläri, E. Pekkala, E. Härmä, K. Kulo and other leading SKP figures in Finland broke with the party and formed an independent 'Left Group of the Finnish Workers', on a programme of freedom from SKP and Comintern direction.[29] SKP rounded on the dissenters in fury as even more dangerous than the social democrats; they declared that 'a conciliatory attitude towards the deserters means helping the deserters',[30] and they have never since forgiven Wälläri, who tends to rank with Tanner as an SKP bogeyman.

How much cause for alarm there really was is extremely hard to assess. Pekkala, Wälläri and the others had a personal following among the workers, however much SKP seeks to deny this.[31] They proved it by capturing control of some party newspapers, notably the Vaasa paper *Työn Ääni*,[32] and then the 'Labour' printing establishment, on which they began to publish their own paper, *Suomen Työmies*.[33] One may surmise that in normal circumstances, if SKP had held to its line of 1928, the Wälläri group had some prospect of displacing the *émigré* leadership over the workers' movement,

but that SKP was saved by its own follies, for in the deluge
of repression which it brought on itself in 1930 the Wälläri group was also swept away. On the other hand, before the cataclysm, SKP had successfully counterattacked
and recaptured *Työn Ääni*, and also held control against
the opportunists at a number of trade union conferences
in 1930,[34] so that SKP might have succeeded in beating
off the revolt in its ranks. But it is significant how easily
SKP, by its own misguided actions, had shattered its internal unity and come back to the 1920 situation; the
party had travelled full circle.

The third consequence of the 'third-phase' policy was
to bring into the open a semi-fascist reaction dedicated
to destroying communist activity in Finland. During the
summer of 1929 SKP had continued to demonstrate its
adherence to the Comintern line for Finland. It had
declared the intensification of the class war, condemned
all conciliatory policies as futile and dangerous, and affirmed that the masses were moving to the Left and
that SKP must move with them.[35] They then proceeded
to give two demonstrations of their own weakness, of
which the first arose from the Comintern call for massive demonstrations against imperialist war on 1 August
1929. The party now agrees that the results were disappointing. 'They succeeded well in some places',[36] but
showed that SKP lacked the ability to mount really massive street demonstrations. To complete their humilia-
tion, the young communists in Helsinki had paraded with
the incorrect, pacifist slogan 'No more war', which was
un-Marxist and utopian.[37] But nothing dismayed the
SKP leaders; they bitterly reproached their fraction in
SAJ for its feeble opportunism, and on 9 August the
central committee affirmed 'the most resolute struggle
against defeatists . . . the withdrawal of SAJ from ILO,
the formation of a revolutionary leadership in the trade
unions'.[38] The immediate result of this was that their
opponents took the first formal steps to set up a non-
communist trade union congress, when they established
the 'Trade Union Delegation' on 29 September.[39] An

SKP conference which met in September could see nothing wrong in the situation that did not stem from the failure of SKP to match the revolutionary enthusiasm of the masses,[40] from excessive 'legalism' or from weakness in exposing the social democrats and the opportunists.[41] The one note of realism was where the party mentioned the need for the workers to organise to meet the physical force of the fascists, but remarking that there was no 'rigid formula' for this left it entirely vague how such defence should be organised.[42]

Things moved to a sudden crisis in November, when the communist prisoners in the Tammisaari forced labour camp began a hunger strike.[43] They had been careful to advertise their intention, because it was meant to become the focus of an international protest against reaction. The facts of what followed are that SAJ issued a call for a general strike in support of the political prisoners and it was a dismal failure, with a 10 to 15 per cent response on the first day and an abrupt collapse thereafter; the only positive result was that the more militant workers identified themselves by coming out on strike and became the targets for immediate reprisals.[44] The other result was that this demonstration of SKP weakness at last nerved the reactionaries to strike back. SKP has two different accounts of what went wrong, though both blame the opportunists: one is that the feebleness of the opportunist leaders of SAJ accounts for the weakness of the strike organisation; the other is that the treacherous opportunists in SAJ deliberately issued a strike call and then positively impeded the efforts of loyal SKP members to make it effective, in other words that the strike call had been a provocation. But no such colourful explanation is needed; SKP militancy, based on a wholly imaginary revolutionary fervour of the masses, had persuaded an admittedly half-hearted SAJ committee to call a strike for which there was no mass support.

SDP seized the opening created by this fiasco to speed up their own plans to start a rival trade union movement. A 'League of Finnish Workers'[45] became the base around which a new grouping of non-communist trade unions formed. On 31 July 1930 these unions, some of which were social democrat, some politically neutral, agreed to set up the *Suomen ammattiyhdistysten keskusliitto*—SAK (which has lasted down to the present day), and affiliated at once to the Amsterdam International. SAK began its official public activity in October 1930; the schism so long apprehended was now a fact.

The initiative had passed to the enemies of SKP towards the end of 1929; they were looking for a suitable pretext to strike, and found it at the end of November when the communist youth movement organised a rally of its study group members at the town of Lapua.[46] It was a badly chosen place for the communists, since it was the centre of a region notorious for fanatical Lutheran pietism, extreme nationalist politics and a tradition of public violence. The young communist participants, many in red shirts, some indulging in ostentatious anti-religious demonstrations, were set on by mobs, and the first meeting of the rally, on 23 November, was broken up by violence and then closed by the police. On 1 December a great national rally was held in Lapua, with Kosola in the chair; it became the first of a series of mass meetings which launched the so-called 'Lapua movement'. In theory this was a spontaneous uprising of honest Finnish farmers; in fact it was financed and organised by Finnish big business as a weapon which would destroy the communist movement, although it could never have worked if there had not existed a genuine popular mass hysteria directed against the communists as the obvious scapegoats, a feeling which was particularly strong in rural society. From the first the movement made it clear that if the Finnish authorities would not suppress the communists, the Lapuans were ready to do the job themselves. SKP's bluff had now been called; they must demonstrate their ability to lead the masses in a revolutionary resistance to the reactionaries, or go under.

When SKP came to review its efforts to resist the fascists, it had to admit that these had been rather feeble.

There was no lack of fiery words. *Työn Ääni* declared on 27 November: 'The whole working class must rise against fascism',[47] but as a later commentator remarked, SKP 'should at once have begun to create a powerful workers' defence force against fascist attacks. . . . SKP made propaganda about self-defence when it should already have moved from propaganda to realisation'.[48]

Their only action displayed the worst sins of legalism; they put down an interpellation in Parliament. The government told them in effect that they had got what they deserved at Lapua, and that self-proclaimed outlaws should not complain if the law did not protect them; even the social democrats supported this government attitude.[49] Under heavy Lapua pressure the government began to legislate: a law on associations aimed against communist cover organisations—and supported by the social democrats—was met with more verbal defiance; the communists in Parliament declared that they would fight the law to the end, and if it were enacted 'the Finnish workers will not obey the law'.[50] New laws on the press, designed to restrain the communist newspapers, were not supported by the social democrats, and were rejected in Parliament in March 1930.[51] In direct response to this, Lapua struck back, and a fascist gang attacked and destroyed the presses of the Vaasa paper *Työn Ääni*.[52] Even after this the response of the Finnish bureau was only to call for protest demonstrations. Some steps were taken to organise guards on other communist presses, to prevent a repetition, but this was done partly with the approval of the authorities.[53] This blatant failure to meet force with force, as they had often boasted they would, is reflected in an enlarged central committee meeting of SKP held in April 1930. In face of the manifest intention of the fascists to destroy them, the main policy statement of this meeting is concerned with the dangers of right-opportunism, 'the struggle against the right-opportunist renegades'; Wälläri rather than Lapua was seen as the main enemy. It was only after the final catastrophe that the central committee acknowledged that 'in practice the whole party walked around with eyes half-closed', that it showed a pernicious passivity in its response to the fascist challenge, and that this was largely because party policy directed the attentions and energies of the party in other directions.[54]

Individual party members did make defiant gestures. On May Day 1930 the communists tried to defy the police prohibitions on their processions, and in Helsinki A. Äikiä boldly invaded the platform of the social democrat rally, denounced the social democrats as allies of fascism, and called for a revolutionary counterattack by the workers.[55] When the social democrat press accused him of huliganism, he replied to the 'morally offended gentry' that 'the working class has its own moral code. . . . . You hired lackies should shut up, you have sold the class interests of the proletariat to the bourgeoisie a thousand times over'.[56] But on the whole SKP waited quietly for the slaughter, and in June the blow fell. The Lapua movement gave the government an ultimatum to close the communist press, and announced that there would be a farmers' march on the capital to enforce their demands. Now at last the communist press and parliamentary group issued unambiguous calls to the workers for organised resistance to fascist violence: 'Fascism is directed against the whole working class. . . . We urge all workers—leftists, social democrats, and non-party— to create and strengthen a common front of workers against fascism'. On 10 June the parliamentary group caused a suspension of the sitting by making a defiant declaration in Parliament.[57] On 13 June, *Tiedonantaja* called for 'a defence committee in every place of work . . . the working people will not be satisfied in future with presenting protests. These are no use by themselves. . . . In every place of work a committee must be elected to organise the means of defence'. In another article in the same issue the paper declares that 'we cannot wait any longer while the fascists carry out their seizure of power. The fascists must be sent home first. The Kosola train must stay in Lapua'.[58] But on the following day all the communist newspapers were closed illegally by the authorities, and when on 15 June SKP issued clear orders to the party for all-out resistance to the fascists there was no longer any means of publishing it.[59]

Lapua was now in control; a new government was installed under Svinhufvud to pass the necessary anti-communist laws, and when Parliament proved slow to act, Lapua thugs seized two communist members of Parliament, E. Pekkala and J. Rötkö, from an actual sitting of a parliamentary committee and carried them off to Lapua; four days later the whole parliamentary group was arrested.[60] Two days before this the farmers' march had taken place; the Lapuans had paraded in arms through the capital and the government had given them assurances that communism would be finally dealt with. The Finnish bureau had considered whether they should try to resist the farmers' march but decided that it was hopeless. In the far north, at Rovaniemi, the Lapuans started a fire and accused SKP of responsibility—a miniature rehearsal of the Reichstag fire technique—and published spurious SKP leaflets urging terrorism, although SKP had always very firmly set its face against individual terrorism.[61] The party claims that a number of communist youths were tortured into confessing responsibility for the fire.

Since Parliament still hesitated to pass the full programme of anti-communist laws, it was dissolved, and a general election held in September 1930. The Lapua thugs were given a free hand by the authorities to clean up the communists; during the summer of 1930 at least a hundred and fifty individuals were attacked and maltreated, forty-two of them being subsequently dumped over the frontier in Russia. Many more people were intimidated into giving up all political activity.[62] In addition, the legal authorities made numerous arrests of communists, and effectively prevented SKP from contesting the election, so that only a handful of communist electoral lists were presented, for which a mere 11,500 votes were cast. In October the new Parliament quickly passed the required anti-communist laws. These in effect enabled the authorities to imprison any communists they could lay hands on, prevented any legal publication of communist literature or newspapers, broke up any legal organisation which the authorities deemed to be run by communists, and prevented communists from legally contesting parliamentary or local government elections.

The effect on the communist movement in Finland was shattering. Its public activity was totally prevented and its underground work rendered so hazardous as to be largely ineffective. During the years of full-scale repression, from 1930 to 1935, the number of communists convicted of treason or sedition was 350 in 1930, 518 in 1931, 454 in 1932, 558 in 1933, 371 in 1934, and 257 in 1935. If one accepts a figure of around two thousand as the probable maximum total of committed and active members of SKP in Finland at any one time before 1945, one can appreciate how crippling was the damage that was inflicted. Inevitably, this is an area in which precise quantification is impossible; as one SKP memoirist points out, there is no record, outside the reminiscences of individuals and the police files, of such SKP activity as was carried on in Finland in the 1930s.[63] But it seems reasonable to conclude that little purposeful, organised activity took place between 1930 and 1939, after which conditions became even more unfavourable. The so-called Lapua laws of 1930 did their job.

One can illustrate what happened from the demise of SAJ. In September 1930 legal proceedings were begun against SAJ as a criminal organisation, and in due course it was condemned, together with all its member unions, and their assets confiscated. SKP ordered that SAJ should continue to operate as an illegal organisation, and this was attempted.[64] In June 1931 Profintern ruled that the 'Finnish Red Trade Unions' should continue their illegal existence, while at the same time communists would seek to infiltrate and disrupt the legal, SAK unions.[65] It was recognised that so far the red trade union movement was not a mass movement but it was intended that it should be, and it was formally affiliated to Profintern.[66] There were plans for ambitious, wide-scale activity. 'Not a single industrial conflict must slip by the revolutionary trade union movement', all strikes must be spread as widely as possible, and the aim was always 'to raise the fighting spirit of the masses'.[67] But in 1932 it had to be recorded that after nearly a year there was almost nothing achieved, the membership of the red trade unions was smaller than that of SKP itself, and penetration of SAK unions was almost non-existent.[68] In 1933 things were no better; SKP was still talking of the need to develop the red trade unions into mass organisations.[69] Then in 1934 SKP changed to a popular front line, and all workers were urged to join the legal, SAK unions; and the red trade union movement was quietly dropped.[70] It is reasonable to assume that for all practical purposes the red trade union movement had never existed outside the imagination of the SKP leaders in exile; certainly it was never a working organisation, and in this respect it is typical of SKP's various efforts at underground work in the early 1930s.

In the summer of 1930 SKP was at its nadir; it had proved to be one of the greatest paper-tigers of all time—incompetent and impotent. This was not the judgement of its enemies, who had their own reasons for continuing to propagate belief in the communist menace, but of the Comintern itself. In a remarkable intervention of July 1930 the Comintern executive committee ruled that SKP had totally failed to meet the fascist attack and that the Comintern itself would assume the leadership of the Finnish proletariat until SKP had managed to correct its errors.[71] SKP was declared to be in need of intensive self-criticism, because it had not purged itself of legalism and social democratic delusions; in the meantime the Comintern would mobilise the Finnish proletariat in the fight against fascism. This meant above all exposing the social democrats, casting off democratic delusions, and getting the masses into action. The parliamentary election would be the first challenge; the workers must on no account vote for the social democrats, but the communists must run independent lists: 'Talk of returning to bourgeois democracy is mere betrayal, which helps the fascist dictatorship . . . the only way out for the working class is revolutionary activity led by the Communist Party to destroy the fascist dictatorship through proletarian revolution'.[72]

This emergency statement of the Comintern was elaborated in a further analysis in November 1930, which declared that because Finland was a key forward position in the preparations of imperialism for war against the Soviet Union, SKP held 'an especially important guard-post'.[73] It had been caught asleep at this post by the fascist attack, 'it had capitulated, surrendered without any serious attempt to fight', and the leadership of SKP was wholly to blame.[74] It had been so sunk in legalism and opportunist error that it had had no effective underground organisation to rally the workers' resistance; the party had not known exactly who its members were, had misunderstood fascism, neglected its work among young people and women, and failed to expose the social democrats. SKP must totally reconstruct its organisation on the basis of a fundamental self-criticism and achieve a 'real change in all its work'; it could learn useful lessons from the exemplary work of the Polish and German communist parties.[75]

The sheer unfairness and unreality of this criticism is breath-taking, for SKP had come to disaster through a faithful attempt to implement the asinine 'third-phase' policies of the Comintern, and was now being told to persist in these absurdities. As the Comintern analysis shows, it based itself on a supposed mass revolutionary disposition in the Finnish workers, and on supposed imperialist war preparations by the Finnish bourgeoisie, both of which existed only in the imagination of the Comintern theorists. But SKP knew its duty by now, and prepared to obey. In August a party conference was held and the correctness of the Comintern analysis confessed to: SKP was guilty of all the sins ascribed to it.[76]

Fourteen closely printed pages of abject confession conclude that in fact the conduct of SKP 'cannot be characterised in any other way than as a surrender before the
fascist revolution'. The party must now lead 'a mass
struggle of workers and poor farmers, a revolutionary
common front and battle alliance' against the fascists.[77]
They went on to spell out how a new underground network would direct the mass struggle, building up a united
front from below, without for a moment deviating into the
opportunist heresy of a united front from above, for the
unremitting exposing of SDP as the 'left sleeve' of Finnish
capitalism must always have priority. It took some forty
printed pages to analyse all the ramifications of this new
action programme.[78]

In April 1931 a Comintern analysis of fascism shows
that it is still not satisfied with the performance of SKP;
it had not even yet shown the Finnish workers that the
pretended opposition to Lapua by SDP and the liberal
bourgeoisie was a fraud, since many workers had obviously
voted for them in the recent elections. In fact, these
elements, far from opposing fascism, 'by their policies
are actively supporting it', because to differentiate between fascism and bourgeois democracy is wrong: 'Both
are the dictatorship of the big bourgeoisie'. SKP had
still not succeeded in leading the workers and small farmers into active resistance.[79] So the Comintern drivelled
on, and when SKP held its party conference in September
1931 it once more swallowed this criticism and confessed
that the party had not yet overcome its crisis;[80] the
pernicious legalist habits rooted during the 'second phase'
were still exercising their baneful influence.[81] There was
indeed objective reason for dissatisfaction with SKP's performance. In the parliamentary election of September
1930, the local elections in December, and the presidential election of January 1931, SKP had achieved nothing,
though this was hardly its own fault.[82] The combination
of legal repression and Lapua violence meant that SKP
had to try to organise a write-in vote, while deprived
of all means of mass communication. Nobody could have

done very much in these circumstances. But the party should have been able to lead the masses out in strikes and protest demonstrations, and the unemployed in particular should have been aroused. The party had to admit that the call for massive demonstrations by the unemployed on 25 February had been a total failure,[83] as had the attempted May Day processions and sundry other demonstrations. So all that SKP could say in September 1931 was that after a year of effort it was now working along the right lines but that progress was slow.

One of their problems was a hard core of left-deviation, which expressed itself as passivity, or waiting for the revolution; a body of ex-red guards had put out a manifesto saying that only revolutionary activity in underground cells was worth pursuing and that attempts to penetrate public organisations or raise demonstrations was wasted effort. This Leftism was to be a continuing nuisance within SKP, and in 1931 they were blaming poor Eino Rahja for it. SKP had to realise that so far it had only been able to issue proclamations, which the masses had not heeded, and that until there was an effective underground net, able to influence the masses, this state of affairs would continue.[84] SKP knew that it had to remedy this, for if the bourgeoisie finally thrust Finland into war with Soviet Russia, 'the Finnish workers must rise with their whole strength, under the leadership of the Communist Party, in a war against war'. Clearly, SKP was still dreaming dreams; their unreality was embodied in a special statement issued to the rural population calling on them to rise against their exploiters and join hands with the proletariat which would help them. The country people had only to turn their eyes to the Soviet Union to see what an alliance of farmers and workers could achieve, for there, fourteen million farmers had 'voluntarily founded great collective farms'.[85] It is difficult to imagine any example less likely to inspire enthusiasm among Finnish small farmers, even if there had been a word of truth in it.

The year 1932 was another year of quiet frustration

for SKP. In February there should have been an opening, when the reactionary front split in the so-called Mäntsälä revolt, as a result of which the right-wing radicals in the Lapua movement broke away from their conservative, constitutionalist partners, and eventually set up their own, openly fascist opposition movement, the Patriotic People's Movement—IKL.[86] SKP had to admit that all it had been able to do during the crisis was to issue statements.[87] Then in June 1932 a favourite dream of SKP came true: in the village of Nivala a group of bankrupt farmers took arms to prevent the forced sale of their holdings—just what SKP had always urged them to do; yet again the party had to concede that they had had nothing to do with this incident and had been unable to influence it.[88] The most the party could claim for 1932 were a few demonstrations—the best were in Turku to celebrate the anniversary of the Paris commune—and a fairly well-organised distribution of illegal literature. The twelve-page duplicated *Announcer* and various other duplicated newsletters aimed at young people, at the conscripts, and at the women were in fact produced and distributed with fair regularity.[89] The *Announcer* had a circulation of five to six thousand, and in 1933 it was supplemented by a printed four-page paper *The Worker*.[90] On the negative side in 1932 the underground youth movement was penetrated by police spies and almost destroyed in a wave of arrests.[91]

When an enlarged central committee meeting was held in the middle of 1932 it could only repeat that SKP was now working along the correct lines but that progress in extending its influence with the masses was slow. They still stressed the war danger, pointing out that the non-aggression pact recently concluded between Finland and Russia made no real difference, and that the war preparations of the Finnish bourgeoisie were undiminished by it—a theme further developed by Kuusinen before the Comintern in September.[92] The preparation of the workers for their role in an imperialist war was therefore still a principal commitment of SKP. In this task they were still plagued by Leftism, which relied on the illusion 'that the red army of the Soviet Union will liberate the Finnish workers from under the yoke of capitalism, without the revolutionary struggle of the Finnish workers and farmers'.[93] This was a 'dangerous and pernicious idea' that must be fought. The meeting put out another statement on the situation in the countryside which regurgitated the old formulae; SKP was 'the real leader of the revolutionary workers and farmers'.[94] Finally, the party was instructed to take note of Stalin's *Some Questions in the History of Bolshevism*, and in the light of it to revise their own attitudes to the history of SKP.

SKP continued along these same tracks through 1933. Despite suggestions that the party had already begun to adopt a popular-front line, the record shows that this is not so.[95] The enlarged central committee meeting of the summer of 1933 affirmed all the old positions and repeated the same story of slow progress in the right directions. In the parliamentary election of 1933 the workers had been instructed not to vote for the social democrats but to give a write-in vote for well-known communists,[96] yet the response had been so slight as to be undetectable.[97] SDP was still defined as 'the main social support of the Finnish bourgeoisie'[98] and its phoney leftists were the party's 'treacherous device for supporting the fascist dictatorship'.[99] The line on trade union work was virtually unaltered; the red trade unions must be built up into mass organisations. But there was one modification: where there was a large and well-established reformist union, the communists were to work inside that, but only so as to form a revolutionary opposition which would expose the reformist leadership as traitors.[100] Much space was devoted to the youth movement, virtually wiped out by arrests, which would have to be rebuilt, and in the process must avoid past errors, which according to the document included every conceivable kind of deviation and tactical mishandling.[101] One newer theme was the need for SKP to attract the liberal petty bourgeoisie, chiefly in order to counter the growing influence of SDP among these people, who could be persuaded by showing them how happy and secure was the life of their kind in the Soviet Union.[102] This whole document is full of the same depressing note of fantasy; for instance, although Finland was just beginning an economic recovery in 1933, this was affirmed to be illusory, and, objectively, the country's economy was held to have worsened, since the Comintern line required that this should be so.[103] Similarly, in reviewing the international scene, SKP assured the Finnish workers that Hitler was being firmly resisted by the German Communist Party and his position was already weakening.[104]

This arid dogmatism was summed up in a set of theses issued to mark the fifteenth anniversary of SKP. These put the first stress on the danger of imperialist war, and warned the party members against the dangers of bourgeois nationalism: 'In defending the Soviet Union, the Finnish proletariat directly defends its own interests'.[105] Revolution and the dictatorship of the proletariat were the only way forward; there could be no democratic transformation to socialism. The masses must be prepared to meet the new era of world war and revolution, which is imminent, by the exposure of the social democrats, without whose help capitalism could not survive. It must be shown how the supposed resistance of the social democrats to fascism is fraudulent, and how only SKP can lead the masses to create 'a workers' and farmers' republic in Finland'.[106] These theses may stand as the appropriate and enduring monument to the most depressing and futile period of the history of SKP.

It is reported that during the enlarged committee meeting of 1933 there had already been arguments over the need for SKP to adopt a new line. Kuusinen had just brought A. Tuominen, a reliable henchman of his own, to Russia with a view to using him in the internal politics of the party. Tuominen says that Kuusinen was suggesting the need for a more flexible trade union policy, since the red trade unions were manifestly useless, and that Manner and Hanna Malm, and the party secretary, T. Antikainen, clung to a rigid revolutionary line. The ghosts of the 1920 schism were active once more.[1] There is little overt sign of such an argument in the published decisions of the meeting, but it is true that shortly after this, Antikainen lost his place as secretary and was sent on a mission to Finland, Tuominen being installed in his place. Shortly thereafter the new popular front line was promulgated. A factor facilitating its adoption was the emergence inside SDP of a new radical Left, centered round the 'Academic Socialist Society'—ASS—and its periodical, *Soihtu;*[2] thus it was basically a movement of intellectuals. As early as the SDP congress of 1933, ASS had suggested joint action with the communists against fascism, while *Soihtu* began to take an increasingly Marxist line. SKP was at first suspicious of ASS and its leader, M. Ryömä, but during 1934 friendly contacts were developed.

The new party line was analysed and defined by an enlarged central committee meeting in 1934, and it called for careful argumentation since it involved glossing over years of virulent abuse of those to whom cooperation was now being offered. Basically it was claimed that the fascist pressure in Finland was growing in severity, and now extended to some elements of SDP, and that this, together with the growing danger of war, provided a basis for common action between communists and all other progressive-minded people.[3] It was of course no obstacle to SKP that its first assertion was the reverse of the truth; the danger from the fascists was manifestly slackening in Finland in 1934. SKP was ready to meet this imagined situation 'with true bolshevik flexibility and bold popular front tactics to develop a broad common struggle of working people against fascism and war'.[4] It was recognised that this policy would meet with resistance inside SKP itself, where many members had understandably come to look on social democrats as irredeemably wicked; these members must be brought to see that while it was true that SDP was everything that the communists had always said it was, and while the campaign to expose its true nature must be maintained, none the less the abuse and sloganising must stop and the party must reason patiently with social democrats and be prepared to work with them at all levels in a common struggle against fascism.[5] SKP set no harsh conditions for this cooperation, and it was to be a genuine partnership.[6] Bourgeois democracy could now be defended and repressive laws fought even if they mainly concerned social democrats.[7] All workers were urged to join the SAK unions, and this time to do it in good faith, without disruptive intent; but it was stressed that this was purely tactical, 'to gain contacts with the broad masses and strengthen the economic struggle'.[8]

It was fortunate that this change of line was quickly followed by an episode ideally suited for developing contacts with the non-communist Left. In 1934, when Antikainen went into Finland, he was swiftly caught by the security police. Antikainen was particularly hated by the Finnish Right because he had been a successful partisan leader against the Karelian incursions of 1922. So in addition to the usual charge of treason, Antikainen was also charged with the murder of one of his white prisoners

by burning him alive, and there was a loud call for the
death penalty. Antikainen's conviction was a matter of
course, although the evidence was conflicting, but SKP successfully turned the trial into an international incident.
A mass campaign against the death penalty enlisted some
sixty bourgeois intellectuals in Finland, and over one hundred and twenty thousand signatures were collected for a
petition. Antikainen got life imprisonment, but the movement to save his life, headed by Professor V. Lassila,
crystallised during 1935 into the 'Human Rights League',[9]
one of the more successful of SKP's popular front organisations.[10] The saving of Antikainen's life through a major
public agitation was the first big success scored inside
Finland by SKP since 1930; it symbolised a slight turning
of the tide.

During 1935 the new line was ratified and elaborated
by the sixth congress of SKP. The ideological task was
simple, because the congress was held directly after the
seventh and last congress of Comintern, which had defined the popular front for the whole movement. As a
party historian notes, all that the sixth congress had to
do was to apply the Comintern theses to Finnish circumstances.[11] It had been hoped to bring in a strong
delegation from Finland to attend the congress, but in the
debilitated condition of the party inside Finland this
proved impossible and only ten delegates were smuggled
out.[12]

The documents of the sixth congress do not suggest that
the party's powers of objective assessment had improved
very much; the fascist IKL is described as 'one of the
strongest of the Finnish bourgeois parties', when in fact
it was by any standards the weakest,[13] and the ruling
parties were described as in close collusion with IKL just
at the point when they were finally breaking away from
association with it. The party declared that the fight
against fascism called for 'a vigorous common struggle of
the working class and all the other elements opposed to
fascism'.[14] The policy of urging the workers to join SAK
was already a success, the trade union movement was

increasing in size, and as it grew would become more open to the adoption of class-war policies.[15] Communists were warned that while they must keep up their criticism of the reformists, they must be honest and loyal in their membership of SAK, and those party members 'who out of sectarianism still oppose joining the public organisations of SAK, must be thrust aside, until they learn to understand the ABC of mass movements'.[16]

The party emphasised that to recruit the workers was only the first step to the creation of a wider popular front, for there were progressives in all the bourgeois parties who could be enlisted on a basic programme of suppressing the IKL, repealing the anti-communist laws, and pursuing a policy of real friendship with the Soviet Union.[17] In discussing this last point the party soared off into fantasy again, alleging that 'nowadays there is scarcely a country in the world which is so closely involved as Finland is with the fascist governments of Germany and Poland, and also with the imperialists of Japan and Britain, that is, in general with the worst enemies of the Soviets'.[18]

SKP therefore saw itself as shouldering a heavy responsibility to the whole nation in its role as the leader of this broad coalition; this made it especially incumbent on the party members to avoid the sins of right-opportunism and of left-sectarianism: 'The remnants of this sectarianism must be eliminated finally'.[19] The style of the language of party propaganda would also have to change to meet the altered circumstances; the subtleties of Marxist dialectics would have to be left on one side in favour of a language plainly comprehensible to the ordinary man. For instance, the defence of bourgeois democracy could be proclaimed without the usual reservations about the need for a real, proletarian democracy as the ultimate aim of the party, nor was it necessary to split ideological hairs over whether Finland was currently a democracy or not; the party could concentrate on showing that if the fascists won, things would get much worse. However, the party had a duty to combat chauvinism,

by showing how in the Soviet Union democracy, prosperity and national freedom flourished, and how all progressive forces had an interest in defending the Soviet
achievement.[20] Finally, the congress reminded the party
that in spite of the popular front the ultimate objective
of the party was unchanged:[21]

> Salvation from capitalist oppression and fascist slav-
> ery for the Finnish workers lies only in soviet power.
> . . . This soviet power has to be created by fighting
> for it. In smashing the power of fascism and capital-
> ism, the Finnish workers must establish their own
> power, the dictatorship of the proletariat. . . . at
> the head of the Finnish toiling masses, this party
> will conquer and create out of Finland—soviet Fin-
> land.

The means had changed, but not the end; even so, the
sixth congress did confirm the liberation of SKP from the
sterile revolutionary extremism of its 'third-phase' policies,
and directed it along more practicable roads. For a time at
least this seemed to produce favourable results.

The history of SKP activity in Finland in the late 1930s
is the history of its popular front activities, whereas in
the early 1930s it had been the story of the work of the
underground cells, such as it was. There exists a beautiful diagram from the year 1935, showing the structure
of the underground party with all its complex interrela-
tions of cells and committees, from the central committee
in Moscow down to the humblest working group in Finland.[22] It is impossible to believe that this splendid
structure had ever corresponded with reality but after
1935, as popular front activity developed, the underground
that did exist was wound up. One factor may be the
apparent cutoff of Comintern funds in 1937, on which
the underground had been heavily dependent.[23] But it
was in part the logical consequence of the whole popular
front idea; already in 1936 the Finnish bureau of the
party began a planned curtailment of secret activity.[24]

The youth organisation, which held a conference in 1936, decided to dissolve itself and the members were urged to join the social democrat youth organisations.[25] Another major organisational change was to shift the main line of communication with Finland to Stockholm,[26] where the party secretary, Tuominen, transferred himself in 1938,[27] initially it is true to investigate irregularities in the use of party funds but then staying and making Stockholm a significant secondary centre for the *émigré* party. It seems that by 1939, SKP in Finland was in a position similar to that developed in the 1920s, that is its whole effective strength was committed to its popular front organisations and it had no real underground networks to fall back on if the authorities closed these down. Even the underground newspapers were discontinued as more satisfactory channels were created in legal, popular front publications.[28]

The popular front movement in Finland was diffuse, but at its centre stood ASS and its periodical *Soihtu*, through which SKP developed good relations with a whole group of progressive intellectuals, notably the social democrats C. Sundström and M. Ryömä, and the writers J. Pennanen and R. Palmgren. Pennanen ran an important literary periodical, *Kirjallisuuslehti*, which became a major outlet for Marxist views, and which SKP subsidised at times.[29] SKP also made contacts with radical SDP branches and organisations; one of the most important of these was the Helsinki 'Comrades Society', and through these, and with help from bourgeois progressives, they ran a series of action committees, of which the one against the death penalty was the prototype, besides the more permanent bodies like the 'Human Rights League', 'the League of Women for Freedom and Peace'[30] and the 'National Committee against War',[31] which raised over a hundred thousand signatures for a peace petition, ran a series of public meetings, and included, besides Ryömä, Palmgren and Pennanen, the social democrat members of Parliament R. Svento and E. Vala. In these activities SKP made many valuable contacts. Some, like Professor

Lassila, were recruited as active fellow-travellers; the professor was introduced to top figures like Kuusinen and Tuominen during a visit to Moscow in 1936, and indeed Intourist trips won over a number of important sympathisers, like the woman social democrat leader S-K. Kilpi.[32] But numerous other people simply got into the habit of working with communists in these popular front bodies, and suffered with the communists the persecution of the authorities and the SDP establishment; after 1944 many of them found it easy to become involved in the public communist movement.

One of the biggest popular front successes was on the trade union front; it could be coincidental, but it is a fact that once SKP had urged the workers to join the SAK unions, their membership began to rise sharply, from under twenty thousand in 1933 to twenty-seven thousand in 1934 and over forty-four thousand by 1936.[33] The communists in the unions behaved very correctly on the whole, no longer trying to subvert the reformist leadership. SKP issued a statement on the winding up of its underground activity in March 1937, and pointed out that 'the party declared two years ago that it was winding up its fractions inside trade unions and putting an end to all the talk that communists had sinister purposes in the trade union movement'.[34] The party now stood for non-party collaboration in the struggle against capitalism and exploitation. It is probable that the communist strength inside the trade unions was quietly building up, for although the reformist control of SAK was not challenged by the communists down to 1944, once circumstances had changed after the war SKP was very quickly able to make a strong bid for control.

In the 1936 parliamentary elections SKP was able, for the first time since 1929, to take a positive part; bodies like the Human Rights League provided a cover for open electoral activity.[35] SKP issued an election manifesto headed 'Beat the Lapuans in the election! Demand civil rights! Stop the fascist war policy'![36] The manifesto stressed the twin dangers of fascism and war, and warned that 'Finland will not be saved from the war danger by the sort of "neutrality" that Hitler's Finnish hirelings recommend. We can only be saved from the war danger if our people actively participate in the struggle for world peace and collective security against the fascist warmongers'.[37] SKP still stood in domestic affairs for a workers' democracy as the ultimate aim but:

> . . . now the workers have a more pressing problem before them—not the taking of power into the hands of the workers, but the defeat of the danger threatening from fascism and war. . . . SKP is ready to fight for democracy and peace with anyone who honestly wishes to join in the struggle.

Since the anti-communist laws still prevented SKP from running candidates of its own, they urged the voters to support all progressive candidates, irrespective of party, who stood for the same common aims as SKP. The party explained that in the current situation it recognised that it could not rally all the workers on the basis of its own communist policies, so it proposed as the minimum programme the suppression of IKL, repeal of the anti-communist laws, a general raising of living standards and active opposition to the danger of war, and suggested that all progressive forces could rally round this.

It is impossible to know what the electoral effect of SKP's intervention was, but some progressives, like Ryömä and Sundström, may have owed their election to SKP support.[38] The eventual result of this election, followed by the presidential election of early 1937 which ousted Svinhufvud, was the installation of a coalition government of social democrats, agrarians and progressives, which ruled Finland until the outbreak of war. This coalition to some extent reflected the aspirations of SKP; tentative efforts were made to improve relations with the Soviet Union, proceedings were begun (but not completed) for the suppression of IKL, and although the anti-communist laws remained, the police harassment of

SKP fell off. In 1937, convictions of communists for treason or sedition fell to ninety-six, and sank further to fifty-four in 1938 and fifty-five in 1939, as compared with figures of five hundred or more for the peak years of repression. SKP also helped to bring down the reactionary Kivimäki government in 1936 by publishing a memorandum drawn up by the security police, who were alarmed at the proliferation of popular front activities. The report named such a wide range of organisations, which it alleged were penetrated by communists, that it included one to which a government minister belonged, and he resigned in protest. In the ensuing scandal, the chief of the security police had to resign and the whole communist scare campaign received a severe setback.[39]

This did not mean that the communists could work inside the popular front unmolested, for the front organisations were always subject to double attack from the security police and the SDP establishment. The Human Rights League was squeezed out after 1936,[40] and so was the League Against War, which was never able to hold its proposed national conference.[41] The movement to recruit volunteers for Spain, in which SKP and ASS were jointly involved, suffered continuous police obstruction, and the four hundred Finns who eventually went to republican Spain had virtually to be smuggled out of the country.[42] *Soihtu* was subjected to several attempted prosecutions, the best known occurring in September 1937 over an article entitled 'Lighthouses of the Revolution' by Palmgren. This included quotations from Lenin and Stalin, but also from Sidney and Beatrice Webb; among the witnesses called by the defence was Professor Lassila, who defended the right to put the revolutionary case in a free society, and the prosecution failed.[43]

A more serious blow fell in March 1937, when the SDP committee declared that ASS and *Soihtu* were communist dominated, and disaffiliated ASS from the party. Some of its members, like Ryömä, accepted expulsion and stayed with ASS; others, like Sundström, recanted and stayed inside SDP; but the effectiveness of ASS as a cover organisation was seriously reduced.[44] ASS claimed that this measure was a blow against the unity of the workers, and that most SDP members were opposed to it, but when the SDP congress discussed the matter in 1939, the expulsions were confirmed. SKP persevered with its efforts, but there is no doubt that the success of the progressive coalition government, the manifest weakening of the fascists, and the growing economic prosperity in Finland in 1937–9, weakened the forces of protest which were the backbone of SKP strength in Finland. For the 1939 general election SKP put forward what was essentially the same programme as in 1936: first of all the dangers of fascism and war must be beaten, then it would be time to think about how to build socialism.[45] They put out a special statement for the farmers denying that SKP stood for the collectivisation of agriculture and affirming their policy of a worker-farmer coalition.[46] Again, one cannot know what effect the SKP effort had on the election; IKL suffered a severe electoral loss and the ruling coalition was triumphantly confirmed in power. One last popular front initiative which aborted in 1939 was launched by a group of friends of Professor Lassila, who died early in that year. This group, which included Sundström and the prime minister's secretary, discussed the formation of a society to promote cultural relations with the Soviet Union, but action was postponed to the autumn; when it was overtaken by the war crisis.[47]

However, before following the party through the war years, it is necessary to look back at its involvement in the affairs of Russian Karelia. The central figures here were two of the most attractive personalities among the émigré leaders, E. Gylling and K. Rovio, both distinguished as close personal friends of Lenin from the years before 1918. Lenin had written of Gylling: 'He would suit as prime minister for any country whatever'.[48] It was therefore quite natural that Lenin should have put Gylling in charge of Karelia, when in June 1920 the Karelian Workers' Commune was set up. Russian Karelia was then in an unsettled state, threatened by incursions from Finland and deprived of its exiguous native bourgeoisie and intelligentsia because most of them had emigrated. This had created a gap which the Finnish refugees could fill. Gylling had set three conditions for his work, which Lenin had accepted: that his bailiwick should have a Karelian-Finnish ethnic majority; that it should use its own official language; and that it should be allowed to exploit its own natural resources. In the years following, Gylling made two serious mistakes. When the commune was formally established, grateful thanks were sent to Lenin, Trotsky and Zinoviev, but not to Stalin; it is surmised that Stalin did not overlook this omission. Secondly, the incoming Finnish administrators pushed aside the original Karelian and Russian bolsheviks and took over all the leading positions themselves; Gylling became chairman of the commune and Rovio the Communist Party secretary, and they then imposed Finnish as the first official language, on the grounds that Karelian was only a dialect of Finnish. This created in Karelia a discontented group which became a potential anti-Finnish opposition.

The position of the commune was strengthened by the peace treaty, in which Russia promised an autonomous regime for the Karelians. Once Gylling and his comrades had repelled the last incursions from Finland in 1922, they set to work to develop the area. For SKP, the Karelian colony had two important functions: first, it absorbed much emigrant manpower and allowed it to be trained in building socialism, so that in Karelia SKP could develop the skilled cadres who would be needed to build up a soviet Finland when the time came, though it suffered the fate of all colonial areas, that is, it tended to become a dumping ground for the misfits and the failures; the ambitious career-makers stayed near the centre of power in Moscow. Gylling is reported as complaining of SKP policy in this respect that 'they only send people to Karelia who have done wrong, or otherwise failed. They are supposed to be good enough for Karelia and so there is an accumulation of unemployable characters there'.[49] But several very able Finns did make careers there, and in doing so escaped the worst frustrations of life in exile. They were able to develop their own army, while the capital, Petroskoi, became a centre of Finnish language culture and publishing, very valuable for SKP. In brief, SKP had in Karelia a splendid opportunity to develop and practice the skill and techniques of building a socialist society.

Secondly, Karelia was a political asset, for SKP consistently held out the hope that it could eventually be united with a soviet Finland. This was promised explicitly in 1921, and again in 1923,[50] and was a constant theme down to 1944, a kind of dowry offered with SKP to the Finnish people. But it was also put forward as a model, supposed to demonstrate here and now the glorious life which the Finnish people could one day enjoy under an SKP regime, and also as a base from which valuable practical assistance would be forthcoming when the revolutionary struggle began.[51] Indeed, so effective was this propaganda that SKP had trouble with workers in Finland, eager to cross the border and enter into their inheritance at once; for while Karelia was in theory a willing haven for refugees from the horrors of bourgeois Finland, the workers were warned 'the Soviet Union cannot unconditionally take in unknown arrivals', a discrete hint of the less than enthusiastic reception of many would-be immigrants at the hands of Stalinist bureaucrats.[52]

Karelia, under the Gylling regime, was a modest success; economic activity developed satisfactorily in what had been a primitive backwater, cultural life and educational facilities were revolutionised by the Finnish immigrants, and Gylling and Rovio seem to have developed a popular style of government, reasonably free from bureaucracy and based on the genuine cooperation of rulers and ruled. In the fairly unsophisticated setting of Karelia, still basically made up of scattered forest communities, this was possible. It was inevitable that the very success of the enterprise aroused mixed feelings in

Russian official circles, who were stirred up by opposition Karelians and fed with hints of the dangerous growth of Finnish chauvinism. Already in 1923, as a security precaution, the commune was absorbed into a larger unit, the Karelian Autonomous Socialist Republic. Gylling and Rovio remained in control but they now had an ethnic majority of Russians which was steadily increased by deliberate migration. By 1929 the Karelian-Finnish elements were under 40 per cent of the population. The Karelian party newspaper pointed out that this was making the autonomous regime unworkable. It was suggested that the dominantly Russian areas should be detached to restore a balance of population.[53]

But Stalinist policy ran the opposite way; as early as 1930 SKP was recognising that there was a danger of bourgeois nationalism developing in Karelia, and this was a portent of what was to come. In the end, disaster came because Karelia, and SKP with it, got involved at an early stage in Stalin's great purge. As long as Kirov ruled in Leningrad, Gylling's regime was safe, for Kirov looked on it with favour. But after Kirov's murder, Zhdanov took over in Leningrad, and almost at once official allegations of rampant bourgeois nationalism in Karelia were unloosed, until first Rovio, then Gylling, were recalled in disgrace to Moscow. The sixth congress of SKP was obliged to note the unfortunate happenings in Karelia and to denounce Gylling and Rovio for their mistakes.[54] Gylling is said to have uttered some bitter comments at being saddled with responsibility for policies which SKP had unreservedly endorsed at the time.

In Karelia, the terror was let loose in two phases, the first managed by Zhdanov's henchman, Irglis. It was affirmed that:[55]

> Rovio and Gylling forgot the path of proletarian internationalism and the tasks it lays down, and objectively got on to the road of bourgeois nationalism. . . . The weaknesses of the party leadership were then skilfully exploited by the class enemy.

The purge was to eliminate all Finnish elements from leading positions in Karelia; the first stage was completed under Irglis by July 1937, when he was himself purged. One of the early victims, O. Vilmi, made a confession which implicated the whole Gylling regime, and this provided all the necessary material for legal proceedings, if that is an appropriate term for what happened. There were no great show-trials; either the Finns were not important enough or, as has been suggested, they proved temperamentally unsuitable for that kind of performance. The victims were disposed of quietly. After the fall of Irglis in 1937 the purge rose to full fury; Gylling and Rovio were now arrested, and the purge spread to Finnish groups all over the Soviet Union. Gylling was condemned for spying for British intelligence, and it is seriously estimated that in the end some twenty thousand Finns were sent to labour camps, where many died, while a few, very tenacious of life, survived, to be released in the 1950s, including it is said Gylling himself. The whole SKP achievement in Karelia was wiped out, the army destroyed, the school system violently russified, the use of the Finnish language virtually forbidden there. Although there was to be a brief wartime revival of the Karelian-Finnish republic, it was a purely limited political manoeuvre; the great creative work of Gylling and SKP was extinguished.

Among the very earliest victims of the Stalin purge were K. Manner and his close associates, including Kuusinen's brother-in-law. This group of fifteen prominent SKP figures was accused of espionage early in 1935. Specifically they were supposed to have betrayed Antikainen to the Finnish police. It is not clear who or what precipitated this prelude to the great purge in SKP. Kuusinen did nothing to stop it, and may not have been sorry to see Manner go—he perished in prison along with his wife Hanna Malm. By 1937, of all the leading *émigré* figures in Russia only Kuusinen survived. Sirola was probably lucky to have died naturally in March 1936; he remained untainted and got a solemn state funeral. Sirola had been almost entirely

employed in training cadres at the Lenin school and is
said to have felt personally responsible as so many of his
colleagues and former pupils fell to the rising purge,[56]
so that this hastened his death.

There remains the interesting problem of why Kuusinen
survived. He was reported to have been in serious danger
when Gylling was arrested in 1937, and to have been
saved at the last moment by Stalin's personal intervention.[57] This seems plausible, since Kuusinen was certainly as 'guilty' as any of the others but had distinguished
himself by many personal services to Stalin. All through
the later 1920s Kuusinen had specialised as a theoretician
closely attached to Stalin; as each of Stalin's victims fell—
Trotsky, Zinoviev, Bucharin—Kuusinen was at hand to
supply a correct Marxist explanation. Tuominen describes
him as fanatically careful, never letting slip any careless
opinion of his own, putting nothing on paper that he
had not first cleared with Stalin, above all never lifting
a finger to try to save any of Stalin's victims, however close
they may once have been to Kuusinen. It is surmised
that a combination of high technical skill and absolute
obedience and reliability, combined with a growing talent
for divining the directions in which Stalin's mind was
working, helped Kuusinen to survive every purge, to survive Stalin himself and die in his bed as an honoured
elder statesman of the Soviet Union.

It is with a sense almost of comic relief that one turns
from the horrors of this massive slaughter of the innocents—because the victims were truly innocent of the
fantastic charges levied against them, they suffered imprisonment and death for no reason at all beyond the
blind workings of Stalin's paranoia—to the crimes that
really had been committed. In 1937 Dimitrov, in his
capacity as Comintern secretary, presented Tuominen as
secretary of SKP with a document, drafted by A. Liedes,
which charged almost every member of the central committee of SKP with gross irregularities in their private
lives, and in the cases of A. Hyvönen, I. Lehtinen and

Y. Enne, then in charge of SKP affairs in Stockholm, with grave misuse of party funds. Dimitrov is reported to have said after reading this indictment, 'I would not have believed that any party leadership could have been so degenerate'. The charges, which involved Kuusinen as well, had some substance, for as might be expected few of the *émigrés* had led impeccable private lives by normal bourgeois standards. An enquiry had to be made, and during it some of the accused are said to have sought safety in accusing others of political deviation. When the dust settled, only one of the accused, A. Hyvönen, was regarded as so compromised that he was put off the central committee, but other key members, like J. Lehto-saari and H. Mäkinen, got sucked into the affair and disappeared into the camps.[58] So when the war opened a new phase in the history of SKP it was only a pale shadow of what it had once been; and who knows how many of those who survived the 1940s to take over the leadership after 1944 did so because during the killing years 1935–9 they were living safely under the white terror of the Finnish bourgeoisie or languishing in its prisons. Had they been living in Stalin's socialist fatherland they might not have been so lucky.

The German-Soviet Pact of August 1939 put Finland in the Russian sphere of influence, and in October Russia proceeded to consolidate her position, first in the Baltic republics and then in Finland itself. The Finnish government was asked to agree to frontier adjustments near Leningrad, and to lease a naval base at Hanko on the gulf of Finland. But instead of submitting, like the Baltic republics, the Finnish government refused to make any substantial concessions and mobilised its army. On the home front, on the basis of emergency regulations, it rounded up most of the active members of SKP and put them into preventive detention, thus effectively paralysing SKP in Finland.[59] A communist commentator remarks that 'there is not much to be said about party activity in wartime', and another remarks that 'the conditions of unbridled terror did not give the Communist Party the possibility of raising the broad masses to struggle against the war'.[60] Thus one major factor in the situation in Finland was that SKP ceased to function before the crisis was properly begun. Its press outlets were closed, the September issue of *Soihtu* which called for a new approach to relations with the Soviet Union was confiscated and the paper closed down, together with the other popular front publications like *Kirjallisuuslehti*.[61] Individual communist leaders, like Y. Leino and Kuusinen's daughter Hertta, who escaped the preventive detention net did so by going into hiding on a remote farm, thus putting themselves out of action just as effectively.[62] The party concedes that 'it is not to be denied that these repressive measures achieved their purpose in that situation'.[63]

The negotiations which preceded the outbreak of war between Finland and Russia on 30 November 1939 show that Stalin and Molotov were baffled by the Finnish resistance, that it was quite unexpected; consequently there is reason to assume that they had not made any very specific plans in advance to overcome something on which they had not reckoned. Certainly one can accept that SKP played no positive role; the party says that 'in the outbreak of the winter war SKP could not influence one side or the other',[64] and for the very good reason, to adopt Stalin's reputed scale of values, that in 1939 SKP had no divisions—it was a nullity in the power game.

What exactly happened next is obscure, but the circumstantial evidence suggests that when the negotiations became deadlocked in mid-November, leaving Stalin without a policy, one faction in the Soviet Union, probably led by Zhdanov and the Leningrad party, supported by the military leadership, persuaded Stalin that Finland could easily be taken over, because as soon as fighting began the Finnish workers would rise up against the bourgeois regime and welcome the red army as liberators. To facilitate this process, a workers' government was to be set up by the leaders of SKP, which would act as the focus for the uprising and would also provide the legal pretext for the intervention; the world was to be told that the Finnish situation was really one of civil war in which a desperate white government had provoked Russian intervention and caused the red army to come to the help of the embattled Finnish workers. This fairy tale was the Russian scenario for the war, and if the expected swift military success had followed, no doubt it would have served well enough.

But this plan suffered from being an improvisation; in the second half of November it was hastily botched up and ran into an unexpected snag. The SKP secretary, Tuominen, then in Stockholm, was to be chairman of the government, but Tuominen, once he was safely abroad, had been shaken by his reflections on the great purges which he had so luckily escaped, and had developed strong doubts about the policies of SKP. T. Karvonen describes how he met Tuominen in 1938 on party business in Stockholm, and had been disturbed then by Tuominen's inclination to question the party line.[65] The last straw for Tuominen was the Nazi-Soviet Pact, and when he got orders to return to Russia in November to take up his new role, he refused, broke with the party and during the war issued calls to the workers to rally to the defence of national independence; since when Tuominen has joined men like Tanner and Wälläri in the lowest rank of SKP's hierarchy of traitors and renegades.[66] Despite this setback, the plan went forward; when the Russian invasion of Finland began it was announced that a Finnish People's government, sitting just inside Finnish territory at the frontier town of Terijoki, had been set up to meet the wishes of the working people of Finland, and had asked the red army to help it to suppress the white fascist clique that purported to be the government of Finland. In the absence of Tuominen, Kuusinen himself had to be chairman; the obscurity of the other ministers—M. Rosenberg, A. Anttila, T. Lehen, A. Äikiä,

I. Lehtinen and P. Prokkanen—reflects the results of the great purge; they were all that was left.[67] This government of the new Finnish People's republic then solemnly entered into a mutual assistance pact with the Soviet Union, conceding what had been asked of the bourgeois government in the negotiations, and in return redeeming the old pledge of SKP that Russia would give the bulk of Karelia to a truly democratic Finland; most of Russian Karelia was ceded to the new republic as a token of goodwill.

The People's government put out a programme in the name of SKP. They started from the assumption that the bourgeois regime, egged on by foreign imperialism, had started the war and thus presented the working people with a chance to destroy it.[68] It is worth noting that Y. Leino, who later broke with SKP, says he really believed in 1939 that it was Finland which had begun the war, and this is still what SKP says in effect. They say that the war was the logical outcome of the anti-Soviet policies of the bourgeois regime, pursued consistently since 1918, and therefore 'SKP's central committee could not do anything other than to take a negative attitude to the war'.[69] The People's government is therefore presented as an honest effort by SKP to save the Finnish people from the probably disastrous outcome of the policies of the bourgeois government. Their programme is interesting on two grounds: first, it stresses Finland's independence, declares that the Soviet Union desires to preserve this and always has, and emphasises that because of its present structure Finland is in any case ineligible to join the Soviet Union: 'The Finnish democratic republic, which is in its political structure quite different from a Soviet state', could not be part of a federation of Soviet republics.[70] The Finnish People's government was in any case only provisional:

> Some comrades may think that we should demand the establishment of a soviet state in Finland: they are mistaken. Such an important proposal as to change fundamentally the whole social structure

cannot be decided by one party, not even by the working class alone. Only the whole nation, all the productive classes, can decide this question.

Therefore the People's government put forward as a basis of discussion a democratic constitution with the overthrow of all fascist institutions, a people's army, some nationalisation of industry, educational and social reforms, land distribution, and state aid for the small farmer and the rural poor. This programme was a continuation of the moderate popular-front line pursued by SKP since 1934. It is true that there are a lot of unanswered questions about the Finnish People's government, partly because neither SKP nor the Soviet Union is at all keen to perpetuate the memory of such a dismal fiasco—indeed in the official Soviet history of the war, Kuusinen's government has vanished into the limbo of un-facts. So it is unclear whether this body ever functioned as a government, how far it had developed any positive plans for taking over the administration of Finland, where it expected to find the necessary internal support, or how it conceived its long-term relationship with the Soviet Union. There is no reason to doubt the honesty of its public professions on this point in those circumstances; Stalinist caution in foreign policy is a well documented fact, as is his fundamental disinterest in promoting revolution, provided Russian interests could be secured by other means. The Finnish People's government would have given Stalin all he wanted at that stage on its stated programme. But the subsequent fates of the Baltic republics and Czechoslovakia leave it legitimate to doubt whether the moderation proclaimed by SKP would long have survived when circumstances changed.

The one thing the People's government did do was to create the nucleus of a people's army; Finnish-speaking remnants in the Soviet Union were actually conscripted and put into distinctive uniforms, not as a fighting force in the war but as the basis for a security force in Finland once the new regime had been installed. Otherwise the activity of the government, beyond the issue of propaganda, is obscure. By the beginning of 1940 the Russian leaders realised that they had made a dreadful mistake, that the People's government evoked no response in Finland and was a burden to them, a positive obstacle to winding up the war. So the Soviet Union entered into negotiations with the real government of Finland and peace was concluded with it on 13 March 1940. The People's government, not without a certain dignity, announced that it would not stand in the way of ending the bloodshed, and formally disbanded.

It might be expected that so total and humiliating a fiasco would have profound repercussions on the fortunes of communism in Finland, but in fact it had so few that it might never have happened. It may have affected the fate of Kuusinen himself; there is some evidence that Zhdanov felt that he had been compromised and let down by SKP, and that after 1940 he had no use for Kuusinen. This is held to be one basic reason why Kuusinen could not return to Finland after 1944 to lead the resurrected communist movement, as would have been natural. But Kuusinen's brief chairmanship of the People's government also meant that official Finland would not willingly have him back; suggestions that Kuusinen be given a visa to visit Finland in the 1950s were rejected by Finnish governments, though his surviving colleagues were allowed back without fuss. Otherwise the People's government made no difference to the attitudes of non-communist Finland, since it merely provided dramatic proof of what they had always alleged, that SKP were traitors and tools of Russian imperialism. But one might have expected to find some nationalist revulsion against SKP among those who were normally tolerant of communism. There is a problem of evidence here; it is not known what left-wing Finns thought about the Kuusinen government at the time, since during the war the government rigorously suppressed all dissenting opinion in Finland. Dissenting opinion hostile to the war did exist—there is scattered evidence of some anti-war strikes and demonstrations, and a few opposition leaflets were circulated—but how large a body of opinion this represented one cannot say.[71] The events of the period after March 1940 suggest that it was by no means insignificant in size. It seems reasonable to assume that the People's government really had no effect at all on the pro-communist Finns, because it had no contact with them; there had never been any links, other than broadcast propaganda, between the Kuusinen government and the communists inside Finland.[72] It had therefore remained an alien phenomenon to them, an event in a vacuum, which the basic mass of radical opinion in Finland simply ignored as having nothing to do with them. The communist movement was to remain the only organised channel through which such people could express their dissent from established policy, and for this reason it retained their support.

The one well-documented protest movement of the winter war probably had nothing to do with SKP at all. In December 1939, M. Ryömä wrote an open letter to Tanner, then the foreign minister, protesting against the war and asserting that the workers were opposed to it: 'The Finnish working class goes to the front against its will, it goes under compulsion, and hopes for peace and friendly relations with the Soviet Union'.[73] For this act of defiance Ryömä was arrested and held in preventive detention, but he stoutly denied under interrogation that he had had any dealings with SKP or with the Kuusinen government.[74] It seems reasonable to accept that this was a desperate personal initiative by a sensitive and overburdened man, and that SKP in its then circumstances would have had no means of exploiting Ryömä's action even if it had been involved. Whether Ryömä was right about the feelings of the workers we cannot know, for as he pointed out in his letter, there was no legal way in which they could have expressed their dissent, if indeed they really felt it.

After the peace treaty of March 1940, SKP in exile was quickly found a new role; already on 31 March the areas newly annexed from Finland were attached to Russian Karelia, to form a new member of the Soviet Union, the Karelian-Finnish Soviet Socialist Republic. Zhdanov, in presenting the new member of the union, stressed that it was meant to develop closer ties with the Finnish people, which to some people might sound sinister. Certainly the new state was virtually put in the nominal charge of SKP; it became, particularly through its broadcasting services in the Finnish language, the main channel for putting over the Russian point of view to people in Finland, and the running of it was the last major task of SKP in exile. The tone of its propaganda strongly suggests that the Karelian-Finnish republic was being held in reserve as a possible basis on which to construct a Russian-dominated Finland if the opportunity for this should ever arise; in effect, it served to keep the Kuusinen government on ice in case it should ever be needed again. But it lost even this vestigial function after 1944, and though its formal existence continued for some years after that, it was eventually quietly wound up and reabsorbed into the Russian federal republic. Kuusinen became the prime minister of the republic and was said to have been very unhappy in his job, for he had Zhdanov, in Leningrad, as his immediate and unfriendly superior. After June 1941 most of the territory of his republic fell under enemy occupation and always he longed to get back to his natural activity, the pursuit of theoretical work in Moscow.[75]

During the brief interval of peace, from March 1940 to June 1941, SKP in Russia did not succeed in establishing any effective links with its sympathisers in Finland. The wartime emergency regulations gave the authorities such sweeping powers over every aspect of national life that the frontiers were effectively sealed off, the post was censored, and even the link through Stockholm was no longer safe. The only direct line open was through the Russian embassy in Helsinki, and not much use could be made of this—the comings and goings at the embassy and the movements of its staff were closely scrutinised by the security police, and no doubt the embassy had more important things to do than act as postman for SKP. Kuusinen and his colleagues had been shunted into their Karelian backwater after their lugubrious failure in the winter war, and there is not much sign that Stalin any longer took them very seriously. One service the Russian government did do for SKP was to secure the release of two leading SKP members from Finnish prisons; T. Antikainen and A. Taimi were returned to the Soviet Union at Russian request, and their experience and ability were a valuable addition to the now somewhat mediocre talents left at the disposal of SKP after the great purges. Taimi was an old man by 1940, but Antikainen would probably have had an important part to play in the history of SKP after 1944, and might well have emerged as its leader in Finland, had he not been killed in a plane accident.

The question of the ultimate direction of Russian policy towards Finland after March 1940 is still one that is hotly debated. On the one extreme is the view that the Soviet Union continued to plan for a takeover of Finland along the same lines as occurred in the Baltic republics, and intended to use the Finnish communist movement as a means to this end. On the other extreme is the SKP view that the Soviet Union had no other intention but to live in peace with Finland on the basis of the treaty, fully respecting her sovereignty and independence. A reasonable interim view, while the archives of the Soviet Union remain shut, is that Stalin, a cautious and consistent man, intended to keep what was due to him by the Nazi-Soviet Pact, that is to keep Finland firmly within a Russian sphere of influence by excluding the influence of all other powers. This would guarantee that even a bourgeois government in Finland, totally isolated and struggling with the formidable consequences of a lost war, would be amenable to Russian pressures. This system worked well enough down to August 1940, after which the German government began to show a sympathetic interest in Finland. Up to then Russian pressures had forced the Finnish government to yield without much difficulty, and there had certainly been no need to call in the very doubtful assistance of SKP. By the autumn of 1940, when it became clear to the Soviet leaders that Finland was no longer responding to pressure, they contemplated sterner action. What exactly this would have involved was never revealed, but Molotov went to Berlin in November 1940 to demand from Hitler a free hand to reassert Russian influence over Finland; it may be he had in mind the enforcement on Finland of a pro-Russian government of a popular front type led by SKP, but this is pure speculation. Hitler vetoed any further proceedings against Finland, and although the Soviet Union continued for a little while longer to try to bluff the Finnish government into submission, it had no success.

An objective consideration of the situation, based on this hypothesis about Russian policy, suggests that Finnish communism would have played a very marginal role in Soviet policy-making. The party in exile had been proved useless, and it was questionable whether the movement inside Finland could be a viable political force in the prevailing circumstances; the record of events suggests that it was not. It will therefore be assumed that there never existed any Russian master plan to which the behaviour of the communists in Finland conformed, but that their behaviour was spontaneously generated by the circumstances prevailing in Finland. When the war ended, the Finnish authorities began to release most of the hundreds of preventive detainees, including many communists. During their months of confinement, these people had been able to discuss what forms of political activity would be appropriate after the war, and a group centered on M. Ryömä had felt that some organisation dedicated to promoting Finnish-Soviet friendship would meet the most urgent need; for in their eyes the war had highlighted the need to promote a new atmosphere in this field.[76] As soon as Ryömä was released he set to work, and in May 1940 had a group of twelve, of whom five were communists, the others mostly popular fronters with ASS connections, preparing a project.[77] On 22 May a formal meeting was held which launched the 'Finland-

Soviet Union Peace and Friendship Society'—generally known as SNS—on a constitution drafted by Ryömä.[78] It was to be a national organisation, dedicated to educational and cultural purposes and aimed at promoting understanding between the two countries.

Ryömä started this organisation in good faith; it was not manufactured by SKP or the Russian embassy. Further, it was soon able to demonstrate that it met a genuine public demand; meetings in Helsinki and the provinces were packed out, and in only five months SNS had recruited some thirty-five thousand paying members in one hundred and fifteen local branches, in the face of every kind of official obstruction.[79] SKP rightly claims that this shows the existence in Finland of a substantial body of opinion which welcomed friendly relations with the Soviet Union.[80] They go on to remark bitterly that 'this mass movement was so dangerous a reply to the official lies about the Finnish people's unanimous hatred of the Soviet Union' that it had to be suppressed. The authorities took a jaundiced view of SNS from the start; it had been planned to resume the publication of Soihtu as the journal of the movement, with an edition devoted to very favourable descriptions of conditions in the Soviet Union, but the government censors held up publication until July, and then heavily mutilated the proposed articles.[81] And although SNS applied for legal registration on 29 May, the authorities held up an official reply until 19 August while they looked around for some legal pretext for refusing it; then they set two conditions for registration, that young persons, and persons with criminal convictions, should be excluded from membership.[82] Superficially these conditions look innocent enough, but they were justifiably refused by the leaders of SNS as intended to wreck the movement. For they would have excluded from participation in the society a very large number of active radicals, since most of such people had some kind of conviction for political offences, and in so far as SNS existed to promote new attitudes towards the Soviet Union the young were obviously one of its best hopes of success. So for a time sns remained in a legal limbo, neither registered nor banned.

But to do justice to the Finnish government, sns had from a very early stage become politically committed, and had gravely compromised its claim to be purely cultural and educational in character. For one thing, the vice-chairman, D. Vilenius, was a dedicated communist with a long record in the party, and other known communists were active at all levels of sns activity. On the other hand, this was entirely natural—one would hardly expect communists not to support such an organisation, and skp can and does claim that sns was not just a communist front; it was always much more than that, but it was also the only public activity in which communists could take part and inevitably they tended to move into positions of influence and guide the way it developed. Another factor that seems to have worried the authorities was the interest which the Russian embassy took in sns, though it has yet to be demonstrated that this interest went beyond the bounds of diplomatic propriety. The sns leaders visited the embassy in May, there was a press conference at the embassy for the Soviet press in June, and another visit by sns leaders to the embassy on 19 June.[83] In addition, embassy officials were present at some sns functions, and late in July the Russian ambassador made a tour of sns provincial branches and met local officials.[84] In addition, the Soviet press and radio showed a keen interest in sns, and in a speech to the Supreme Soviet on 1 August, Molotov said bluntly that the repressive attitude of the Finnish authorities towards sns was damaging Finnish-Russian relations.[85]

In ordinary circumstances it would be entirely right and proper for a foreign embassy to show interest in the proceedings of a relevant friendship society; it is, of course, done all the time. If sns had been only what it professed to be—an educational and cultural body—no exception could have been taken to the interest displayed by the official organs of the Russian state. But by June 1940, sns had made some explicitly political gestures, which made embassy participation in its proceedings of questionable propriety. Whether in fact, as sns always maintained, contacts with the embassy were entirely innocent or whether it did in reality take political instructions from the embassy cannot yet be determined. But it strains credulity to believe that the embassy made no attempt to suggest political lines that sns might follow, or that the sns leaders would have felt any scruples in acting on such advice. After all, the society was dedicated to the proposition that the policies of the Soviet Union were designed to promote peace and the best interests of all nations.

sns began to circulate overtly political material after only a few weeks of its existence; a circular condemned the winter war as 'unnecessary, senseless, unfortunate, and criminal'[86] sns officially welcomed the events in Estonia which led to a Russian takeover, and some members said openly that this was an example for Finland to follow; finally sns issued and published a letter to the speaker of Parliament, on 26 June 1940. This declared that:[87]

> Instead of the government working to get relations between Finland and the Soviet Union on a confidential and friendly basis, it tries on the contrary to obstruct developments which are in the vital interests of our people . . . they try to prevent the open expression of that broad public opinion which supports the friendly relations of these countries. . . . For these reasons, the society regards the present government as unwilling and unable to manage the relations of Finland and the Soviet Union in the way demanded by the interests of the Finnish people.

The government met this challenge by the arrest of Ryömä and Vilenius, and the sns replied with a series of meetings and demonstrations, some of which led to public disorders, and in two cases to the police opening

fire. Whether these were cases of deliberate provocation
by one side or the other is now keenly contested, but it
seems irrelevant, since it takes two sides to make a riot.
What was important was that SNS and the government
measured their strength, and the government won. By
the end of August the SNS leaders were again at the
embassy and, it is said, were reproached for their failure
to get real mass support on the streets.[88]

In September the government began to consolidate its
victory. The matter of SNS registration was referred to
the courts, and a new wave of arrests took twenty-seven
SNS leaders into preventive detention, including both the
national organisers.[89] On 2 September, SNS had managed, in the face of formidable difficulties, to publish its
first printed newspaper, *Kansan Sanomat*,[90] the thirty-
five thousand copies of which were sold out at once. The
second issue was confiscated by the police, the third met
a similar fate, and the paper was then officially banned.
What seems to have given most offence were the unfavourable comparisons consistently drawn in the paper
between conditions in Finland and the supposedly superior conditions prevailing in the Soviet Union—this was
indeed a constant theme of SNS propaganda.[91] Local
SNS branches managed to publish newspapers locally. One
such Helsinki paper was still coming out in December
1940 but the attempt to start a national press for the
movement had been strangled at birth.

Still in an ambiguous legal position, SNS held a national congress from 25 to 27 October, which defiantly
elected the imprisoned Ryömä chairman and made extensive plans for future activities. Stress was put on the
need to establish new branches and to get all the nominal
members fully active: 'There is enough work for everybody who really wants to advance the Finnish workers'
movement'. The ultimately political character of SNS
showed through in this phrase, although they claimed to
enlist the progressive bourgeoisie as well.[92] But the days
of SNS as a legal organisation were numbered: on 23
December the courts declared that SNS was an illegal

organisation, and on 31 December the committee sent out a circular to the branches to disband.[93] A defiant statement on the government's actions said that 'the decision is a new demonstration of the crude attacks of the bourgeoisie and its government on the interests of peace and democracy. In addition it is also a new demonstration of hostility towards our great neighbour, the Soviet Union'. They promised that in spite of everything the work would continue.[94]

From this point on the evidence becomes very dim, since the former SNS branches which did not break up went underground. A petition for the release of political prisoners was circulated early in 1941, and even in August a circular attacking the war came out in the name of SNS,[95] but so far as systematic work was carried on into 1941 it seems to have focused on agitation among conscripts against a renewal of war, and attempts to organise for resistance through mass refusals of call-up. A number of associations of working-class servicemen were developed in connection with SNS branches, and as early as September 1940 they had had their own central coordinating committee.[96] Their work, though obscure, bore some fruit, for in the new war, which began in June 1941, there was a significant amount of refusal of call-up and of desertion, which had some degree of organisation behind it.

But in spite of this it is clear that the brief renaissance of communist activity in Finland had been smashed by the authorities by the beginning of 1941. With the destruction of SNS the party in Finland had lost the possibility of large-scale coordinated action, and being cut off from any effective outside support or guidance the movement disintegrated into a scattering of uncoordinated underground cells. The story of SNS seems to confirm that there was built in to Finnish society after 1918 a permanent opposition to the established order, which would express itself whenever organisational opportunities for doing so existed. The communists, even when they were isolated and lacked any clear central direction,

were able, as the only movement uncompromisingly dedicated to fighting the establishment, naturally and without effort to assume the leadership of such organisations.
No matter how often or with what superficial success
bourgeois Finland destroyed the communist's organisation, as soon as the pressure relaxed even slightly it
sprang to life again with undiminished vigour.

When Finland joined in Hitler's attack on Russia in
June 1941, the resulting war was obviously different in
character from the winter war. Although official Finland
cultivated the myth of a separate Finnish-Russian war,
the outcome of the conflict was entirely dependent on
the result of the world war. So this time SKP could
plausibly claim to be a part of the great international
crusade against fascism and for democracy, and on this
basis expect to win support inside Finland even from
non-communist elements. SKP itself is in two minds
about its performance after 1941; it is naturally proud
that it alone, under incredibly adverse circumstances, has
a record of consistent, active resistance to the disastrous
war.[97] But they also have to concede a degree of failure,
because theoretically it should have been possible for
SKP to lead a movement of mass resistance to fascism,
as in occupied Europe, and it could not fulfil this historic duty: 'The movement of resistance in Finland did
not acquire the character of a mass, armed partisan war,
as in other countries occupied by the fascists'.[98] This
self-criticism is sometimes almost abject: 'There is not
much to be said about party activity in wartime . . .
one must speak the truth, that our party at that time
was not able to carry out the tasks set it by history'.[99]

The basic factor in the situation was that almost the
entire active membership of the party was in prison or
under preventive detention. The only two leading figures
who managed to escape the police and give some kind
of central direction were Y. Leino, who escaped in September 1941 and organised some underground activities
right through to the end of the war, and E. Hietanen,
who worked among army deserters as a partisan.[100] The

party line on the war was laid down by T. Antikainen, in a speech over the radio on 8 July 1941. He said that the Finnish government had deliberately allied itself with Hitler in a war of aggression, and they would be defeated. The Soviet Union 'does not want to fight the Finnish people . . . the Soviet Union does not want to threaten Finland's independence or sovereignty . . . the Soviet Union does not wish to intervene in Finland's internal affairs'. This line was elaborated in a statement circulated by SKP in September 1941:[101]

> The present war was not a war of defence on Finland's part . . . but a ruthless war of plunder against the Soviet Union and the whole world . . . the democratic front is fighting for those values which are important for the happiness and the future of small nations, peace and the freedom and independence of nations. . . . Our only salvation from the threatening catastrophe that is before us is to get a quick peace. . . . Hostilities with the Soviet Union must be ended and the German troops driven out of the country.

SKP activity inside Finland was of two kinds: first, they managed to produce and circulate a fair quantity of propaganda, leaflets and underground newspapers, much of this was Leino's work, though he does not claim any great successes for it.[102] Some anti-war strikes and meetings were held, and in 1944, for example, the city of Turku was placarded with calls to end the war. The total effect of all this is anyone's guess; the party claims that it 'made possible the formation of an anti-war opposition in Finland and prepared the ground for the change which was accomplished at the end of the war'.[103] It agrees that this movement was 'broken up, for the greater part unorganised, and without purposeful political direction', but claims that in the circumstances of terror and repression it was a respectable achievement: this seems a reasonably fair assessment.

But the really heroic and spectacular work was the effort to organise mutiny and sabotage, and stir up armed resistance to the war. SKP propaganda constantly urged this; the underground paper *Socialist Herald*, in June 1942 calls on the soldiers to leave the front, workers to go on strike, farmers to withhold deliveries to the authorities, men on leave to go absent, deserters to start up a partisan war. The success achieved was not inconsiderable—it is alleged the numbers who deserted or refused to enlist rose as high as thirty thousand; certainly it ran into many thousands, and some of these were organised into armed bands which carried out attacks on the police or the German troops and committed acts of sabotage.[104] Some of these deserters were conscientious objectors, and some were purely self-interested draft-dodgers, but in so far as this 'forest guard' had any consistent organisation or purpose it was the result of communist activity.[105] The solid reality of this work is attested by the roll of the martyrs; SKP counts twenty members executed for opposition to the war, after trial by court martial, including some women. Most of them went to their deaths with exemplary courage, shouting or singing their defiance of the class enemy in the face of the firing squads, as the police records testify. There were certainly others disposed of summarily for acts of mutiny in the immediate vicinity of the front line. SKP has every right to take pride in its martyrs, all of them genuine volunteers for their cause, and all ready to sacrifice their lives to it. They are SKP's enduring monument to its campaign of active resistance to the war.

The pace of resistance naturally began to pick up after Stalingrad, as realisation that the war was lost spread to all levels in Finland. For the first time, with the emergence in the ranks of the social democrats and the trade unions of a 'peace opposition', the possibility of a broad popular front opened up. SKP statements about its share in the growing legal opposition to the war in 1943–4 are ambiguous. One party historian speaks of 'the peace movement which was active among the workers and other groups of the people, which the Finnish Communist Party led', and claims that the social democrat opposition 'came to act in the government and Parliament as the interpreter of the wish for peace raised by SKP'.[106] But another declares that 'the peace opposition was not in close touch with the broad masses who opposed the war', but unlike them was defeatist, thinking in terms of forming a government in exile in Sweden rather than forcing their own government to make peace.[107] The truth is that the emergence of an opposition to the war in the social democrat movement was inevitable as soon as it was clear that the war was going badly, and the communists, because of their anti-war record and their connections with the Soviet Union, naturally became involved with it. And it may well be that the change of attitude in SAK and its chairman Vuori in 1943 reflects the result of communist agitation among the members of SAK unions against the war.

But it is necessary to keep this movement in perspective; the decision to make peace with the Soviet Union owed nothing to the efforts of SKP, however heroic, and everything to the defeats inflicted on the Finnish army in the battles of June 1944. When Germany had demonstrated her inability to remedy the situation, the Finnish leaders installed the commander-in-chief, Mannerheim, as president, and concluded an interim peace settlement with Russia in September 1944. One of the clauses of this interim peace required the release of political prisoners and the abolition of restrictions on the freedom of democratic organisations, which opened the way for SKP to begin a new phase in its history as a legal public movement in Finland.

Looking back over the twenty-five years of relentless struggle between SKP and the legal government of Finland, one has to recognise that in the end SKP won. It had been superficially wiped out more than once, but each time after a brief interval the movement had sprung to life again, showing that the roots from which it came had not been eradicated. In the course of the battle at least 4,412 communists had been convicted of treason or sedition down to 1942, some five thousand different organisations had been legally suppressed between 1922 and 1934, thousands of people had suffered fines or short sentences for lesser offences, particularly offences against the press laws, and then there were the wartime victims.[108] Yet by the standards of the twentieth century it had been a humane struggle; certainly the security police had often mistreated those in their custody, as had prison officials on occasion, while during the war the conditions in the preventive detention camps, particularly the remote camp at Sääsmäjärvi, had often been deplorable, and during the period of the Lapua terror the authorities had done nothing to protect communists from the attentions of fascist hooligans. But by comparison with what happened in the concentration camps of occupied Europe, or Stalin's labour camps, conditions for political prisoners in Finland had been very mild and the loss of life over a twenty-five-year period very small. Apart from the wartime executions only a handful died in custody under dubious circumstances, and communist allusions to official plans to kill off their prisoners by ill treatment fail to carry conviction because the figures show such a low rate of fatalities. This brings us back to the final irony, that the real killer of Finnish communists was Stalin; beside his efforts those of the Finnish bourgeoisie pale into insignificance. In 1944, precisely because they had been secure and protected in Finnish prisons and camps, there was a body of communist leaders alive and in a position to take up the new tasks.

# 6. THE FIRST PHASE OF THE LEGAL COMMUNIST MOVEMENT, 1944-5

The imprisoned communists were being released in September and October of 1944, and they joined their comrades who emerged from hiding.[1] They had to face the task of re-starting SKP from nothing: they had no money, no premises, no newspapers or printing facilities, and at most some two thousand nominal members on which to build.[2] A. Aaltonen, the first chairman, and V. Pessi, the secretary, had at first to work as building labourers to support themselves.[3] The communist leaders were soon meeting every evening in a room in Helsinki, and it is reported that there were hours of careful theoretical debate before it was decided to set up a legally registered party. The great majority of these people were of the same type, largely self-educated, working-class men and women, usually of the post-1918 generation, with a period of party training in Russia during the Stalin era, followed by brief spells of underground work in Finland and years of imprisonment. They had been trained as underground organisers in the Stalinist, bureaucratic tradition, and had no experience of running a public movement. Such were Aaltonen and Pessi, Hertta Kuusinen—really bourgeois in origin, but an honorary proletarian because of her father—M. Janhunen and M. Huhta; the odd man out was Y. Leino, who had never been to Russia nor undergone formal party training. This group opened negotiations with the authorities, and in order to meet the requirements for registration called a party conference which met on 4 and 5 October 1944.

About thirty delegates representing the survivors of the old underground movement ratified the line worked out in the preliminary discussions and agreed that SKP should come out into the open. They debated what sort of a public party it was to be; the leaders had already resolved that the party should drop its revolutionary tactics and adopt constitutional ones, and the conference now decided that SKP must be a mass party, which would form the vanguard of the working class; but there was a minority who argued for a small, select party of élitists. Some of the majority, like Leino, suggested forming an entirely new workers' party, in which SKP would be merged, but this was rejected. The conference elected a new central committee, because, as a party historian remarks with unconscious irony, 'the central committee elected at the last party congress in 1935 had been reduced by a number of factors'.[4] In the new committee the direction was firmly in the hands of the Stalinists. Aaltonen was chairman, a strong ambitious character, Pessi, a much more flexible figure, was secretary, Janhunen and Huhta were tame supporters, while Hertta Kuusinen, a formidable figure in her own right, was often taken to be standing in for her father. Significantly, Leino was not elected; even then he did not quite fit in with the rest.[5] From this point on the leadership of SKP was remarkably stable; Aaltonen, Pessi and H. Kuusinen continued to direct the fortunes of the party into the 1960s. This basic group was re-inforced in 1946 when some three hundred exiles returned from the Soviet Union to reinforce the home communists, adding three important figures to the ruling group, T. Lehen, A. Äikiä and I. Lehtinen, without changing its basic character.[6]

The new committee issued a manifesto defining the new party line, and the title proclaimed that it was to be a popular-front line: 'A joint endeavour for freedom, a better life, and a brighter future for our people'.[7] The party said that it was now open to public inspection:

. . . we have nothing to hide. We state our demands and our principles openly for everyone to criticise. We ask for the support and assistance of all those who approve these principles . . . our party's existence is a necessity produced by the class war, a condition of victory in the struggle against capitalism. Its work is founded on scientific socialism —the theory of Marxism-Leninism, whose validity is continually being proved in real life.

They went on to define their short-term programme: a new foreign policy based on friendship with the Soviet Union, the destruction of domestic fascism and the real democratisation of the country, full employment, the transfer of the burdens arising from the war to those who had caused it, land for the rural poor, the restoration of real wages to prewar levels, and educational and social reform.[8]

There is plenty of evidence that the new line was rejected by a hard-core, leftist minority in SKP, representing the survivors of the old underground days who could not adapt to the new way of life, and who gave intermittent trouble for some time. Pessi denounced them at a very early stage as 'extreme Left elements' who were looking to the Soviet Union to do their job for them. They had failed to understand that 'the Soviet Union does not touch our internal affairs . . . we have to look after our own business, and we can do it'. These people were talking of setting up the Soviet system in Finland, but 'our country is nowhere near ready to change to such a system, much as we would wish for it. The overwhelming majority of the Finnish people does not want to change to a soviet system'.[9] These were the party members who during the original discussions in September had held out for a policy of proletarian dictatorship, to be backed by the red army.[10] They were again denounced in the party's new official journal, *Kommunisti*, in early 1945, for advocating waiting until the Russian tanks rattled through the streets of Helsinki; they were asking, 'why doesn't the red army clear the fascists out of our country once for all, when there is now every opportunity for it?' The party told them that these were fantasies, mere excuses for doing nothing: 'We have got to rebut the fascist allegations that our activities are directed from the Soviet Union'.[11]

But this opposition caused most trouble over party recruiting.[12] Initially SKP tried to hold to the old rule that a new member must be sponsored by two existing members, must submit an account of his life in writing, and undergo a period of candidate membership. These formalities understandably frightened off both recruits and sponsors, in addition to which the opposition faction was positively obstructing recruitment in some branches.[13] In the end the central committee had to intervene, and issued a general invitation to all honest supporters of the communist programme to join the party, without formalities if necessary.[14] The central committee said that it could not be deaf 'to the thousands of honest people who are trying to join SKP as members. . . . The party committee proclaims an invitation to all active, self-sacrificing, anti-fascist fighters to join the ranks of SKP'. The result was ten thousand new members in two months, and a membership of twenty thousand by the end of 1945, utterly revolutionising the structure of SKP membership.[15] Of course some undesirables got in; some were unscrupulous careerists climbing on what they took to be the winning band-wagon, others irresponsible anarchists, 'whose behaviour and language frightened off honest workers and farmers from the party', but the worst of these were eventually weeded out.

SKP, after some hesitation by the authorities, got its legal registration on 31 October 1944.[16] On 1 November the party held the first of its long series of public meetings in the Helsinki Exhibition Hall,[17] and displayed its new line to a mass audience. The speakers called for a popular front and said that as a public affirmation that a new era had begun, the existing government should make way for a better one. SKP claimed to speak for all the working people, and Pessi delivered a warning that 'the masses of the people want action, quite a different kind of action from what they have had hitherto. And if they cannot get it with official consent, they will launch a movement to smash the obstacles which stand in the way of their activity'.[18] Pessi could speak with confidence, for by this time the formation of a broad popular front movement was well under way. It was first embodied in a revived SNS, which sprang up quickly in October and soon had a membership of seventy thousand, and could at last publish its newspaper *Kansan Sanomat*, which had aborted in 1940.[19] The structure of SNS was formally completed on 18 October and represented a fusion of old SNS elements with a parallel movement headed by J. K. Paasikivi, a conservative statesman who also enjoyed the confidence of the Russian government to an extraordinary degree. Thus the new SNS was very broad based—Hertta Kuusinen remarks how strange it was 'to begin to revive the old persecuted society in company with hardened capitalists'. SNS was still technically a cultural body, but since its central concern became the proper implementation of the interim peace treaty it had to develop an appropriate domestic political programme which ran parallel with SKPS.[20]

But SKP envisaged something much bigger than a revived SNS; what they aimed for was to detach SDP from its wartime leadership under Tanner and to draw it into a popular front. There were already in 1944 two dissident groups of social democrats, the so-called 'group of six', led by K. H. Wiik, which had been expelled from SDP and imprisoned during the war, and the elements that had taken part in the peace opposition movement. These latter were actually in a majority in the SDP committee in September 1944, and put out a manifesto calling for the withdrawal of Tanner and the wartime leadership of SDP.[21] SKP began to negotiate with both of these groups about forming a popular front, and a preliminary conference on 5 October envisaged a coordinating body in which all working-class organisations would take part. They decided to hold a congress on 29

October, though when it met only the Wiik group and
SKP took part—the peace opposition held aside in the
hope of bringing over SDP as a whole after the party
council met in November. Wiik had been given the job
of drafting a programme for the new organisation but
he wanted it to be a specifically socialist organisation,
with a Marxist programme, and he expected SKP to
merge into it.[22] SKP on the other hand wanted the
broadest possible popular front, in which it would retain
its own independence and which the bulk of the social
democrats would be able to join. Zhdanov, who had
just arrived in Helsinki as the head of the United Nations
Control Commission, was called in to advise, and finally,
with his approval, they rejected Wiik's concept and accepted instead an idea that Leino says was his, founding
a 'Finnish People's Democratic League'—SKDL.[23]

The principles of the new organisation were set out
in a manifesto on 2 November. It was not to be a
party but a 'connecting link' between political parties and
other appropriate bodies:[24]

> . . . a tie between citizens and organisations which
> are democratic in ideas and act on democratic prin-
> ciples, to illuminate democratic ideas among the
> people of Finland, and to organise joint action
> among them to increase the economic prosperity,
> the political freedoms, and the cultural level of
> the people.

The first chairman of SKDL was Wiik, with his colleague C. Sundström as deputy chairman, but a communist, T. Tuominen, as secretary. Leino says that SKP
meant to control SKDL from its inception, and they have
indeed always done so, but this may be the results of
circumstances rather than deliberate intent.[25] For the
original project did not work out as planned; in November, at the council of SDP, Tanner regained control with
the aid of a group of younger anti-communist members
led by V. Leskinen.[26] Therefore the expected adherence

of the bulk of SDP to SKDL did not happen, and although SKP may have wished for 'honest cooperation on equal terms',[27] events left the party in a position of dominance inside SKDL. Its only political partner at first was the Wiik group, who later formed their own Socialist Unity Party, affiliated to SKDL; this expressed Wiik's original concept of one united Marxist party but never attracted any mass support.

The other components of SKDL were assembled by the end of 1944. On 8 November SKP organised a national farmers' congress, which drafted a programme based on extensive land reform and became a farmers' section within SKDL.[28] Then ASS joined, as did the 'Comrades Societies', started up by SKP for ex-deserters and former red guards.[29] Finally, in December, the 'Finnish Women's Democratic League' was set up in SKDL, and became in effect the women's section of the communist movement.[30] But what chiefly decided the character of SKDL was that after the SDP council had restored Tanner's control over the party, individual SDP branches began to leave their party and join SKDL; in the end nearly a hundred did so, and this began to change SKDL into something more like a political party instead of the co-ordinating body originally envisaged. Soon SKDL began to form its own local branches and to enlist individual members and so took on most of the outward forms of a regular political party.[31]

This process has left SKDL something of a political hybrid. Pessi, speaking in January 1945, insisted that it was neither a 'communist auxiliary' nor an 'independent party'; he said, 'it is not a party at all, but an anti-fascist bloc, an alliance', and he rightly pointed out that SKDL and SKP had distinct programmes, distinct rules for membership, and separate identities, although they held certain aims in common. But Pessi was here expressing what the communists had hoped SKDL would be, not what it was, for since the expected adhesion of the bulk of SDP never happened, SKDL became, against its founders' intentions, essentially a political party directed by

SKP as its dominant member. From time to time SKP has considered whether SKDL and SKP do not overlap to such an extent that one or the other could be dispensed with. In the early years Leino came to the conclusion that SKP should simply merge into the larger body, and persuaded Zhdanov of this, but when it was referred to Moscow, O. W. Kuusinen emphatically vetoed the idea and insisted on the need to preserve an independent communist party as the vanguard of the proletariat.[32] In the end the chief role of SKDL has been to act as the electoral and parliamentary organisation for SKP, a role which it first developed for the elections of March 1945.

Before those elections were held, SKP had been taken into the Finnish government for the first time in history. The circumstances in which this happened were of course far from normal, since at that point SKP was still unrepresented in Parliament. Under the terms of the interim peace treaty, a United Nations Control Commission had been set up in Finland with extensive rights of interference in Finnish internal affairs; in effect no major political issue could be decided in the years 1944–7 without consulting the control commission;[33] as Leino puts it, 'the government came to act in continuous close contact with the control commission'. The Castrén government, which had concluded the interim peace treaty, was essentially a continuation of the wartime coalition government. The communists generally accept now that it was honestly trying to fulfil the treaty, though some still allege that it was secretly working to preserve the old order.[34] When Zhdanov arrived in Helsinki on 5 October 1944, he made it clear that he felt there should be a new government which would symbolise and guarantee a complete break with the past, and it is reasonable to assume that he indicated that to give a place to SKP would be an appropriate gesture.[35] On 7 November the two opposition social democrats who were members of the Castrén government, Vuori and Fagerholm, brought down the government by resigning.[36]

A new government was formed under the conservative

Paasikivi, the nominee of Zhdanov. The Soviet Union, or more probably Stalin himself, had decided that this elderly right-wing politician was the most reliable public figure in Finnish politics from the Russian point of view, and they backed him consistently. It never occurred to them that any member of SKP might take a leading role, but on the other hand they committed SKP to the rather incongruous position of having to support Paasikivi, because, as Hertta Kuusinen said, 'he alone of right-wing politicians had acted for and represented a new line of policy'.[37] There were ten new men in this first Paasikivi government, and of the seven social democrats four were of the anti-Tanner wing of the party.[38] SKP was only consulted after the SDP opposition to communists being in the government had been broken down; then the leftist writer Hella Wuolijoki was commissioned to conduct negotiations with Hertta Kuusinen.[39] SKP asked for three or four places in the government but were offered only 'one relatively unimportant post'. They accepted this and further agreed that it should go to Leino, a more acceptable figure to his prospective colleagues than the Moscow-trained Kuusinen, or M. Huhta, who were first suggested by SKP.

In these circumstances, and in view of the grudging attitude of the other parties, it is no surprise that SKP gave even this reconstructed government a very qualified blessing, particularly since they knew that many of their own members objected on principle to going into any coalition with the bourgeoisie.[40] The party therefore issued a statement to justify its action, on the ground that the government represented a new line in foreign policy and that by taking part in it SKP could keep an eye on what was happening. But the government was on probation as far as SKP was concerned: 'Events will show how the present government approaches its tasks. That will also decide what sort of an attitude the Communist Party will adopt towards it'.[41] SKP wanted 'in every way to help the people to escape from the situation into which a criminal war policy has led our country.'[42] In short, as a party historian says, 'the party thus did not tie its hands, or promise too much'.

The party could not expect to play much of a role in government until it had been able to show how great its real strength was; this it proceeded to do in two fields, of which the first was the trade union movement. The chairman of SAK, E. Vuori, had recognised in October 1944 that SAK would have to come to terms with the communists and suggested that there was no real obstacle to this: 'It is more a question of prejudice and mutual distrust. If these can be overcome . . . it should be possible to get a common basis for the political aspirations of the working class'.[43] SKP for its part was in a conciliatory mood; it urged all workers to join their SAK unions and promised that the party would not seek sectional advantages in the unions:[44] 'SKP does not seek to form any kind of party organs inside the trade union movement, but opposes such attempts on the part of others. In this sense the trade union movement is ·non-party'. Membership of SAK rose very fast after the war, and many of these new members were SKP sympathisers so that union branches began to repudiate their old leaders.[45] In December 1944 negotiations were begun between SKP and SAK and soon reached agreement; SAK publicly repudiated its wartime attitudes, would join in demanding the rooting-out of the remnants of fascism, would seek to promote a new trade union international which would include the Russian trade unions, would base its propaganda work on Marxist ideas, and would promote new leadership elections in member unions. In future, all parties would be represented on SAK committees, and provisionally two communists were coopted to SAK's committee, V. Tattari as a vice-chairman and M. Huhta as the member in charge of propaganda.[46] By the spring of 1945 SKP was well satisfied with the way things were going; as member unions held their congresses SKP was making considerable gains and the old leaders were being displaced so that SKP had good hopes that when the next regular congress of SAK was held they might have a majority.[47]

But the crucial test of SKP's political strength was the parliamentary election held on 17 March 1945. In some ways the SKDL campaign was obviously handicapped by inexperience, the rawness of its organisations, and its lack of press facilities and premises, though opinions differ on how far these factors actually reduced its vote.[48] On the other hand there were favourable factors: the national radio was put under the sympathetic supervision of H. Wuolijoki, and underwent such a drastic change of tone that Paasikivi had to intervene to preserve religious broadcasting.[49] More important were a number of statements by public figures which seemed to imply that the national interest would be served by supporting SKDL. On 20 January, Orlov, a leading member of the control commission, said that the election would be a measure of Finnish goodwill towards the United Nations;[50] after the Yalta Conference on 2 March, Vuori made a radio address in which he implied that revolution, or United Nations intervention might follow if the election showed that reaction in Finland was too strong.[51] Finally Paasikivi made a radio speech on the eve of the poll, which called for the return of a parliament of 'new faces', and could also be taken as encouragement to vote for SKDL.[52]

SKDL, acutely conscious of its incomplete organisation, but also remaining consistent with its popular-front line, proposed an electoral alliance to SDP on 13 January.[53] The essence of the offer was that Tanner and the wartime leaders of SDP should withdraw from public life; the SDP committee rejected the offer by one vote, ignoring the pleas of J. Keto and M. Pekkala in favour of the alliance and Pekkala's hints about some ominous Russian troop movements. As a consequence, Pekkala and Keto led a sizeable minority of SDP supporters into the SKDL camp and made their own electoral alliance with it.[54] This brought in some valuable extra support to SKDL but still left it essentially fighting the election by itself. The SKDL election manifesto put the emphasis on cultivating good relations with the United Nations, a complete purge of fascists, wider democratic freedoms, placing the burdens of reparations on the war profiteers, full employment, and the restoration of the 1938 level of real wages.[55] Thus SKP, faithful to its popular-front line, had dropped its own programme, which as M. Janhunen reminded the party stood for 'socialism and a soviet system as its political form, but only when the nation desires it. . . . So long as the nation itself is not convinced that the soviet system is better than the bourgeois system, we shall not put forward our own programme'.[56] This was the basic price which SKP had to pay for electoral success: on a poll of 75 per cent, SKDL got 398,000 votes, or nearly one-quarter of the total cast, and forty-nine parliamentary seats out of two hundred, as compared with a social democrat vote of 426,000. When two of the SDP members of Parliament decided to join SKDL, its group, with fifty-one members, became the largest single group in Parliament. It was an impressive result, and the party treats it as such,[57] though on 23 March the central committee issued a statement saying that the result 'does not reflect the real political situation in our country'. This might sound sinister, a repudiation of the democratic process, but it appears to mean no more than that the alleged handicaps under which SKDL had campaigned had held back their vote, for the party went on to express its satisfaction that now 'the future development of our country depends in a decisive fashion on the attitude of our party'. Leino hastened to correct any false impressions through an interview with the Swedish press correspondents, in which he said that a multi-party parliamentary system was 'the only conceivable one' for Finland.[58]

The question was one of how SKP should develop its success and on this the party was still split; throughout the first half of 1945 the leadership had to campaign against continuing Leftism in the party, and tried to sell to the suspicious minority its new programme of parliamentary and governmental cooperation with other parties. For instance, H. Kuusinen explained in March 1945 that the achievement of democracy comes before socialism and that each country, as Lenin had said, 'finds for itself the forms through which it realises its social reconstruction'.[59] A month later she was telling the party:

> . . . in the present phase Leftism has become the real chief danger. . . . It is not a matter of tactics that we now recommend democracy on the basis of a bourgeois economic system. It corresponds with the needs of the working people. . . . The direct seizure of power is not in reach. The working people are not ready for it, it does not correspond with the desires of our people.

K. Heikkilä complained that 'many comrades still try in their behaviour to cling to the line of policy which was the party line in the circumstances prevailing fifteen years ago', and their wild radical talk was damaging the party by frightening off potential allies.[60] It looks as though the stubborn old-guard leftists apprehended that the party was selling its revolutionary heritage for a very dubious mess of pottage, and it may yet prove that in the long run they were right about this.

The leaders were not to be deflected from their course, and took the initiative after the election in forming a broad-based coalition, on the basis of a document known as 'the Big Three Agreement', concluded on 13 April between SKP, SDP and the Agrarian Party.[61] Its contents may be summarised as: commitment to support a foreign policy based on the United Nations and cooperation with the Soviet Union; the complete elimination of the remnants of fascism in Finland, which would involve identifying and calling to account those responsible for the war, and a purge of the civil service, army and police establishments; a controlled economy, putting restraints on big capitalism and using nationalisation where appropriate; and tax reform, and fiscal and social policies designed to help the poorer sections of the community. SKDL has broadly adhered to this programme ever since, 'although it was not either a socialist or a communist document'. Pessi said of it: 'It is of enormously important significance. I am certain that many of us at the moment do not understand its great significance'. But what did it in fact signify? Originally it had been conceived of as a SKDL-SDP agreement, a working class unity programme. But SKDL, almost certainly prompted by the control commission, had insisted on bringing in the Agrarian Party as well, making concessions on points like nationalisation to secure their support. The agrarians were pleasantly surprised at being wooed; their parliamentary group stated that SKDL had 'to our great astonishment, shown understanding and sympathy towards us'. The agrarian leader, U. Kekkonen, repeated in a press interview how impressed they had been to discover 'that communists and national democrats showed themselves to be ordinary people who only wanted to act for the country's best'.[62]

Thus SKDL had made concessions to secure this arrangement, but why? They knew that the more conservative elements among the agrarians and the social democrats were insincere in their acceptance of the programme, and subsequent events proved this to be so. To put it bluntly, these people entered the agreement to keep the control commission satisfied, and as soon as it was safe to do so they would repudiate their connections with SKDL. Pessi indicates that SKDL was aware of this but confident that when the time came it would be possible to appeal to the mass membership of its partners to keep the leaders in line. Certainly if this could have been done, if the Big Three programme had really been carried through, Finnish politics would have shifted strongly to the Left and the power of capital, and of its representatives in the bourgeois parties, would have been permanently weakened. Thus what the leaders of SKP chose was, provided that the partners did not deceive it, the certainty of major reforms and a strong progressive government at the price of abandoning all effort to win a majority for a real socialist policy after a period of prolonged opposition. But as it turned out SKDL was cheated and ended up with the worst of both worlds.

Once the Big Three Agreement was concluded a new government could be formed. Paasikivi continued as prime minister, but now Leino was joined by two other communists, M. Janhunen and Y. Murto;[63] in addition two allied social democrats, M. Pekkala and R. Svento, were ministers, giving SKP and its allies almost a third of the seats in the government. SKP insisted that Leino should be minister of the interior, and this has often been interpreted as sinister, because it carried control of the police; almost at once the bourgeois press began to picture Leino as the intended communist strong man.[64] But as is so often the case, SKP's insistence was perfectly reasonable in the circumstances, as Leino has pointed out:[65]

> SKP had wanted the ministry of the interior. With the aid of a new minister of the interior it wanted a change of direction in internal politics, to deprive the bourgeoisie of one of its most important weapons in supporting reactionary policies, the police force. . . . My purpose was to give an airing to the so-called forces of order, because they certainly needed it. . . . In some parts of SKP it was thought that the situation should be taken advantage of and the path of illegality should be followed. But these elements did not get to the surface.

Despite all that was subsequently alleged, there are no serious grounds for challenging Leino's statement. Considering what SKP had suffered from the attentions of the Finnish security services over twenty-five years, their desire to see them re-constructed is entirely understandable and not at all sinister. SKP could not always depend on the control commission to stop the reactionaries mak-

ing a comeback. It is worth noting that SKDL's government partners made no objection—they fussed more
over the Defence Ministry, which went to M. Pekkala.[66]
It is also worth noting that at this very moment, when
SKP was supposed to be laying the foundations of its
future revolutionary takeover, the energies of its leaders
were largely taken up with combatting and repressing the
surviving revolutionary enthusiasm in their own ranks
and converting their followers to constitutional politics.
This process was substantially completed during the summer of 1945; in April a party council was held and the
new line explained to it by Pessi and the central committee. The statement to the council confirmed that the
future lay with a broad progressive coalition, so that SKP
must avoid behaviour or speech offensive to its partners,
must develop its contacts with the masses and throw
open its ranks to all comers: 'Let us make of SKP a mass
party, not only through its political influence but also in
structure'.[67] Pessi, in laying down the democratic, popular-front line, affirmed that SKP needed allies to defeat
the reactionaries: 'A democratic direction can only be
supported on the majority of the people, by establishing
cooperation among the representatives of its working elements'.[68]

All this was finally and solemnly ratified when the
seventh congress of SKP, the first to be held in Finland,
met from 19 to 23 October 1945. Preparations had been
thorough; the congress had been postponed from the
spring, partly because of the election, partly no doubt to
get the Left opposition under control. An article in *Kommunisti*, on getting ready for the congress, stressed that
success depended on choosing the right sort of delegates.[69] Congress had 352 delegates, representing 308
branches and a membership of twenty thousand; of these
83 per cent were industrial workers and only 8 per cent
farmers and 2 per cent intellectuals. The congress agreed
that the membership was still too small, and the structure
unbalanced, and pledged the party to put this right;[70] it

also noted how these thousands of new recruits would
need careful education in Marxist ideology.

The main work of the congress was set out in Pessi's
long keynote speech, and was then embodied in the text
of the final resolutions, which in turn have been the basic
charter of SKP policy ever since.[71] Defending the new line,
Pessi declared:

> If our party could not change its current policies
> to correspond with a changed situation, it would not
> deserve the name of a real Marxist-Leninist workers'
> party, because in that case it would not be the
> executant of a living Marxist-Leninist doctrine but
> a bookish sect hiding behind a dead dogma.

So much for the Leftists, who had been successfully
eliminated and did nothing to disturb the unity of the
congress. The new view of democracy was reinforced in an
important speech by Leino, where he said:

> . . . although soviet democracy is the highest kind
> of democracy, it is not the only kind of democracy,
> any more than the soviet system, although it is the
> best form of socialism, is the only form of organisa-
> tion of a socialist society.

Leino defended SKP's participation in government as a
guarantee of democratic policies: 'We may lack experience and skill, but even so the communists are the most
reliable guardians of democracy in the country'.

The basic policy rested on the analysis that the war
had transformed the world situation by destroying fascism
and weakening the forces of reaction everywhere, although
the remnants of fascism remained to be disposed of. In
Finland, although fascism had been greatly weakened it
had not lost the power or the will to fight, especially as
'in the civil service and the army they still have a dominant position'. The basic need therefore was a 'continuing
struggle between the forces of reaction and democracy'

and SKP sought to rally the widest possible coalition of democratic forces to ensure that reaction would be defeated. In foreign affairs, the keystone was friendship with the Soviet Union; there must be no deviation into 'agitation for forming a so-called Scandinavian bloc, which reactionaries in Sweden and at home are proposing'.

At home, the first steps in the crushing of fascism were to be the trial of those responsible for the war, and the democratisation of the police, the judiciary and civil service by extensive changes of personnel. Then the Big Three programme must be driven through Parliament. On the economic front the two themes were the need for a planned economy, which would require some degree of nationalisation, and control from below through a works committee movement, giving direct worker participation and laying the foundations for industrial democracy. In this way the capitalists would be prevented from sabotaging the economy, while the profits of the nationalised industries could be used to reduce the tax burden. A comprehensive programme of land reform to help the small farmer, of educational reform to eliminate reactionary influences in the schools, and social reforms to relieve the poor and needy would be worked out. At the same time, communists must strengthen the democratic forces on the ground by joining trade unions, the SNS, youth and women's movements, so that the party was in constant contact with the masses and winning their acceptance. Communists must demonstrate that they honestly accept responsibility for working the existing society: 'They must watch over production and the interests of the democratic state, because there is now no other way to safeguard the interests of the workers'—the building of socialism was not possible in the existing situation. The congress confirmed the leadership in office, except that A. Uusitalo replaced Aaltonen as chairman; Leino came into the central committee, as did the SNS pioneer Ryömä, now at last a member of the party. Thus in twelve months SKP had transformed itself from a revolutionary opposition into a pillar of the new establishment, and it was no wonder if some members found the transition hard to take. But it had to be proved whether SKP could really operate the organs of a bourgeois society to promote its own policies, or whether in fact the bourgeois establishment was not exploiting SKP and cleverly muzzling a potentially dangerous and subversive enemy.

To all appearances, during 1945 SKP was profiting out of the new order, because it proved able to enforce its own policies against persistent opposition from the defenders of the old order. The first priority had been given to destroying the remnants of fascism, and this meant first of all bringing the wartime leaders to public account for their actions, a process which culminated in the war responsibility trial. Aaltonen had suggested the need for this as early as 1 November 1944, in a speech to a party rally,[72] and on 27 November SKDL formally declared that the political leaders were as guilty as any war criminals and should answer to a special people's court.[73] But the real attack opened on 23 January 1945, when a question was put down in Parliament; Paasikivi responded by announcing that a committee would be set up under a distinguished lawyer, E. Hornberg, to look into the whole question of responsibility for the war.[74] In addition he appealed to the wartime leaders to withdraw from public life, which they did. It is assumed that Paasikivi hoped that this would be enough, and that Hornberg could then decently bury the whole business.[75] SKP acquiesced, but since their newspaper had already regretted that 'the war-guilty have only one life each, so that they cannot receive a heavy enough sentence', and had described Hornberg as 'this posing old reactionary with his exalted gestures', they clearly were not ready to let the matter drop.[76] Indeed, as Leino points out, SKP had everything to gain: 'For us communists, it was naturally sheer profit that certain leaders of other parties should be branded as criminals and eliminated from the game'. Even so, they would not have won if the Russians, through the control commission, had not made it clear that they expected something to be done.[77] Presumably in connection with this, SKP renewed the domestic pressure on the issue in June, putting down another parliamentary question,[78] while their press threatened sterner measures; they asserted that if the guilty were not punished 'in a manner corresponding to legal and democratic principles, a catastrophe, the violent explosion of tension, will be the regrettable but unavoidable consequence of unpardonable indifference'.[79]

The Soviet Union had by this time expressed official dissatisfaction over the war guilt issue in Finland, and during July SNS was used to bring out masses of demonstrators with demands for action.[80] Pessi declared 'the demand is not born of vengeance, but is founded on the people's sense of justice',[81] while H. Kuusinen in Parliament named the five principal accused, giving an assurance that SKDL was not interested in a witch-hunt after petty offenders.[82] But when the Hornberg committee did report in August, it enraged SKP on two grounds: first, by suggesting that under existing law nobody could be prosecuted successfully for any major offence; second, by saying that the question of the outbreak of war in June 1941 could not be considered apart from the question of the winter war.[83] SKP in the government insisted that the report be suppressed and it has never been published to this day. The street agitation was stepped up; on 10 August a delegation came to the government with the threat of a general strike if justice were not done;[84] but again it was the control commission which tipped the scales by indicating to Paasikivi that in its opinion the terms of the interim peace treaty required effective proceedings against those responsible for the war.[85]

This meant that the game was up, and Parliament obediently passed a law on 11 September setting up a special court composed of members of Parliament to try those responsible for the war. SKP had won the game and now only needed to make sure that there was no backsliding. In this they had the constant support of Zhdanov, who on 30 November called in representatives of the Big Three parties and told them how pleased the control commission was that they were collaborating so well, assuring them pointedly that 'the success of Finnish democracy is dear not only to you but also to us'. This suggests very strongly that the control commission had inspired the original initiative by SKP to conclude the Big Three Agreement. Zhdanov said bluntly that the control commission had been incredibly lenient in leaving Finland free to deal with her own war guilt problem, but there must be no evading the need for strict judgement and sentences: 'This is a question of the honour and moral duty of Finland before humanity'. The Soviet Union did not seek revenge, if it did the bill would be a terrible one, but they expected a clear admission of past mistakes. He then demanded: 'Why had the carrying through of this matter been the monopoly of SKDL? That is a dangerous path, because faithfulness towards treaties is a matter for the whole nation'. Zhdanov concluded by warning them that the whole future of the relations between Finland and the Soviet Union was at stake.[86]

In these circumstances, SKP could not go wrong. Their policy was the only true patriotism. With a little more pressure from the control commission the accused were duly convicted and sent to prison in February 1946. Yet this very convincing demonstration of strength by SKP may be deceptive, for it is doubtful if they would have got very far without the backing of Zhdanov and the control commission. It has been suggested that the whole affair was in fact the first stage in a plot by SKP to take power, that the trial was a preliminary softening up of their opponents, and that Zhdanov personally, independently of the Soviet government, was backing them.[87] The evidence for this is so flimsy and circumstantial that it will convince none but the inveterate enthusiasts for conspiracy theories of history. On the contrary, there is every indication that the Soviet Union required this public repudiation of past men and measures; and as Leino says SKP had every reason to go along with them, for the whole business was a vindication of all that SKP had stood for in opposing the war. The critics of the affair represent the stubborn Finnish refusal to acknowledge that the war responsibility trial was a perfectly justifiable proceeding. Certainly it was exploited by the communists for partisan advantage, but as Zhdanov said: 'Why should the leading men of the state not be subject to punishment? What is there in the idea that they should be that is un-socialist or undemocratic'? Perhaps Zhdanov was not the best qualified man to preach justice or democracy to the Finns, but his question remains a very good one.

Another impressive achievement of SKP in 1945 was the reconstruction of the security police. The original and natural policy of SKP on this was to demand the abolition of their old enemies, and this is implied in the central committee statement of 22 February 1945, which was followed up by an extensive public agitation, to which the government yielded by setting up the Sukselainen committee to look into the question, two of whose members, P. Koskinen and V. Sippola were communists.[88] The committee reported on 31 May that the security police were necessary but that 'the spirit of the institution should be changed'.[89] By this time, Leino was already installed as minister of the interior and there was no more talk of abolition. A new and politically acceptable chief of police, K. O. Brusin, was appointed on 23 April, and the chairman of SKP, Aaltonen, became his deputy on 19 May, without waiting for the committee, while Sippola became the head of the surveillance section.[90] The new chiefs then proceeded to re-construct the force, and by December 1945 it had been purged and reformed. Estimates of the SKDL membership of the new force, commonly referred to as Valpo, range from 45 to 60 per cent; Leino says that 'the new faces were naturally, as far as could be, communists' and adds that inevitably there was some loss of professional efficiency.[91] The change may be gauged by an article in Kommunisti in June, which says that the new Valpo is

'the guardian of democracy, the country, and order . . .
work in the institution is a work of honour', which makes
it clear enough that some party members were having
trouble adjusting their attitudes to the police; and it
goes on, 'we must remember that we are no longer in
the opposition, but in a position of power and influence'.[92]

This success was not unflawed; there was difficulty
over the chiefs. Valpo had four heads in two years before
E. O. Tuominen took over in 1946.[93] Aaltonen did not
get on well with Leino, who accuses him of running
away from responsibility—'he was not fundamentally a
bold man'[94]—and the control commission often grumbled
at Valpo's amateurish proceedings.[95] Leino concludes
that 'Valpo in SKP hands never became the kind of weapon
that had been hoped for',[96] and he thinks that SKP may
in the end have done itself more harm than good, since
'they had not the skill to use it to advantage in the right
way', while their enemies, through Valpo's blunders, got
a succession of first-rate propaganda opportunities to
smear SKP's public reputation—as early as October 1945
parliamentary questions were being put about Valpo's
alleged improprieties.[97]

During these postwar years, SKP always maintained that
its enemies harboured sinister plans for making an armed
comeback, and the great proof of this was the intermina-
ble 'arms dumps affair'.[98] The basic truth about this is
that in the near-panic conditions of late 1944, certain
military men reaching as high as the general staff made
and partially carried through a scheme to secrete weapons
on the demobilisation of the army so as to be able to
resist a possible communist takeover. It was an ambitious
plan, involving enough weapons for two divisions—1,250
different caches and about six thousand persons.[99] When
no insurrection occurred, it is claimed that the organisers
were quietly disbanding their organisation when its existence became known; the communist newspapers made
their first allusions to it on 20 February 1945. In May
the army was compelled to open an official enquiry into

the matter, which quickly uncovered the whole thing and clearly intended to cover it up again.[100] This could not be done because by then the control commission had come to hear of it and had demanded a thorough investigation.[101] On 10 June the two ringleaders were arrested and were eventually followed by some fifteen hundred other victims; the affair was to be the principal occupation of Valpo during most of its existence.[102] SKP naturally felt that it had found a certain winner and proceeded to exploit the affair for all it was worth. Leino dramatically revealed it to Parliament during the debate on the war guilt issue in June, as evidence of how hardened and unrepentant the reactionaries were. He said: 'I have to tell Parliament that there has been prepared in this country a reactionary attempt at armed violence and very important and influential sections of our society have taken part in the preparations, specifically in the army'.[103] From then onwards the 'arms dumps affair' was lovingly kept alive and cherished as proof that the reactionaries were dangerous and that eternal vigilance and fresh purges were always necessary.

Another major success for SKP in 1945 came when SDP agreed to go into alliance with SKDL for the local government elections due in December, a major breakthrough for the popular-front line; there was to be a common programme and joint electoral committees.[104] The results for SKDL were excellent; they polled 274,000 votes, as against 265,000 for SDP, while the combined vote of the bourgeois parties was 620,000. The workers' alliance got 4,500 seats, of which 2,500 went to SKDL, and it took control of 225 local councils, in addition to which were the thirty-three councils where SKDL by itself had an absolute majority.[105]

In the midst of all these promising developments there were a few warning signs that there were disadvantages attendant on becoming part of the ruling establishment. Early in 1945 the first big strike wave broke out in postwar Finland, reaching a peak in March and April when thirty-three major strikes involved over fifteen thou-

sand workers.[106] These strikes were all unofficial, but
SKP was still free then to speak for the workers and
support their demands, which was its traditional attitude.
But soon after this the responsibilities of being in the
government began to tell. During the summer SKP agreed
to the setting up of a council to control prices and incomes, though stipulating that there must be a majority
of workers' representatives on it and that the communists must have two of them. At first the council seemed
to work all right; despite the bitter opposition of Paasikivi the council recommended, and the government accepted, that there should be a general increase of wages
which would fulfil SKP's pledge to restore real wages
to the level of 1938.[107] The council also enforced officially the payment of bonus rates for overtime and Sunday work, another substantial advance for the workers.
The employers did not take kindly to the new dispensa-
tion, and in July and August a new series of strikes
broke out over the interpretation and application of the
government's settlement, but generally SKP could endorse
these, even welcome them as showing the masses supporting the measures of the government against the reactionaries by direct action.[108]

However, there were limits to the encouragement of
workers' militancy; for one thing, strikes might hold up
reparations deliveries to the Soviet Union under the interim peace treaty, so that in May 1945 Pessi had had
to warn workers that the maintenance of production
must have priority and that in general strike action was
not appropriate in current circumstances—strange language indeed from a leader of SKP.[109] In August a test
case came up when the footplate men threatened to strike
for wages above the new government norms.[110] In the
discussion of the problem in the government, the communist ministers were in total disarray; Leino wanted stern
action against the footplate men, Janhunen feared that
if their demands were met it would wreck the new wage
settlement and open the way to inflation, but hoped to
buy off the strike with minor concessions, while Murto

thought that a railway strike would be such a disaster that they would have to give in. The government first tried offering small concessions, but the men scorned these and went on strike. The government then became tough, conscripted the strikers, sent troops into the depots, and broke the strike. The crisis was overcome but it did SKP's image among the workers no good to be associated with this kind of action, and this was made worse when it became clear during the autumn that the communist representatives on the council could not stop it agreeing to compensatory price increases which had eroded much of the improved wages by the end of the year.[111] An economic statement issued by SKP in December 1945 was thoroughly defensive; it accused the capitalists of sabotaging the government's policy while SKP was getting the blame for its failure; the party pinned its faith for the future on the growing powers of works committees in industry to prevent such sabotage, to promote rationalisation, to increase production and to reduce costs.[112] But in January 1946 SKP was involved in a worse crisis when the government decided to take a forced loan by ordering the cutting in two of all bank notes. One-half of everyone's ready cash had to be deposited with the government. This naturally hit the workers worst of all, and the SKP ministers got a flood of reproaches from their supporters. One commentator thinks that they suffered irreparable damage through the cutting of the bank notes: 'When the bank notes were cut, so were the wings of SKDL from the point of view of future elections'.[113] If this was so, the trouble lay in the future; at the beginning of 1946 the communists appeared to be riding the crest of the wave and about to move into a leading place in the government.

# 7. THE PEKKALA GOVERNMENT AND THE LEINO CRISIS, 1946-8

In late February 1946 Paasikivi succeeded Mannherheim as president and this necessitated the formation of a new government. The Agrarian Party proposed U. Kekkonen for prime minister, but SKDL refused to consider another bourgeois for the post[1] and suggested the former social democrat, Vuori, who proved unacceptable to SDP because he was a renegade, or their own Leino, who was rejected by all the others, presumably because he was felt to be too strong a personality. Consequently the name of the former social democrat minister, M. Pekkala, was put forward. Paasikivi was against him, describing him as 'a nice man who can tell a good story in pleasant company, but I do not know any other abilities he has'.[2] The control commission had to be consulted and they were at first dubious, as was Pessi, who thought Pekkala too weak. Then the Russians changed their minds, SKP fell into line and M. Pekkala was prime minister. He was undoubtedly a disastrous choice for the communists; a very bourgeois social democrat by background with no taste for class-war politics,[3] grudgingly accepted by SKP as 'the leftest prime minister it is possible to get',[4] but above all a weak and irresolute man who quickly displayed his longing for a quiet life in his taste for indolence and procrastination. Pekkala was too fond of drink and good company, so that Paasikivi once remarked: 'Just as his private life is a mess, so his indolence and irresponsibility are messing up public affairs'. Either Leino himself or Pekkala's brother Eino—'a straight and courageous man . . . one of the best men of the left-wing workers' movement'[5]—would have been better choices.

In the new government there were six SKDL ministers, five agrarians and five social democrats, of whom three were Leftists.[6] So SKP could plausibly claim that the new government represented a shift to the Left while preserving the basis of the Big Three Agreement; the only significant alteration in the government programme was the emphasis it put on the need for a further purge in public life. SKP claimed that 'the events arising out of the change of government have notably advanced the common interests of the democratic forces'.[7] But SKP was wrong. Under the feeble chairmanship of M. Pekkala, internal cohesion in the government was quickly lost. As Leino says: 'Pekkala's government was not born under a happy star. Distrust and quarrelling appeared while the government was still being formed and they continued to get worse the longer it went on'.[8] It would have helped if Leino's SKP colleagues, Janhunen and Murto, had been abler men, but they were two honest party work-horses, who added nothing significant to communist influence in the government.[9] Later, when Leino himself began to break under the strain and quarrelled with the party, SKP's direct influence in the government virtually collapsed. They were in any case at the permanent disadvantage of being rank beginners in the game of parliamentary politics, playing against a team of experienced professionals; only outstanding abilities in the communist representatives could have offset this.

While the government negotiations were in progress, the first regular congress of SKDL was being held, from 23–5 March 1946. Its most important work was to set up a number of committees to draft a definitive programme for the next congress to consider.[10] It was claimed that there were already more than seventy-five thousand members, of whom 57 per cent were industrial workers while only 31 per cent were in rural branches, a weakness the movement aspired to correct. The ambiguous character of SKDL was emphasised by the formal admission to it of the new Socialist Unity Party, composed of ex-social democrats.[11] This group provided the new chairman of

SKDL, J. W. Keto, but the communist T. Tuominen remained secretary. Leino was, by a prior decision of the
central committee of SKP, omitted from the SKDL committee and he regards this as the beginning of his break
with SKP. There was in fact a serious policy difference involved, since Leino was pressing for SKP to merge into
SKDL, a proposal vetoed from Moscow—rightly from Moscow's point of view since it would have weakened their
ability to control things.[12]

Keto, addressing the congress, pointed out the ambivalent character of SKDL; it was both 'a first step
towards a united workers' party' and a federation which
progressive non-socialist groups could join.[13] SKP preferred to stress the latter aspect; it said that those SKP
members who urged that SKDL should be committed to
socialism misunderstood its purpose as a broad anti-
fascist front.[14] But the idea of a single organisation for
the working class was still very much alive in 1946. When
SDP held its congress in June a substantial opposition led
by K. A. Fagerholm and the two Kilpis declared openly
for cooperation with the communists, but the majority
were against any close connections. SKDL issued a statement on 8 July which said that 'the time has come
when the unification of the workers is once more possible,
and not only possible but unconditionally necessary'.[15]
SKP responded to this by proposing that the opposition
social democrats come into SKDL,[16] and on 22 July
SKDL formally proposed to SDP negotiations for a closer
union.[17] In reply, SDP offered to negotiate, but only with
SKP, an obvious wrecking tactic to break up SKDL and
isolate SKP, which the latter naturally refused; the party
insisted that collaboration must be with SKDL.[18] The
exchange went on for some time longer, but in SKP's
view it failed 'because of SDP's holding back' and the
party suggested that probably SDP had never been negotiating in good faith.[19] It is difficult not to agree with them;
SDP leaders saw themselves as engaged in a life and death
struggle with the communists, in which no holds were
barred, while SKP still cherished a naive faith that in the

long run the tendency to working-class unity could not be resisted.[20] The end result was that the SDP opposition split; one part led by Fagerholm went back to SDP and the others, led by A. Wirtanen and the Kilpis, eventually joined SKDL.[21]

History was to show that the Pekkala government and the Big Three Agreement on which it was based were traps in which SKP got caught, for it was consistently cheated by its partners, used for their convenience, and finally thrown over. One may illustrate something of this from the story of the nationalisation issue. SKP had begun in 1944 from its prewar position that monopolies and major enterprises should be nationalised, while small enterprises and independent craftsmen were guaranteed immunity.[22] In early 1945 it was the social democrats who were making aggressive noises about nationalisation, even hinting that SKP was holding back on the issue,[23] when in reality moderation was dictated by the need to secure the Agrarian Party, who were basically opposed to nationalisation, for the Big Three Agreement. Even so, the agreement clearly lays down that where it is necessary to achieve a planned economy nationalisation of major enterprises will be carried out. At that time SKP took the view that other things, mainly democratisation, should have priority. The government had discussed the matter of nationalisation on 6 February 1946 and agreed to set up a committee of thirteen bourgeois and thirteen SDP and SKDL representatives to recommend what should be nationalised. It is to be assumed that the bourgeois members always intended this to be a delaying device, and that before 1946 was out SDP had lost all its original enthusiasms for nationalisation. The record is that nothing was nationalised except the national airline and that in 1948, when the committee was wound up, SDP was still only proposing pilot schemes in certain food and tobacco enterprises; SKP rightly sees these proposals as attempts to evade the main issue.[24]

SKP first became seriously concerned over this matter in June 1946, when they expressed their suspicions of double-dealing, and said that it was 'time for all who have inscribed socialism on their banner to be asked what they are going to do in practice'.[25] By early 1947 the communists' eyes were fully opened and they decided to bring forward in Parliament nationalisation proposals that would expose the saboteurs. Kuusinen himself, writing from Moscow, decreed that the time had come to press the issue, and SKDL drafted a bill to nationalise forty of the biggest private companies, representing 45 per cent of all private capital invested in industry. Naturally, their coalition partners said that they would wait for the committee to report, and so the SKDL bill was rejected out of hand; nobody outside the SKDL group voted for it.[26] Thus SKDL met with total frustration; they might congratulate themselves that they had now exposed the double-dealing social democrats, but what they had in fact exposed was that SKP was being successfully cheated over a clear provision of the Big Three Agreement and that it was powerless to do anything effective about it.

It is true that the record of the Pekkala government is not entirely negative; it maintained full employment and allowed the workers to keep real wages reasonably in line with the inflation; it also passed some twenty major reforming laws, among the more important being an extension of the eight-hour day, annual paid holidays, compulsory works committees with elected workers' representation, regulation of shop and office conditions, and family allowances; other measures were in draft when the government fell. SKP can justifiably claim that the Pekkala government did more for the workers and the underprivileged in Finland than any other Finnish government.[27] But those measures advocated by SKDL which would really have struck at the roots of bourgeois power in Finland—a purge of the civil service and army, educational reform, nationalisation, drastic land redistribution, control of capital movements—all of which fell within the scope of the Big Three Agreement, were all successfully blocked by the opposition. SKP won many tactical successes but suffered strategic defeat; they were not as clever as their opponents, who knew how to sacrifice the inessentials in order to preserve what mattered.

But it must not be supposed that the communists were political innocents; they had always assumed that the leaders of the agrarians and the social democrats would try to double-cross them, but equally they assumed that SKP could undermine these leaders by appealing directly to their mass following.[28] Events were now to put this theory to the test. That reaction was far from beaten was shown on May Day 1946 when right-wing elements in Helsinki caused street disorders and even threw stones at the control commission building.[29] The Russians complained vigorously that Valpo was falling down on the job; Aaltonen was held responsible, and soon after was replaced along with other police officials. But to SKP the disorders were a gift, since they showed the power of reaction and the need for further purges,[30] and the party appealed to the masses to help: 'The working people must now put serious questions', and act themselves 'to destroy the defences of reaction'. By early June 1946 a formidable mass movement had been whipped up to demand a more vigorous purge, an end to the security of tenure of officials, nationalisation and land reform.[31] There were organised mass lobbies of the government and Parliament on 1 and 5 June, and a mass rally outside Parliament on 7 June. SKDL welcomed this movement, which it had largely organised, as 'a powerful mass movement against reaction and for carrying forward a democratic development . . . SKDL committee urges its organisations everywhere to give active support to the rising mass movement'.[32] This was SKP's answer to the obstruction of its opponents, but what could it achieve? Immediately, only the replacement of the prefect of Uusimaa province by a man more acceptable to SKDL, and a sympathetic talk on the radio from M. Pekkala.[33] The later claim by the party that 'the democratic forces achieved the removal from the organs of the police and justice the more compromised persons' has little substance.[34]

On 30 June, SKP held a party council and later issued a statement that:[35]

> . . . the practical implementation of measures necessary for the democratic development of our country is proceeding too slowly . . . the dismissal of fascist officials has been carried out to a quite insignificant extent. This has compelled broad democratic circles to intervene. . . . The questions raised by the mass movements are fully justified, and the government and Parliament must do everything to resolve these questions in the way demanded by the people.

The council laid down tasks for the party: to finish the purge, to advance nationalisation and land reform, and to build workers' unity.[36] It has been noted that they got nowhere with the last three items; could they enforce the purge? To help in this, the 'arms dumps affair' was pushed forward. In a speech on 11 July Leino indicated that it had proved to be a very serious and widespread plot,[37] and the government agreed to set up special tribunals to deal with the cases, which would run into hundreds. Yet the draft law for this purpose, drawn up by E. Pekkala, was very moderate and deliberately provided for many mitigating circumstances which the courts could take into account.[38] The law passed Parliament early in 1947 and the lengthy court proceedings began to roll forward. Leino had also improved his police organisation after the May Day disturbances, creating in Helsinki a small picked force, the mobile police, distinguished by their possessing submachine guns and being safe party supporters.[39] The opposition was far from being intimidated and put down a parliamentary question alleging illegalities by Leino and Valpo, which was debated on 4 November.[40] Leino was conciliatory, conceding that there might have been some minor irregularities, but he pertinently reminded his hearers of some of the wilder practices of the old security police against the communists. The minister got a substantial vote of confidence, and Pessi, on behalf of SKP, claimed a major victory, but significantly noted the unfortunate 'passivity' of the democratic forces and the need for them to swing over to active aggression. For although SKP had tried to raise a campaign of popular demonstrations to support Leino, nothing like the impressive performances of June could be managed. The purge campaign, after a promising start, had run out of steam, and SKP had therefore failed in this as well.

One of the more curious episodes of 1946 was the so-called 'peace crisis' which broke in August, when Finland had to send delegates to Paris to make her representations about a definitive peace treaty. Paasikivi, as president, had the constitutional right to direct foreign policy, and he tried to use this—unsuccessfully—to exclude M. Pekkala, Leino and other SKDL representatives from going to Paris on the delegation, then—successfully—in instructing the delegation to suggest a revision of the territorial provisions of the treaty in Finland's favour and a reduction of the burden of reparations. Paasikivi did this without formally consulting the government, so that the SKDL ministers got no opportunity to express an opinion about it. Enckell, the foreign minister, in his speech at Paris obeyed Paasikivi's instructions, despite misgivings expressed by Leino and Pekkala when they discovered what he was going to say. The Soviet Union took deep offence at the speech, which they interpreted as a manoeuvre by Finland to enlist the sympathies of the western powers and also as an insult to the Soviet Union which maintained that the existing treaty terms were generous.[41] SKP bungled the matter because most of its leaders happened to be out of the country, Pessi and H. Kuusinen being in Moscow, and the remaining leaders at home allowed their newspapers to approve the Enckell speech, no doubt reflecting the virtually unanimous Finnish feeling on the matter. But when the Russians in both Paris and Moscow made their resentment clear, SKP had to change its line and adopt the Russian view that the

Enckell speech was a provocation inspired by the reactionaries. Pessi wrote: 'Those same circles which . . . led the country into war now without a twinge of conscience talk about the interests of the people. We know that this is false. The aim of the campaign is to sow enmity towards the Soviet Union'.[42]

On this basis a public agitation was got up; SKP publicly dissociated itself from Enckell, mass meetings of workers were held, and a delegation was sent to see Paasikivi.[43] The agitation was much easier to get going because a second issue had come up much nearer to the workers' interests: there were clauses in the draft treaty which guaranteed basic political freedoms in Finland; the non-communist delegates at Paris wanted to ask for these to be taken out, because they were a slur on Finland's reputation, as her constitution already guaranteed such rights. But to the communists, who could remember how they had been treated under this same constitution before 1944, this seemed an insolent mockery and they easily got the workers out to demand the retention of the safeguards written into the treaty. As Leino says, these clauses 'were regarded as giving SKP the possibility of continuing to act as a legal movement. These peace-treaty clauses safeguarded this in the communists' opinion'.[44] Experience suggests that they were right; subsequently, when Finnish governments have contemplated measures to control 'extremism' in politics, the press, or the trade unions, SKP has successfully brought up the peace treaty and the threat of Russian intervention to see that it is observed and this has sufficed to discourage such measures.

On the whole, SKP was able to turn the 'peace crisis' to advantage; they forced their opponents to back down, for the question of treaty revision was dropped, and they had appeared publicly as the true defenders of friendly relations with the Soviet Union and of the rights of the workers against the reactionaries. They had also, of course, demonstrated the extent to which they were subject to control from Moscow and were subservient to a foreign power, but while this infuriated their enemies it seemed to do them little harm with their supporters. How far it may have alienated potential sympathisers in the middle is anyone's guess.

We must now turn to the struggle for the control of the trade unions. Here SKP was inhibited from playing its usual role as the unconditional champion of the workers' demands, however extreme, by its responsibilities in the government. In March 1946 the Pekkala government had approved an economic stabilisation plan which involved a wage and price freeze, but on condition that there should also be effective planning of the economy, including the direction of capital.[45] SKP maintains that it supported this programme in good faith, and that their later campaigns to drive up wages came only after their partners had sabotaged the plan by refusing to legislate effective economic controls or to work a real system of controlled prices. Thus when, in May 1946, the farm workers struck in defiance of an arbitration award, M. Pekkala went on the radio like any good bourgeois and condemned their anarchistic defiance of society.[46] Still, in 1946 SKP was reasonably confident that it would shortly win control of SAK, for the delegate elections for the congress due in 1946 were running strongly in favour of the communists,[47] to such an extent that the SDP-controlled SAK committee insisted on postponing the congress to 1947, on the grounds that there had been electoral irregularities.[48] When SKP tamely agreed to this, according to them to preserve the unity of the workers' movement, they made a shocking blunder; Leino claims that SDP was astonished at its easy victory. This gave SDP almost a year in which to counter-attack and swing the SAK elections in their own favour. Once more a naive SKP was outmanoeuvred by a subtler opponent, unless, remembering their easy predominance in SAJ in the 1920s, the party was overconfident and imagined that there was nothing to fear.

By the autumn of 1946 the stabilisation programme was under heavy strain and worker unrest at price rises was again being expressed through strikes. In October the workers at the Arabia porcelain factory came out on unofficial strike, or more accurately sat-in; SKP supported them and managed to make the strike political when the workers added nationalisation and a purge of industrial managers to their demands.[49] SKP tried, without success, to get other workers out in support of the Arabia strikers. The party's apparently two-faced attitude to the stabilisation programme seemed more justifiable after December, when the majority in the government overruled the communist ministers and approved a new round of price increases. Even so, in 1946 inflation had been held down to about 15 per cent and real wages had more or less kept up with it.[50]

The fight for the trade unions hotted up in 1947, for the SAK congress was set for 15 June and a series of delegate elections was taking place. The party was reminded by its leaders how important these were in March; the party claimed that its sole aim was 'to keep the trade union movement an undivided, united, and battle-worthy organisation of wage labourers'.[51] There was a significant incident over a social democrat campaign leaflet entitled 'We Have Had Enough', which summarised communist policy as 'lying promises, price rises, and compulsory democracy'.[52] Leino ordered Valpo to stop the circulation of the leaflet, but the social democrats appealed to the government and Leino had to give way. SKDL made its counter-bid on 29 March, proposing a general wage increase, the abolition of control on wages, the retention of controls on prices, and justified this on the grounds that an effective system of economic planning had been sabotaged by their partners.[53] Employers could very well meet the bill for higher wages by reducing profits or increasing efficiency. Marx had already shown that higher monetary wages were not necessarily self-defeating, as the social democrats alleged. Even so it was the social democrats who won; when the SAK congress met, the social democrats had some 170 delegates out of 300,[54] and for the new SAK committee the

communists had to concede a social democrat majority
of 7 to 5. Thus they had lost this vital power struggle,
as they allege because of the cunning manipulation by
SDP of a number of small 'undemocratic' unions,[55] but
really because SKP had blundered in accepting the post-
ponement of the 1946 congress and had then failed to
win the large and crucial metal workers' union. Their
enemies used the victory to forbid member unions to
participate in mass actions without SAK endorsement,
and to reserve the right of unions to support political
parties, defeating the SKP demand that trade unions
should be non-party. All that SKP could win for its
policies were resolutions denouncing wage restraint, demanding nationalisation, and urging increased workers'
participation in the management of industry through
works committees.[56] There was no disguising the fact
that the SAK congress had been a major defeat for the
communists.

But SKP had also suffered another shock in the government crisis of 1947. The peace treaty was signed in
February 1947, and when it had been ratified it would
mean the withdrawal of the control commission and the
normalisation of internal politics in Finland. When the
council of SKDL had met in January 1947 it had complained openly that its partners were not honestly working the Big Three Agreement, and there is some evidence
that about this time the social democrats and the agrarians had come to an understanding that when the control
commission left they would force a reconstruction of
the government, with equality of places for the partners
and a social democrat as prime minister.[57] A well-placed
observer of these years, an agrarian himself, takes it for
granted that the other parties only tolerated a powerful
SKDL influence in the government because of fear of
Russian reactions.[58] The effects of the signing of the
peace treaty, which was welcomed by SKP because it
guaranteed both Finland's international position and also
her internal liberties,[59] were not immediately apparent,

since for reasons that are obscure the Russians held up ratification for some months.

It is equally obscure why, on 10 April, the agrarian ministers precipitated a government crisis by resigning on an issue of economic policy. It could have been a warning shot in retaliation for the new militant wages policy announced by SKDL;[60] it is also possible that Paasikivi had given them to understand that now the peace treaty was signed Russian intervention in internal politics could be discounted so that they could go ahead with re-constructing the government.[61] In this case they were mistaken; the control commission had no hesitation in making clear that a social democrat as prime minister was unacceptable to them, nor for some reason would they accept the SKDL sympathiser, V. Meltti, whom Leino and H. Kuusinen suggested. The other parties would not accept a stronger man, either Leino or E. Pekkala, in place of M. Pekkala, so that in the end, after nearly six weeks of haggling, the old government was re-installed.[62] Perhaps the whole crisis was simply caused by a fit of nerves in the Agrarian Party: on the one hand they feared that by remaining associated with SKDL they were losing supporters to the conservative Kokoomus Party, which was excluded from the government; on the other they were afraid of an SDP-SKDL workers' government which would exclude them altogether. There had been some renewed talk of this but SKDL rejected the idea as impractical, since a workers' government would lack a parliamentary majority and be at the mercy of bourgeois support.[63] The whole idea could well have been a trick by SDP to break up the Big Three coalition. In any case, once it was found that Russia insisted on the preservation of the existing political structure, the crisis ended in effect.

SKP was convinced that there had been a deliberate plot to put it out of the government[64] and insisted more strongly than ever that Big Three collaboration was the only way to keep the reactionaries excluded from power. The Russian press backed them up; *Novaja Vremja* wrote of a reactionary conspiracy to change Finland's political course which had been defeated. The forces of the old order would have to wait a little longer before an attempt to dislodge SKP from the government could succeed. It was now the turn of the communists to strike back and during the summer of 1947 the party began to promote more energetic policies. In May 1947 Pessi and H. Kuusinen had been in Moscow, and Leino says that they were told by Zhdanov that the time had come for SKP to assert itself more forcefully, and in particular to get the masses out on the streets to put pressure on the reactionaries.[65]

On their return the party leadership analysed the situation. They worked on the assumption that the underlying international situation would work in their favour because the Soviet Union would compete successfully with the United States in the economic field and would gradually pull ahead. But they also had to accept that the current position of SKP in Finland was a difficult one, because while 'formally in alliance with other parties' the communists were 'in fact isolated. The communists alone have carried all the burden of the current struggle for the peoples' interests'. The biggest danger was that by staying in the government, where they were a permanent minority, the communists would get identified with policies which they had in fact opposed. But like humanity everywhere they decided to go for the best of both worlds, ignoring the inconsistencies this involved. 'The tactics will be that we do not give up our places, nor do we give up the sovereignty of the party, so that we preserve our freedom to criticise. . . . We must not become hostages to the government.' They believed that by staying in the government, 'we get a better view, we can unravel from that position the plans of the enemy'. Thus SKP wanted to be both government and opposition at the same time. They saw clearly that this was the best they could do as long as SDP remained united. But they were confident that in the long run internal contradictions would cause SDP to break up, and for that reason SKDL was important, as showing how communists can work together with non-communists in a single organisation. When the Soviet Union had outstripped the United States the social demo-crat position would weaken dramatically, 'and in this situation, SKDL will have new meaning'.[66] It was not an unreasonable analysis, except that the basic premiss proved to be false; if SKP were ever to be anything but a permanent minority opposition the tactics suggested were about the best they could adopt, but they would require for success a high level of skill and flexibility, which Sta-linist bureaucrats like Pessi and Aaltonen were ill-equipped to provide.

The party scored one easy success in July 1947, when Finland was invited to attend the Marshall Plan Con-ference in Paris. The invitation came on 4 July and the following day the control commission indicated that Russia opposed acceptance, and so, naturally, did SKP. The party opposed acceptance in the government and organised workers' demonstrations against it on the grounds that it was an imperialist trap: 'It is intended to segregate us from the Soviet Union in an econom-ically and politically hostile camp'.[67] Paasikivi, the non-SKDL ministers, and the majority in Parliament would have accepted without hesitation, but the peace treaty was still ominously unratified by Russia and in the end Paasikivi took it on himself to refuse the invitation.[68] SKP had helped to win a clear victory for their Russian patrons—or perhaps one may think that the Russians had won a clear victory for SKP. Either way, SKP's policy had been imposed on its partners and enemies alike. Yet they might have thought that when the protecting hand of the control commission was gone this might prove a Pyrrhic victory. And in September the Soviet Union did at last ratify the treaty, and many observers believe that this had been held up to prevent Finland from accepting Marshall aid and that ratification was Finland's reward for being sensible over this.[69]

The new communist effort to increase its power by

getting the masses to take a more active part in politics was assisted during the summer of 1947 by a new outbreak of industrial unrest, one of the biggest strike waves ever seen in Finland. During July and the two succeeding months over 113,000 workers came out on strike and over half a million working days were lost.[70] These strikes, beginning with the transport workers' strike in Turku in July, were all unofficial because SAK refused to endorse them, and they were bitterly condemned by SDP which went so far that in a statement of 17 September, the social democrats said they would support workers who acted as strike-breakers by remaining at work.[71] The bourgeois press and the conspiracy theory historians present the whole mass movement as artificially incited by the communists. In fact the main trigger was the ending of rationing in mid-1947 and the consequent jump in basic food prices. The keen observer will certainly note that while the social democrat ministers had fought to retain rationing, SKDL ministers did not;[72] for conspiracy theorists this is obviously significant.

But the uncommitted observer may be prepared to accept that basically the workers' unrest was spontaneous and thoroughly justified, even if SKP tried to make the most of it. Leino alleges that the party leadership wanted to stoke up the social tension and were angry with him because he had ordered the police to show restraint and avoid confrontations with the strikers.[73] This may be so; what is fact is that on 20 August the central committee of the party formally endorsed the strike movement; they denied that SKP had caused it, on the contrary they had always fought for the kind of planned economy and 'strong democratic order' that would make such disturbances unnecessary. But the reactionaries had sabotaged economic planning and the capitalists had brought this trouble down on their own heads: 'The dissatisfaction of the masses is justified', and wage restraint must be ended. SAK was only injuring itself by its opposition to the movement, and SKP would, 'in spite of the flood of abuse, continue the struggle to carry to victory this democratic policy, which accords with the interests of the whole nation'.[74] Leino says that the SKP leaders were split over how far they should go; he was for moderation in exploiting mass unrest, Aaltonen and H. Kuusinen were more extreme and accused Leino of lack of nerve. This difference certainly did not appear in any of the party's public pronouncements; the basic policy remained that wages should be left free while price controls were maintained.[75]

The non-communists were understandably furious over the whole movement, which seemed to them to be the deliberate product of the worst kind of communist perfidy. They found one interesting line of attack when they claimed that the strikes were endangering reparations deliveries to the Soviet Union. The social democrat leader, Fagerholm, speaking on 10 August, said that 'every strike is an act of sabotage against our reparations obligations. By what right do the communists seek to worsen our relations with the Soviet Union'?[76] This kind of hysteria is routine in any situation where the workers try to assert their rights by industrial action, and as usual was quite unfounded. The official body dealing with reparations stated in September that deliveries were in no danger, nor were the general allegations that the strikes were destroying the economy valid; on the whole the Finnish economy had a very good year in 1947 in spite of them.

The government was clearly not well placed to cope with the unrest, being so deeply divided internally, and after some vain efforts to deal with it piecemeal it summoned a conference of party chiefs and trade union leaders on 16 September.[77] The SAK delegates stood out for the social democrat line of re-establishing full wage and price controls; they wanted an immediate 25 per cent increase in wages, and for this to be tied to the cost of living index and adjusted automatically in future. The SKDL ministers, like E. Pekkala, professed pious horror at such a blatantly inflationary scheme; he thought that it should not even be a basis for discussion. H. Kuusinen stuck to the official party line; there should be a legal minimum wage, but above that wages should be left to free bargaining. In these circumstances no agreement was possible, so the government issued an appeal to the nation, pointing out that the general economic situation was slowly improving, promising that the government would seek to remedy outstanding injustices, but urging that nobody could gain from unrestricted inflation. They begged for restraint and patience, and rather pathetically threatened to resign if this was not forthcoming. These were exactly the kind of woolly, meaningless platitudes that all weak and divided governments indulge in. One must observe that the attitude of the communist delegates at this conference was moderate and responsible. There is no trace of the desire to exploit a socially explosive situation by extremist demands which Leino hints at in his memoirs. It was now the social democrat trade union leaders who were the trouble-makers.

On 20 September SAK threatened to call a general strike if its scheme were not adopted by the government. The government made one more effort to bluff them out of it by threatening resignation and then hastily re-convened the conference and on 26 September agreed to a settlement which was a substantial victory for SAK and the social democrats.[78] There was to be a general 10 per cent wage increase, with more for the lowest paid workers, and these new wages were in future to be tied to the index. In addition, a scheme of family allowances was to be introduced.[79] But this was not just defeat for the government, it was a blow to SKP; the party's own economic policy had been rejected in favour of one which it had condemned. Further, after leading the strikers during the worst of the struggle, the communists saw SAK step in and in a few days satisfy the workers with what was essentially a social democrat solution.[80] The communists had borne the heat of the battle but the social democrats had snatched the fruits of victory. SKP talked bravely in the autumn of

1947 about how it would renew the wages struggle if necessary, but in fact the strike movement died away.

The communists were now in deep trouble, part of it with their own mass following. Leino prints a letter which he received from a woman supporter in the countryside. She pointed out how to people like her it appeared that the party had paid too high a price for its alliance with the Agrarian Party, since concessions to them had meant that food prices went up and the rich farmers grew wealthier, while the poor consumers could not afford to buy the food, and they were increasingly blaming the government—and the communists as part of it—because the rich seemed to get away with everything. This atmosphere was not improved by the kind of bureaucratic SKP officials who came into the countryside to explain matters. Ordinary voters were put off by their stupid behaviour. The voters 'look at what kind of people and leaders they are. And I look as well, and sometimes these poor people's advocates horrify me'.[81] Nor was the party policy adequate: 'There should be something more than slogans to draw the masses to the party'. This letter was written in April 1947, and in December another local party member, K. Leino, wrote to the minister a long analysis of what was going wrong in the party.[82]

First of all, like many of the party faithful, he had never been able to understand why the party had not seized power in 1944–5. The present democratic line could surely lead nowhere as long as the bourgeois order remained intact. It was true that the peace treaty now guaranteed certain basic rights, but democratic methods meant a long haul and he doubted if the workers had the necessary staying power; already 'wide sections of the workers are getting cynical and indifferent'. The workers were baffled because their standard of living was not improving: 'The democratic line promised good and splendid things at the beginning. The workers have been let down. They do not believe words any more, they demand results, they demand the fulfilment of promises'. Discontent was now focused on the party leadership and the workers could be heard frequently consigning them to the devil. He conceded that of the two possibilities, insurrectional tactics or parliamentary tactics, the party was now irrevocably committed to the latter, but these could only succeed if the support of the social democrat workers could be enlisted. 'If we find the right forms of action, the situation is saved. They must be found in the united strength which only the solidarity and unity of the working class can provide. SKP has adopted the democratic line and it is equally responsible for its success or failure'.

The malaise among the mass following which these two letters illustrate showed itself in the local elections held in December 1947. The party had staked a lot on these, calling in September for a major effort, including a big new recruiting drive for a 30 per cent increase of membership as the immediate target. In November, Pessi warned the party how important the elections were and how, since SDP had refused an electoral alliance this time, they would be much more difficult to fight.[83] The results were disappointing, it is true that SKDL polled twenty thousand votes more than in 1945, but their share of the total poll fell back to twenty per cent, while the social democrats got 25 per cent. The party's electoral position had slipped badly, with only six months left before the parliamentary elections. The party surveyed the results and concluded that it was not succeeding in putting its policy over to the voters or explaining how the party was not responsible for the failings of the government. The disadvantages of being in government without a predominant voice were beginning to show.

On top of this SKP had to struggle with a new crop of difficulties, not of its own making, for like all other communist parties it got caught up in the developing cold war. Already, when a government delegation headed by M. Pekkala went to Moscow in November 1947, there were nervous rumours of some new Russian demand on Finland.[84] These were well founded, for when Pekkala met Molotov on 6 November, expecting to talk about trade and reparations, Molotov said that the Soviet Union was interested in concluding a mutual assistance treaty with Finland.[85] Since the Finnish delegation had no instructions on this the matter was not pursued, but a few days later the western press reported that treaty negotiations were actually taking place and a hasty government statement had to be issued admitting that the subject had been raised in Moscow.[86] The communist press was less restrained and said that the press reports were a vile imperialist provocation, as did the Russian press.[87]

However, in Finland itself Leino addressed a public meeting and told the audience that SKP would certainly welcome a mutual assistance pact with the Soviet Union, which it saw as an opportunity that should be seized; it would save Finland from the danger of being drawn into the imperialist camp.[88] This launched a major SKP campaign in favour of the idea of the mutual assistance pact.[89] Foreign observers concluded that while the Finnish government would seek to avoid any treaty obligation, the communists were trying to force its hand. As the cold war feeling intensified in Europe, tension and uncertainty inevitably built up in Finland too and were doing the image of SKP among the public at large no good at all. There was a growing sense of vague menace from the Soviet Union, and with it the fear that SKP might prove to be a Trojan horse. By early 1948 it is fair to describe the atmosphere inside Finland as hysterical; it was thick with rapidly accumulating rumours and under the strain the government coalition was falling to pieces. On 9 November 1947 the social democrat O. Hiltunen had pronounced the coalition to be unworkable: 'In truth, from a parliamentary point of view, it is the weakest government we have ever had, because each government party is trying to do the others down when it can'. Communist behaviour in particular had made the position of the government impossible and the present sham coalition must soon fall apart.[90]

In fact by this stage SDP was looking for a suitable pretext for renouncing formally the Big Three Agreement, which finally came in May 1948.[91]

But on top of all these troubles, SKP had been hit by a paralysing dispute in the central leadership of the party which centred on Leino. Like most crises of its kind it had a variety of causes. There is no reason to disbelieve Leino when he says that he had never got on well with Aaltonen and Pessi, and it is obvious that Leino's wife, H. Kuusinen, had played an important bridging role in keeping them together. But in 1947, according to Leino, his wife began to turn against him,[92] suggesting that he ought to go for a long rest in the Soviet Union. Then there had undoubtedly been some clashes over policy; the central committee had not been wholly satisfied with Leino's attitude to the 1947 campaign to whip up popular pressures, and to some extent then, and on numerous other occasions, Leino as the minister responsible for law and order had been torn between his duty to the party and the demands of his office, because he asserts that he had always opposed what he calls 'the politics of hooliganism'.[93] But there was yet another factor which Leino does not mention, that he was drinking heavily, and on occasion was absent from his office for days on end. At least some of those who knew him well will affirm privately that he had undergone a deep deterioration as a person. All these factors must have worked together, but there was almost certainly some cause for his wife to be suggesting a cure in the Soviet Union, particularly as he also had growing trouble with his eyes. On the other hand one remembers leading communists who did go to Stalin's Russia for their health and did not recover. Certainly, by the end of 1947 the party central committee had decided that Leino had become a liability to them and wanted to replace him in his key government post.

In December Leino went to Moscow, accompanied by Pessi and his wife; he was confronted by Zhdanov and Malenkov and read an official communist reprimand for neglect of his duties and for disobeying party orders, and told that the Russian leaders expected his resignation (though Leino himself does not believe this, he believes that his wife and Pessi had turned them against him). He was ordered to go back to Finland, resign on health grounds, and then return to the Soviet Union for a cure.[94] He did go back, and on his return the central committee of SKP read him another reprimand and suggested a long course of self-criticism, but told him to stay at his post temporarily. The pressure of events probably forced this course on the party, and in the end, instead of a clean break, Leino tended to drift away from the party. He has evidence that he stopped paying his party dues in April 1948, though he was still a candidate for SKDL in the elections of July 1948 and he did not separate from his wife until later in the year. There is evidence that the Kokoomus Party knew that there was some kind of difficulty between Leino and the party in January 1948, though they did not know what the quarrel was about.[95] Leino says that Aaltonen was denouncing him as a potential Titoist but this seems premature, for Titoism was not yet an official heresy in the communist world.[96] Certainly, the original party plan, that Leino resign at once and be replaced as minister of the interior by Murto, with H. Kuusinen going into the government in Murto's place, could not be realised.

At this point it must be said that most Finnish and foreign writers on the events of early 1948 in Finland, apart from the communists themselves, have assumed that SKP, aware that it would lose the parliamentary elections in July, planned to take power by force before the election could be held. It is alleged that while the Russians softened up the bourgeoisie by forcing the mutual assistance pact on them, the communists, relying on their control of the police and the Ministry of the Interior, would stage in Finland an almost exact parallel of the events of 1948 in Czechoslovakia. It is the contention of this book that there is no satisfactory evidence that such a plan ever existed, much less that any attempt was made to execute it, but that on the contrary the communists fell victims to the manoeuvres of more skilful opponents. One might think that the trouble over Leino, who would have been the key figure in any such plan, would in any case have made it a non-starter. But the argument will be that there is no positive evidence to show that there ever was a communist takeover bid and a great deal of evidence to the contrary; though it is notoriously difficult to prove a negative proposition, namely that no communist plot ever existed in 1948. At least history records that no such plan ever got off the ground even if it had once existed as a theoretical concept.

It seems obvious enough that to execute a design of that kind would, for instance, require some overt efforts to prepare the minds of the rank and file for insurrectionary action, whereas as has been shown the party had expended a great deal of time and energy on the precise objective of rooting out insurrectionary ideas in the party. Certainly there were party members who still harboured such ideas, but they had been officially, publicly and repeatedly attacked and discredited by the party.[97] One has to consider, unless it is held to be a deliberate deception, an article in *Kommunisti* published in mid-February 1948.[98] This discussed the coming parliamentary elections and stressed that SKDL must make a major effort in them 'to overthrow the present majority in Parliament' which had become 'the main obstacle to the country's democratic development'. The whole emphasis of the article is on the voters and how to persuade them; there is no hint that there is any other way of defeating the reactionaries. At the end of February the magazine carries on its cover the slogan, 'SKDL is now moving from defence to attack and calls all of you into the democratic and popular battle . . . to smash the reactionary parliamentary majority by a SKDL election victory'.[99] This issue also carries an article on the Czech crisis and says that while Czechoslovakia shows what can be done at the appropriate stage of development, that is that a national front movement can make a breakthrough directly into the building of socialism, Czechoslovakia differs from Finland in important respects. Specifically, in Czechoslovakia, unlike Finland, land reform and nationalisation had already broken the economic power of the bourgeoisie and hence its effective powers of political resistance. If SKP had had any idea of doing in Finland what its comrades had just done in Czechoslovakia, this article would scarcely have appeared in the party's official journal.

At this point the mutual assistance pact crisis began; SKP had campaigned steadily in favour of a pact since November but nothing had happened at the official level until on 22 February 1948 Stalin sent a personal letter to Paasikivi which invited Finland to conclude such a pact. The letter was not made public until 28 February but the news of it leaked out earlier and set off a flood of alarmist speculation.[100] Paasikivi, on the other hand, kept very cool, and entered on a long round of consultations with political leaders. Statements were put out with the assurance that such a pact would not involve any interference in the internal affairs of Finland, as when he told the foreign press corps on 22 March that the Finnish elections would certainly be held as planned, and on 13 March the prime minister, Pekkala, gave a long and reassuring radio address on the subject.[101] Pekkala told the public that any treaty would be subject to the full process of ratification by Parliament and that there were absolutely no grounds for the current wave of alarmist rumours. Of all the political groups in Finland only SKDL unreservedly and publicly welcomed the idea of a treaty. They got up a considerable campaign in favour of it;[102] 135 separate delegations were brought to Helsinki from the provinces to lobby the government and Parliament, and on 1 March a national delegation went to Paasikivi to urge acceptance of the Russian offer.[103] The communists proclaimed that this was an acid test of who really favoured good relations with the Soviet Union, and that the popular delegations showed that 'the broad masses of the people were clear that it

was not just a question of a mutual assistance pact but
of the future of the entire relationship of Finland and
the Soviet Union'.

After so much expenditure of nervous and emotional
energy, the actual negotiation of the treaty was an anti-
climax. Paasikivi and the political leaders worked out
in advance the sort of terms they could accept and who
should go to Moscow to negotiate for them.[104] During
these discussions a problem arose for SKP because Paasikivi insisted that Leino ought to go, while clearly in
view of what had happened Leino's presence in Moscow would be an embarrassment. Leino has preserved
the scribbled note which H. Kuusinen passed to him
during the discussions which ran[105]:

> You must know yourself that you should not let
> yourself be chosen for the delegation, although we
> understand that you could manage things best. You
> must try to get one of the others to go along—or if
> the delegation is widened to include members of
> Parliament, then me.

However, Paasikivi had the decisive voice in the matter and Leino went, and there is indeed some evidence
that embarrassments did occur because of it. But the
actual negotiation of the treaty terms caused no trouble
at all; at the decisive meeting with Molotov on 5 April
the proposed Finnish text was readily accepted as the
basis for the treaty.[106]

The essential point which was gained, from the Finnish point of view, was that the treaty operates only in
case of an attack by Germany, or countries allied with
Germany, coming through Finnish territory. It is provided that in the first instance Finland will defend her
own territory, and has no obligations outside her own
boundaries, and if Russian assistance is needed to help
in the defence of Finnish territory that help will be the
subject of separate, mutual agreement between Finland
and Russia. Thus Finland is not involved in the general

defence of the Soviet Union, while the Soviet Union has no automatic rights of intervention on Finnish territory. Both domestic and foreign opinion felt at the time that Finland had got away with the minimum of restrictions on her sovereignty and her neutrality.[107] It is difficult to relate these proceedings to any proposed scheme for a communist takeover in Finland. Would Stalin have gone through this elaborate diplomatic transaction with the government of bourgeois Finland, which ended in the most public assurances of mutual esteem and respect, if he had known that there was a serious intention of overthrowing that government and installing in its place a communist regime, with which much more favourable terms could have been made? Only if one is prepared to assert that it was all deception; but in that case was it a subtle effort to distract attention and put the bourgeoisie off their guard, and if so could it also be part of a war of nerves to weaken their will to resist? It might be interpreted along some such lines but it seems rather implausible.

Meanwhile, inside Finland, the general mood of hysteria had been producing some odd effects. skp was not immune to it, for some elements in the party were imagining the existence of right-wing plots; they were agitated about the alleged stocks of weapons still in private hands and they had produced a document, which Leino prints without vouching for its genuineness, which contained a rather improbable plan to set up a government of resistance to an envisaged communist insurrection, backed by Russian troops. This was to be led by the convicted wartime leaders, liberated from prison for the purpose, and in its turn would get armed support from the west.[108] The communists were taking this sort of thing seriously enough to be circulating party branches in March and April about precautions to be taken against the dangers of an armed rising by the reactionaries, but these were purely defensive in tone.[109] One must accept that there existed in Finland in 1948 groups of activists both in the communist movement and among its enemies who were having nightmares about the plots which they imagined the other side was hatching. They were insignificant in numbers but important because their existence, and the ideas they had about their opponents, served to build up and sustain a general atmosphere of rumour and nervous tension.

Before Leino went to Moscow at the end of March, he had been sufficiently worried by the possibility of extremists on either side starting trouble that he spoke with the commander-in-chief, General Sihvo, and suggested that he might take some security precautions. This was in fact done; some reservists were called up, the armoured division was moved closer to the capital, and security measures at government arms dumps were tightened. Then, on 25 March, H. Kuusinen made a speech to a party rally which discussed the recent events in Czechoslovakia. She analysed the situation in very much the same terms as the article in *Kommunisti* already cited, and concluded that 'that must also be our road'.[110] It is interesting to see how the speech went quite unremarked for several days and then quite suddenly the non-communist newspapers and politicians seized on it, blowing it up into crisis proportions. They said Kuusinen had revealed what SKP was really after, because the party knew that it would lose the elections and was determined to hang on to power by other means. This gross misinterpretation of what had been said gained wide and immediate currency; even the SKDL members of the delegation in Moscow were disturbed when they came to hear of it, and Leino in his memoirs says 'in that situation, such a speech was either the utmost irresponsibility or a deliberate incitement to insurrection'.[111]

Since that time the speech has become one of the sacred myths of Finnish history and nobody stops any more to look at what Kuusinen actually said and what it could reasonably be taken to have meant. Like any well-trained communist speaker, Kuusinen was expounding the party line to the faithful; the 'road' which had been taken in Czechoslovakia was the road to socialism and it had been opened up for the Czechs because they had already broken the power of the reactionaries to resist. Finland had not yet achieved this necessary precondition of advance, but eventually of course it would come, and the road to socialism would then be Finland's road as well. When challenged on her speech by a Swedish newspaper, Kuusinen made her meaning perfectly clear and re-affirmed what had always been the party line, that they would accept the verdict of the coming elections, that they would seek to preserve the widest possible popular front against reaction, and that this democratic and parliamentary policy would hold good until there was a clear majority of the people of Finland ready to proceed to the building of socialism.[112] It is in any case in the highest degree improbable that an able and experienced party orator like H. Kuusinen would ever have departed from the party line in a major speech, not even in a momentary fit of enthusiasm. She became, in fact, the victim of what communists would call a provocation; her explanations were of no avail because, as a bourgeois commentator remarks, 'in circles other than those of SKDL there was no desire under any circumstances to accept her explanation as true'.[113] She would not be the first left-wing politician to have been deliberately misinterpreted in a predominantly hostile press.

The sensation over the Kuusinen speech marks the crescendo of a public campaign to represent SKP as 'seeking a minority dictatorship to oppress the majority of the Finnish people', and this campaign had a great measure of success. It served to undermine the nerve of Leino, whose position must in any case have been a very unhappy one personally at this point; T. Heikkilä, who was the prime minister's secretary, describes how a distraught Leino got the habit of seeking him out and unburdening himself in long rambling discourses, emphasising his own integrity and talking wildly about the dangers from extremists.[114] It was this talk that finally got to Paasikivi's attention and may have stimulated the president to issue secret and constitutionally dubious orders to the army commander, Sihvo, and the Helsinki chief of police, Gabrielsson, to take further security precautions. On the night of 26 April the army ordered increased guards on all government armouries, a warship appeared in the harbour opposite the presidential palace, a general police alert was given, and the submachine guns of the mobile police, widely thought of as a kind of communist praetorian guard, were transferred from the usual armoury to a cellar in the government quarter of Helsinki.[115]

The communists reacted that same night by sending a delegation to the government to ask what was happening, but the government knew nothing since Paasikivi had acted over their heads. The next day the storm broke, although both Sihvo and Gabrielsson, following instructions, denied that there had been any crisis, that the police alert was a practice and the military precautions routine. But the whole anti-communist press leapt to the conclusion that a communist seizure of power had been narrowly averted. When the government assembled on the evening of 27 April, Paasikivi read the ministers a lecture on how public order had deteriorated and must now be restored; the ministers were in no position to argue with him because they did not know what all the fuss was about, as indeed they could not, because it was about nothing. Only Leino grumbled, as well he might, about police measures being taken without the minister of the interior being informed.[116] SKP issued a statement saying that all talk of a communist *coup* was 'the most blatant provocation against the communist party. The party demands a fundamental investigation and the prosecution of the rumour mongers'.[117] Leino gave a speech over the radio on 28 April in which he said that the only planned resort to violence that he had heard of had originated in right-wing circles, alluding no doubt to the memorandum which he had acquired.[118]

The government felt obliged to meet the communist demand for a thorough enquiry and a committee was appointed to look into the whole affair, which reported late in June 1948.[119] This report has never received the

attention it deserves, because after questioning newspaper
editors and security officials the committee could find no
facts which justified the alert of 26 April or confirmed
any of the accompanying talk of a communist plan to
seize power. The only reasonable conclusion is that this is
because there was in fact no such plan. The following
passage from Leino's memoirs seems to make good
sense:[120]

> The whole time that I was in the committee of SKP,
> nobody suggested to me the making of a revolution.
> In Finland the circumstances were not as favourable
> to revolution as in the so-called satellite countries.
> . . . SKP's leaders had had no desire to start a seizure
> of power, even when conditions were most favoura-
> ble. When they came out of prison at the end of the
> war, they were so eager for a comfortable existence
> that it attracted unfavourable attention in extremist
> working-class circles . . . desire for power they cer-
> tainly had, but they did not want to endanger the
> comfortable position they had attained.

And one may put beside this the observations of T.
Heikkilä, a sound and well-placed but thoroughly bourgeois observer, who gives his impression of 'the insurrectionary endeavour of the Finnish communists'. Heikkilä dismisses the whole story as a fabrication: 'There
never was such an attempt, not even a plan.' Heikkilä
believes that Paasikivi was angered and disturbed by what
he saw as the feebleness and incompetence of the Pekkala government and that he cynically exploited the state
of rumour and tension to strike a blow for authority, more
especially his own. M. Pekkala asked Paasikivi where he
had heard about the supposed *coup* and on what grounds
he had acted. Paasikivi is said to have replied that the
whole city was full of rumours about it and that fortunately 'my wife happened to hear them at the hair-
dresser'.[121]
    While SKP was engaged on a vain attempt to establish

its innocence, another blow struck it. Three years before, on 20 April 1945, Leino had received from the control commission an urgent demand for the arrest and transfer to the Russian authorities of twenty persons, alleged to be war criminals; some of these people had been Finnish nationals.[122] Leino, then quite new to his job, complied with the order without getting formal endorsement of his action by the government, though he discussed it informally with leading ministers, who agreed that he had had no choice.[123] On 19 May 1948 the constitutional committee of Parliament reported on the incident and said that Leino's conduct had been technically illegal. SKDL, not without some reason, described the whole affair as deliberate anti-Soviet muck-raking.[124] But the Kokoomus Party saw a chance to make political capital and moved a vote of no confidence in Leino, while the government declined to go to Parliament to defend him; there is evidence that M. Pekkala quite deliberately stayed away from the crucial debate, alleging that it was a waste of time to try to defend Leino. The vote of no-confidence was carried by 81 votes to 61, with only fifteen social democrats voting with the majority of the SKDL group in Leino's support.[125]

Leino should have resigned at once, but the following day he could not be found and thus he appeared to be defying the constitution. He says himself that he was still waiting for an official notification of the vote but it seems more likely that he expected Paasikivi to intervene in his favour. After all, the grounds for his dismissal were grotesquely unfair, and indeed Paasikivi, who knew all about the original incident, seems to have recognised this.[126] But since, when the government met two days after the vote, Leino had still not submitted his resignation, Paasikivi had no choice but to dismiss him formally. This started a new political crisis. Leino's behaviour was a gift to the anti-communist propagandists, seeking to prove that communists had no respect for the constitution, while the non-communist parties saw an opportunity to get the Ministry of the Interior, and with it the control of the police, out of communist hands. It must be assumed that SKP was not sorry to see Leino go, but they must insist that he be replaced by another communist. To make sure of this they began a major public agitation, and since they could not afford to expose their internal quarrels to public view this took the form of a campaign for Leino's reinstatement, in which, it must be said, Leino played a full part, showing that his break with the party was by no means completed even then.[127]

But behind the scenes, within the government, SKP was not asking for Leino to be reinstated, which was obviously impossible, but only insisting that they should keep the Ministry of the Interior and the same number of places in the government. The social democrats in particular were absolutely insistent that the interior be taken out of communist hands and were ready to bring the government down, offering to form a purely social democrat minority government in its place. There was now an open power struggle. SKDL had managed to get over a hundred thousand workers to strike in support of Leino and had set up a committee to organise this into a general strike, but they must have decided that the prospects of success were poor because when it became clear that Paasikivi was ready to appoint a social democrat Ministry the communists backed down and accepted a compromise.[128] E. Kilpi, a former social democrat, a very unfrightening figure and not a member of SKP, became minister of the interior, so that it remained in SKDL hands. H. Kuusinen entered the government as minister without portfolio, so that the overall political balance remained unchanged. SKP seems to have deceived itself into believing that it had scored a success, and it is true that the failure to wrest control of the police from SKDL hands rankled with their opponents. But when they claimed that 'our workers have again shown their strength', and that 'the masses understood that the question of the communists being in the government is essentially a question of democracy' and went on to say that the communists would meet any new efforts of the reactionaries with the same kind of mass response, they were showing a foolish overconfidence.[129]

Before the election in July SKP tried a manoeuvre to boost their electoral appeal. The three communist ministers wrote a formal letter saying that there was reason to think that the Soviet Union would now listen favourably to a request for a reduction of the burden of reparations.[130] The Soviet government, which one assumes had inspired the move in the first place, was receptive, and agreed on 2 June to reduce the balance of reparations outstanding by half, a gift worth 73.5 million dollars to the Finnish people. It was probably a miscalculation to think that SKP could earn much credit by securing a reduction of what most Finns believed to be a monstrous injustice, and in addition the way in which it was done caused some damage inside SKDL, for M. Pekkala seems to have resented the way in which the SKP ministers had taken the initiative in the matter, perhaps feeling that they had tried to monopolise the credit which he felt ought to go to him as prime minister. It was certainly observable that Pekkala's efforts on behalf of SKDL during the election campaign seemed half-hearted—this could have been his customary indolence but perhaps he was sulking over the lack of respect shown for him by his SKP colleagues.

Yet in spite of all their difficulties, SKP went into the 1948 election fairly confident of success. The party historian says that 'SKDL went into the election sure of victory. It was generally believed that the achievements under the democratic line and their significance for the future of our people was clearly understood by all our citizens'.[131] The SKDL election manifesto was based firmly on the Big Three Agreement. The basic problems for the immediate future were defined as building even closer friendship with the Soviet Union, completing the purge of fascists, which would require the ending of security of tenure for government servants, and 'a new spirit' which must be introduced into 'official propaganda, in the schools, and the whole of our cultural life'.[132] SKDL claimed credit for the very good economic recovery since

1945 but said that they could do even better if they had
the power to impose effective price controls, carry further
tax reforms, and carry out their progamme of nationalisation and land reform. The reactionary elements in SDP
and the Agrarian Party had been able to block these measures in the outgoing Parliament and they aspired even to
reverse what had been achieved since 1945. Therefore it
was up to the voters, by supporting progressive candidates
everywhere, to break down the obstacles to further advance.

Considering the misfortunes which had overtaken them
in the months preceding the election, and in particular
the sustained scare campaign against their alleged undemocratic intentions, SKDL held on fairly well in the election
of 1948. They lost some twenty-three thousand votes overall, or just 3 per cent of their 1945 total, though this was
unevenly distributed. SKDL actually increased its vote in
the thinly populated north but in some constituencies in
the south their vote fell by as much as 20 per cent. The
net result was to cut their parliamentary representation
to thirty-eight seats, while both the social democrats
and the agrarians made gains. Clearly the whole responsibility for the less popular aspects of the policy of the
Pekkala government had been visited by the electorate
on SKDL.[133] SKP had to concede defeat; they admitted
that 'the united forces of reaction have won a notable
victory in the elections . . . their main aim, to smash the
people's democrats, they could not achieve'.

After the election the government had to be reconstructed, and SKDL expected to be included—indeed they
declared openly that to keep them out would be an
overtly anti-Russian act and damaging to relations.[134]
It is doubtful whether this was a very well-chosen line of
argument in the aftermath of electoral defeat. However,
the social democrats and the agrarians were willing to
continue the coalition, but on their own terms, which
would reduce the communists to junior partners in the
government. They proposed to take six places each themselves and leave four for SKDL, but on condition that the

Ministry of the Interior be in non-communist hands. SKDL would have been ready to accept four places but insisted that the Ministry of the Interior must be one of them.[135] Alternatively, SKDL offered to form a workers' government with the social democrats and representatives of SAK, but no acceptable compromise emerged. It is to be assumed that basically the other parties preferred that SKDL be excluded from government entirely and did not want their offers to be accepted. In the end the social democrats formed a one-party minority government under K. A. Fagerholm, and SKDL went into very vigorous opposition. They were to stay there for eighteen years, though they could hardly have envisaged this in 1948, and perhaps if they had would have accepted a place in government on any terms. But the communists felt with good reason that it could do no good to be associated with policies which they would not be in a position to influence decisively and they were confident of getting back into government in a reasonably short time. They were not to know that the developing cold war would make collaboration between communists and non-communists virtually impossible everywhere for years to come.

From 28 to 30 August 1948 SKP held its eighth party
congress, which was able to take stock of the changed
circumstances. It was made clear in advance of the congress that the party line was unchanged; the basis of SKP
policy remained the broadest possible union of democratic
forces within the framework of a bourgeois society.[1]
H. Kuusinen presented the analysis that conditions in
Finland were not yet ready for socialism, because the bourgeoisie had not lost its will to power and the masses had
not yet developed the strength or the will to master it.[2]
SKP had made mistakes over the past years through its
inexperience in parliamentary and government work, but
its greatest failing had been the inability to lead the
masses effectively and to coordinate their actions with
those of the party inside the government so as to beat
down the opposition of the reactionaries.[3] There was still
trouble with Leftists in the party, who continued to oppose the democratic and reformist policies of the party
and were expressing their opposition through a 'mood of
hopelessness and passivity'.[4] The party would fight this
by a drive to win new membership and to raise the level
of its ideological preparedness. The congress accepted
new party statutes which emphasised that all the members must be fully active, that all must work with the
non-party masses, and that all study Marxism-Leninism.[5]
To implement the educational side of this the party set
up a central school in September 1948 which offered one
month courses for full-time students, while the Sirola
Correspondence College and district party correspondence
courses met the needs of those who could only study part-

time. But after some three years of this educational drive the party was still complaining that a majority of its members had not availed themselves of the facilities and apparently denied the need for this kind of study.[6]

The short-term task of the party was to bring down the Fagerholm government. In H. Kuusinen's words: 'This government must be got rid of, and the sooner the better'.[7] The Russian press had taken the lead in August in describing the Fagerholm government as a tool of imperialism and its mission as 'quietly to prepare the psychological and political conditions for a repetition of that destructive role which Finland played between the two wars'.[8] SKP enlarged on this analysis:[9]

> The government's purpose is, in the economic field, to bind the Finnish economy ever more closely to the depression-ridden economy of the west, to strengthen the power of big capital and add to the millionaire profits of the capitalists. In the political field, the aim of the reactionary bourgeoisie is to purge from state institutions the few democratic employees and to limit the general and political freedoms of the workers.

The early actions of the Fagerholm government lent a degree of plausibility to these charges: government institutions were being purged of SKDL sympathisers, the control of the state radio was completely changed,[10] Valpo was dissolved and a new security force, the security police, put in its place,[11] while the other branches of the police were purged. The 'arms dumps affair' was quickly wound up and the convicted men amnestied, and before long the politicians convicted in the war responsibility trial began to be released from prison. Trade with the Soviet Union declined and in the autumn of 1948, for the first time since the war, there was significant unemployment in Finland. Thus there were plenty of grounds on which SKP could seek to rally the masses to resist any return to the bad old days. The party hoped that in doing so it could prove that it had the power, through its influence over the masses, to make Finland ungovernable without SKP participation and thus force its way back into the government.

But in fact SKP rendered its self-appointed task, the leadership of a united democratic front, almost impossible, and by exactly the kind of mistake that had proved to be fatal after 1928—a blind and unreasoning loyalty to policies laid down in Moscow. It must be made clear that this did not then have any serious effect on the hard-core support which SKDL enjoys among the Finnish masses. No matter what inconsistencies, idiocies and humiliations adherence to the international party line involved, no matter how much SKP made itself appear to be a puppet organisation manipulated from Moscow, the loyal support of 20 per cent or more of the Finnish electorate was unaffected. What was affected adversely was the hope, proclaimed at the eighth congress, of adding to this hard core of support significant elements from the social democrat workers, the small farmers and the progressive bourgeoisie which was frustrated because these people accepted the identification of SKP with a slavish devotion to Russian interests—an image which the bourgeois and social democrat press and publicity assiduously cultivated.

There is no doubt that the relationship of SKP to the Soviet Union is unusually close for a communist party outside the actual Soviet bloc. A number of factors contribute to this: on the Russian side there is a special relationship with Finland arising from her being a border state, and expressed in the mutual assistance treaty and in the readiness of the Russian government to interfere in Finland's internal affairs whenever they feel their interests are threatened. Although the Soviet Union is very careful not to involve SKP in its official relations with the Finnish government, the party does get involved indirectly, as when in 1948 Russian propaganda treated the exclusion of SKP from government as an anti-Soviet manifestation.

SKP is not now, of course, run directly from inside Russia, as it was between 1930 and 1944, and the party has always sought to deny that it is in any sense subservient to foreign interests. A. Äikiä, parodying the words of a famous Finnish nationalist, declared that 'we are not Russians, we do not want to become Americans, we are therefore Finns, and for that reason fight for Finnish independence'.[12] One can also accept Leino's assessment that the party does not receive any substantial monetary assistance from Russia.[13] But sheer geographical proximity makes it easy for SKP delegations to go to Russia to be briefed, or for Russian delegations to come to Finland. The sheer number of such recorded exchanges of visits since 1944 testifies to the maintenance of intimate personal contacts between the leaders of SKP and the leadership of the Russian Communist Party; in addition to which there was still, in Moscow, the by now almost legendary O. W. Kuusinen, the intimate of Stalin, who was peculiarly well placed to keep SKP in line. He contributed a fair number of articles and pamphlets over the years to re-inforce the ideological purity of the party.

Thus perhaps more readily than most communist parties in the west, SKP identified itself unreservedly with a rigid acceptance of the Russian position in the cold war, in a way which created immediate obstacles to cooperation with uncommitted progressive opinion. For SKP was forced to deny that there could be any honest uncommitted opinion; it accepted that the world was divided into two camps, the camp of peace and progress led by the Soviet Union, and the camp of imperialism and war led by the United States. SKP recognised no third world, would admit no neutrality. This was spelled out early in 1948 in a book by Äikiä, whose title, A Third Way?, speaks for itself. The whole book is built round the proposition that 'there is no third way between the camps of the forces of peace and the warmongers . . . the third way leads straight to capitalist reaction.' It follows, for instance, that there is no real progressive policy in which the communists have no share, because 'communists are the most consistent supporters of both democracy and socialism, and any other party which supports the enlargement of democracy and the building of socialism is forced of necessity into joint action with the communists'.[14] O. W. Kuusinen wrote on the same theme in 1949 when he said: 'Delusions about some "third way" come only from the efforts of right-social democrats, who try to conceal from the workers that they belong with the associates of bourgeois reaction. Thus the "third way" is only the fine covering for a policy of reaction'.[15]

In this way SKP drummed into the minds of the Finnish public that they gloried in their unswerving devotion to the Soviet Union. Without a moment's hesitation they solemnly condemned Tito and the Yugoslav heresy. They proclaimed that Russia was the best guarantee of the survival of democracy in Finland, because through the peace treaty the Soviet Union 'sets direct limits to the revival of fascism and warmongering in our country';[16] they asserted that 'the real patriotism' for which SKP stands involves the intimate collaboration of the Finnish and Russian proletariats 'in a broad international democratic camp led by the Soviet Union'. The most spectacular expression of SKP's loyalty was the way in which the party joined in the personality cult of Stalin. Hertta Kuusinen wrote of Stalin: 'In himself he represents that tendency, that class, and that party, whose task is to change the world into a happy dwelling place for humanity'.[17] One can understand too why it was difficult for Finns who could remember the winter war, and had observed what had happened to the Baltic republics, to accept Pessi's claim that:[18]

> . . . ever wider social circles in Finland acknowledge comrade Stalin's great work in developing friendly relations between our countries . . . the great example of comrade Stalin as the defender of the equality of all nations great and small, obliges the communist parties of all countries to multiply their endeavours to protect national independence and liberty. . . . The Finnish Communist Party and the

whole of the democratic movement in the country will not spare any effort to carry out, for their own part, the counsel of our beloved teacher and leader.

Thus in 1948 SKP set out to win the allegiance of all progressive forces and simultaneously armoured itself in the repulsive Stalinist dogmatism which doomed its efforts to failure. The first battle in SKP's war on the Fagerholm government occurred in October, when a strike broke out in the Arabia porcelain factory in Helsinki. The local union branch began the strike in defiance of SAK, which then declared Arabia an open shop and invited the workers to break the strike. SKP naturally backed the strikers and made it a test of strength. For several days, from 22 to 25 October, there were violent clashes between strike pickets and the police who were escorting strike-breakers into the factory. SKDL put down questions in Parliament, and lobbied Fagerholm and Paasikivi, but the strike was broken, and to consolidate the victory the government successfully prosecuted a number of the strikers for resisting the police.[19] This first encounter had ended in defeat for SKP, but they were not discouraged. They concluded that the episode only showed 'that in the present situation every wage demand becomes a political struggle', and defeat only proved that the communists must be better prepared next time. The workers had begun to move in protest at the Fagerholm government and SKP must build up their movement from below since SAK refused to support them.[20]

As 1949 began the party was reasonably confident. The emergence of major unemployment should put some militancy into the workers and the Agrarian Party, unhappy at being out of office, was already criticising the Fagerholm government for its poor relations with the Soviet Union and might be willing to help bring it down.[21] H. Kuusinen published a major analysis of the situation early in 1949:[22] both SDP and the Agrarian Party were really petty-bourgeois parties which were being used by the big capitalists for their own ends. Therefore SKP could expose this situation and detach their mass following from the leadership. She repeated that socialism could be achieved peacefully, as the example of Czechoslovakia proved, but this needed the breaking of the will to rule of the capitalists, the detachment from them of the petty bourgeoisie who were their allies, and the organisation of the majority of the workers to will the overthrow of capitalism. All these conditions must be fulfilled; in the interim period, reform policies could strengthen the workers and weaken the enemy but they are not an end in themselves unless they really alter the power structure. SKP sought these ends through its parliamentary work and wanted to be in the government to gain access to information. But in the end, while the class war lasts it is the action of the masses that is decisive: 'The masses are the force on which the whole movement rests. The most important weapon of the Communist Party is their self-conscious activity, its leadership of them and participation in the deciding of every question, however insignificant'. Since it is commonly alleged that in the course of 1949 SKP was trying to turn industrial unrest into a revolutionary overthrow of the existing order, it is worth stressing again that SKP specifically ruled out on Marxist grounds even a Czech type of revolution in current Finnish conditions; the time for that had not yet come. Their aim was to get back to the *status quo* of 1948 and regain a place in a coalition government, for 'government without the communists has always been reactionary government'.[23]

In fact their main emphasis had been put on international affairs, and above all on the peace movement; the party council of March 1949 gave this priority.[24] Äikiä alleged that the government was preparing Finland as an advanced base of imperialism and breaking the peace treaty by permitting the uncontrolled dissemination of anti-Soviet propaganda. He denied that SKP was acting as an informer and provocateur in Russo-Finnish relations as the government was claiming. SKP attended the Paris Conference which launched the peace movement and collected 270,000 signatures for its peace appeal.[25] The peace movement was also the central theme for the party's May Day slogans and rallies.

From 28 June to 1 July SKDL held its second congress, which is important because it adopted a basic policy document for the movement. This programme, which was adopted unanimously, had been drafted by a committee of four, two communists and two ex-social democrats. It was characterised by its concrete, non-ideological nature, which was inevitable, as a communist observer notes, because 'it is impossible to reconcile communist ideology with the spirit of the old social democrat party and the agrarian-christian rural spirit'.[26] So Palmgren, who introduced the programme to the congress, emphasised that it contained no references to socialism: 'The word socialism does not appear here at all. This programme really involves the achievement of progressive measures on the basis of the existing society'.[27]

The programme begins by stressing that good relations with the Soviet Union are the foundation of everything, and then accepts the existing bourgeois democratic system but claims that its democracy is 'to a great extent nullified' by the surviving economic power of big capital.[28] The programme aims to break down this power and achieve real democracy, which will be a necessary preliminary for the 'final liberation of the working people'.[29] Among the essential democratic rights which need to be secured are the right to strike and hold demonstrations, through which the workers can give 'direct expression of their will'. The programme proposed a planned economy with extensive nationalisation, tax reforms which would lighten the burdens on the working people, land reform and a system of government aid which would help the dairy-based economy of the small family farm, complete social security, and a free health service. The machinery of government was to be democratised, security of tenure for civil servants ended, and some element of election introduced into the selection of the judiciary. The army would be reformed and democratised to fit it for its role under the mutual assistance treaty, while cultural life would be protected from capitalist perversion.[30] The document was adopted as a definitive programme for SKDL 'which will last as long as the present social and political system', and it expressed what SKP stands for in immediate practical terms. It rests on the need, at this stage of development, for the workers to enlist the aid of the small farmers and the progressive intellectuals, on the assumption that by working together these groups can realise their immediate aims. While this situation lasts, the question of socialism and the ultimate aims of SKP are held in abeyance.[31] Finally, the SKDL congress indicated the overriding immediate objective, to bring down the Fagerholm government and re-install a government of 'all the progressive forces' which would unambiguously support the peace policies of the socialist camp; the presidential election, due at the beginning of 1950, might be the means to realise this.

But the dominant event of 1949 in Finland was the great strike movement which began in the northern city of Kemi. There are two opposing myths about this sequence of events: the anti-communist myth is that SKP was responsible for starting the strike movement, that it consistently perverted it for political ends, and that it planned to develop it into a general insurrectionary movement to reverse the democratic verdict of the 1948 election. The communist myth is that the Fagerholm government, acting on the orders of American imperialists, deliberately provoked the strike with the intention of attacking the living standards of the workers. They would also weaken the trade union movement, discredit SKP, nullify the democratic safeguards embodied in the peace treaty, and launch a general repression to make Finland a secure base for the imperialist warmongers: 'The Kemi insurrection-provocation was a consistent follow-up of the *coup*-provocation staged in Helsinki in the spring of 1948'.[32] Neither of these fantasies is worth much credence by itself, though both reflect and distort aspects of what really happened.

The background was that the economic situation in

Finland was deteriorating in 1949, and the paper and wood industries were having difficulties in their export markets for the first time since the war. In March 1949 the Kemi Co., whose timber and pulp interests dominated the Kemi region, with the approval of the government began pressing for a change in the wages structure, seeking specifically to move from flat-rate to piece-work wages.[33] This might be considered provocative, for Kemi had always been a citadel of communism and militancy, where in 1948 SKDL had got 53 per cent of the vote. But in addition, prices were rising fast in 1949, local rents in Kemi were being raised, the price of bread increased sharply in June, and in July devaluation threatened further major increases in the cost of living, so that the workers had plenty to be militant about. The wage negotiations had dragged on until 25 June, when the employers singled out a small group of a few hundred workers and proposed for them new piece rates which could have meant reductions in earnings of up to 40 per cent. The local trade unions declared a strike for 1 July unless the company made a better offer, and when this began they spread it to ever-wider groups until by 20 July some three thousand Kemi workers were on strike, making it virtually a general strike in the Kemi area. SKP had given the strike full support from the first, as would be expected in accordance with their declared policies, and there is no question that the party led the strike movement throughout. It is worth noting that on 12 July the committee of SAK, while declining to endorse the strike, did not oppose it either, while on 13 July the official social democrat newspaper wrote that the whole responsibility for the trouble rested with the Kemi Co., which was trying to revoke a valid wages agreement. This vindicates the communist claim that they had not started the trouble.[34]

So far it had been a straightforward industrial dispute, and it seems to have been the social democrats who introduced a political element when, through SAK, they tried to intervene and settle the dispute over the heads of the communist strike committee. When these attempts failed, and the communists remained firmly in control of the strike, SAK and the government began to take the line that the strike was both unofficial and illegal and that the employment of strike-breakers was permissible. On 2 August the first disorder occurred when a delegation of strikers invaded the company offices at Kemi, made some disrespectful remarks and gestures, but left without doing any damage before the police, who had been summoned, could intervene. From this point the situation deteriorated very fast. An official mediation attempt foundered because the government mediator would not recognise the communist-led strike committee. On 11 August the first black-legs arrived, and sensational scare stories were circulated in the non-communist press that the log-jam being built up because of the strike was of such proportions that it could not be cleared before the river froze in the autumn and would cause a major disaster at the spring thaw. There seem to be no very substantial grounds for this horror story; although the strike did continue beyond the disaster date indicated, the predicted catastrophe did not materialise. But it served to justify the government issuing orders under its emergency powers that the strikers must go back, and since SKP led the workers in defying this order there was an open confrontation between the strikers and the constitutional authorities.

Although the strike had not produced any serious disorder in Kemi, the government began to take security measures; some troops were alerted, and on 17 August fresh police precautions were ordered to protect strike-breakers, including the issue of submachine guns to some of the police. On 18 August the strikers held a meeting, at the end of which some of them decided to go along and see if there were strike-breakers at work. A large procession formed and moved towards the site. The authorities allege that it was their intention to commit violence, specifically to throw any strike-breakers they found into the waters of the Kemi river. The communists insist that it was an entirely peaceful and spontaneous demonstration, and there is certainly a lack of firm evidence that the strike meeting had made any decision on the matter. About the action of the authorities there is no ambiguity: a cordon of armed police was drawn up to block the path of the procession, and with this it duly collided. There are two versions of what happened then: the police say that incited by its communist leaders the procession defied repeated calls to disperse and attacked the cordon so that the police had to fire in the air to stop them; the communists say that the police, in effect, ambushed the procession and began shooting into it without any real attempt to allow it to disperse. At most they will concede that some workers may have hurled abuse and stones at the police.[35]

An impartial observer will surely think that it was irresponsible of the strike leaders to permit the procession when violence could easily break out if it did come across any strike-breakers, but there is the evidence that the authorities were panicky and that some among them were looking for a showdown with the strikers. It is beyond dispute that the police did open fire, that two strikers were killed, one by a police bullet, and others were wounded. The authorities immediately declared a state of emergency in Kemi, ordered the troops to move in, raided the Communist Party offices, and arrested the strike leaders.[36] The result was an anti-climax; the state of emergency had to be cancelled when it became clear that there was no threat to public order and on 22 August the government publicly announced that the Kemi Co, had been legally in the wrong in seeking unilaterally to alter a valid wages agreement. To this extent the strikers were successful; the proposed wage-cutting scheme had to be withdrawn.[37]

But the communists now tried to build on what had happened, and encouraged and directed a wave of unofficial strikes designed to force SAK into presenting a demand for a general wage increase. Although at the peak of this movement some sixty thousand workers were

out, the government and SAK stood firm, on the grounds
that the strikes were politically motivated and illegal.[38]
The communists concede that the government won, because as they see it once the wage cut proposal was
withdrawn many of the social democrat workers withdrew
their support for the continuing strike movement.[39] Then
it was the turn of the government and SAK to counter-
attack. In September the SAK committee began to expel
member unions which had supported the strikes, on such
a scale that the membership of SAK fell from 350,000
to 200,000.[40] The government launched charges of insurrection, based on the incidents of 2 and 18 August,
against some hundred and fifty people in Kemi, and their
trial began on 7 September; it dragged on into the new
year, when sixty-three of the accused were convicted and
given prison sentences.[41] But even while the trial was
on the charges had carried so little conviction that the
government was proposing an amnesty, which was finally
passed in March 1950. Parallel charges were brought
against SKP officials and newspapers for inciting disorder
and bringing the government into contempt, but these
were mostly abortive. SKDL fought back in Parliament;
they attempted to impeach the minister of the interior
for what they claimed was a whole string of illegal actions[42]; yet when Pessi came to try to strike a balance,
he had to take most comfort from the thought that the
social democrat leaders in the government and SAK had
been 'exposed', and that the attempts to pin legal charges
of insurrection on SKP were so manifestly unfounded that
they could not be sustained.[43] Y. Murto insisted that
SKP was proud that it had led the strikes but claimed that
all talk of insurrection was absurd—the strikes had simply
expressed the very real grievances of the workers, and if
only the social democrat workers had stood firm the strike
wave could have succeeded.[44] In fact, neither side can
show convincingly that the events of 1949 were the result
of deep-laid plots by their opponents. The truth is that
once the initial discontents of the workers came to a head
at Kemi, both SKP and their opponents tried their best

to turn the situation to political advantage and that the end result was pretty much a draw. But there may well be substance in Pessi's claim that fear of the Soviet Union invoking the civil rights clauses of the peace treaty restrained the authorities from carrying their repressive measures too far.[45]

As cold war feeling intensified, SKP tended to draw ever closer to its Moscow support. Although SKP was never a member of Cominform, it endorsed all the Cominform theses, confirmed its condemnation of Tito, approved the Rajk-Kostov trials, and deduced from them that SKP itself must be vigilant against the danger of similar infiltration by agents of imperialism.[46] To guard against this a major purge of party membership was carried through under cover of a re-issue of party cards. H. Kuusinen noted that SKP had a peculiarly low level of ideological education and still lacked practical experience in guiding the masses, so that it needed the help 'which the whole world communist movement, led by the Soviet Union's experienced and high quality Communist Party, the example and guide for the world communist movement, offers'.[47] But of course the ultimate source of light was the man described in December 1949 as:[48]

> . . . the Lenin of our times . . . the comrade and friend of all the deprived and oppressed, the man who has the head of a scientist, the features of a worker, and the simple dress of a soldier. It is fortunate that the country of socialism and the international workers' movement has a leader like him.

Already, Stalinist paranoia in the party had reached the level where the SKP central committee solemnly declared that the current government efforts to attract western tourists to Finland was only a cover for anti-Soviet espionage by the imperialists.[49]

After the strikes, one of the first political tasks set by the party concerned the presidential election of January 1950. The bourgeois parties would have been willing to re-elect Paasikivi without an election, but SKDL would not agree unless it were re-admitted to the government and it had enough votes in Parliament to force a formal election.[50] In view of SKP's later adoption of Paasikivi as almost one of themselves, it is interesting to recall that in 1949 he was a man 'who had belonged to the blackest wing of reaction . . . and his politics have been consistent with this'. SKP could not forgive Paasikivi for having installed the Fagerholm government and told the electors that 'Paasikivi's election means a new demonstration against a policy of friendship between Finland and the Soviet Union, a continuation of the present reactionary direction'.[51] For the election SKDL ran M. Pekkala, and did quite well, with 337,000 votes and sixty-seven electors in an electoral college of three hundred, which was three more than SDP got.[52] The basic electoral strength of SKDL was clearly unbroken, and in the event the election did work in their favour; Paasikivi was re-elected with social democrat support but agreed to a change of government. His new prime minister, the agrarian leader U. Kekkonen, was a man who always favoured conciliation with the Soviet Union, and if possible with SKP as well, and Kekkonen would have been willing to take SKDL back into the government. The social democrats however would not serve with the communists and in the end Kekkonen formed an agrarian minority government.[53] But the new government ostentatiously repudiated its predecessor, amnestied the Kemi strikers, negotiated a new trade agreement with the Soviet Union, and many of its ministers signed the Stockholm peace appeal. In July SKP denounced these moves as mere window-dressing, because no real change had occurred—the difference between Fagerholm and Kekkonen was 'rather apparent than real', a case of 'one master—two servants'.[54] But when it came to deeds rather than words it is significant that in November 1950, when the SDP tried to force their way back into power, SKDL used its votes to save the Kekkonen government, though this did them no good in the

end, because in January 1951 SDP was taken into a new
Kekkonen government—once more the arch-agents of
American imperialism were in the seats of power.[55]

When the party council met from 11 to 13 March 1950
it still put first the struggle for peace.[56] SKP had held a
national peace congress in October, had circulated a peace
address round the country, and had organised a 'herald of
peace' who ran round the country to publicise the movement,[57] while they eventually got eight hundred thousand
signatures for the Stockholm peace appeal of 1950.[58] The
party stressed that for the peace movement to succeed,
workers unity was essential and the party must see that
its influence extended everywhere. The members were
warned that 'communists must not isolate themselves in
their own organisations in any field, but must strengthen
their organised power to make SKP able to lead the united
forces of democracy in the battle against reaction'.[59] But
the mere desire to take the lead was not enough. The
council recognised the very poor rate of penetration by the
party in rural areas, while in the key field of trade union
activity SKP was repeatedly frustrated and outmanoeuvred.
When the Fagerholm government fell, the social democrats felt free to harass its successor so as to force their
own way back to power. Suddenly SAK became militant; in
May 1950 an official rail strike successfully beat the
government and helped to force a general wage increase.[60] SAK continued to make militant noises, even
issuing a threat of a general strike, until the details were
settled to its satisfaction. At one time, in August 1950,
SAK had a hundred thousand workers out on strike.[61]

This gave SKP a very difficult part to play. They wanted
to discredit the SAK leaders and represent their militancy as phoney, yet they had to support all strikes,
although this might mean that SAK got the credit for
their success.[62] But the party did not flinch; in a statement of 30 September they reminded their members
that it was their duty to support the SAK-led strike
movements. But this did make it difficult for SKP to
fight the SAK leadership; where they did, as in the long

campaign for the re-admission of the unions expelled in 1949, or in their campaign to keep SAK in the World Federation of Trade Unions with the communist countries, they had little success. Indeed, they had to fight very hard to stop SAK authorising the setting up of new, non-communist unions to replace the ones expelled, while at the end of 1950 the communists could not prevent SAK making a new agreement with the government for a wage and price freeze.[63]

Final defeat in this sector came to SKP at the SAK congress in 1951. SKP claims that the elections for this congress were rigged; they say that SAK created ghost unions with imaginary memberships to swell the establishment voting power, while the expelled unions naturally could not take part. The result was certainly a clear majority for the social democrats,[64] and it would be nothing unusual if some pretty dubious tactics contributed to the outcome—the sort of tactics which SKP had pioneered in the old SAJ in the 1920s. The congress was naturally a series of defeats for the communist line; the policies adopted at the last congress were repudiated, the wage freeze was confirmed, the expulsions of the communist unions were confirmed, SAK resigned from WFTU, and the social democrat control of the whole SAK organisation was strengthened. SKP did its best to put a brave face on the matter—'the army is not dispersed although the headquarters is in enemy hands'[65]—but the reality was that in a straight fight for the control of the trade union movement, SDP had won. The position of the 1920s was now reversed: if SKP led its followers out of SAK they would appear as the splitters.[66] SKP could not even keep up the basic militancy of the workers and there was a dramatic decline in strike activity in the early 1950s.[67]

The year 1951 found SKP firmly embedded in its Russian-inspired rut. There was a general election in July, and the election manifesto starts from the situation created by the cold war, asserting that Finland has been led into the wrong camp and complaining that fascists and imperialists freely exercised their dangerous and provocative activities: 'There are only two ways to choose, one way of terror, hunger and war, the other way of better living, democracy and peace'. The manifesto makes all domestic issues aspects of the international struggle.[68] O. W. Kuusinen sent a reminder from Moscow that 'the defence of peace is now the most vital matter for all levels of the population, but I would like to emphasise: the most important tasks and responsibilities in this matter fall to the workers. The Finnish working class now faces a historic test of its maturity'.[69] The actual election result was quite encouraging; on a reduced percentage poll SKDL got over 390,000 votes, an absolute increase on 1948, and received forty-three seats,[70] but since the social democrats still refused to consider them as possible partners in government the communists were no nearer their main objective. But it is interesting to see how three years of sterile cold war politics had not adversely affected SKDL's popular following.

In November 1951 SKP held its ninth congress, and this simply elaborated the endless theme that the struggle for peace must have priority, that all domestic issues are subsumed in the peace problem, and that only the unity of the working people can defeat the warmongers.[71] Pessi elaborated these themes both in his report to the congress and in his summary of its significance afterwards: 'The most important of the congress decisions, the central business, was developing the work for peace'.[72] Finland, like Sweden, was already fully integrated in the imperialist camp, the civil defence organisation was a covert fascist militia, dangerous bodies like 'The Finnish Military-psychological Society' were in secret contact with NATO, and Finland's joining GATT and the World Monetary Fund were subtle moves by the imperialists. Because the unity of the working people could alone defeat these sinister developments, party members must do everything to win over those misguided workers who followed the social democrat leaders. To succeed in this, zealous party members must refrain from spoiling things by abusing

SDP, for they must always 'behave in a comradely and calm manner towards social democrat workers and their leaders'.[73] It was equally wrong to press social democrats to become converted to communism, if conversion was made a condition of cooperation.

The most interesting part of an otherwise tedious congress was the report on the internal affairs of the party. Here the congress expressed alarm because the growth aimed at by the last congress had not been realised; they had indeed increased their membership in the countryside, but some bourgeois members had fallen away—no doubt repelled by arid Stalinist polemics.[74] There were two other disturbing phenomena: one was the rising age of the party membership; in five districts the members had an average age of forty, so that 'our party absolutely needs rejuvenation'. The other was that the conduct of party business in the branches had become sterile and tedious, so that a majority of members stayed away from party meetings and a tiny minority had to do everything; again the Stalinist spirit was clearly doing its work and killing the party at its roots. Naturally the party resolved to put this right, though it was not explained how, except to insist that party work should be firmly rooted in the places of employment, where contact with non-party workers would be automatic and the party could exercise real leadership.[75] Progress in breathing new life into party work at the branch level was evidently slow, for Aaltonen noted in 1952 how the party had not adopted 'Comrade Stalin's wise counsel on the decisive influence of organisational work for the realisation of the party line', and complained that at all levels party committees and meetings barely functioned, that the secretary simply dictated an agenda which was automatically endorsed, making a mockery of party democracy.[76]

The year 1952 was an uneventful one for SKP. In January, Kekkonen made a speech in which he floated the idea of a neutral bloc in Scandinavia.[77] This had no appeal at that time for SKP, since it was committed to the dogmas that there was no third way, but the party noted with pleasure that their enemies were now divided over foreign policy.[78] The ending of reparations deliveries was a help to everyone in Finland, but on the other hand German re-armament was becoming an issue, and in May the central committee pointed out that it had an obvious bearing on the mutual assistance treaty.[79] Finland's success in the Miss World competition drew some very severe communist comment on the spread of decadent American cultural values at the expense of decent Finnish standards, which wound up with the conclusion that 'the fight against American anti-culture is part of the fight for peace. And in it, laughter is a powerful weapon'. If SKP had ever understood that last point they might have been much more successful than they were in influencing uncommitted opinion.

The great event of the year was the nineteenth congress of the Russian Communist Party. This was eagerly anticipated as likely to provide important pointers to future developments.[80] Naturally it did, and SKP's members were guided into drawing the appropriate conclusions. Pessi specially recommended Stalin's paper on the economic problems of socialism in the Soviet Union, for he was sure that the success of the Russian five-year plan would at last convince the Finnish workers of the superiority of the socialist system.[81] Pessi also gave a splendid example of how Stalinist paranoia leads to total divorce from reality, when he sought to illustrate Stalin's thesis that the bourgeoisie in small countries will always sell out the national interest to the imperialists by reference to a new and totally innocent Finnish law on the local autonomy of the Åland islands, which Pessi alleged—without the remotest justification—was intended to facilitate their use as an imperialist base. SKP also took to heart Stalin's warning to the nineteenth congress that bourgeois nationalism was lurking in some communist parties, and this may be connected with the otherwise unexplained dismissal of the prominent R. Palmgren from the editorship of the paper *Vapaa Sana* in January 1953.

The hysteria underlying so many SKP pronouncements was very clear in the months preceding the death of Stalin. An article on American subversion in Finland asserted that the scholarships offered to Finnish students at American universities were simply a scheme to recruit spies for the imperialist cause, while MRA was just a cover organisation for spreading imperialist propaganda.[82] The death itself brought an article from O. W. Kuusinen on, 'J. V. Stalin—the great leader of nations', whose 'whole lifetime was one great uninterrupted struggle for the success and happy future of the working people'. He stressed Stalin's thesis that everywhere the bourgeoisie had sold itself to reaction, so that even bourgeois democracy was now only defended by the communist parties.[83] I. Lehtinen contributed a memorial article entitled 'I Heard Stalin Speak', which regretted those occasions when it had been a mere radio broadcast that she had heard, so that 'atmospherics stole away valued words', but 'his calm voice and strong delivery created, even at a distance, close and direct contact'.[84]

Bourgeois Finland was in trouble in 1953, for the Korean war boom had turned to recession, unemployment was high, and the government was beset by chronic budget deficits and scandals in high places. SKP did its best to rouse the workers to fight, through demonstrations and strikes, but they had to concede that it was not easy.[85] In July 1953 Kekkonen re-formed his government and proposed a massive policy of retrenchment, sacking civil servants and cutting social services, including family allowances. To this SKP replied with a new call to the masses, on 2 August, to resist the cuts;[86] and in fact the cumulative opposition to the cuts of the many vested interests resulted in the fall of the government in November and family allowances were saved. The party got an encouragement from the local government elections in September, in which they had made much of the responsibility of local authorities for organising effective unemployment relief, and SKDL got more than four hundred thousand votes for the first time in any national election. SDP did quite well too, for it had joined in opposing cuts in the social services, but SKP was confident that their secret links with imperialism could be exposed and their supporters won over.[87]

However the solution of the government crisis did not please SKP, for the president appointed a caretaker government, including for the first time since the war ministers from the conservative Kokoomus Party, the embodiment in the eyes of SKP of the blackest reaction. SKP, which maintained that Kekkonen had been replaced for being too friendly to the Soviet Union, called this a 'right-wing seizure of power' and pushed their own solution of a revived Big Three coalition.[88] However, Paasikivi had also called a general election for early in 1954, and since the bourgeoisie were manifestly deeply divided, and after its successful campaign to save the family allowances, SKP had good hopes for the election.[89] In February a statement from the central committee announced a major effort to attract social democrats into cooperation with SKDL, because the reentry of Kokoomus into government showed the need for a united front of the workers to resist further advances by reaction. The statement denies that SKP is seeking the destruction of SDP, while conceding that 'thoughts of that kind have been put forward on occasion, but for decades now have been rejected as wrong and harmful'. SKP assured the social democrats that it sought genuine partnership; under conditions of socialism it was proper for communists and social democrats to merge into a single movement, as they did in the people's democracies, but under capitalist conditions unity of the workers is not organisational but takes the form of joint actions. Since there can be no conflict of interest between one worker and another, this collaboration is entirely natural. This appeal to the social democrats became the central theme of 1954. The party admitted that communists had often been guilty of using offensive language against social democrats, thus failing in 'their class duty to workers who think differently', but it would not happen any more.[90] The communists did not even ask, at this stage, that social democrats should join SKDL: 'We do not ask social democrats to abandon their principles to achieve unity'. Unity would grow in three stages: first work side by side, then assimilate one another's ideas, finally achieve organisational unity.[91]

The SKDL election manifesto for 1954 is very similar to that of 1951. There are still only two choices, imperialism and war or the Soviet Union and peace, and workers' unity is still the key to success. Otherwise specific policy proposals stand unchanged.[92] There was a high turn-out of voters in 1954, and SKDL improved its vote, but this still left it at forty-three seats, and the party had to recognise that it was not winning over any substantial new working-class vote from the social democrats.[93] Still, the central committee expressed satisfaction with the result and predictably suggested a Big Three government, which was as predictably refused. Instead there was a prolonged government crisis, since although the other parties could agree to exclude SKDL they could not agree on much else, and it took until October for Kekkonen to emerge with his fifth government. He got tacit SKDL support, for now both SKP and the Soviet Union were grudgingly acknowledging that Kekkonen was the best bourgeois friend that they had. SKP put it rather meanly when they said that Kekkonen was not by conviction devoted to friendship with the Soviet Union but:[94]

> . . . because of pressure from the mass of peace-loving Finnish farmers, and as a representative of certain commercial interests among the bourgeoisie, he reckons that for the moment the development of good relations and especially trade relations with the Soviet Union is to Finland's advantage.

In fact, relations with Russia were blooming in 1954. There was a new trade agreement, a large Russian credit for Finland, and although the Kekkonen government declined an invitation to attend a security conference in Moscow it made suitably friendly noises. It would seem that the post-Stalin leadership in Moscow was beginning to see a potential role for Finland as a showpiece for peaceful coexistence, and as some kind of a bridge between east and west. H. Kuusinen, in a speech on 25 July 1954, noted that 'the special position of Finland as the neighbour of a Soviet Union friendly to our people, and on the border of the two world market systems, gives the Finnish people exceptional possibilities for safeguarding peaceful construction and democratic development, prosperity and the fostering of a progressive culture'.[95] In this speech one can detect the glimmerings of a change of line; perhaps there was a 'third way' for Finland after all, though it was not quite time for this yet.

For SKP held its tenth congress from 2 to 5 May 1954, and Pessi was still quite clear that there were only two camps and that, for instance, the Nordic Council for Scandinavian Cooperation, which Finland wanted to join, was 'a branch movement of the Atlantic aggressive alliance'; Finland must stay away from it, though SKP would welcome a genuine Scandinavian break with the imperialist camp. The peace movement was still of vital importance, although 'our party does not seek to control the peace movement or keep anyone out of it'. The central aim of SKP was the broadest possible progressive front, and nothing should be allowed to stand in the way of this. SKP stood for proletarian dictatorship still, but this only means that during the transition to socialism the democratic majority will take and hold power. But in any case, SKP is not now proposing socialism but an alliance for a real bourgeois democracy within a capitalist system. The Soviet Union for its part does not confine cooperation in Finland to SKP but is ready to have dealings with all friendly groups. Pessi summed up the position as follows:[96]

> Take any question you like, and you see that the
> cooperation of democratic forces is possible. It is
> possible because our Communist Party is not a
> sectarian party, which wants to be a 'perpetual
> opposition', but a true Finnish mass party, which
> wants to take part with all the other democratic
> forces in Finland in building a happy Finland.

Still, there was to be no retreat on the essential points
of ideology, as a set of new party statutes made clear.[97]
The party is defined in these as 'the organised advance
guard of the Finnish working class . . . its activity is
based on the teachings of Marx, Engels, Lenin and
Stalin', and although all party decisions are made 'on
the basis of free discussion', democratic centralism is
still the rule.[98] The purpose of the party is to combine workers, farmers and intellectuals in a struggle to
democratise political, economic and cultural life in order
to 'overthrow capitalism and create a socialist society
as the first phase of communism'. Even so there is a
clear mood of *détente* in this tenth congress, and this
was to be cautiously extended, following step by step
the line laid down in the Soviet Union.

As one follows SKP through the year 1955, one cannot
but admire the sheer imperturbability with which its
old Stalinist leaders proclaimed that what they had once
sworn was black had in fact been white all the time.
There was the case of the rehabilitation of Tito, res-
olutely damned in 1948 and 1949, and steadily abused
ever since. Now SKP welcomed the recognition of Yugoslavia as fully entitled to follow her own road to socialism. *Kommunisti* claims that this should not surprise anyone, because it was well known that 'all the countries
in the democratic camp are independent, not vassals'.[99]
The fall of Malenkov required a fresh diet of words to be
eaten; it was interpreted as showing the principle of
collective leadership at work. This was not unreasonable,
but unfortunately the party could not leave it at that but

324 THE COMMUNIST PARTY OF FINLAND

added that the principle of collective leadership had always been operative in the communist movement:[100]

> This was in force in the time of Lenin and Stalin, although both these great men enjoyed such prestige . . . that the people and the responsible leadership did not find it necessary to move them from the higher posts to a less demanding one. On the contrary, in the years of danger more than usual power was concentrated in their hands, because they were trusted without limits.

This account of Stalin's position came less than a year before the exposures at the twentieth congress. It must always baffle the outside observer that the leaders of SKP apparently could not appreciate how little credit such evasive and contradictory explanations must carry, and in consequence how their own integrity was impugned by them; even the credulity of the party faithful must have been somewhat shaken. It must have been further shaken in October when the central committee made a statement about the international situation, welcomed the Geneva spirit and revealed, rather hesitantly, that perhaps it would be all right after all for Finland to join the Nordic Council, so roundly denounced at the beginning of the year, provided certain reservations were adopted.[101] What had happened was that the Khruschev government had made a spectacular deal with Paasikivi, by which, in return for extending the term of the mutual assistance treaty, Finland got the return of the Russian military base on her territory at Porkkala and a hint that she could now go ahead and join the Nordic Council. SKP of course was not consulted about this reversal of Russian policy; it was not the first time that the party had faithfully defended an unpopular line of Russian policy and then had the mat pulled from under their feet by a sudden change of mind in Moscow, leaving the Finnish communists sprawling in undignified disarray. They just had to put the best face on it that they could.[102] Their dog-like loyalty to the Moscow line was so often poorly rewarded by the ungrateful beneficiary.

But it seems that the leaders of SKP were quite oblivious of the damage they were suffering—on the contrary they persuaded themselves that their popular support must be increasing as the cold war thawed out. In July 1955 they began to look forward to their prospects in the presidential election, due in January 1956. Quite regardless of what they had been saying about Paasikivi in 1950, they now praised him for his 'personal share in turning Finnish policy into peaceful paths and developing friendship between Finland and the Soviet Union'.[103] However, Paasikivi was not standing again, so they concluded that a workers' candidate should have a good chance, and in August they nominated the former social democrat E. Kilpi as the SKDL candidate, proclaiming that their aim was to secure for him the largest electoral vote.[104] Since all the parties were running their own candidate in this election, there would be a fair trial of strength, and in normal circumstances their ambition would have been a reasonable one. The election manifesto billed Kilpi as 'the man of peace', suggesting that all progressives should find him acceptable, and in December the party showed clear confidence that Kilpi would get a big vote. The result was a disaster, for the SKDL candidate got fewer electoral votes than any other, only fifty-six, as against seventy-two for Fagerholm and eighty-eight for Kekkonen, who was elected.[105] The party found it difficult to explain this away, for their percentage vote was only 18.7 per cent against the 21.4 per cent which Pekkala had received in 1950. They said that since all the candidates had pretended to be friends of the Soviet Union, there had not been a true measuring of political strength and that some of their voters had supported Kekkonen because he was known to be acceptable to the Russians and had the best chance. But one suspects that what the voting revealed was that SKP was beginning to suffer from what would now be called a credibility gap, as one revelation followed another until the climax was reached in the aftermath of the twentieth congress.

The twentieth congress, and the Khruschev speech denouncing Stalin, had a delayed-action effect; immediately, SKP had no difficulty in endorsing the public proceedings and the new lines on peaceful coexistence, the possibility of different roads to socialism, and of the peaceful transition to socialism, for these were not novel doctrines—it was more a matter of shifting emphasis. As the party remarked, 'revolution—peaceful or not—will still be revolution'.[106] But the reckoning was only postponed. In April 1956 the SKP leaders went into conference with the Russian leaders about the implications of de-Stalinisation,[107] and after a further period of delay, which must have seen some agonised discussion within a group composed of dedicated and life-long Stalinists, the central committee published its changed attitude in August 1956. They wished to make it clear that SKP not only recognised its past errors but also had a genuine desire to make a fresh start. Therefore they announced that the party was to have a new basic programme, to be presented to the party congress in 1957, but that this programme would be evolved in open public discussion, which would prove that SKP was indeed a democratic party and that the Stalinist past was dead and buried.[108] This intention was fully carried out; a draft for a new programme was circulated to party branches in October and an enlarged central committee meeting considered their comments on it in December, after which a revised draft was circulated and opened to discussion in the party press before being presented to the congress.

On 18 August the party issued a statement dealing with the cult of personality.[109] This confirmed that the personality cult of Stalin had led to mistakes and that his authoritarianism had stifled initiative and creativeness in the movement. The party conceded that, as *Kommunisti* put it, 'SKP's attitude to Stalin had in no

way departed from the cult of Stalin that had developed',
but this would now be put right:[110]

> It has begun boldly to correct the errors and wrongs
> caused by the personality cult of Stalin, which was
> alien to Marxism, and by the weakening of the
> collective leadership of the party.

In token of their repentance the Finnish victims of the
Stalin purges would be rehabilitated, so that figures like
Gylling, Rovio, Manner and many others ceased to be
un-persons, and as a party historian puts it, 'the actions
and careers of those in the ranks of the workers' movement who had been wrongly condemned were assessed
in the light of historical truth'. Unfortunately this was
exactly what the party did not do, so that the apparent
frankness and honesty of its confession failed to carry
conviction. What the party was doing was to substitute
for one falsified version of history—Stalin's—another
equally falsified version—Khruschev's. It was all very well
for SKP to apologise to Yugoslavia for having condemned
and abused her on the basis of 'one-sided and misleading
information'.[111] What this failed to explain is why for
so many years the truth about Yugoslavia, which had
been freely available, had been not just ignored but
fiercely denied. Having made its confession and done its
best to repair past errors, Leino says that the party even
offered to take him back into the leadership, though he
refused.[112] SKP assured the members and the public
that there would be no going back on the principles of
collective leadership and the right of party members to
express their views without restraint; the very recognition
of these principles guaranteed their continuance and this
has indeed proved to be the case in the Finnish party.

But there was no denying that all this had an immediate adverse effect on the party; as *Kommunisti* put
it, 'it is understandable that the coming to light of
Stalin's personal mistakes and the miscarriages of justice
that occurred under his leadership was an upsetting sur-

prise to tens of thousands of party members, supporters and friends', which seems a fairly mild way of putting it. The extent of the damage was indicated in the local government elections of 1956, which SKP tried to turn into a mass protest at growing economic difficulties.[113] The outcome was depressing; the SKDL vote sank from over 400,000 to 350,000[114] and the party recognised that this reflected loss of morale in its ranks; many of its supporters had been shocked into inactivity, while their enemies skilfully exploited the upheavals in the communist world.[115] But the leadership was not dismayed; these were purely transitory phenomena they claimed, and events have proved them right. In fact, considering the battering that it had received, SKP survived the Hungarian crisis remarkably well; the leadership endorsed the Russian thesis that events in Hungary had developed into a counter-revolution which justified Russian intervention.[116] Although SKP, like all other communist parties, had had its misgivings, it could boast with some justification that 'dividing up the communists into "Stalinists and Titoists", or "nationalists and internationalists", is a wish-fulfilling dream of our enemies, without any basis in truth'. There were of course both nationalists and Titoists in SKP, and even more in SKDL, and some of them broke with the movement, but the orthodox leadership succeeded in preventing any major defections and the organisation and discipline of the majority carried the party safely through the crisis of de-Stalinisation, postponing a final reckoning for more than another ten years, as the successful eleventh congress of the party was to demonstrate.

The year 1956 had also seen an event which briefly brought encouragement and relief to the hard-pressed SKP, the Finnish general strike of 1 to 20 March.[117] The general strike began as a dreadful mistake. At the beginning of 1956 SAK launched demands for a general wage increase, backed by SDP, which was showing its strength in anticipation of the negotiations for a new government that would have to be formed when President Kekkonen assumed office on 1 March. The leaders of SAK had backed their demand with a rather routine threat of a general strike, as they had on some previous occasions, in the confident expectation that there would be no need to carry it out. They had, however, mistimed it, since the old government reasonably declined to enter into a far-reaching settlement which would bind its successor, and when the ultimatum ran out on 1 March the strike began.[118] The SAK leaders were embarrassed, and their social democrat backers were furious, because a general strike must lead to some degree of cooperation with communist trade unionists, and for precisely the same reason, SKP leapt at the opportunity to show what workers' unity could mean in practice. It was obvious that the SAK leaders had not meant to carry out their threat from their failure to draw up precise instructions for the conduct of the strike. This gave local strike committees, on which communists could often take the lead, considerable scope for independent action. Trouble centered on road transport, for the lorry and bus drivers had not joined the strike.[119] The strikers tried to counter this by stopping petrol supplies, while the authorities in turn tried to maintain them, leading to numerous clashes around filling stations and a certain amount of violence. The communists and other activists were successful in maintaining the morale and militancy of the bulk of the strikers, and finally nerved the SAK leaders to make the ultimate threat to cut off public heating, which in Finland at that time of year could not be ignored. On 19 March the new government capitulated and agreed to the full wage increase demanded, and that the new rates should again be tied to the index and adjusted automatically in future.[120]

The general strike of 1956 has been described, with justification, as 'a solid and magnificent show of force' by the Finnish working class, and SKP was surely right in drawing the moral that it had proved how a united front of all the workers could achieve great things. The aftermath was therefore to be a great disappointment to

them, and was undoubtedly a betrayal of the workers'
legitimate expectations. The government began to increase prices and taxation so that much of the gain in
real wages was wiped out, in spite of the index tie. The
communists had early pointed out that to consolidate
the victory a system of effective price controls would be
necessary. But this was as nothing to the disaster caused
by the tensions and recrimination inside the non-communist part of the trade union movement after the
strike, and the strain it had put on their relations with
the social democrats. For the Finnish trade union movement began to break up. It must be stressed that SKP
did not want this, and did all it could to prevent it, but
in vain. On the one hand a number of powerful unions,
disgusted at the ambivalent policies of SAK, decided they
could do better by themselves and resigned from SAK.[121]
Then the surviving main body of SAK became involved
in a quarrel with SDP over the political repercussions of
the strike. In May 1957 that part of SAK faithful to the
SDP establishment broke away from the majority and
eventually set up a new trade union federation. The
majority of SAK then broke off its relations with SDP
in turn, causing a split to develop in the party. After
the 1957 congress of SDP there emerged an independent
social democrat grouping, dominated by the SAK leaders,
E. Skog and A. Simonen, and this contested the 1958
general election as the 'Social Democratic League'.[122]
Again it must be said that SKP had not encouraged or
wanted this social democrat schism. From their point of
view the schism split the trade union movement when
SKP wanted it to be united and in general made the
achievement of any kind of workers' unity even more
difficult. The schismatic social democrats offered nothing
from the ideological point of view—as the communists
noted, 'the Skog group has no clear or consistent political
line' but eventually the group did drift into partnership
with SKDL, chiefly to preserve itself from electoral ex-
tinction in the 1960s; it tended increasingly to range
itself with SKP on foreign policy issues, accusing SDP

of being fundamentally anti-Soviet, just as the communists did. So that although on balance the Skog group has been an embarrassment and a nuisance to SKP, they could not reject it as a partner.

The eleventh congress of SKP was held from 29 May to 2 June 1957, and was preceded by the first genuine public debate ever held by the communists on fundamental policy issues. T. Lehen, a leading party theorist, discussing in an article 'What Sort of a Programme Do We Need?', suggested that it ought to define the Finnish road to socialism and specify the various interim measures that would be needed before they could start out on it: 'We need a basic programme in which there is clearly defined that democratic road to socialism which the communists maintain is the only possible one'.[123] Among the issues prominently discussed in advance were how far socialism could be achieved by peaceful means,[124] what was the correct meaning of democratic centralism, and what was implied by free discussion within the party. At the end of it all the congress was assured that a real Marxist programme had emerged.[125]

The basic programme presented to the congress opens with definition and analysis: SKP is the 'party of the working class' which seeks to apply Marxist-Leninist theory to the particular circumstances of Finland.[126] The programme analyses the international situation in terms of the two camps, and one task of the party is to keep Finland out of the clutches of the imperialists and to support the forces making for peace headed by the Soviet Union. On the domestic front, Finnish capitalism remains the obstacle to progress but Finland is already fundamentally ripe for the advance to socialism, which will be achieved by overthrowing the dictatorship of the bourgeoisie and substituting 'workers' power, the dictatorship of the proletariat', and this must be powerful enough to beat down any attempts at a counter-revolution. This transformation will come about through a combination of parliamentary with mass action, and it is stressed that both are necessary, but any violence involved will be entirely the fault of the bourgeoisie if it ventures to resist. The revolution will immediately implement nationalisation, land reform, industrialisation based on planned economic development, promote co-operative movements in agriculture and distribution, and guarantee full rights to trade unions. There would be an end to unemployment and complete social security. These measures would create a socialist society which in turn would develop into a communist society.

The interim programme, which was valid as long as the capitalist structure of society remains, was in effect the SKDL programme with a certain amount of elaboration. SKP declares that it stands 'unconditionally for the national independence of our country', and that the rate and timing of the change from capitalism to socialism is 'for the Finnish people itself to decide'. It will depend wholly on the extent to which all the progressive forces work together, for every stage must be carried through in 'unbroken cooperation with the working people'. The whole programme was, as Pessi said, 'a programme for the common action of the working people'.[127] This programme is, as the party claims, solidly Marxist; it relates to the specific circumstances of Finland and defines a Finnish road to socialism, and its execution is to be entirely on the basis of the popular front, which will embody the will of a democratic majority. It therefore excludes outside intervention or any armed seizure of power by a minority, although it insists that at the critical point of the transfer from capitalism to socialism, parliamentary action by itself will not be enough but will be supplemented by the direct intervention of the masses. The programme as a whole is very consistent with what SKP had claimed to stand for since 1944, as modified by the ideas of the twentieth congress.

Pessi opened the eleventh congress with a general review, in which he stressed the popular front theme: 'The communists, in spite of many differences, do not consider the social democrats or any other party which has mass worker support as an enemy. Only the enemies of the common good of the workers are our enemies'.[128] He reported a party membership of forty-eight thousand, somewhat below the peak of earlier years; it was also still weak in the countryside and contained too few bourgeois intellectuals. Further, it was still disturbingly old; even the average age of recruits to the party was thirty-five.[129] Then the congress began a discussion of the programme which reflected those points in it that had caused most difficulty during the drafting process. There had been strong argument over whether to define the party as the 'party of the working class';[130] the critics had felt this to be a restricting definition, but Hyvönen assured them that members of other social classes are welcome to join[131] while Lehen reminded the congress that this only reflected the leading role of the proletariat, which came about not because industrial workers are better than farmers, or understand things more easily, but simply because the proletariat is better organised for taking the lead in mass actions.[132]

But it was the process of transformation to socialism that had caused most debate, and it was revealed that the original draft of this section had had to be re-written in its entirety.[133] What had most worried the rank and file members was the dangers of weakening the revolutionary character of this change. So the leaders, in their comments, emphasised that 'the capitalist class does not voluntarily give up its privilege' but will have to be compelled, and that a 'democratic road' does not at all imply that action is to be restricted to parliamentary elections and to discussions and votes within the walls of Parliament. The party would of course 'like to see a parliamentary majority lead the transformation, but mass action will be needed'.[134] On the other hand, 'proletarian dictatorship' had sounded too harsh for some critics, who would have preferred to speak only of 'workers' power', but it was thought reasonable to use both terms.[135] On the question of a peaceful transfer to socialism, there was agreement that for Finland this was 'within the bounds of possibility'.[136] But opinions still differed within the party on how strong the possibility was. One delegate remained obstinately pessimistic: 'I do not want to argue that it would not be possible at some historical point of time to take power into the workers' hands peacefully', but he doubted very much whether the capitalist structure was 'so rotten that it would collapse of itself'.[137]

The enemies of SKP, commenting on this debate, naturally accuse the party of being evasive over this crucial issue; but this is unfair, for the party's position is abundantly clear. It does not expect the bourgeoisie to give up power without a struggle, but it does hope that when the critical stage is reached, the power of the united front of the workers and all other progressive elements will be so manifest that actual violence will be avoided. On the other hand, if the bourgeois minority insists on a fight, SKP will accept. Provided that one can accept SKP's assurance that the transformation is not to be attempted until there is a clear majority of the nation in favour of it, this process would be entirely democratic though it might be formally illegal or unconstitutional in bourgeois terms.

The eleventh congress also adopted a new set of party statutes. These confirmed the doctrine of democratic centralism as necessary, because basically SKP was a fighting organisation. Proposals that for central committee elections there must be more candidates than places, thus giving a choice, were rejected,[138] but most of the discussion concerned the need for, and the limits on free debate and criticism. Examples were freely given of how bureaucratic attitudes in the leadership stifled discussion in the party,[139] but the prevailing view was that the principle of collective leadership was well established in SKP. It was pointed out with some justice that SKP had never really had a personality cult of its own. No one had ever worshipped A. Aaltonen or V. Pessi—the very idea is absurd. SKP had always been so close to the fountainhead of all wisdom in Moscow that it had had no room to develop a local vicegerent of its own. Indeed there was complaint at the congress that the party was over-reacting: 'Pictures of our leaders have disappeared from the party press to such an extent that the question arises whether to start a special publicity campaign to make the leaders known'.[140] In general, speakers favoured freedom of criticism but some condemned those party members who 'seem to feel the need to shout out that I can do what I like'. The party must insist that criticism was Marxist-Leninist and constructive; for those who thought this unduly restrictive the example of Hungary gave an awful warning.[141] Survivals of bureaucratic attitudes must be seen in their context; they had been bred into the leadership in its underground days and patience was needed while the party grew out of them.[142]

One has to conclude that the eleventh congress of SKP made an honest effort to apply de-Stalinisation to itself, to define its objects and methods for all to see, and to erect a real party democracy. If this effort was not wholly successful it was not for lack of good intentions but because no significant change of personnel at the top had occurred. All the old guard leaders, Aaltonen, Pessi, Hertta Kuusinen, Janhunen, Murto and Ryömä, were continued in power by the congress.[143] Since they had shown in the past that they had conformed obediently to a line laid down from outside, and had been willing to change their beliefs as directed, it was difficult to be entirely confident that in their hearts they were immutably committed to the ideals of the twentieth congress. They had a long and contradictory past record to live down.

The congress revealed that once again the future of SKDL had been under review. Pessi remarked that while 'we naturally have not the power to decide whether SKDL is to exist or not',[144] the central committee was of the opinion that SKDL did have a role to play quite distinct from that of SKP, which was the organised vanguard of the working class. H. Kuusinen insisted that SKDL had a real life of its own: 'In its ranks there are tens of thousands who do not belong to our party'.[145] Her fear was that perhaps SKP played too large a part in SKDL, for although at branch level only 30 per cent of the members of SKDL were also members of SKP, in the controlling committees of SKDL the places were 'at present too much occupied by communists', and this was to some extent SKP's own fault. She urged that 'we must trust them more. Where this has been done, there SKDL's work is more alive'. It was not clear, she said, how SKDL might develop in the future, but for the present it was necessary.[146]

Most non-communist commentators tend to assume that the sort of attitude being expressed by Hertta Kuusinen was sheer hypocrisy, and that SKDL was not and never had been anything but a front manipulated by SKP. But this is surely too unsophisticated a view of the matter. One can see in Kuusinen's remarks the lineaments of a genuine idealism; SKP did want SKDL to be a real expression of the popular front in action—it was in truth more the enthusiasm and assiduity of the SKP members inside SKDL that gave them their controlling influence rather than any cynical or sinister conspiracy by the party. None the less one knows that if at any point SKDL had shown signs of escaping from SKP control, or striking out on a line of its own, SKP would have been alarmed and distressed. It just shows that communists are like everyone else—they sometimes subscribe to ideals which they would find intolerably inconvenient if they were realised. This does not make them more cynical or less sincere than non-communists, it simply shows their common humanity.

Finland was in continuous economic difficulty in 1957,
plagued by inflation and a persistent shortage of government revenue. Governments tried to meet this with the
usual stabilisation programme for wages and prices, by
deflation and in the autumn of 1957 by devaluing the currency. As always these measures provoked unrest among
the wage earners and unusually high levels of unemployment. Massive relief projects were necessary to bring this
under control, which further aggravated budgetary problems, but even so in the winter of 1957–8 unemployment
was at a new postwar peak of nearly one hundred thousand.[1] SKP therefore found the conditions very favourable
for the party to come forward as the champion of the
rights of the workers, particularly since SAK was now in total disarray and the social democrats moving toward their
schism. In March 1957 SKP called on the workers to reject
the latest stabilisation plan and fight for better wages,[2]
and in June they scored a major parliamentary victory
when a plan to reduce family allowances by a 'compulsory
savings' scheme was frustrated by the filibustering tactics of the SKDL group.[3] In August, and again in September, the party urged the workers to resist the deflationary
policies of the government,[4] with such success that they
could now plausibly claim that they had fought the
bourgeoisie to a standstill and shown that the orderly
government of the country was impossible without them.
President Kekkonen virtually conceded this and urged the
inclusion of SKDL in a new government, but the social
democrats still refused absolutely to enter a coalition
with the communists so that a caretaker government of

civil servants was appointed until the elections due in 1958.

In January 1958 industrial production was down by 20 per cent compared with a year before, and on 10 January some government payments had to be suspended for lack of cash.[5] SKP felt strongly that a breakthrough was at hand; they hammered away at the theme that only their own inclusion in the government could bring about an improvement[6] and denounced as false and pernicious such ideas as Finland joining the common market or a free trade area as a solution to her economic difficulties.[7] SKP saw these so-called third force schemes as cunning traps set by American imperialism—the imperialist bogey had lost none of its terrors—and the communists pushed their own alternative of more trade with the Soviet Union and the socialist world.[8] They said that a recent party delegation to Moscow had discovered vast possibilities for increasing trade, and that the Finnish government had only to ask for them to be realised. On this occasion SKP's optimism about its electoral prospects was well founded. The party won its greatest electoral success ever, over 450,000 votes and fifty seats in Parliament, a quarter of the whole, making SKDL the biggest party. The two social democrat factions held fifty-one seats between them, thus producing a workers' majority in the Parliament of 101 to 99. Naturally SKP issued a call to revive the Big Three coalition to work for economic recovery through trade with Russia, and to use the workers' majority in Parliament to carry a new programme of social reform.[9] But all these suggestions were to be frustrated, except that a few reform measures like the paid-holidays law of 1960 did get through this Parliament.

President Kekkonen properly asked the SKDL leader Kilpi to try to form a workers' government with the social democrats, but neither of the social democrat factions would agree. Instead they began to work for an all-party, anti-communist coalition, and forced this solution on a manifestly reluctant president, when Fagerholm formed a grand coalition on 29 August. This was weakened from its inception by the hostility of the president, which meant that his own Agrarian Party was split in its attitude to the government. The fury of communist opinion at being cheated of the legitimate fruits of electoral victory was boundless. They swore to bring the Fagerholm government down: 'The working class must teach democracy and parliamentarianism to those who have preached it in words for so long'. The party called on the workers to take direct action but this time they had another important ally behind them, for the Russian ambassador, in a quite unprecedented way, made it clear that the Soviet Union expected SKDL to be taken into the government, though one cannot yet find out the exact terms or the degree of pressure behind his lobbying.

Why then did the other parties in Finland persist in their absolute refusal to work with the communists? One must conclude that to a large extent they fell victims to their own propaganda. Both the bourgeois parties and the social democrats had insisted for many years that the democratic pretentions of SKP were fraudulent, that the communists were simply the stooges of Moscow, that 'their purpose is to shove this country down the same road as Czechoslovakia and Hungary'.[10] They had, in short, declared that it was impossible to cooperate with communists because the latter would always be acting in bad faith, and there is some evidence to show that they had successfully convinced their own rank and file members. A local survey of the attitudes of social democrat voters in 1958 shows that only 16 per cent of them were willing to see a coalition with the communists.[11] Some of the comments made by non-communist voters and their view of SKDL are also relevant. A social democrat says: 'They are feeble-minded, they praise only the Soviet Union and want the same system for us'. Another social democrat says: 'They are after revolution, they are unpatriotic and cause chaos'. While a conservative voter says: 'It is not a Finnish party, it depends on foreign manipulators, it cannot be trusted with the nation's interests'.[12] These remarks illustrate some of the attitudes of mind that made coalition impossible in 1958; the other parties had worked for years to create the image of the communist bogeyman, of SKP as the tools of Moscow, and they could not suddenly unsay it now even though this picture bore no relation to the actual SKP of 1958. And in justice it must be said that the communists had been guilty of numberless stupidities that had played into the hands of the enemy.

The outcome was that SKP in 1958 had to be content with the negative satisfaction of helping to destroy the Fagerholm government. There was rarely an unhappier Finnish government than this one, despite its large parliamentary majority. The president remained implacably hostile to it, and the Soviet Union opened up a full-scale campaign to bring it down. The Russian authorities pressed for a visa for O. W. Kuusinen to visit Finland and took offence when it was refused; the Russian ambassador suddenly left Helsinki without the usual diplomatic courtesies and did not return; various Finnish-Russian negotiations ground to a halt; and the Soviet press adopted a very unfriendly tone. On the domestic front the problems of the economy were still intractable. The government was looking for a solution through deflation, a 'national starvation programme' as SKP labelled it,[13] and SKP's repeated calls to the workers and SAK to fight for their threatened living standards looked increasingly likely to succeed. By December 1958, when winter unemployment was rising, SKP was able to organise mass demonstrations against the government. A large public meeting outside Parliament on 9 December threatened:[14]

> We the workers, small farmers, and deprived groups will rise up again and again in ever-growing strength, and go on presenting our demands until the country learns to respect the nation's will.

At this point, the Agrarian Party, urged on by President Kekkonen, called out their ministers and brought the government down. It was a sterile victory for SKP, though very satisfactory to the Soviet Union which had demonstrated its power in Finland. A new agrarian minority government quickly set about appeasing Russia, but inevitably the defeated coalition partners were adamantly opposed to any cooperation with SKDL, so there could still be no question of its entering a government. So the communists had only limited grounds for congratulation; as they said, the new government was obviously an improvement, since it meant the defeat of the Fagerholm plot to take Finland into the imperialist camp, but it still stood for the same reactionary internal policies.[15] It was to take nearly eight more years of patient waiting before SKP at last persuaded the politicians and their voters that it could be an acceptable partner in government, and that its help alone offered a hope of real political stability after an unbroken series of unstable minority administrations.

The reason why, in the end, the communist claim to share in the government of Finland could not be denied, if the democratic system were to function properly, was the sheer size and stability of the communist vote. Though this receded slightly from the peak of 1958, it remained so big that in effect the communists could prevent the parliamentary system working without them. It is therefore important to understand the character of this support. The most striking feature about it is its persistence and consistency over the years; broadly speaking the same groups of voters in the same parts of the country have been voting for SKDL since 1945, and they correlate quite strongly with the groups which voted for STP in the 1920s. From this it is apparent that it matters little or nothing what variations there are in the line being followed by SKP—they do not have more than a marginal effect on its hold over the electors. Stalinist or de-Stalinised, with all its absurdities and contradictions, SKP holds the loyalty of its rank and file. It is only at the top, among the bourgeois intellectuals who have always been very weakly represented in Finnish communism, that fluctuations in support follow events like the Hungarian revolution or the exposures of Stalin. On the other hand, SKP never wins any significant new mass support either. It has consistently bid for the votes of social democrat workers and agrarian small farmers, with its liberal popular front line and its attractive reform proposals, but it has consistently failed to win them over.

The massive SKDL vote falls into two well marked categories, of which the first is that of the 'backwoods communists' of north and east Finland. They are predominantly small farmers whose farming operations are heavily uneconomic and who make a living by casual, seasonal labour, mainly in the forests in winter. Even with this they rarely achieve a satisfactory standard of living compared with the affluent society of south Finland. They suffer both poverty and insecurity because the conditions of forest work are liable to wide fluctuations; they also feel isolation, as they are a minority apart from the mainstream of Finnish life. Their resentments are heightened by the fact that every political party pays lip-service to developing the north but only the SKDL, with its attractive concrete proposals, can honestly say that it has had no chance to apply them. It so happens that the years 1945–8, when SKDL was in government, were years when capital flowed into the north to repair wartime devastation and when the world demand for timber was insatiable, so that the north had a brief boom. The northerners have undoubtedly come to feel that there is no place for them in the social and political system as it is, and support SKDL because it alone clearly stands in opposition to the established order. So in these areas SKDL gets 26 per cent of the urban vote and 45 per cent of the rural vote, and in many parts of the north enjoys an absolute majority. For these people, to vote SKDL is the natural way to protest at their exclusion from the prosperity and progress of postwar Finland.[16]

But an analysis like this oversimplifies the picture. A detailed study of voting behaviour in the Kuopio region, which is very much a part of backwoods Finland, reveals interesting variations of pattern.[17] For instance, there are backwoods parishes round Ilomantsi which are as poor, isolated and backward as any, where SKDL gets almost no support; there are others, like Marttisenjärvi, where SKDL gets up to 80 per cent of the vote. In this latter case it may be significant that there is an unusually high proportion of forest owned by big private companies. The Kuopio area shows clearly that voting patterns are affected not only by economic circumstances but also by political tradition. The area is divided into two parliamentary constituencies, both with a substantially similar social and economic structure; yet SKDL does consistently better in the west constituency than in the east and always has done. In 1954 it took 29.8 per cent of the votes in the west against only 17.3 per cent in the east,[18] and this pattern was apparent in the 1920s as well, although the bourgeois parties get much the same percentage of the vote in both constituencies. From this it seems that one factor is how the traditional socialist vote of pre-1917 split between the social democrats and the communists, and there does not seem to be any consistent pattern about this. In the town of Varkaus, one of the biggest industrial centres in the west Kuopio constituency, which was the scene of strong radical activity in 1917 and experienced one of the most brutal examples of the white terror in 1918, one would expect the communists to get the workers' vote, but in fact it is the social democrats who are predominant.[19]

Backwoods communism is therefore a complex phenomenon. It is a protest vote of the relatively deprived, it is a historic tradition, it is sometimes a hard-headed calculation. There is evidence that when voters do leave SKDL in these regions, they often pass over to the agrarians, which suggests that their support for SKDL has little to do with socialism but stems from the belief that the communists will get things done, as they often can through their control of local government, and changes with the hope that perhaps the agrarians, with their links to the centres of national authority, might do even more. The backwoods vote gives SKDL the bulk of its rural

vote; it makes no comparable inroads in the more pros-
perous farming communities of south Finland, where the
agrarians have an unshakeable grip. For instance in
Korpilahti, a farming parish near Tampere, a strong centre
of communist power and where the farmers also depend
considerably on supplementary industrial earnings, so that
it might be expected that SKDL would have some chance
of success, it gets very few farmer votes and its share
tends to drop all the time as the dominant agrarians
increase their hold. In this parish 61 per cent of the SKDL
voters are industrial workers resident in the area.[20] It is
unlucky for SKP that the support which it enjoys in the
thinly populated north carries little weight in national
elections; there are simply not enough voters up there.

Thus the communist vote really rests, as would be expected, on the industrial workers of the south and is essentially an urban vote. One reason why SKDL does well
with these people is that it works hard for its vote. In the
industrial city of Tampere SKDL is distinguished from all
other parties by its high level of organisation, so that 21
per cent of its voters also participate in the work of some
SKDL organisation, as against 13 per cent of the social
democrats.[21] Yet in the 1958 election the workers' vote
in Tampere was split almost evenly between SKDL and
the two social democrat factions.[22] This pattern is repeated over the whole of south Finland; with minor variations the communists and the social democrats each have
about half of the votes of the industrial workers. Investigation in Tampere suggests no obvious social or economic
explanations. Naturally most of the communist voters are
manual labourers, but not necessarily the less skilled or
the poorer paid ones.[23] On the contrary, since on the
whole SDP is much stronger with the women industrial
workers, who tend to be less skilled and lower paid, the
pattern is rather the reverse. What does seem to distinguish the communist worker is a wider experience of
unemployment.[24] It looks as though SKDL does better
with the more highly paid but less secure workers—like
the building workers, who are often on piece-rate earnings

—than it does with the more secure but lower paid workers on time-rates in the big factories; and in Finland these latter are often women.

But one is bound to look for other than economic reasons why one worker votes SKDL and another votes SDP. It is possible to pick up clues from some of the things which voters say about their parties. In the light of questions put to SKDL voters in Tampere in 1958, it looks as though over 70 per cent of its supporters identify communism with the cause of the working class: 'This party pursues the interests of the people'—'It has tried to do something for the workers in Parliament'—'It is a party close to the workers, which is most strongly abused. A man must be a communist if he is to be able to demand his wages'—'The only party for our sort of people which works for progress'.[25]

It is in remarks such as these that one can find the clue to why so many workers vote communist in Finland. The Finnish working class has been brought up since 1903 on a tradition of class-war politics, reinforced by their memories of the experiences of 1918, and workers see themselves as an interest outside of and opposed to the established order of bourgeois Finland. Those who support SKDL see the movement as the only one which embodies this concept of separateness and hostility. It is interesting that most SKDL voters in Tampere in 1958 were well satisfied with their party—over 70 per cent of those asked,[26] though they had their grumbles—'We should have expected more real action'—'Perhaps SKDL lays into things too crudely, but that may be necessary in politics'—'SKDL is a little too extreme'—but none of this was going to stop these people voting for it.

In all the recorded comments of communist voters there is very little reference to communist ideology. They do not say they support the communists because they want socialism, they seem to support it because they identify with the movement; it is 'their' party, it alone stands for them against the bourgeois enemy. This is surely why the fluctuations of communist party politics have no significant impact on SKP's mass support. For the communist voter the party is 'the workers' party, where all are equal and pull together', or 'it supports the interests of the workers most realistically. I am a worker myself'. It follows for him that no other explanation of support is necessary.[27]

To complete the picture it is obviously relevant to look at what the social democrat workers say, and it appears that they talk about their party in a surprisingly similar way. They say that SDP 'is the party that looks after the workers, and is more reasonable than SKDL'— 'It is the workers' party but does things moderately'— 'It pursues the workers' ideals with moderation, the others do it by violence'.[28] It seems clear that the extremism of some of SKDL's tactics, while attracting some supporters also repels people who might otherwise be sympathetic. When all the evidence is reviewed it has to be admitted that nobody can be certain why so many Finns vote for SKDL, while others who might be expected to do so vote social democrat instead. One can only point to a number of factors which seem to be involved. But it can be concluded that as long as SKP continues to satisfy the workers that it stands for them, and against the established forms of society and politics, it will hold the allegiance of both its backwoods and its industrial vote. These people seem to realise that nothing fundamental will change for the better until society as a whole changes, and by voting SKDL they give expression to this feeling. It is difficult to see how anything that SKP may do, within the bounds of reasonable political probability, will make much difference to its support one way or the other. SKP and the social democrats must live with the fact that they are yoked together as the joint heirs of the old Finnish workers' movement, and that their divisions are condemning it to sterility just as their cooperation can win successes. On the whole, SKP, the demands of Moscow permitting, has been readier to accept the implications of this situation than has SDP.

SKP entered the 1960s, after de-Stalinisation, as a party of radical democratic reform, which sought to attain its

ends through the widest possible democratic and progressive coalition, an objective finally achieved in 1966. There
was just one serious danger to the successful pursuit of this
policy, that posed by the loyalty of SKP to the foreign
policy line of the Soviet Union, which has finally thrust
the party into crisis and threatened schism in 1969. Signs
of the kind of trouble that might emerge were present in
1959. The Sino-Russian quarrel was emerging over the interpretation of the Chinese communes and Khruschev's remarks about them to his twenty-first congress. *Kommunisti*
had to explain these away as only part of 'the process of
dialectics' and dismissed as malicious those people who
would 'like to detect or hope for differences between the
two greatest communist parties of the world'.[29] A further
diet of words was being accumulated for future eating.
A much more serious problem is raised by the endorsement of the Russian myths about the activities of the
aggressive West German warmongers. Finland is involved
in these myths, because the West German aggressors are
supposed to be planning to use Finnish territory for their
war against the Soviet Union and the reactionaries in
Finland, and more specifically the Kokoomus Party, are
supposed to be actively involved in their plans.[30] Thus
when Pessi discussed this problem before the party congress in 1960 he affirmed that West Germany 'once more
cherishes plans dangerous to our country as well', and that
it was the duty of SKP to frustrate the intrigues of the
Finnish Right with Germany. Pessi said that because
Finland had a duty under the mutual assistance treaty
to help Russia in resisting a German attack through her
territory, Finland ought to support the German policies
of the Soviet Union designed to avert this, ought to
encourage Norway and Denmark to leave NATO, and
ought to work for the setting up of an atom-free zone in
Scandinavia.[31] The adoption of this distinctive foreign
policy line cuts SKP off from the other political parties
in Finland, which are committed to a more balanced
concept of neutrality, and helps to keep alive the belief

that skp is unpatriotic and a tool of Moscow. And when, as in the so-called 'note crisis' of 1961, Finland gets actively involved in east-west tensions, skp finds itself in a very embarrassing position with respect to those non-communist elements in Finland whose cooperation it is seeking. But skp can no more exempt itself than any other political body from the drawbacks of publicly maintaining a view of the situation which does not correspond very closely with reality. skp could not hope to shake off this foreign policy incubus as long as the world communist movement remained as it was in the early 1960s.

But this apart, skp seemed set fair in 1960 when the twelfth party congress met. As on the previous occasion, there had been advanced public debate of the issues which were to come up. In December 1959 an enlarged central committee had approved a set of theses on the growing power of monopoly capital in Finland. These were circulated and discussed in the movement and then adopted at the party congress.[32] The theses maintain that the economy of Finland is geared to a monopoly power based on the timber and timber-processing industries. This monopoly is virtually in the hands of an alleged twenty families, who also control the two great private banks, employ nearly half of the country's labour force, are increasingly reaching out into other industries like textiles, and are getting a grip on the distributive machine.[33] This monopoly power was the real enemy, and the prospects of final victory over it were good because in the first place the class antagonism between the monopolists on the one side and the workers and small farmers on the other must intensify, so that all these people can be more readily aroused to fight the monopolists; but in the second place the monopolists will also arouse the antagonism of the lesser capitalists, excluded from their cartels, and increasingly themselves oppressed and exploited by the monopolists. So in time even these strongly anti-socialist forces can be brought to see that their best interests will be served by supporting a broad, all-inclusive front against monopoly power. The task of SKP in the 1960s was to arouse and inspire the emergence and activity of such a front.

The party congress, which met from 15 to 18 April 1960,[34] heard a report from Pessi which was almost complacent. He was especially proud of the fact that at a time when both the social democrats and the agrarians were struggling with internal dissension, SKP was solidly united. Pessi claimed that 'there are not any kind of political or personal conflicts in the central committee and the political committee of our party. The party leadership has been solid and united'.[35] The party still had its problems: the membership, which was approaching fifty thousand, was still not big enough, there were cases of party branches that were closed in upon themselves and had not recruited anyone new for years, and a majority of party members were still disinclined to undertake the necessary theoretical studies.[36] So the process of recruitment should be further eased and the level of party education improved, and the party's work so arranged that theory and practice go together.[37]

Pessi discussed the practical problems of working with non-communists: SKP reserves the right to exercise a controlling influence from inside some mass organisations, where this is necessary and appropriate:[38]

> Communists should direct activity, after proper consideration by the party, in at least some local, mass democratic bodies or in national organisations, in order to promote the realisation of the objectives which those organisations have assumed.

But SKP is still offering genuine collaboration on equal terms with all progressive forces, and most of all with the social democrats. The suspicions of the social democrats that SKP has ulterior motives in making this offer are groundless. Perhaps in the time of the Big Three Agreements 'faults and mistakes had appeared on both sides, and in this respect changes must take place'.[39] But SKP does not interfere in the internal affairs of SDP, it has no interest in fostering the current schism, and it will work freely with all genuine workers' representatives because the unity of the working class is a great overriding priority.[40]

The congress re-affirmed that the existing situation in Finland was one that required alleviations within the capitalist order, and that consequently the question of the transition to socialism does not yet arise, although the ultimate need for it remains; when the time does come, if the working class is united the transformation can definitely take place without violence.[41] SKP has absolutely no interest in promoting a violent transition. The party recognised that the social democrats cannot agree with SKP over the attitude to be adopted towards the socialist countries but this need not be an obstacle to cooperation between the parties.[42] This was followed up in August 1960, after the conference in Bucharest of communist parties, when SKP re-affirmed its belief in and attachment to the peaceful coexistence of different political systems and the correctness of parliamentary methods for communist parties under the conditions of capitalism.[43]

Thus the twelfth congress cleared the decks for coalition by seeking to put to rest the old fears about SKP; and the same themes were prominent at the congresses of SKDL in 1961 and 1964. SKDL proclaimed that the acceptance of a policy of friendship with the Soviet Union, of the widening of political and economic democracy, and of the need for widening social and cultural progress, constituted the sole conditions for membership of the movement, and that SKDL would work with anyone who accepted these aims.[44]

On this basis, SKP and SKDL soldiered on into the 1960s, keeping up their solid popular vote in the general election of 1962 and suffering a marginal decline in 1966, partly because they were then in electoral alliance with the dissident Social Democratic League, and the alliance worked rather in favour of the latter, but still proving that the communists maintained their hold on between

21 and 24 per cent of the Finnish voters. Then at last the other parties accepted the logic of the electoral statistics, accepted SKP's professions of peaceful reformist intent, and the long awaited Big Three coalition was restored, though with SKDL playing a much humbler part in it than in 1945–8, and without the attempt to summon up mass pressures to intimidate their partners, which had been such an off-putting feature of the previous coalition.

To those who have followed the story of SKP so far it may well seem that the party has never had much luck. The year 1966 should have been the year of its culminating triumph, when the eighteen-year campaign to re-enter a popular front type government finally succeeded. But this very success combined with other factors to make 1966 the beginning of a new and prolonged crisis for the party. It is still too early, and the evidence is too sparse, to attempt a description and analysis of this latest phase which is still continuing. But briefly, it seems that SKP found once more that to be a minority partner in a coalition government made it a hostage for its enemies and damaged its relations with its own voters. The communist ministers found themselves saddled with responsibility for unpopular policies, such as devaluation, which they were too weak to oppose inside the government, and were precluded from attacking effectively outside it. By being in the government they seemed increasingly to become identified with that very establishment which their traditional supporters rejected. Secondly, like all communist parties, SKP was damaged by events in Czechoslovakia in 1968, and its new liberal course was put under severe strain. Thirdly, the party experienced an internal power struggle.

This became open and public at the congress of the party held in January 1966, when reformers held a majority of the delegates and forced the retirement of the Stalinist chairman, Aimo Aaltonen. He was replaced by a representative of the new, post-Stalin generation of communists, Aarne Saarinen. This started a power struggle, which still rages, between the survivors of the old Stalinist leadership and their disciples who find their hard-line policies attractive, and the reformist majority. So far the reformists have tended to win ground steadily, but at the cost of driving the party, on more than one occasion, to the verge of open schism. These developments eventually forced SKP out of the government once more, but worse, they seem to have shaken the allegiance of the party's hard-core voters. At the last two parliamentary elections, it has become apparent that the communist vote is declining and that the party is in serious electoral trouble. But one recalls that it has survived and overcome worse crises than this, and if at the moment its future looks more uncertain than at any time since 1944, it would be a bold historian who would prophesy what the outcome of the present crisis will be.

# NOTES

## 3 The Communist Party of Sweden

1 The contents of this study are based in essentials on, Ake Sparring, *Från Höglund till Hermansson. Om revisionismen i Sveriges kommunistiska parti* (Stockholm, 1967).

2 K. Bäckström, *Socialismens programfrågor* (Stockholm, 1943), p. 122.

3 *Ibid.*, p. 127.

4 K. Kilbom, *Cirkeln slutes. Ur mitt livs äventyr*, III (Stockholm, 1955), pp. 12ff.

5 *Ibid.*, p. 10: see also K. Kilbom, *I hemligt uppdrag. Ur mitt livs äventyr*, II (Stockholm, 1954), pp. 283ff.

6 R. Casparsson, *LO. Bakgrund, utveckling, verksamhet* (Stockholm, 1966), pp. 283ff.

7 According to T. Nerman, *Kommunisterna* (Stockholm, 1949), pp. 174ff., the Kilbom group calculated that after the split they kept eleven thousand of the members of the old party, while four thousand followed Sillén. Later skp has claimed that only an insignificant minority followed Kilbom. The first election after the split bears out Nerman's statement.

8 A. Wretling, *Kommunistiska partiet 20 år* (Stockholm, 1937), p. 42.

9 But not altogether. In his noted memoirs, the former Comintern agent Jan Valtin, *Out of the Night* (London, 1941), says that still, in the beginning of the 1930s, skp was the most independent section of the Comintern, partly in consequence of the fact that skp was economically independent. It was Valtin's assignment in Sweden to 'free' the party of its economic assets, in which he eventually succeeded.

10 P. Meurling, *Kommunismen i Sverige* (Stockholm, 1950), p. 95.

11 S. Linderot, *I kamp för fred och frihet* (Stockholm, 1941), p. 15.

12   *Ibid.*, p. 18.

13   In fact, both Moscow and Berlin wanted to preserve this independence of Sweden, which is clear from the diplomatic correspondence between the two capitals after the German invasion of Norway; but who could trust promises at that time?

14   S. Linderot, *I kamp för fred och frihet*, pp. 11–3, 15–7.

15   S. Linderot, *Bönder och arbetare* (Stockholm, 1943), p. 6.

16   *Vårt Program. Med kommentarer av Hilding Hagberg* (Stockholm, 1944).

17   S. Linderot, *Demokratins handlingsprogram* (Stockholm, 1946), p. 27.

18   *The programme of the Communist International*, 1 September 1928.

19   *Program och resolutioner antagna vid kommunistiska partiets kongress 1921* (Stockholm, 1921), pp. 11ff.

20   *Vår Tid*, no. 3 (1945), p. 2.

21   *Ibid.*, no. 2 (1945), p. 1.

22   S. Linderot, *Svensk arbetarrörelse i brytningstid*, pp. 413ff.

23   S. Persson, *Vad läget kräver av Sveriges arbetare* (Stockholm, 1945), p. 24.

24   S. Persson, *Repliker till Linderot-Lager-Hagberg* (Stockholm, 1954) (stencil). The city of Stockholm is run by an executive board of five '*borgarråd*' (appointed by the city council).

25   S. Linderot, *Demokratins handlingsprogram*, p. 24.

26   S. Linderot, *Ny kurs* (Stockholm, 1943), p. 16.

27   S. Linderot, *Svensk arbetarrörelse i brytningstid*, pp. 434ff.

28   See note 16 of this chapter.

29   *Anteckningar från internordisk konferens i Stockholm, 29–30 December 1945* (stencil).

30   S. Linderot, *Demokratins handlingsprogram*, pp. 13, 25.

31  *Material för föredrag om fjortonde partikongressen* (Stockholm, 1948), p. 6.

32  *Vår Tid*, no. 8 (1948), p. 2.

33  L. Kihlberg, *Den ryska agenturen i Sverige* (Stockholm, 1950).

34  *Ny Dag*, 12 October 1963.

35  See, for example, S. Linderot, 'En olöst taktisk uppgift', *Vår Tid*, no. 5 (1952).

36  S. Persson, *Repliker till Linderot-Lager-Hagberg*, p. 14.

37  *Vår Tid*, no. 9 (1950).

38  Here it can be noted that the reputation of the Swedish social democrats in Moscow—thanks to Swedish neutrality— was somewhat better than that of the sister parties in the countries which joined NATO. Judging by many signs, Stalin was satisfied with Swedish foreign policy, which helped to stabilise the situation in the north.

39  S. Persson, *Till försvar för kommunismen* (Stockholm, 1953), p. 22 (stencil).

40  *Vår Tid*, no. 6 (1955), p. 203.

41  *Ibid.*, no. 3 (1956), pp. 81ff.

42  *Ny Dag*, 2 March 1956.

43  *Vår Tid*, no. 3 (1956), pp. 81ff.

44  *Ibid.*, pp. 97ff.

45  *Ibid.*, no. 5 (1956), p. 172.

46  *Nutid-Framtid. Arbetarrörelsens programdebatt* (Stockholm, 1957), pp. 132ff.

47  Sveriges kommunistiska parti, *Programförklaring* (Göteborg, 1964), p. 15.

48  See, for example, Erik Karlsson's article in *Ny Dag*, 14 April 1956.

49  *Ny Dag*, 15 October 1963.

50  *Vår Tid*, no. 5 (1956), pp. 171ff.

51 *Ny Dag*, 27 September 1962.

52 *Ibid.*, 2 October 1962.

53 *Ibid.*, 30 October 1962.

54 *Dagens Nyheter*, 31 May 1965.

55 This attitude to what was then the most burning question in the communist movement was of a conspiratorial character, which is underlined by the fact that the communiqué was never published in *Ny Dag*, but only in the periodical *Vår Tid*, no. 2 (1963), pp. 45ff., with its very limited circulation.

56 *Ny Dag*, 25 September 1963.

57 I have given a detailed account of this debate in my essay, 'Continuity, change, and the Sino-Soviet dispute', in *Communism in Europe*, II, ed. W. E. Griffith (Cambridge, Mass., 1964).

58 Material from SKP's 1967 congress will be found in *Samling Vänster i Svensk Politik. Material fran Vänsterpartiet kommunisternas (Sveriges kommunistiska parti) 21:a kongress 13–16 maj 1967 (Stockholm, 1967)*

59 The party leadership's first comments, *Ny Dag*, no. 45 (1968), struck a fairly optimistic note, and it was not until the end of the year that Hermansson was ready with a detailed analysis of the election, *Ny Dag*, nos. 54, 55 (1968), where he sums up briefly: 'The election defeat has created a great problem, it would be ridiculous to pretend anything else'.

PART TWO: THE COMMUNIST PARTY OF FINLAND
1 *The Historical Background*

1 In Finnish, *Suomen sosiaalidemokraattinen puolue*: cited hereafter in the text by the usual Finnish initials SDP. The programme of 1903 was adopted by a congress held in the town of Forssa, hence it is usually referred to as the 'Forssa programme'.

2 Its official name in Finnish was *Kansanvaltuuskunta*, literally 'People's Deputation'.

3 I. Hakalehto, *Suomen kommunistinen puolue ja sen vaikutus poliittiseen ja ammatilliseen työväen liikkeeseen, 1918–
1928* (Porvoo, 1966), p. 12; A. Hyvönen, *Suomen Kommunistinen puolue, 1918–1924* (Helsinki, 1968), p. 29.

4 Hakalehto, p. 13; Hyvönen, p. 29.

## 2 The Creation of the Finnish Communist Movement

1 Hyvönen, pp. 36–8.

2 SKP:n *taistelun tieltä: muistelmia, kuvauksia ja aineistoa*
SKP:n 15 *vuotistaipaleelta*, ed. T. Antikainen (Leningrad,
1934), pp. 142–3 (hereafter cited as *Antikainen*).

3 Hakalehto, p. 14; Hyvönen, pp. 34–5; *Vapaus*—literally
'freedom'.

4 V. Pessi, 'SKP:n synty', SKP *taistelujen tiellä: vuosikirja I*
(Helsinki, 1945), p. 9. SKP published a series of eleven of
these year books in the period 1945–55, and they are
cited hereafter as *TT*.; A. Tuominen, *Sirpin ja vasaran tie*
(Helsinki, 1957), p. 105.

5 Hyvönen, p. 40; Hakalehto, p. 14; T. Lehen and others,
*Kipinästä tuli syttyi: SKP vuodesta 1918 nykypäivään*
(Helsinki, 1958), p. 7.

6 *Antikainen*, p. 10.

7 Hyvönen, p. 42.

8 *Ibid.*, p. 43.

9 *Ibid.*, p. 44; *Antikainen*, p. 10; Lehen, p. 7; Hakalehto, p.
15.

10 Hyvönen, pp. 43–4; *Antikainen*, pp. 9–10.

11 The offence of '*valtiopetos*' under Finnish law is rendered
as sedition; in more serious cases the charge was '*maanpetos*'
—treason.

12 Lehen, pp. 9–10.

13 *Antikainen*, p. 10.

14 Hyvönen, p. 46. What happened to the three who voted

for the theses, but did not apparently take part in the congress, seems to be unexplained.

15 Hyvönen, p. 45.

16 *Ibid.*

17 *Ibid.*, p. 49.

18 *Ibid.*, p. 50; Hakalehto, p. 16.

19 *Suomen Kommunistinen puolue. Puoluekokousten, konferenssien ja keskuskomitean plenumien päätöksiä* (Leningrad, 1935), p. 11 (hereafter cited as *PKKPP*).

20 Hyvönen, p. 53.

21 *Ibid.*, p. 52.

22 *TT*, X (1954), p. 116ff.; *PKKPP*, pp. 12–8; *Kommunisti*, nos. 35–6 (1945); Hyvönen, p. 53.

23 Hakalehto, pp. 70–4; Hyvönen, pp. 81–2; Lehen, pp. 49–50.

24 Lehen, p. 49.

25 In Finnish, *Helsingin työväen yhdistys.*

26 R. H. Oittinen, *Työväenkysymys ja työväenliike Suomessa* (Helsinki, 1954), p. 176.

27 *Antikainen*, p. 74; Oittinen, p. 177; Hyvönen, p. 67.

28 Hakalehto, p. 211; Tuominen, p. 101.

29 *'Kumous'*—literally 'revolution'.

30 Hyvönen, pp. 56–7.

31 Hakalehto, p. 24; *Antikainen*, p. 41.

32 Lehen, p. 44.

33 *Ibid.*, p. 36.

34 Hyvönen, p. 61; Lehen, p. 38; *Antikainen*, p. 38.

35 Hyvönen, p. 60.

36 *Antikainen*, p. 34; Tuominen, p. 110.

37 *Antikainen*, p. 41; Lehen, p. 44.

38 Lehen, p. 46; *PKKPP*, p. 497; 'Finnish bureau' translates the Finnish '*Suomen byroo*'.

39 'The red voting ticket' translates the Finnish '*Punainen vaalilippu*'.

40 *Iz istorii Kommunisticheskoi partii Finljandii* (Moscow, 1960), pp. 8, 29; Hyvönen, p. 76; A. Äikiä, 'SKP taistelussa Suomen kansanvaltaisen kehityksen puolesta', *TT*, X (1954), p. 49.

41 *PKKPP*, p. 23.

42 *Antikainen*, p. 43.

43 Hyvönen, p. 78; Hakalehto, p. 149; *Antikainen*, p. 106.

44 Hyvönen, p. 79; Hakalehto, p. 150.

45 Hyvönen, p. 100; K. Korhonen, *Naapurit vastoin tahtoaan. Suomi Neuvostodiplomatiassa. Tartosta Talvisotaan. I, 1920–1932* (Helsinki, 1966), p. 37; *PKKPP*, p. 496.

46 Hakalehto, pp. 76–8.

47 Tuominen, pp. 111–3.

48 Hyvönen, p. 82.

49 Hakalehto, pp. 80–1.

50 Tuominen, p. 119.

51 *Ibid.*, p. 118.

52 Lehen, p. 54; *Iz istorii* . . . , p. 35.

53 Lehen, p. 54.

54 Hyvönen, p. 103; *Antikainen*, p. 226; Lehen, p. 58.

55 Hyvönen, p. 107.

56 *Ibid.*, p. 109.

57 *Antikainen*, pp. 110–4; 'Socialist Journal'—in Finnish '*Sosialistinen Aikakauslehti*'.

58 Hyvönen, p. 102.

59 J. Nousiainen, *Kommunismi Kuopion läänissä* (Joensuu, 1956), p. 63.

362 NOTES

60  Hakalehto, p. 154; *Kaksi vuosikymmentä Suomen sisäpolitiikkaa 1919-1939*, ed. P. Tommila (Porvoo, 1964), p. 72.

61  Hakalehto, p. 214.

62  Tuominen, p. 132.

63  Hyvönen, p. 121.

64  *Ibid.*, p. 124.

65  *Ibid.*, p. 129; Antikainen, p. 76.

66  Hyvönen, p. 131.

67  *Ibid.*, p. 137; Tuominen, p. 130.

68  Hyvönen, pp. 139–40.

69  Hakalehto, pp. 152–3.

70  *PKKPP*, p. 29.

71  Tuominen, p. 120.

72  Hyvönen, pp. 125, 142; Hakalehto, pp. 154–5; Lehen, p. 59.

73  E. Hiitonen, *Vääryyttä oikeuden valekaavussa* (Hyvinkää, 1953), p. 157; Lehen, p. 65; Antikainen, p. 78. 'Finnish Socialist Workers' Party' translates 'Suomen sosialistinen työväen puolue'; this party is referred to in the text as STP, as are the other radical parliamentary organisations of the 1920s which were its successors.

74  Hiitonen, p. 155.

75  *Ibid.*; O. Borg, *Suomen puolueideologiat* (Porvoo, 1964), p. 82; Hakalehto, p. 158.

76  Borg, p. 82.

77  Hiitonen, p. 157.

78  Tuominen, p. 134.

79  Hiitonen, p. 158; Hyvönen, p. 148; Hakalehto, p. 160.

80  Hyvönen, p. 149; Hiitonen, p. 180; Hakalehto, p. 160; Lehen, p. 61; Tuominen, pp. 136–7.

81  Tuominen, p. 137; Hakalehto, p. 160.

82 Hyvönen, pp. 152–3; Hakalehto, p. 161.

83 Oittinen, p. 211; Hakalehto, pp. 219–21; Tuominen, pp. 138–44.

84 Hakalehto, p. 247.

85 Tuominen, p. 146.

86 *Ibid.*, p. 169.

87 Hyvönen, p. 160; *Antikainen*, pp. 12–3; *PKKPP*, pp. 32, 63–4.

88 Hyvönen, p. 161; Hakalehto, p. 46; Tuominen, p. 180; *Antikainen*, pp. 138–57.

89 *Antikainen*, pp. 156–7.

90 Hyvönen, pp. 156–7, 173; Hakalehto, p. 45.

91 Tuominen, p. 172.

92 Lehen, p. 65; *Iz istorii* . . . , p. 42.

93 *PKKPP*, p. 35.

94 *Ibid.*, p. 36; Hakalehto, p. 47; *Antikainen*, p. 19; Lehen, p. 65.

95 *PKKPP*, p. 37; Tommila, p. 102.

96 Lehen, p. 65; *Iz istorii* . . . , p. 42.

97 *PKKPP*, p. 37.

98 *Ibid.*, pp. 37–8.

99 Tuominen, p. 172; Hyvönen, p. 163.

100 Lehen, p. 63.

101 Hyvönen, pp. 164–5.

102 Tuominen, p. 209.

103 K. Heikkilä, 'Vainovuosilta', *TT*, I (1945), p. 72.

104 Hyvönen, p. 202.

105 Tuominen, p. 242.

106 *Ibid.*, pp. 291–306; Hyvönen, p. 166; Hakalehto, p. 34.

107 Tuominen, p. 247.

108 *Ibid.*, p. 265.

109 *Ibid.*, p. 287.

110 Hyvönen, p. 176.

111 *Ibid.*, p. 177.

112 *Ibid.*, p. 173.

113 *Ibid.*, p. 175.

114 *Ibid.*, p. 180; PKKPP, pp. 60–3.

115 Hyvönen, p. 181.

116 *Ibid.*, p. 182; PKKPP, p. 40.

117 *PKKPP*, pp. 42–4.

118 *Ibid.*, p. 48.

119 *Ibid.*, p. 50.

120 *Ibid.*, p. 54.

121 *Ibid.*, p. 55.

122 Hakalehto, p. 25; Lehen, p. 76; Tuominen, p. 306.

3   The Struggle for Survival in Finland, 1921–8

1 Hakalehto, p. 164; A. Tuominen, *Maan alla ja päällä* (Helsinki, 1958), p. 18.

2 Tuominen, p. 20; Hakalehto, p. 166.

3 Hakalehto, pp. 94–6.

4 *Ibid.*, p. 97.

5 Tuominen, p. 24.

6 *Ibid.*, pp. 24–6; Hakalehto, pp. 82–3.

7 Tuominen, pp. 106–11; Hakalehto, p. 98; Korhonen, p. 63.

8 PKKPP, p. 78; Korhonen, p. 86; *Antikainen*, p. 304; Hakalehto, p. 100.

9 *Antikainen*, p. 237.

10 *Ibid.*, p. 242.

11 Hakalehto, p. 166.

12 *Ibid.*, p. 169; Tuominen, pp. 40–1; Hyvönen, p. 207.

13 Hakalehto, p. 169; Tuominen, p. 46; Hyvönen, p. 208.

14 Tuominen, p. 49; Hyvönen, pp. 211–4.

15 Tuominen, p. 49; Hyvönen, p. 213.

16 Hakalehto, p. 170; Hiitonen, p. 188; Tuominen, pp. 55–8; Hyvönen, p. 215.

17 Tuominen, p. 81; Hyvönen, p. 215.

18 Tuominen, pp. 118–27.

19 Hakalehto, p. 170; Tuominen, p. 93.

20 Hyvönen, p. 236.

21 *Ibid.*, pp. 238–9.

22 *Ibid.*, p. 239.

23 *Ibid.*, p. 223; Tuominen, p. 91.

24 Hyvönen, pp. 227–8; Tuominen, p. 93.

25 Hyvönen, p. 229.

26 *Ibid.*

27 *Ibid.*, pp. 226, 229; Tuominen, p. 93; Hakalehto, p. 171.

28 Hyvönen, p. 232.

29 *Ibid.*, p. 234; Hakalehto, p. 172.

30 Hyvönen, p. 235; *PKKPP*, p. 76.

31 Hyvönen, p. 241; Hakalehto, p. 174; Nousiainen, p. 17.

32 Hyvönen, pp. 243–4; *TT*, IV (1948), p. 42.

33 Hyvönen, pp. 245, 259.

34 *Ibid.*, p. 246.

35 *Ibid.*; Hakalehto, p. 174.

36  Hakalehto, p. 174.

37  Hyvönen, pp. 250–2; Hakalehto, p. 175.

38  Hyvönen, p. 254; Lehen, p. 72.

39  Hyvönen, p. 238.

40  Hakalehto, pp. 178–9; Lehen, p. 73.

41  Hakalehto, pp. 182–3; Tommila, p. 33.

42  Lehen, p. 74.

43  Hiitonen, p. 183.

44  Hyvönen, p. 256; Tuominen, p. 176.

45  Tuominen, p. 177.

46  'Suomen suojelusliitto'—literally 'League for the Defence of Finland.'

47  Tuominen, p. 178; Tommila, p. 32; Hyvönen, p. 270.

48  Hyvönen, p. 262; Hakalehto, p. 185.

49  'Workers' Party of Finland' translates 'Suomen työväen puolue'—thus still STP.

50  Hyvönen, pp. 265–8.

51  Hiitonen, p. 189.

52  Ibid., p. 190; Hakalehto, p. 185; Tommila, p. 34; Hyvönen, p. 272.

53  Hiitonen, p. 204; Hakalehto, p. 186; Hyvönen, p. 289.

54  Hiitonen, pp. 203–12; Hyvönen, pp. 280–90; Tuominen, pp. 185–95; Lehen, p. 82.

55  Antikainen, p. 238.

56  Lehen, pp. 76, 87.

57  Ibid., p. 65.

58  Ibid.

59  A. Hyvönen, 'SKP ja talonpoikaiskysymys', TT, X (1954), p. 98.

60 *Ibid.*, p. 101; *PKKPP*, p. 79.

61 Hyvönen, *op. cit.*, pp. 104–5; Hyvönen, *Suomen Kommunistinen puolue* . . . , p. 297; *PKKPP*, p. 80.

62 *PKKPP*, p. 78.

63 Korhonen, p. 86; Hakalehto, p. 186.

64 *Antikainen*, p. 236.

65 'Helsinki Workers' Local Organisation' translates 'Helsingin työväen paikallisjärjestö'.

66 *Antikainen*, p. 243; Lehen, p. 90.

67 *Antikainen*, p. 242.

68 *Ibid.*, p. 245.

69 *Ibid.*, p. 243.

70 Hakalehto, pp. 116–9; Hyvönen, p. 296.

71 *Antikainen*, p. 258.

72 Hakalehto, pp. 120–1.

73 *Antikainen*, p. 256.

74 *Ibid.*, p. 257.

75 Lehen, p. 88.

76 Hakalehto, p. 187; Lehen, p. 89.

77 Hakalehto, pp. 188–9.

78 *Ibid.*, p. 193; Lehen, p. 93.

79 Lehen, p. 94.

80 Hakalehto, p. 189; Tommila, p. 113.

81 Hakalehto, p. 190; *Antikainen*, p. 14.

82 *PKKPP*, pp. 83–4.

83 Hakalehto, p. 191.

84 *Antikainen*, pp. 263–4.

85 *Ibid.*, p. 265.

86 *Ibid.*, pp. 293–4.

87 Hakalehto, p. 191; *Antikainen*, p. 254.

88 *Antikainen*, p. 252.

89 Lehen, p. 85.

90 Hiitonen, p. 220; T. Karvonen, 'Salaista ja julkista nuorisotoimintaa', *TT*, IV (1948), p. 191.

91 *PKKPP*, p. 121; Hakalehto, p. 131.

92 Hakalehto, pp. 131–2; Karvonen, *TT*, IV (1948), pp. 100–9; Lehen, pp. 120–4; Tommila, p. 109.

93 Hakalehto, pp. 18, 20.

94 *Antikainen*, p. 14.

95 M. Waltari, *Neuvostovakoilun varjossa* (Helsinki, 1943), p. 55.

96 *Ibid.*, pp. 57–8.

97 *Antikainen*, p. 260.

98 *Ibid.*, p. 258.

99 *PKKPP*, p. 88; *Antikainen*, p. 259; Hakalehto, p. 58. pp. 101–4.

100 A. Hyvönen, 'skp ja talonpoikiaskysymys', *TT*, X (1954),

101 *PKKPP*, p. 97; Hakalehto, p. 66.

102 *PKKPP*, pp. 91, 109; Hakalehto, p. 58.

103 *PKKPP*, p. 93.

104 *Ibid.*, p. 103.

105 Hiitonen, pp. 185–7.

106 Hakalehto, pp. 225–6.

107 *Ibid.*, p. 225.

108 *Ibid.*, p. 250.

109 *Ibid.*, p. 254.

110 *Ibid.*, pp. 231–7.

111 *Ibid.*, p. 262.

112 *Ibid.*, p. 261.

113 A. Hyvönen, '30-vuotias SKP:n taisteluhistorian päävaiheet', *TT*, IV (1948), p. 48; M. Janhunen, 'SKP työtätekevien voimien kokoojana . . .', *TT*, X (1954), p. 83.

114 Hakalehto, pp. 271–2.

115 Tuominen, p. 199; *Antikainen*, pp. 246–7.

116 *Antikainen*, p. 247.

117 Tuominen, p. 200.

118 Hakalehto, pp. 279–80.

119 *PKKPP*, p. 119.

120 Hakalehto, p. 283.

121 Tuominen, pp. 205, 210; Lehen, p. 170; Hakalehto, p. 286.

122 Tuominen, p. 211; Hakalehto, p. 287.

123 Tuominen, pp. 212–4; *PKKPP*, p. 151; Hakalehto, p. 288.

124 Hakalehto, p. 286; Tuominen, p. 222.

125 *PKKPP*, pp. 142–4.

126 'Farmers' News' translates '*Talonpojan Sanomat*'.

127 Tuominen, pp. 231–8.

128 *PKKPP*, p. 153.

129 *Ibid.*, pp. 140–1, 145, 160.

130 *Ibid.*, pp. 157–9.

131 Korhonen, pp. 155–9.

132 *PKKPP*, pp. 166–8.

133 *Antikainen*, p. 403.

134 Hakalehto, pp. 105–8; *TT*, X (1954), p. 141.

135 Hiitonen, p. 223; Hakalehto, p. 109; Tommila, p. 114.

136 Tuominen, p. 297.

137  *Antikainen*, p. 18; Hakalehto, p. 20; *PKKPP*, pp. 166–9.

138  Tuominen, pp. 297–8.

139  *Antikainen*, p. 401.

140  Hakalehto, p. 293.

141  *Ibid.*, p. 294.

142  Tuominen, pp. 267–8.

143  Hakalehto, p. 295; Tuominen, p. 274.

144  Tuominen, pp. 278–9.

145  *Ibid.*, p. 302.

146  *Ibid.*, p. 290; Hakalehto, p. 299.

147  Tuominen, p. 295.

148  *Ibid.*, pp. 291–2.

149  Hakalehto, p. 300.

150  *Ibid.*, p. 301; *Antikainen*, pp. 437–8.

151  Hakalehto, p. 302; Tuominen, p. 316.

152  *PKKPP*, p. 172.

153  *Ibid.*, p. 185.

154  Tuominen, p. 317.

155  *Antikainen*, p. 404.

156  Hakalehto, p. 121; Tommila, p. 115; A. Taimi, *Sivuja eletystä* (Petroskoi, 1954), p. 252; Hiitonen, p. 227.

157  *Antikainen*, p. 367.

## 4  The Destruction of Communism in Finland

1  *Antikainen*, p. 430.

2  *Ibid.*, p. 450.

3  *Ibid.*, p. 430.

4  *Ibid.*, p. 431; *PKKPP*, p. 216.

5 *Antikainen*, p. 433; *PKKPP*, pp. 216–31.

6 Lehen, p. 130.

7 Hakalehto, p. 122.

8 *PKKPP*, p. 198.

9 *Ibid.*, p. 205.

10 *Ibid.*, p. 207.

11 *Ibid.*, pp. 211–3.

12 *Ibid.*, pp. 214–5.

13 'Vientirauha'—literally 'export-peace'.

14 Lehen, p. 129.

15 *Antikainen*, p. 450.

16 N. Wälläri, *Antoisia vuosia* (Helsinki, 1967), p. 58.

17 *Antikainen*, pp. 17, 438; *PKKPP*, p. 235.

18 *Antikainen*, p. 441.

19 Hakalehto, p. 302; Lehen, p. 132; *Antikainen*, pp. 442, 445, 450; *PKKPP*, pp. 209, 506.

20 A. Hyvönen, '30-vuotias SKP:n taisteluhistorian päävaiheet', *TT*, IV (1948), p. 54.

21 *Antikainen*, p. 442.

22 Lehen, p. 132.

23 *Antikainen*, p. 443; N. Wälläri, *Myrskyssä ja myötätuulessa* (Helsinki, 1951), p. 32.

24 *Antikainen*, p. 443.

25 *Ibid.*, p. 20.

26 Lehen, p. 129.

27 *PKKPP*, p. 252.

28 *Antikainen*, p. 408.

29 Tommila, p. 115; Lehen, p. 129; *Antikainen*, p. 407; *PKKPP*, pp. 252, 267–9.

30 *PKKPP*, pp. 271–2.

31 Lehen, p. 129.

32 *'Työn Ääni'*—literally 'The voice of Labour'.

33 *Antikainen*, p. 501; Tommila, p. 116; *'Suomen Työmies'*—literally 'The Finnish Worker'.

34 Lehen, p. 132; N. Wälläri, *Antoisia vuosia*, p. 63.

35 *Antikainen*, pp. 22, 433; *PKKPP*, p. 479; Korhonen, p. 199.

36 *PKKPP*, pp. 249, 290; Lehen, p. 134.

37 *PKKPP*, p. 265.

38 Wälläri, p. 59.

39 Oittinen, p. 186; Lehen, p. 127.

40 *PKKPP*, p. 238.

41 *Ibid.*, pp. 236, 239.

42 *Ibid.*, p. 248.

43 Tuominen, pp. 334–6; N. Parkkari, 'Puoluetyö vankilassa', *TT*, I (1945), p. 93.

44 *PKKPP*, pp. 267, 272, 290–1; *Antikainen*, pp. 491–2; Tuominen, pp. 337–8.

45 Wälläri, p. 70; Lehen, p. 127; *'Suomen työläisliitto'*—literally 'Workers' League of Finland'; *'Suomen ammattiyhdistysten keskusliitto'*—literally 'Central League of the Trade Unions of Finland', invariably referred to as SAK.

46 Lehen, p. 135; Hiitonen, pp. 244–5.

47 Lehen, p. 136.

48 *Antikainen*, p. 496.

49 Hiitonen, p. 246; Tommila, p. 153.

50 *Antikainen*, p. 406; Tommila, p. 60.

51 Tommila, p. 155.

52 Hiitonen, p. 248.

53 *Antikainen*, pp. 497–8; Lehen, p. 147; Tommila, p. 157.

54 *PKKPP*, p. 294.

55 Lehen, p. 142.

56 *Ibid.*, p. 144.

57 *Antikainen*, p. 407.

58 *TT*, X (1954), p. 58.

59 *PKKPP*, p. 297.

60 Hiitonen, pp. 276–7.

61 *PKKPP*, p. 294; Lehen, p. 142.

62 Tommila, pp. 165–6.

63 L. Kantola, 'Erään puoluejärjestön työstä', *TT*, III (1947), p. 183.

64 A. Hyvönen, '30-vuotias SKP:n taisteluhistorian päävaiheet', *TT*, IV (1948), p. 68; *PKKPP*, p. 310; *Antikainen*, pp. 466, 469.

65 *Antikainen*, p. 469.

66 *PKKPP*, pp. 352, 365; Tommila, p. 117.

67 *PKKPP*, p. 367.

68 *Ibid.*, p. 390.

69 *Ibid.*, p. 421.

70 A. Tuominen, *Kremlin kellot* (Helsinki, 1957), pp. 266–7.

71 *PKKPP*, pp. 303, 484–8; Korhonen, p. 203.

72 *PKKPP*, p. 303.

73 *Ibid.*, p. 489.

74 *Ibid.*, p. 490.

75 *Ibid.*, pp. 491–5.

76 *Ibid.*, pp. 284–98; *Antikainen*, pp. 21–2.

77 *PKKPP*, p. 303.

78 *Ibid.*, pp. 306–43.

79 *Antikainen,* pp. 456–65.

80 *PKKPP,* p. 344.

81 *Antikainen,* p. 24.

82 E. Karpinen, 'Tähdenvälejä SKP:n illegaaliselta toiminta-ajalta', *TT,* III (1947), pp. 179–82; *Antikainen,* p. 471; *PKKPP,* p. 510.

83 *PKKPP,* p. 371; *Antikainen,* p. 472.

84 *PKKPP,* p. 351.

85 *Ibid.,* pp. 376–9.

86 'Patriotic People's Movement' translates *'Isänmaallinen kansanliike'*—hence *IKL.*

87 *PKKPP,* p. 383.

88 *Ibid.,* p. 511.

89 *Antikainen,* p. 428.

90 *Ibid.,* p. 598; *'Announcer'* translates *'Tiedonantaja',* and *'The Worker'* translates *'Työmies'.*

91 *PKKPP,* p. 433; *Antikainen,* p. 428.

92 *PKKPP,* pp. 380, 394; Korhonen, p. 249.

93 *PKKPP,* p. 394.

94 *Ibid.,* pp. 397–407.

95 Tuominen, pp. 265–8; M. Janhunen, 'Yleispiirteitä SKP:n historian eri vaiheista', *TT,* I (1945), p. 18.

96 Tommila, p. 117.

97 *PKKPP,* p. 418.

98 *Ibid.,* p. 415.

99 *Ibid.,* p. 416.

100 *Ibid.,* p. 430.

101 *Ibid.,* pp. 433–7.

102 *Ibid.,* pp. 439–42.

103 *Ibid.,* p. 414.

104   *Ibid.*, p. 413.

105   *Ibid.*, p. 444.

106   *Ibid.*, p. 452.

## 5   The Popular Front and the War

1   Tuominen, pp. 265–7.

2   M. Ryömä, '. . . yhteis-ja kansanrintamaliikkeestä 1930-luvulla', *TT*, II (1946), pp. 115–8; 'Academic Socialist Society' translates '*Akateeminen Sosialistinen Seura*'—hence ASS; '*Soihtu*'—literally 'the Torch'.

3   *PKKPP*, p. 455.

4   *Ibid.*, p. 456.

5   *Ibid.*, pp. 457, 468, 472; A. Hyvönen, 'SKP työväen yhtenäisyyden puolustajana 30-luvulla', *TT*, III (1947), p. 34; *Kommunisti*, nos. 15–16 (1948), p. 362.

6   *PKKPP*, p. 469.

7   *Ibid.*, p. 468; *Kommunisti, loc. cit.*

8   *PKKPP*, p. 459; *Antikainen*, p. 27.

9   'Human Rights League' translates '*Ihmisoikeuksien Liitto*'.

10   Lehen, pp. 190–1; M. Ryömä, '. . . yhteis-ja kansanrintamaliikkeestä 1930-luvulla', *TT*, II (1946), pp. 120–2.

11   'SKP:n VI puoluekokouksen (v.1935) päätös . . .' , *TT*, X (1954), p. 148.

12   Tuominen, pp. 154–7.

13   *TT*, X (1954), p. 150.

14   *Ibid.*, II (1946), p. 119; III (1947), p. 39; X (1954), p. 152.

15   *Ibid.*, X (1954), p. 153.

16   *Ibid.*, p. 153.

17   *Ibid.*, II (1946), p. 119; III (1947), p. 40; X (1954), pp. 89, 153.

18  *Ibid.*, X (1954), p. 159.

19  *Ibid.*, p. 160.

20  *Ibid.*, pp. 163–70.

21  *Ibid.*, p. 171.

22  Waltari, p. 35.

23  *Ibid.*, p. 43.

24  Lehen, p. 177.

25  *Ibid.*, p. 189; T. Karvonen, 'SKNL', *TT*, I (1945), p. 47.

26  Tuominen, p. 272.

27  *Ibid.*, pp. 386–7.

28  A. Mäkinen, 'Maanalaiset sanansaattajat', *TT*, I (1945), p. 61.

29  Lehen, pp. 183–6; *'Kirjallisuuslehti'*—literally 'Literature paper'.

30  'The League of Women for Freedom and Peace' translates *'Naisten rauhan ja vapauden liitto'*.

31  'The National Committee Against War' translates *'Sotaa vastustavain kansalaistoimikunta'*.

32  Tuominen, pp. 296–7.

33  *TT*, IV (1948), p. 70.

34  *Ibid.*, X (1954), p. 184.

35  *Ibid.*, II (1946), p. 122.

36  *Ibid.*, IV (1948), p. 77; X (1954), pp. 62, 172.

37  *Ibid.*, X (1954), pp. 62, 176.

38  S. Karttunen, *Ystävyys vastatuulessa* (Helsinki, 1966), p. 16; Lehen, p. 194.

39  Lehen, p. 192; Tommila, p. 182.

40  *TT*, II (1946), p. 122.

41  *Ibid.*, p. 123.

42  L. Vilenius, 'Toiminta tasavaltalaisen Espanjan hyväksi', *TT*, III (1947), pp. 191–9.

43  Hiitonen, pp. 404–5; Karttunen, p. 20.

44  M. Ryömä, '. . . yhteis-ja kansanrintamaliikkeestä 1930-luvulla', *TT*, II (1946), p. 127; IV (1948), p. 75; Karttunen, pp. 32–3.

45  *Kommunisti*, no. 11 (1945), p. 11.

46  *Ibid.*, nos. 15–6 (1948), p. 362.

47  Karttunen, p. 22; Hiitonen, pp. 405–6.

48  Tuominen, p. 347.

49  *Ibid.*, p. 36.

50  Hakalehto, p. 65; *PKKPP*, p. 81; 'Kyntömiesten oikeuksien ja vaatimusten puolustaminen', *TT*, X (1954), p. 125.

51  *PKKPP*, pp. 342–3, 354, 394.

52  *Ibid.*, p. 343.

53  Tuominen, p. 354.

54  A. Hyvönen, 'skp työväen yhtenäisyyden puolustajana 30-luvulla', *TT*, III (1947), pp. 41–3; Tuominen, pp. 316–7.

55  Tuominen, p. 370.

56  *Ibid.*, pp. 278–87.

57  *Ibid.*, pp. 184–7.

58  *Ibid.*, pp. 336–44.

59  Lehen, p. 199.

60  M. Janhunen, 'Yleispiirteitä skp:n historian eri vaiheista', *TT*, I (1945), p. 19; V. Smirnov, 'Finljandia', *Antifashistkoe dvizhenie soprotivlenija v stranax Evropy v gody vtoroi mirovoi voiny*, ed. V. P. Bondarenko and P. I. Rezonov (Moscow, 1962), p. 649.

61  Karttunen, p. 20; Lehen, p. 198.

62  Y. Leino, *Kommunisti sisäministerinä* (Helsinki, 1958), p. 12.

63 Lehen, p. 199.

64 *Ibid.*, p. 200.

65 *Ibid.*, p. 177.

66 Tuominen, p. 390.

67 M. Jakobson, *The Diplomacy of the Winter War* (Cambridge, Mass., 1961), pp. 165–70; G. Mannerheim, *Muistelmat* (Helsinki, 1952), II, pp. 140–6.

68 'Kansanhallituksesta ja sen tehtävistä', *Kommunisti*, nos. 15–16, p. 362; Leino, p. 11.

69 Lehen, p. 205; T. Lehen, 'Maanalaisen SKP:n kanta sodan ja rauhan kysymyksessä', *TT*, X (1954), pp. 43–4.

70 Lehen, p. 207; *TT*, IV (1948), p. 85; X (1954), p. 70; *Kommunisti*, nos 15–16, p. 362.

71 Lehen, p. 200; *Antifashistkoe dvizhenie* . . . , p. 649.

72 Lehen, p. 207.

73 Karttunen, p. 7.

74 *Ibid.*, p. 35.

75 Leino, p. 146.

76 Karttunen, p. 27.

77 *Ibid.*, p. 37.

78 *Ibid.*, p. 40; Hiitonen, p. 410; Waltari, pp. 69–70; 'Finland-USSR Peace and Friendship Society' translates '*Suomen-Neuvostoliiton rauhan ja ystävyyden seura*',—hence SNS.

79 Karttunen, pp. 49–53; Waltari, p. 83; *Antifashistkoe dvizhenie* . . . , p. 649.

80 Lehen, p. 208; *Antifashistkoe dvizhenie* . . . , p. 649.

81 Karttunen, p. 45; Hiitonen, p. 411.

82 Karttunen, p. 81; Hiitonen, p. 421; Waltari, p. 78.

83 Karttunen, pp. 46, 139; Waltari, pp. 71–2.

84 Waltari, pp. 73–4.

85 *Ibid.*, p. 75.

86 Karttunen, p. 65; Waltari, p. 72.

87 Karttunen, pp. 65, 70; Waltari, p. 73; Hiitonen, p. 414.

88 Karttunen, p. 140; Waltari, p. 77.

89 Karttunen, p. 83; Hiitonen, pp. 421–2.

90 Karttunen, p. 60; Waltari, p. 78; 'Kansan Sanomat'— literally 'People's News'.

91 Karttunen, pp. 61–3.

92 Ibid., p. 73; Waltari, pp. 80–1.

93 Karttunen, p. 103.

94 Waltari, p. 97.

95 Karttunen, p. 68; Waltari, p. 98.

96 Karttunen, p. 120; Waltari, p. 100.

97 Lehen, pp. 213–4; Antifashistkoe dvizhenie . . . , pp. 652–3; L. A. Ingulskaja, 'Rabochii klass Finljandii i demokratizatsija strany (1944–48)', Rabochee dvizhenie v Skandinavskix stranax i Finljandii, ed. I. M. Maiskii (Moscow, 1965), pp 134–5.

98 Antifashistkoe dvizhenie . . . , p. 652.

99 M. Janhunen, 'Yleispiirteitä SKP:n historian eri vaiheista', TT, I (1945), pp. 19–20.

100 Leino, p. 186.

101 Kommunisti, nos 1–2 (1946), p. 16.

102 Leino, p. 19.

103 Antifashistkoe dvizhenie . . . , pp. 654, 658; Rabochee dvizhenie . . . , p. 133.

104 Lehen, p. 212; Rabochee dvizhenie . . . , p. 132; T. Lehen, 'Maanalaisen SKP:n kanta sodan ja rauhan kysymyksessä', TT, X (1954), p. 31; E. Salomaa, Tavoitteena kansanvalta: Suomen työväenliikkeen vaiheita vuosina 1944–1960 (Helsinki, 1964), p. 9; Oittinen, p. 248.

105 Antifashistkoe dvizhenie . . . , p. 654; 'forest guard' translates 'metsäkaarti'.

106 Salomaa, p. 8.

107 H. Kuusinen, 'SKDL—laajan demokraattisen rintaman järjestö', *TT*, VIII (1952), p. 69.

108 *Antifashistkoe dvizhenie* . . . , pp. 646–7; K. Heikkilä, 'Vainovuosilta', *TT*, I (1945), p. 72.

## 6 The First Phase of the Legal Communist Movement, 1944–5

1 L. Hyvämäki, *Vaaran vuodet 1944–48* (Helsinki, 1958), p. 28; Lehen, p. 216; Salomaa, p. 22.

2 Lehen, p. 218.

3 *Ibid.*, p. 219.

4 *Ibid.*, p. 220; Salomaa, p. 38; A. Aaltonen, 'Julkisuuteen', *TT*, III (1947), p. 47.

5 Lehen, p. 220; Leino, p. 187.

6 Leino, p. 188.

7 'Yhteistyön, kansamme vapauden, paremman elämän ja valoisamman tulevaisuuden puolesta', *TT*, XI (1955), p. 107; M. Tiilikainen, 'Kolme julkisuuden ja rauhan vuotta', *TT*, III (1947), pp. 49–50; H. Kuusinen, 'SKP ryhtyy sodan jälkeen kokoamaan rauhan ja kansanvallan rintamaa', *TT*, XI (1955), p. 20; *Rabochee dvizhenie* . . . , p. 136; Y. E. Miettinen, 'Borba kommunisticheskoi partii Finljandii za demokratizatzija strany v 1944–1948 godax', *Novaja i noveishaja istorija*, no. 3 (1964), p. 9; Salomaa, p. 40.

8 Tiilikainen, *TT*, III (1947), p. 50.

9 V. Pessi, 'Tilanteen ja tehtävien tarkastelua', *Kommunisti*, no. 1 (1944), p. 4.

10 Leino, p. 34.

11 'TS', 'Pois vahingollinen intoilu', *Kommunisti*, no. 5 (1945), p. 16.

12 *Iz istorii* . . . , p. 147.

13 *Kommunisti*, no. 4 (1945), p. 6; Lehen, pp. 237, 247.

NOTES 381

14 Salomaa, p. 42; Lehen, p. 247.

15 Lehen, p. 248.

16 Hyvämäki, p. 31; *Rabochee dvizhenie* . . . , p. 136; Aaltonen, *TT*, III (1947), p. 48.

17 Lehen, p. 232; Tiilikainen, *TT*, III (1947), p. 54; H. Kuusinen, *TT*, XI (1955), p. 8.

18 Aaltonen, *TT*, III (1947), p. 48.

19 Salomaa, p. 46; Hyvämäki, p. 35.

20 Salomaa, p. 47.

21 *Ibid.*, p. 30; Hyvämäki, p. 34.

22 Salomaa, p. 49; Borg, p. 42; SKDL, *Kymmenvuotias Liitto* (Helsinki, 1959), p. 6; Leino, p. 28; Lehen, p. 229.

23 Leino, p. 29; 'Finnish People's Democratic League' translates 'Suomen kansan demokraattinen liitto'—hence SKDL.

24 *Kymmenvuotias Liitto*, p. 6; *Rabochee dvizhenie* . . . , p. 139; Salomaa, p. 49.

25 Leino, p. 29.

26 *Ibid.*, p. 194; Hyvämäki, p. 34; Salomaa, p. 31; *Kymmenvuotias Liitto*, p. 8.

27 H. Kuusinen, *TT*, XI (1955), p. 10.

28 *Kymmenvuotias Liitto*, p. 96; Miettinen, *Novaja i noveishaja istorija*, no. 3 (1964), p. 17; Salomaa, p. 50; *TT*, XI (1955), p. 175.

29 Salomaa, p. 60.

30 Salomaa, p. 59; 'Finnish Women's Democratic League' translates 'Suomen naisten demokraattinen liitto'.

31 Salomaa, p. 51.

32 Leino, p. 197.

33 *Ibid.*, p. 68.

34 *Rabochee dvizhenie* . . . , p. 146; Salomaa, pp. 22–3, 35.

35 Leino, pp. 35, 36.

36 Hyvämäki, p. 36.

37 T. Heikkilä, *Paasikivi peräsimessä: pääministerin sihteerin muistelmat 1944–1948* (Helsinki, 1965), p. 67.

38 Hyvämäki, p. 36.

39 Leino, p. 31; Lehen, pp. 241–2; Salomaa, p. 76.

40 Lehen, p. 243.

41 *Ibid.*

42 *Rabochee dvizhenie* . . . , p. 153; Hyvämäki, p. 38; Lehen, p. 243.

43 Salomaa, p. 65.

44 *Kommunisti*, no. 46 (1945), p. 11.

45 Salomaa, pp. 32, 62–3, 69.

46 *Rabochee dvizhenie* . . . , p. 145; Salomaa, p. 69; N. Wälläri, *Myrskyssä ja myötätuulessa*, p. 146.

47 M. Huhta, 'Ammattiyhdistysliike', *Kommunisti*, no. 20 (1945), p. 10; *Rabochee dvizhenie* . . . , p. 145.

48 Lehen, p. 252; Leino, p. 189; Salomaa, p. 84; Y. Soini, *Kuin Pietari hiilivalkealla: Sotasyyllisyysasian vaiheet 1944–1949* (Helsinki, 1956), p. 59.

49 Heikkilä, p. 69; Hyvämäki, pp. 50–1; Lehen, p. 253.

50 Hyvämäki, p. 44.

51 *Ibid.*, p. 52; Soini, p. 60.

52 Hyvämäki, p. 53.

53 *Ibid.*, p. 45; Lehen, p. 250; Salomaa, p. 85.

54 Salomaa, p. 86; Hyvämäki, pp. 45–7; Lehen, pp. 250–1.

55 *Kommunisti*, no. 5 (1945), p. 6; *Rabochee dvizhenie* . . . , p. 150; Miettinen, *Novaja i noveishaja istorija*, no. 3 (1964), p. 9; Salomaa, p. 83.

56 M. Janhunen, 'SKP:n vaaliohjelmasta', *Kommunisti*, no. 4 (1945), p. 14.

57 Salomaa, pp. 89–90; Lehen, p. 256; *Rabochee dvizhenie* . . . , p. 150.

58 Hyvämäki, p. 55.

59 *Kommunisti*, no. 9 (1945), p. 3, nos. 14–5, p. 10.

60 K. Heikkilä, 'Vasemmistolaisista', *Kommunisti*, no. 16 (1945), p. 3; Lehen, p. 254; Leino, p. 51; Salomaa, p. 93.

61 Hyvämäki, p. 57; *Iz istorii* . . . , p. 166; *Kymmenvuotias Liitto*, p. 31; Lehen, p. 258; Leino, p. 126; *Rabochee dvizhenie* . . . , p. 151; Salomaa, p. 95.

62 Soini, p. 65.

63 Hyvämäki, p. 59; Lehen, pp. 258–9; Salomaa, p. 96.

64 Leino, p. 50.

65 *Ibid.*, p. 51.

66 *Ibid.*, p. 49.

67 *Kommunisti*, nos 14–5 (1945), p. 9; Lehen, pp. 261–2.

68 H. Kuusinen, 'skp ryhtyy sodan jälkeen kokoamaan rauhan ja kansanvallan rintamaa', *TT*, XI (1955), pp. 15–6.

69 E. Salonen, 'Valmistautumisesta puolueemme VII edustajakokoukseen', *Kommunisti*, no. 41 (1945), p. 7.

70 *Kommunisti*, nos 44–5 (1945), p. 21; *Rabochee dvizhenie* . . . , p. 137; Salomaa, p. 119.

71 *Kommunisti*, nos 44–5 (1945), pp. 9–14; *Iz istorii* . . . , pp. 163–6; *Rabochee dvizhenie*, p. 137; M. Tiilikainen, 'Kolme julkisuuden ja rauhan vuotta', *TT*, III (1947), pp. 53–60; *TT*, XI (1955), pp. 113–9.

72 Soini, p. 28.

73 *Ibid.*, p. 34; Miettinen, *Novaja i noveishaja istorija*, no. 3 (1964), p. 11.

74 Soini, pp. 57–8; Hyvämäki, p. 47; Salomaa, p. 79.

75 Heikkilä, p. 145.

76 Soini, pp. 49, 58.

77  Leino, p. 93; Soini, pp. 81–6.

78  Miettinen, Novaja i noveishaja istorija, no. 3 (1964), p. 12.

79  Soini, p. 68.

80  Hyvämäki, pp. 63–6.

81  Kommunisti, no. 29 (1945), p. 3.

82  Soini, p. 89.

83  Heikkilä, p. 184.

84  Hyvämäki, p. 68; Soini, p. 111.

85  Heikkilä, p. 171.

86  Leino, pp. 98–105.

87  Soini, pp. 373–7.

88  Ibid., p. 75; Hyvämäki, p. 50; Lehen, p. 253; Leino, p. 116.

89  Leino, p. 116.

90  Soini, p. 76; Hyvämäki, p. 79; Salomaa, p. 102.

91  Leino, p. 117; the new force was called in Finnish 'Valtiollinen poliisi'—literally 'State Police' and hence Valpo.

92  Kommunisti, no. 24 (1945), p. 5.

93  Leino, p. 132.

94  Ibid., p. 134.

95  Ibid., pp. 130–1.

96  Ibid., p. 134.

97  Hyvämäki, p. 86; Leino, p. 135.

98  'The arms dumps affair' translates 'Asekätkentöjuttu'.

99  Salomaa, p. 103; Hyvämäki, p. 81.

100  Hyvämäki, p. 82.

101  Leino, p. 129.

102  Hyvämäki, pp. 83–4; Leino, p. 129.

103 *Kommunisti*, no. 29 (1945), p. 5.

104 Salomaa, p. 120; Hyvämäki, p. 88; *Kommunisti*, no. 30 (1945), p. 5.

105 Hyvämäki, p. 88; Salomaa, p. 120; H. Kuusinen, 'Kansanvallan kehitysvaiheita vuodelta 1946 Suomessa', *TT*, II (1946), p. 6; L. Suonpää, 'Kommunistit kunnallispolitiikassa', *TT*, VII (1951), p. 90.

106 Salomaa pp. 80–1; *Rabochee dvizhenie* . . . , p. 157.

107 Salomaa, p. 109; *Rabochee dvizhenie* . . . , p. 158.

108 *Kommunisti*, no. 24 (1945), p. 3.

109 *Ibid.*, no. 20 (1945), p. 6.

110 Heikkilä, p. 112.

111 Salomaa, pp. 111–2.

112 *Kommunisti*, nos 51–2 (1945), p. 8.

113 Heikkilä, p. 121.

7 *The Pekkala Government and the Leino Crisis, 1946–8*

1 Hyvämäki, p. 103; 'Hallituksen vaihdos', *Kommunisti*, nos 7–8 (1946), p. 6.

2 Heikkilä, p. 218; Leino, p. 138.

3 Leino, p. 138.

4 Heikkilä, p. 201.

5 *Ibid.*, p. 153.

6 G. von Bonsdorff, *Suomen poliittiset puolueet* (Helsinki, 1957), p. 481; Salomaa, p. 133.

7 'Hallituksen vaihdos', *Kommunisti*, nos 7–8 (1946), p. 6.

8 Heikkilä, p. 208; Leino, p. 152.

9 Heikkilä, p. 208.

10 Salomaa, p. 124; Borg, p. 43.

11 Oittinen, p. 256; Salomaa, p. 125.

12 Leino, pp. 197–8.

13 Borg, p. 45.

14 'SKDL:n linja', *Kommunisti*, nos 7–8 (1946), p. 18.

15 *Kommunisti*, no. 14 (1946), p. 9.

16 *Ibid.*, no. 17 (1946), p. 6.

17 M. Tiilikainen, 'Työväenliikkeen yhtenäisyys', *TT*, II (1946), p. 67.

18 Hyvämäki, p. 122.

19 Y. Murto, 'SKP taistelussa työväenluokan yhtenäisyyden puolesta', *TT*, VIII (1952), p. 32.

20 Murto, *TT*, VIII (1952), p. 35.

21 Hyvämäki, p. 122; Salomaa, p. 127; Oittinen, p. 259.

22 M. Tiilikainen, 'Kolme julkisuuden ja rauhan vuotta', *TT*, III (1947), p. 61.

23 A. Äikiä, *Kolmas tie?* (Helsinki, 1948), pp. 34–6.

24 Äikiä, pp. 37–48.

25 Tiilikainen, *TT*, III (1947), p. 61.

26 *Ibid.*, p. 62; *Rabochee dvizhenie* . . . , p. 161; Miettinen, *Novaja i noveishaja istorija*, no. 3 (1964), p. 16; Salomaa, p. 149.

27 Salomaa, p. 134; *Rabochee dvizhenie* . . . , pp. 165–6.

28 H. Kuusinen, 'SKDL—laajan demokraattisen rintaman järjestö', *TT*, VIII (1952), pp. 73–4.

29 Hyvämäki, p. 109; Leino, pp. 71–2; V. Pessi, 'Fasismi lyötävä lopullisesti', *Kommunisti*, no. 10 (1946), p. 3; H. Kuusinen, 'Kansanvallan kehitysvaiheita vuodelta 1946 Suomessa', *TT*, II (1946), p. 8.

30 J. Parkkari, 'SKP:n puolueneuvosto kokoontuu', *Kommunisti*, no. 11 (1946), p. 3.

31 Hyvämäki, pp. 110–2; Salomaa, p. 147; Miettinen, *Nova ja i noveishaja istorija*, no. 3 (1964) p. 14.

32 Hyvämäki, p. 111.

33 *Ibid.*, p. 112.

34 Miettinen, *Novaja inoveishaja istorija*, no. 3 (1964), p. 14.

35 *Iz istorii* . . . , p. 169.

36 M. Tiilikainen, 'Valtava työ odottaa', *Kommunisti*, no. 13 (1946), p. 3.

37 Hyvämäki, p. 123.

38 Heikkilä, p. 252.

39 Hyvämäki, p. 134.

40 Hyvämäki, pp. 122–8; V. Pessi, 'Asekätkijäin asianajajain tappio', *Kommunisti*, no. 21 (1947), p. 8; Leino, p. 166.

41 Heikkilä, pp. 281–2; Leino, pp. 153–5.

42 Miettinen, *Novaja i noveishaja istorija*, no. 3 (1964), p. 20; Salomaa, p. 138; Hyvämäki, pp. 116–7; *Kommunisti*, no. 17 (1946), p. 11; H. Kuusinen, 'Kansanvallan kehitysvaiheita vuodelta 1946 Suomessa', *TT*, II (1946), p. 12.

43 Hyvämäki, p. 118.

44 Leino, p. 158.

45 Salomaa, p. 149.

46 Hyvämäki, p. 106.

47 Leino, p. 195; H. Kuusinen, 'Kansanvallan kehitysvaiheita vuodelta 1946 Suomessa', *TT*, II (1946), p. 9; Y. Murto 'SKP taistelussa työväenluokan yhtenäisyyden puolesta', *TT*, VIII (1952), p. 31.

48 Leino, p. 195.

49 Hyvämäki, p. 121; Salomaa, p. 152; *Rabochee dvizhenie* . . . , p. 159.

50 Salomaa, p. 151.

51 L. Junttila, 'SAK:n edustajakokous', *Kommunisti*, no. 5 (1947), p. 123.

52 Hyvämäki, p. 137.

53 Äikiä, pp. 94, 101; M. Tiilikainen, 'Kolme julkisuuden ja rauhan vuotta', *TT*, III (1947), p. 67.

54 Hyvämäki, p. 141; 'SAK:n edustajakokous', *Kommunisti*, no. 12 (1947), p. 295.

55 Salomaa, p. 153.

56 *Rabochee dvizhenie* . . . , p. 145; *Kommunisti*, no. 12 (1947), p. 295.

57 Leino, p. 168.

58 Heikkilä, p. 221.

59 'Lopullinen rauhansopimus varmistaa kansamme onnellisen tulevaisuuden', *TT*, XI (1955), p. 130.

60 Heikkilä, p. 221.

61 Leino, p. 169.

62 Heikkilä, p. 221; Leino, p. 171.

63 *Iz istorii* . . . , p. 174; 'Työväenhallitus', *Kommunisti*, no. 11 (1947), p. 271.

64 'Sisäpoliittisesta tilanteesta', *Kommunisti*, no. 9 (1947), p. 223.

65 Leino, p. 202.

66 *Ibid.*, pp. 201–2.

67 *Ibid.*, p. 172; Heikkilä, p. 297; Salomaa, p. 139; Miettinen, Novaja i noveishaja istorija, no. 3 (1964), p. 21; Hyvämäki, p. 157.

68 Heikkilä, p. 296.

69 Leino, p. 173

70 Hyvämäki, p. 143; Salomaa, p. 152; *Rabochee dvizhenie* . . . , p. 160; Heikkilä, p. 256.

71 Äikiä, p. 98.

72 Heikkilä, p. 256.

73 Leino, p. 172.

NOTES 389

74 'Työtätekevän kansan tyytymättömyys', *Kommunisti*, nos 15–6 (1947), p. 363.

75 Leino, p. 203; Äikiä, p. 106.

76 Hyvämäki, p. 142.

77 Heikkilä, p. 257.

78 *Ibid.*, pp. 263–4.

79 Hyvämäki, p. 143.

80 M. Huhta, 'Hinta-ja palkkapolitiikka', *Kommunisti*, nos 19–20 (1947), p. 483.

81 Leino, p. 182.

82 *Ibid.*, pp. 180–2.

83 A. Mäkinen, 'Vastaisku vihollisillemme', *Kommunisti*, no. 18 (1947), p. 423; *Kommunisti*, no. 21 (1947), p. 502.

84 Heikkilä, p. 299; Hyvämäki, p. 157.

85 Leino, p. 207; Heikkilä, pp. 300–1.

86 Heikkilä, p. 304.

87 Hyvämäki, p. 157.

88 Heikkilä, pp. 304–5.

89 Äikiä, p. 170.

90 Heikkilä, p. 222.

91 Hyvämäki, p. 181.

92 Leino, p. 203.

93 *Ibid.*, p. 240; Heikkilä, p. 226.

94 Leino, p. 242; Hyvämäki, p. 159.

95 Leino, pp. 246–8.

96 *Ibid.*, p. 245.

97 Hyvämäki, p. 174.

98 'Eduskuntavaalien poliittinen tausta', *Kommunisti*, no. 3 (1948).

99 *Kommunisti*, no. 4 (1948); M. Tiilikainen, 'Demokratian suurvoitto', *Kommunisti*, no. 6 (1948), p. 131.

100 Hyvämäki, p. 161.

101 *Ibid.*, p. 175; Heikkilä, pp. 310–2.

102 *Kommunisti*, no. 5 (1948), p. 107.

103 Salomaa, pp. 140–2; Miettinen, *Novaja i noveishaja istorija*, no. 3 (1964), p. 21; Hyvämäki, p. 164.

104 Leino, pp. 216–28.

105 *Ibid.*, p. 247.

106 *Ibid.*, pp. 234–5; Heikkilä, pp. 323–5.

107 Heikkilä, p. 256; Leino, p. 236.

108 Leino, p. 249.

109 Hyvämäki, p. 176.

110 *Ibid.*, p. 174; Leino, p. 255.

111 Leino, p. 255.

112 Heikkilä, p. 225.

113 *Ibid.*, p. 226.

114 V. Kanto, 'Kolmen vuosikymmenen taipaleelta', *Kommunisti*, nos 7–8 (1968), p. 162; Heikkilä, p. 227.

115 Hyvämäki, p. 176; Heikkilä, p. 227.

116 Heikkilä, pp. 229–30.

117 *Ibid.*, p. 230.

118 Hyvämäki, p. 176; Heikkilä, p. 231.

119 Salomaa, p. 156; Heikkilä, p. 241.

120 Leino, pp. 192–3.

121 Heikkilä, p.230.

122 Leino, p. 119.

123 Salomaa, p. 158.

124 Hyvämäki, p. 177.

125 Heikkilä, p. 233; Leino, p. 256.

126 Leino, pp. 256–7.

127 Hyvämäki, p. 179; Leino, p. 257.

128 Salomaa, p. 159; Hyvämäki, p. 179; Heikkilä, p. 256.

129 'Uusiin voittoihin', *Kommunisti*, no. 10 (1948), p. 223.

130 Leino, p. 255; Heikkilä, p. 233.

131 Salomaa, p. 162.

132 *Kommunisti*, nos 7–8 (1948), p. 212; Salomaa, p. 160.

133 'Vaalitulosten merkitys', *Kommunisti*, nos 13–4 (1948), p. 295; Salomaa, p. 163.

134 *Kommunisti*, nos 13–4 (1948), p. 299.

135 Salomaa, p. 165; *Kommunisti*, nos 15–6 (1948), p. 339.

## 8 Finnish Communism in the Cold War and Its Aftermath

1 *Kommunisti*, nos 15–6 (1948), p. 236; A. Aaltonen, 'SKP:n voiman kasvu', *TT*, VIII (1952), p. 16; H. Kuusinen, 'SKP ryhtyy sodan jälkeen kokoamaan rauhan ja kansanvallan rintamaa', *TT*, XI (1955), p. 39.

2 *Kommunisti*, nos 15–6 (1948), p. 347.

3 'Edustajakokous on puhunut', *Kommunisti*, no. 17 (1948), p. 379.

4 *Kommunisti*, nos 15–6 (1948), p. 236.

5 'Puolueen uudet säännöt', *Kommunisti*, nos 15–6 (1948), p. 351.

6. V. Pessi, 'SKP:n ideologisen ja organisatorisen työn käisityksestä', *TT*, VI (1950), p. 25; A. Mäkinen, 'Ideologisesta kasvatustyöstä SKP:ssa', *TT*, VII (1951), p. 71.

7 *Kommunisti*, nos 15–6 (1948), p. 341.

8 Salomaa, p. 167.

9 *Ibid.*, p. 174.

10 *Ibid.*, p. 170.

11 Oittinen, p. 260; 'Security Police' translates 'Suojelupoliisi'.

12 A. Äikiä, 'Kansalaisrintama Suomen riippumattomuuden ja rauhan suojelemiseksi', *TT*, VIII (1952), p. 48.

13 Leino, p. 195.

14 Äikiä, pp. 7, 185.

15 O. W. Kuusinen, *Suomen työväenliikkeen opetuksia* (Lappeenranta, 1949), p. 32.

16 *Kommunisti*, nos 15–6 (1948), p. 347; O. W. Kuusinen, pp. 58–9.

17 *TT*, VI (1950), p. 30.

18 *Kommunisti*, no. 4 (1953), p. 179.

19 Salomaa, pp. 176–8.

20 'Tehtävistämme nykyisessä vaiheessa', *Kommunisti*, no. 21 (1948).

21 Salomaa, p. 172.

22 *Kommunisti*, no. 1 (1949), p. 31.

23 'Miksi maan politiikkaa on muutettava', *Kommunisti*, no. 2 (1949), p. 67.

24 'Vappu—rauhan juhla', *Kommunisti*, no. 4 (1949), p. 193.

25 Salomaa, p. 186; 'Rauhan turvaaminen on työtätekevien joukkojen tehtävä', *Kommunisti*, no. 5 (1949).

26 Borg, p. 47.

27 *Ibid.*, p. 46.

28 *Kommunisti*, no. 7 (1949), p. 389.

29 *Kymmenvuotias Liitto*, p. 30.

30 *Ibid.*, pp. 23–38; Salomaa, p. 189; *Kommunisti*, no. 7 (1949), p. 389.

31 *Kymmenvuotias Liitto*, p. 38.

32  M. Ryömä, 'Amerikkalaispolitiikan epäonnistuminen Kemissä', *TT*, VI (1950), p. 74.

33  Salomaa, p. 190; K. Murto and K. Kaukonen, *Oikeus konepistoolin piipussa* (Helsinki, 1951), p. 10; K. Kaukonen, 'Kestätko Kemi, me autamme', *TT*, XI (1955), p. 81.

34  Salomaa, p. 190; Murto and Kaukonen, pp. 11–5.

35  Murto and Kaukonen, pp. 37–40.

36  Salomaa, pp. 192–3; Ryömä, *TT*, VI (1950), pp. 76–7; Kaukonen, *TT*, XI (1955), pp. 84–6.

37  Kaukonen, *TT*, XI (1955), p. 86.

38  Salomaa, p. 192.

39  *Ibid.*, p. 196; Y. Murto, 'Käydyn lakkotaistelun arviota', *Kommunisti*, no. 10 (1949), p. 577.

40  Salomaa, p. 197.

41  Murto and Kaukonen, p. 87.

42  Ryömä, *TT*, VI (1950), p. 80.

43  V. Pessi, 'Maamme työväki taistelussa leivän puolesta', *Kommunisti*, no. 9 (1949), p. 513.

44  Y. Murto, 'Käydyn lakkotaistelun arviota', *Kommunisti*, no. 10 (1949), p. 577.

45  Pessi, *Kommunisti*, no. 9 (1949), p. 513.

46  H. Kuusinen, 'Lujan rauhan ja kansandemokratian puolesta', *TT*, V (1949), p. 82; 'Taistelumme perustehtävistä', *Kommunisti*, no. 1 (1950), p. 1.

47  H. Kuusinen, *TT*, V (1949), p. 82.

48  'Aikamme Lenin', *Kommunisti*, no. 12 (1949), p. 705.

49  *Kommunisti*, no. 1 (1950), p. 7.

50  Salomaa, p. 198; *Kommunisti*, no. 11 (1949), p. 642.

51  *Kommunisti*, no. 3 (1950), p. 145.

52  Salomaa, p. 201.

53 *Ibid.*, p. 206.

54 'Yksi isäntä—kaksi renkiä', *Kommunisti*, no. 7 (1950), p. 402.

55 'Kaikki voimat vastaiskuun', *Kommunisti*, no. 2 (1951), p. 65.

56 *Kommunisti*, no. 4 (1950), p. 246.

57 M. Viri-Tuominen, 'Rauhanpuolustajien liike laajenee Suomessa', *TT*, VI (1950), p. 47.

58 Salomaa, p. 205.

59 *Kommunisti*, no. 4 (1950), p. 249.

60 Salomaa, p. 207.

61 *Ibid.*, p. 209.

62 *Kommunisti*, no. 5 (1950), no. 10 (1950), p. 593.

63 Salomaa, p. 212; *Kommunisti*, no. 5 (1950), no. 3 (1950), p. 145.

64 *Kommunisti*, no. 5 (1951), p. 274; Salomaa, p. 223.

65 *Kommunisti*, no. 5 (1951), p. 274.

66 Salomaa, p. 224.

67 *Ibid.*, p. 216.

68 *Kommunisti*, no. 5 (1951), p. 267.

69 A. Aaltonen, 'Työpaikka kommunistisen puolueen linnakkeena', *TT*, VII (1951), p. 52.

70 Salomaa, p. 227; 'Rauhan leirin voitto Suomessa', *Kommunisti*, nos 7–8 (1951), p. 385.

71 *Kommunisti*, nos 11–2 (1951), p. 385; H. Kuusinen, 'IX puoluekokouksen edellä', *TT*, VII (1951), p. 35.

72 V. Pessi, 'SKP:n IX edustajakokouksen päätökset', *TT*, VIII (1952), p. 5; *Kommunisti*, nos 11–2 (1951), p. 624.

73 Salomaa, p. 221; *Kommunisti*, nos 11–2 (1951), p. 624.

74 *Kommunisti*, nos 11–2 (1951), p. 655.

75 *Ibid.*, p. 672; Aaltonen, *TT*, VII (1951), p. 51.

76  A. Aaltonen, *Kommunisti*, no. 4 (1952).

77  Salomaa, p. 219.

78  *Kommunisti*, no. 2 (1954), p. 105.

79  *Ibid.*, nos 6–7 (1952), p. 321; K-M. Rydberg, 'Miss Cosmopolitan', *TT*, VIII (1952), p. 148.

80  'Suurten voittojen edustajakokous', *Kommunisti*, no. 9 (1952), p. 465.

81  V. Pessi, *Kommunisti*, no. 11 (1952), p. 610.

82  H. Yrjölä, *Kommunisti*, nos 1–2 (1953), p. 20.

83  O. W. Kuusinen, 'J. V. Stalin—suuri kansain johtaja', *TT*, IX (1953), pp. 5, 10; V. Pessi, *Kommunisti*, no. 4 (1953), p. 179.

84  I. Lehtinen, 'Kuulin Stalinin puhuvan', *TT*, IX (1953), p. 110.

85  'Yhtenäisin voimin rauhan ja kansanvallan puolesta', *Kommunisti*, no. 5 (1953), p. 209.

86  *Kommunisti*, no. 9 (1953), p. 422.

87  H. Kuusinen, 'Kunnallisvaalit viitoittavat tietä', *Kommunisti*, no. 11 (1953), p. 545.

88  Salomaa, p. 219; M. Ryömä, 'Taantumuksen vallankaappaus ja nykyisen politiikan kriisi', *Kommunisti*, no. 12 (1953), p. 609.

89  *Kommunisti*, no. 1 (1954), p. 6.

90  *Kommunisti*, no. 2 (1954), p. 72; 'Työväen yhteistoiminta on välttämättömämpää kuin koskaan aikaisemmin', *TT*, XI (1955), p. 151; *Iz istorii* . . . , p. 183.

91  'Työväen luokan toimintayhtenäisyys', *Kommunisti*, no. 3 (1954), p. 129.

92  *Kommunisti*, no. 2 (1954), p. 89; Salomaa, p. 227.

93  *Kommunisti*, no. 4 (1954), p. 200.

94  *Ibid.*, no. 5 (1954), p. 257.

95  *Kymmenvuotias Liitto*, p. 8.

96  V. Pessi, *Kommunisti*, no. 11 (1954), p. 563.

97  *Kommunisti*, no. 12 (1954), p. 719.

98  Nousiainen, p. 19.

99  'Maailmantapahtumia', *Kommunisti*, nos 6–7 (1955), p. 363.

100  *Ibid.*, no. 3 (1955), p. 129.

101  *Kommunisti*, no. 11 (1955), p. 604.

102  *Ibid.*, p. 612.

103  'Presidentinvaali lähestyy', *Kommunisti*, nos 6–7 (1955), p. 321.

104  'Mistä vaaleissa on kysymys', *Kommunisti*, no. 9 (1955), p. 465.

105  Salomaa, pp. 232–3.

106  *Kommunisti*, no. 3 (1956), p. 81.

107  *Suomen Kommunistisen puolueen XI edustajakokous*, Helsinki 29.5–2.6.57 (Kotka, 1957), p. 69.

108  *XI edustajakokous*, pp. 71–2.

109  Salomaa, p. 231; 'Puolue työväen johdossa', *Kommunisti*, no. 9 (1956), p. 417.

110  *Kommunisti*, no. 9 (1956), p. 420.

111  *Ibid.*

112  Leino, p. 260.

113  'Suurten tapahtumien vuosi', *Kommunisti*, no. 1 (1957), p. 3; Salomaa, p. 231.

114  Salomaa, p. 248; 'Vaalien jälkeen—eteenpäin', *Kommunisti*, no. 11 (1956), p. 545.

115  *XI edustajakokous*, p. 65.

116  *Kommunisti*, no. 1 (1957), p. 5.

117  *Iz istorii* . . . , p. 109.

118  Salomaa, p. 235; Wälläri, *Antoisia vuosia*, pp. 275–6.

119  *Kommunisti*, no. 4 (1956), p. 148; Wälläri, p. 276.

120  Wälläri, p. 277.

121  *Ibid.*, pp. 281–3.

122  Salomaa, p. 248.

123  T. Lehen, 'Millaisen ohjelman tarvitsemme?', *Kommunisti*, no. 1 (1957), p. 12.

124  *Kommunisti*, no. 5 (1957), p. 156.

125  A. Hyvönen, 'Marxilainen ohjelma', *Kommunisti*, no. 6 (1957), p. 188.

126  *Kommunisti*, nos 9–10 (1957), p. 344.

127  V. Pessi, 'Sosialistisen Suomen puolesta', *Kommunisti*, no. 12 (1957), p. 387.

128  XI *puoluekokous*, p. 48.

129  *Ibid.*, pp. 63, 67.

130  *Ibid.*, p. 75.

131  *Ibid.*, p. 250.

132  *Ibid.*, p. 362.

133  *Ibid.*, p. 79.

134  *Ibid.*, p. 82.

135  *Ibid.*, p. 83.

136  *Ibid.*

137  *Ibid.*, pp. 286–7, 364.

138  *Ibid.*, p. 94.

139  *Ibid.*, pp. 194, 315.

140  *Ibid.*, p. 315.

141  *Ibid.*, p. 316.

142  *Ibid.*, pp. 394–5.

143  *Ibid.*, p. 450.

144  *Ibid.*, p. 67.

145   *Ibid.*, p. 245.

146   *Ibid.*

9   *Finnish Communism Enters the Sixties*

1   Salomaa, pp. 242–3.

2   *Kommunisti*, no. 6 (1957), p. 183.

3   *Iz istorii* . . . , p. 196; Salomaa, p. 241; XI *puoluekokous*, p. 427.

4   *Kommunisti*, no. 13 (1957), p. 429; no. 14 (1957), p. 451.

5   P. Pesonen, *Valtuutus kansalta* (Porvoo, 1965), p. 21.

6   A. Aaltonen, 'Uusi taisteluvuosi', *Kommunisti*, nos 1–2 (1958), p. 3.

7   *Kommunisti*, no. 3 (1958), p. 59.

8   *Ibid.*, no. 9 (1958), p. 257; no. 10 (1958), p. 283.

9   Salomaa, p. 249; *Kommunisti*, nos 12–3 (1958), p. 349.

10   Pesonen, p. 133.

11   *Ibid.*, p. 141.

12   *Ibid.*, p. 135.

13   K. Vuori, 'Kansan näännyttämisen ohjelma', *Kommunisti*, no. 15 (1958), p. 421.

14   'Käänne parempaan on turvattava', *Kommunisti*, no. 1 (1959), pp. 3, 20.

15   *Kommunisti*, no. 1 (1959), p. 35.

16   E. Allardt, 'The social sources of Finnish communism: traditional and emerging radicalism', *International Journal of Comparative Sociology*, V, no. 1 (1964), pp. 57–8.

17   Nousiainen, p. 111.

18   *Ibid.*, p. 12.

19   *Ibid.*, p. 52.

20  Pesonen, pp. 42–4.

21  *Ibid.*, p. 37.

22  *Ibid.*, p. 27.

23  *Ibid.*, p. 33.

24  *Ibid.*, pp. 84, 90.

25  *Ibid.*, p. 123.

26  *Ibid.*, p. 127.

27  *Ibid.*, p. 291.

28  *Ibid.*, p. 292.

29  A. Nojanen, *Kommunisti*, no. 4 (1959), p. 142.

30  *Kommunisti*, no. 2 (1960), p. 65.

31  *Suomen Kommunistisen puolueen XII edustajakokous:*
    *15.4–18.4.60* (Kotka, 1960), p. 98.

32  *Iz istorii* . . . , p. 202; 'Taistelu suurpääoman valtaa vas-
    taan', *Kommunisti*, no. 1 (1960), p. 3.

33  *XII edustajakokous*, pp. 38, 139.

34  *Ibid.*, p. 13; *Kommunisti*, no. 4 (1960), p. 139; no.
    5 (1960), p. 195.

35  *XII edustajakokous*, p. 91.

36  *Ibid.*, pp. 64, 70.

37  *Ibid.*, pp. 109, 117.

38  *Ibid.*, p. 112.

39  *Ibid.*, p. 122.

40  *Ibid.*, p. 123.

41  *Ibid.*, pp. 124–6.

42  *Ibid.*, p. 126.

43  Miettinen, *Novaja i noveishaja istorija*, no. 3 (1964),
    p. 23; *Kommunisti*, no. 7 (1960), p. 293.

44  Salomaa, pp. 263, 291.

# BIBLIOGRAPHY

BIBLIOGRAPHY

DENMARK AND NORWAY

1 General

Alsterdal, A., *Den nya vänstern* (Stockholm, 1963).

Sparring, Johansen, Holmgaard, and Mati, *Kommunismen i norden og krisen i den kommunistiske bevegelse* (Oslo, 1965).

2 Denmark

Christiansen, E., *Men det gik anderledes* (1960).
Jensen, R., *En omtumlet tilvaerelse* (1957).
———, *Hvem er Axel Larsen?* (1961).
Larsen, A., 'Danmarks kommunistiske parti', *Den danske Rigsdag, 1849–1949*, III (1950).
———, *Den levende vej* (1958). Collection of speeches and articles.
Madsen, C., *Vi skrev Loven* (1968).

3 Norway

Gustavsen, F., *Rett på sak* (1968).
Langfeldt, K., *Moskva-tesene i norsk politik* (1961).
Løvlien, E., *Opgjøret med det annet centrum* (1950).
Norges kommunistiske parti, *Vårt partis politik under krigen* (1945).
*Norges kommunistiskes partis historie*, I (1963). The subsequent volumes of this official party history have not appeared.
Zachariassen, A., *Fra Marcus Thrane til Martin Tranmael* (1962).

FINLAND

1 Original sources

Suomen kansan demokraattinen liitto, SKDL:n, *Sosiaalidemokraattisen ja Maalaisliiton eduskuntaryhmien yhteistyösopimus* (Helsinki, 1945). The text of the Big Three Agreement.
Suomen Kommunistinen puolue, *Puoluekokousten, konferenssien ja keskuskomitean plenumien päätöksiä* (Leningrad, 1935). A collection of the resolutions of SKP congresses, conferences and central committee meetings from the origins of the party to the enlarged central committee meeting of 1934.
———, *Kommunisti* (1944–60). The official journal of the legal SKP since 1944, published sometimes fortnightly, sometimes monthly, and containing all the official pronouncements of SKP and a certain amount of other historical material.
———, *Suomen Kommunistisen puolueen XI edustajakokous,*

*Helsinki 29.5–2.6.57* (Kotka, 1957). The official printed record of SKP's eleventh party congress of 1957.

———, *Suomen Kommunistisen puolueen XII edustajakokous: 15.4–18.4.60* (Kotka, 1960). The official printed record of SKP's twelfth party congress of 1960.

———, SKP *taistelujen tiellä, vols I–XI* (1945–1955): *Suomen Kommunistisen puolueen vuosikirja*. A series of eleven year books published by SKP and devoted to the history of the party, which contain both original materials and secondary accounts.

———, SKP:n *taistelun tieltä: muistelmia, kuvauksia ja aineistoa* SKP:n *15 vuotistaipaleelta* (Leningrad, 1934), ed. T. Antikainen. A collection of original materials and secondary accounts bearing on the history of SKP from its origins down to the year 1933.

The author also gained a number of useful insights from a conversation with Kansanedustaja Hertta Kuusinen in 1968.

## 2 Books and articles

Allardt, E., 'Social sources of Finnish Communism', *International Journal of Comparative Sociology*, V, no. 1 (1964).

Bonsdorff, G. von, *Suomen poliittiset puolueet* (Helsinki, 1957).

Borg, O., *Suomen puolueideologiat* (Porvoo, 1964).

Braunthal, J., *History of the International*, II (1914–43) (London, 1967).

Hakalehto, I., *Suomen Kommunistinen puolue ja sen vaikutus poliittiseen ja ammatilliseen työväen liikkeeseen, 1918–1928* (Porvoo, 1966).

Heikkilä, T., *Paasikivi peräsimessä* (Helsinki, 1965).

Hiitonen, E., *Vääryyttä oikeuden valekaavussa* (Hyvinkää, 1953).

Hodgson, J. H., *Communism in Finland: a history and interpretation* (Princeton, 1967).

Hyvämäki, L., *Vaaran vuodet 1944–48* (Helsinki, 1958).

Hyvönen, A., *Suomen Kommunistinen puolue 1918–1924* (Helsinki, 1968).

Ingulskaja, L. A., 'Rabochii klass Finljandii i demokratizatsija strany (1944–48gg)', *Rabochee dvizhenie v skandinavskix stranax i Finljandii*, ed. I. M. Maiskii (Moscow, 1965).

*Iz istorii Kommunisticheskoi partii Finljandii* (Moscow, 1960).

Jakobson, M., *The Diplomacy of the Winter War* (Cambridge, Mass., 1961).

Karttunen, S., *Ystävyys vastatuulessa* (Helsinki, 1966).

Korhonen, K., *Naapurit vastoin tahtoaan: Suomi Neuvostodiplomatiassa Tartosta Talvisotaan*, I, 1920–32 (Helsinki, 1966).

Kuusinen, O. W., 'Suomen Sosialidemokratian johtajille', *Sosialistinen Aikakauslehti*, 16 April 1920.

———, *Suomen työväenliikkeen opetuksia* (Lappeenranta, 1949).

Leino, Y., *Kommunisti sisäministerinä* (Helsinki, 1958). This book has a curious history: it was ready for distribution in 1958 when, following an intervention by the Russian ambassador, the edition was destroyed and only a handful of copies survive. At present the wishes of the family of Y. Leino prevent any new attempt at publication. Readers who imagine in view of this that the book is full of lurid political indiscretions will be sadly disappointed: it is a fairly average specimen of politicians' memoirs.

Miettinen, J. E. I., 'Borba Kommunisticheskoi partii Finljandii za demokratizatsija strany v 1944–48 godax', *Novaja i noveishaja istorija*, no. 3 (1964).

'Mitä tahtoo suomalainen kommunistinen puolue?', *Suomalaisten kommunistien sarjajulkaisu*, no. 5 (Petrograd, 1918).

Murto, K., and Kaukonen, K., *Oikeus konepistoolin piipussa* (Helsinki, 1951).

Nousiainen, J., *Kommunismi Kuopion läänissä* (Joensuu, 1956).

Oittinen, R. H., *Työväenkysymys ja työväenliike Suomessa* (Helsinki, 1954).

Parkkari, N., *Suomalaisissa keskitysleiressä vv. 1940–1944* (Helsinki, 1955).

Pesonen, P., *Valtuutus kansalta* (Porvoo, 1965).

Pessi, V., 'Na strazhe interesov naroda', *Problemy mira i sotsializma*, no. 2 (1958).

Renvall, P., 'Neuvosto-Karjalan suomalaisuuden kriisin alkuvaiheista', *Historiallinen Aikakauskirja* (1944).

Rozdorozhny, I., '40 let Kompartii Finljandii', *Agitator*, no. 17 (1958).

Salomaa, E., *Tavoitteena kansanvalta: Suomen Työväenliikkeen vaiheita vuosina 1944–1960* (Helsinki, 1964).

Smirnov, B., 'Finljandija', *Antifashistkoe dvizhenie soprotivlenija v stranax Evropy v gody vtoroi mirovoi voiny* (Moscow, 1962).

Soikkanen, H., 'Sosiaalidemokraatti vai kommunisti?', *Suomalainen Suomi*, XXIX (1961).

———, 'Työväenliikkeen jakautumisongelma itsenäisyyden alkuvuosina', *Turun Historiallisen Yhdistyksen julkaisu*, XV.

Soini, Y., *Kuin Pietari hiilivalkealla: Sotasyyllisasiain vaiheet 1944–1949* (Helsinki, 1956).

Suomen Kansan Demokraattinen Liitto, *Kymmenvuotias Liitto* (Helsinki, 1959).

Suomen Kommunistinen puolue, *Kipinästä tuli syttyi: muistiinpanoja Suomen Kommunistisen puolueen 40 vuotistaipaleelta* (Helsinki, 1958).

Taimi, A., *Sivuja eletystä* (Petroskoi, 1954).

Tanner, V., *Kahden maailmansodan välissä* (Helsinki, 1967).

Tigerstedt, O., *Statspolisen slår till* (Helsinki, n.d.).

Tommila, P., *Kaksi vuosikymmentä Suomen sisäpolitiikkaa 1919–1939* (Porvoo, 1964).

TsKKPF, '40 let rabochii revoljutsii v Finljandii', *Novaja i novei-shaja istorii*, no. 2 (1958).
Tuominen, A., *Sirpin ja vasaran tie* (Helsinki, 1957).
————, *Maan alla ja päällä* (Helsinki, 1958).
————, *Kremlin kellot* (Helsinki, 1957).
Waltari, M., *Nevvostovakoilun varjossa* (Helsinki, 1943).
Wälläri, N., *Myrskyssä ja myötätuulessa* (Helsinki, 1951).
————, *Antoisia vuosia* (Helsinki, 1967).
Äikiä, A., *Kolmas tie?* (Helsinki, 1948).

# INDEX